Lumber Widths and Thicknesses

Lumber is ordered by thickness, width, and length. When you order in U.S. or imperial measurements (2 inches x 4 inches x 8 feet, for example), the thickness and width figures (in this instance 2x4) refer to nominal size—the dimensions of the piece as it left the saw. But what you get is the smaller, actual size remaining when the piece has been planed smooth; in actual fact, a piece 1½ inches x 3½ inches x 8 feet. (Length is not reduced by the processing.)

Metric measurements, on the other hand, always describe the actual dimensions of the processed piece.

Nominal size in inches	Actual size in inches	Actual size in millimeters
1x3	¾ x 2½	16 x 64
2x2	1½ x 1½	38 x 38
2x4	1½ x 3½	38 x 89
2x6	1½ x 5½	38 x 140
2x8	1½ x 7¼	38 x 184
2x10	1½ x 9¼	38 x 235
4x4	3½ x 3½	89 x 89
4x6	3½ x 5½	89 x 140

Tiles and Tiling

This formula (based on 23-centimeter square tiles and a room 5 meters long by 4 meters wide) will help you to determine how many tiles you need to cover a room:

1. Divide 100 centimeters (1 meter) by 23 (100 ÷ 23 = 4.35 tiles per meter).
2. Find the number of tiles per side by multiplying length and width respectively by tiles per meter (5 x 4.35 = 21.75; 4 x 4.35 = 17.4).
3. Calculate the area in tiles (21.75 x 17.4 = 378.45, or about 380 tiles).
4. Add 10% for fitting (380 + 10% = 418).

Sheet Vinyl Flooring and Carpeting

To estimate your sheet vinyl flooring and c meters:

1. Measure the room's longest and widest alcoves in the measurements), adding 7.5 ce good measure. Your calculation will be something such as:

   5.18 meters + 7.5 centimeters = 5.26 meters (width)
   5.79 meters + 7.5 centimeters = 5.87 meters (length)

2. Calculate the area of the room (5.26 meters x 5.87 meters = 30.87 square meters). You will need 31 m^2 to cover the room.

Metric Plywood Panels

Plywood panels generally come in two standard metric sizes: 1,200 millimeters x 2,400 millimeters and 1,220 millimeters x 2,400 millimeters (the equivalent of a 4 foot x 8 foot panel). Other sizes are available on special order. With sheathing and select sheathing grades, metric and inch thicknesses are generally identical. The metric sanded grades, however, come in a new range of thicknesses.

Metric thicknesses

Sheathing and Select Grades		Sanded Grades	
7.5 mm	(5/16 in.)	6 mm	(4/17 in.)
9.5 mm	(3/8 in.)	8 mm	(5/16 in.)
12.5 mm	(1/2 in.)	11 mm	(7/16 in.)
15.5 mm	(5/8 in.)	14 mm	(9/16 in.)
18.5 mm	(3/4 in.)	17 mm	(2/3 in.)
20.5 mm	(13/16 in.)	19 mm	(3/4 in.)
22.5 mm	(7/8 in.)	21 mm	(13/16 in.)
25.5 mm	(1 in.)	24 mm	(15/16 in.)

The Family Handyman®

Interior Remodeling

D. LAZZARONI
AMARETTI DI SARONNO

THE FAMILY Handyman®

Interior Remodeling

Projects That Will Bring New Life to Every Room in Your Home

THE READER'S DIGEST ASSOCIATION, INC.
Pleasantville, New York / Montreal

A READER'S DIGEST BOOK

Produced by Roundtable Press, Inc.
Directors: Susan E. Meyer, Marsha Melnick
Executive Editor: Amy T. Jonak
Project Editor: William Broecker
Editor: Tom Neven
Assistant Editor: Megan Keiler
Design: Sisco & Evans, New York
Production: Steven Rosen

For The Family Handyman
Editor in Chief: Gary Havens
Special Projects Editor: Ken Collier
Associate Editor: Gregg Carlsen

For Reader's Digest
Executive Editor: James Wagenvoord
Editorial Director: John Sullivan
Design Director: Michele Italiano-Perla
Managing Editors: Diane Shanley, Christine Moltzen
Editorial Associate: Daniela Marchetti

Library of Congress Cataloging in Publication Data
The family handyman interior remodeling.
p. cm.
Includes index.
ISBN 0-89577-791-6
1. Dwellings—Remodeling—Amateurs' manuals. I. Family handyman.
TH4816.F352 1995
643'.7—dc20 95-22069

Printed in the United States of America

A Note from the Editor

Home remodeling, as a segment of the American economy, has grown nonstop for 50 years. It's been virtually recession-proof, and immune from foreign competition. Home-growing is a home-grown, all-American phenomenon!

A lot of that growth has to do with do-it-yourselfers. You and I are the toughest competition the pros have. We demand the same quality products, fixtures, and materials that the pros use. We demand, and use, the same tools.

We also expect the same results. We think—no, we know—that we can do our own remodeling better than some pros, while saving as much as 60 per cent of the cost of hiring a professional. That's better than doubling the use of every D-I-Y dollar, a pretty good investment by any accounting.

Of course, we've all made mistakes along the way to remodeled kitchens, baths, and family rooms. I've personally made most of the possible mistakes—some of them several times. And I know very well that those mistakes cost time and money. But they also teach: They're part of the tuition of the school of life.

Of course, it's nice to learn some things without going through the agony of trial and error. That's why I recommend this book to you. Every chapter comes from the pages of *The Family Handyman* magazine. Every project was actually built before we wrote about it. Sometimes we rebuilt it, to make sure we got it right.

Finally, before we let the project appear in this book, the editors went over the details once again. We've made sure the hints actually help, that the measurements all add up—and that you can finish each project with a maximum of pleasure and satisfaction. So go to it— build!

Gary Havens
Editor, *The Family Handyman*

Contents

Introduction

Whether you've lived in your house for a few months, a few years, or a few decades, there are probably things you'd like to change. This book has something to satisfy the urge to change or improve things in every room of the house.

Perhaps the kitchen is looking dingy, or there's no place to store the myriad gadgets and other conveniences that make life simpler. Maybe you'd like to bring your bathroom up to date with a new sink or shower, or perhaps that small room near the back door would make a great second bathroom. These and many other projects are explained step by step on the following pages with clear, informative photographs and illustrations. There are projects and ideas for the bedroom, living room, dining room, basement, and attic as well as the kitchen and bathroom.

While making these home improvements you'll also learn new do-it-yourself skills. From putting on a gleaming coat of glossy paint to working with copper pipe, from laying glass blocks to basic framing carpentry, your confidence and abilities will grow with every project you tackle.

Whatever job you're doing, keep safety foremost in your mind. Always wear eye and ear protection when working with power tools, hammering nails, or demolishing walls. Keep your tools sharp, clean, and well maintained; they'll work better and last longer. Follow the manufacturer's directions for operating power tools. For reasons of clarity, some photographs in this book show power tools with safety or blade guards removed. When you work, always use the safety guards on all tools.

For comfort as well as safety, think ahead. Send the family to grandma's or some other pleasant place for the weekend before you turn off the water main to start that big pumbing project. Don't rip out your old kitchen cabinets until the new ones have been delivered and you have made sure they are the right size. There's nothing like planning and checking details to make a project go smoothly.

The Kitchen

Refinish Kitchen Cabinets
Transform the look of your kitchen in one bold stroke—repaint or stain the cabinets. The results will be impressive.
12

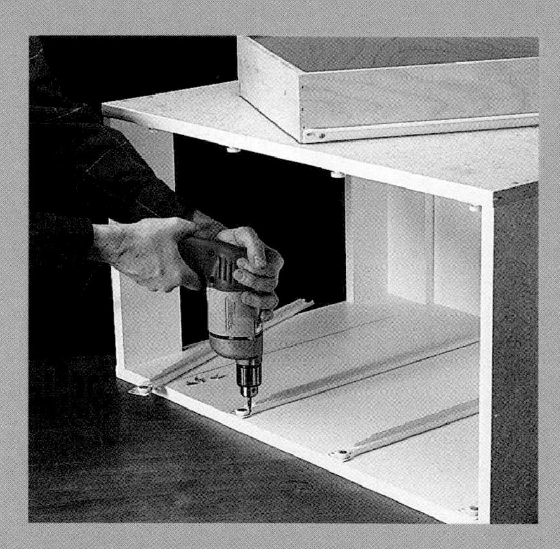

Build Euro-style Kitchen Cabinets
For a custom-fitted kitchen, build your own cabinets. The European style is easy to build and has a sleek, modern look.
46

Replace a Countertop
The countertop takes the brunt of kitchen work. Refurbish the work area with a new stock or custom-made top.
18

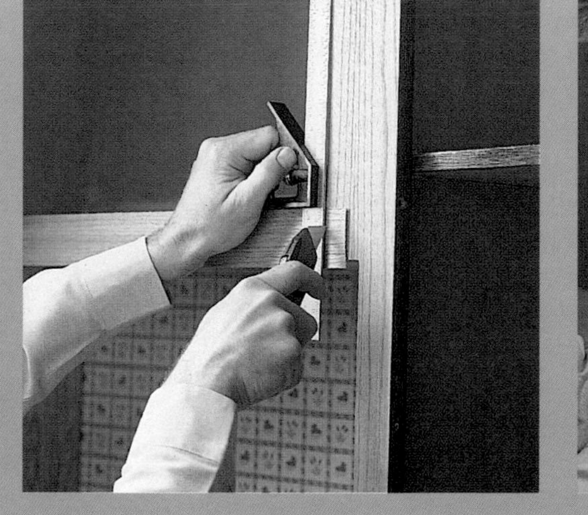

Reface Kitchen Cabinets
Put new fronts and doors on existing cabinets—it's the easy and economical way to give your kitchen a true facelift.
24

Install Stock Kitchen Cabinets
Ready-made cabinets can be used in any configuration. They're the fast, economical way to complete a new or remodeled kitchen.
34

Improve Kitchen Storage
Every kitchen has wasted space in the cabinets. Try these clever ways to put space to use with a minimum of work and cost.
56

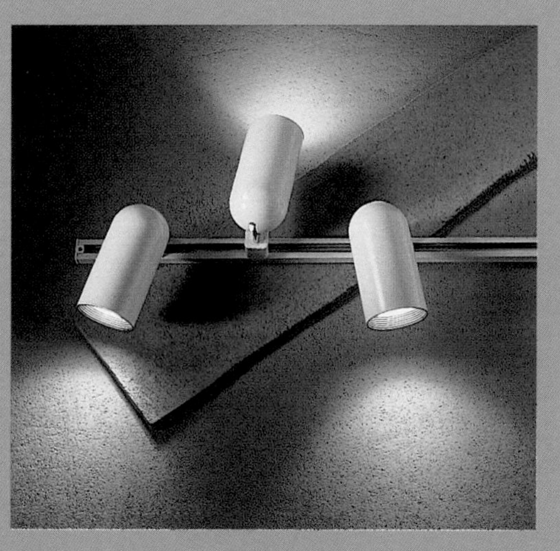

Lighting Your Kitchen
To be efficient and inviting, your kitchen needs general, task, and accent lighting. Here's how to evaluate and improve your kitchen's lighting.
62

Refinish Kitchen Cabinets

For many families the kitchen is the most popular room in the house—a place where everyone gathers to cook, eat, talk, or do schoolwork. But this pleasant room can take a beating from all that activity. Refinishing the cabinets with gleaming enamel paint or stain and replacing the cabinet hardware is an easy way to make it a bright, attractive spot once again.

Painting kitchen cabinets a glossy white is an easy and inexpensive way to spruce up a kitchen that needs brightening. Proper preparation and careful work are the keys to outstanding results.

DO IT YOURSELF AND SAVE

You can save almost two-thirds the cost of what a professional would charge by doing this work yourself. Painting or staining cabinets is not especially difficult. If you work methodically and take your time, you can do a professional-looking job.

REFINISHING OPTIONS

You can choose from three basic approaches to refinishing your cabinets:

▶ Paint over the old finish.

▶ Strip off the old finish, and then paint with enamel.

▶ Strip off the old finish, then bleach and stain the wood.

Whichever approach you use, take the time to do it right. Remove doors and drawers to work on them, and take off all the hardware. Install new knobs, handles, and hinges at the end of the project. Tarnished and dirty hardware will diminish the look of the finished project after all the hard work you have put into refinishing.

Paint over the old finish

Clean the cabinets thoroughly. A solution of trisodium phosphate (TSP) will do an excellent job of removing the greasy film that is common in kitchens. If this chemical is banned in your community, you can use laundry detergent or a TSP substitute instead.

▶ Sand every inch of the cabinets with 100-grit paper to roughen up the surface. Then sand the edges of any chipped areas to feather them out. Vacuum and use a tack cloth to remove the dust, then apply a shellac-based primer to seal the old surface.

▶ If necessary, repair the surface by filling chips or gouges with latex spackling compound (Photo 1). Fill any holes with wood putty. Sand the patches smooth and clean up the dust.

▶ Now put on the new finish. First apply a coat of enamel undercoater, then a coat of gloss or semigloss enamel, sanding and removing the dust between coats. Use the techniques explained in Applying Enamel, page 16.

This method of redoing cabinets is fast—it takes about two or three days. Unfortunately, the paint doesn't bond to old paint as well as bare wood, and it can chip off. This approach is fine, however, if you don't bang and slam your cabinet doors and drawers and you aren't necessarily looking for the longest-lasting paint job possible.

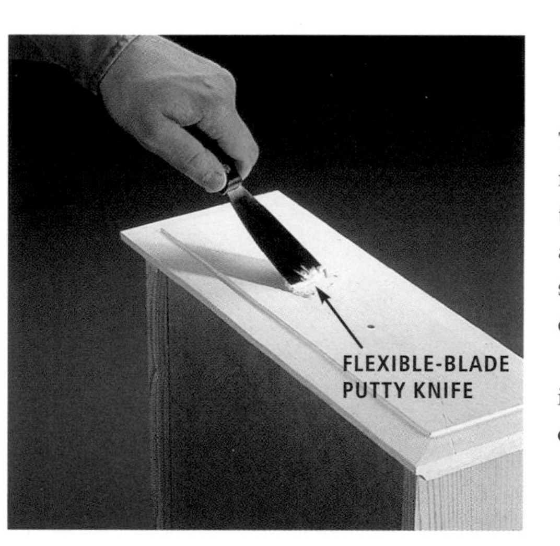

Photo 1. Repair the wood surface after the primer coat dries. Use wood putty for holes and latex spackling compound for gouges.

Strip, then paint with enamel

Stripping and painting is a good middle course in refinishing cabinets. There are just two major steps to this process:

▶ Strip off the old finish as explained in Stripping the Finish, page 14.

▶ Apply two coats of enamel undercoater, then paint the cabinets with a gloss or semigloss enamel; see Painting Cabinets, page 14.

This approach provides a long-lasting finish. It takes about a week, and with average use the finish should last ten years or more. Best of all, it can easily be repainted.

Strip, bleach, and stain

Although it is the most difficult and time consuming, this method can completely transform the appearance of your cabinets. The whole procedure takes about a week and involves two steps:

▶ Strip off the old finish as explained in the text on page 14.

▶ Bleach the wood and apply a stain. These finish techniques are explained in Staining Cabinets, page 17.

This approach can change the color of the cabinets dramatically and will allow the grain of the wood to show through. The stain can be any color, but if you choose white stain, as shown on page 17, you can achieve a "pickled" or whitewashed look on the cabinets.

The final appearance depends on the original color of the wood and how much of the old color you can remove.

TOOLS

- Natural- or synthetic-bristle paintbrush
- Drop cloths
- Putty knife
- Tack cloth
- Sanding block
- Wire-bristle brush
- Paint buckets
- Sawhorses
- Rubber gloves

MATERIALS

- Semigloss or gloss enamel paint
- Enamel undercoater
- 100-, 120-, and 150-grit sandpaper
- Steel wool
- Paint stripper
- Wood putty
- Latex spackling compound

Stripping Safety

If you use a solvent-base stripper, check that burners and pilot lights are turned off before you begin. Don't smoke; wear rubber gloves and safety goggles; and make sure the room has plenty of cross-ventilation. An open window at one end and a fan at the other is a good system. Even better, take doors outside and work on them there.

STRIPPING THE FINISH

Kitchen cabinet finishes are usually easy to remove although, like all stripping, the job makes a mess.

▶ Remove all cabinet hardware such as knobs and hinges before beginning, and protect countertops and the kitchen floor with drop cloths. Lay old newspapers over the drop cloths to absorb the stripping residue.

▶ Remove paint with either a traditional solvent-base or a water-base stripper. Remove varnish and stain with a solvent-base stripper, or a mixture of equal parts of lacquer thinner and denatured alcohol.

▶ Follow the manufacturer's directions and apply the stripper by brushing in one direction only. Let it sit until the finish begins to bubble.

▶ Scrape the bubbling finish off with a dull putty knife. Take your time; the stripping operation itself isn't difficult, but it is quite time consuming.

For crevices, use medium steel wool with a solvent-base stripper, or a plastic scrub pad with a water-base stripper. If an existing stain does not come off with the finish, scrub it out of the pores of the wood with a solvent and a metal-bristle brush (Photo 2).

▶ Clean the stripped wood as suggested by the stripper manufacturer. If you used an alcohol–lacquer thinner solution, clean with straight denatured alcohol. When the surfaces are dry, lightly sand them with 120-grit sandpaper.

▶ Let the stripping residue dry, then throw it out in the trash.

Photo 2. Strip the old finish. If necessary, use a metal-bristle brush to lift the old stain and finish out of the pores of the wood.

PAINTING CABINETS

Primers and undercoaters can be sanded smooth, but the finish coat of enamel has to be perfect—there's no repairing it. A gloss enamel paint reveals careless technique without mercy. It exaggerates drips, brush marks, flecks of dirt, brush hairs, and all other possible imperfections of a paint job. You can't sand a glossy surface without destroying the gloss, and touch-up spots will be glaringly obvious. Semigloss paints present the same problems, although they are a bit more forgiving of minor errors.

Preparation

Here are a few rules to follow to achieve a great painted finish:

▶ Choose the right paint. Water-base latex enamel is easier to clean up and it lacks the strong odor of an oil-base paint, but it does not wear as well as an alkyd or oil-base paint. An oil or alkyd enamel flows out onto the surface better, leveling itself free of brush marks. When using these paints, the undercoat must be an alkyd-base paint too.

The finish paint can be a gloss or semigloss luster. A semigloss surface wears as well as a glossy one does, and it is less shiny under bright lights.

▶ Buy a good brush. Use a top-quality natural- or synthetic-bristle brush for oil enamel. It's not hard to tell brush quality—just look at the price tag. A good brush costs several dollars; a cheap one might cost only a dollar or two. However, a top-quality, expensive brush is really cheaper in the long run. With proper care, a good brush will provide many years of service.

Among the best natural bristles are so-called china-bristle brushes, made with hair from an Asiatic species of hogs. If you choose a water-base paint, use only a brush with synthetic bristles. Natural bristles will swell as they absorb water from the paint, which will make it difficult to get a smooth finish.

▶ Work in a dust-free area. Before you start painting, clean up all of the dust and grit you can from the area. When you work, restrict traffic near the wet paint, to avoid creating air currents that carry dust.

▶ Use a tack cloth. After every sanding of bare wood, primer, or undercoater, first vacuum off the dust, then use a tack cloth to remove the fine particles that remain (Photo 3).

You can buy a tack cloth—a piece of fabric impregnated with a chemical that makes it sticky—at any paint store, or you can make your own tack cloth by soaking a lint-free cloth in turpentine and letting it air-dry until it's tacky to the touch.

▶ Strain the paint. This is essential. All paint should be strained—even undercoater and finish enamel fresh from the can. Strain it into a clean container, using either manufactured paper filters, available from paint stores, or an old nylon stocking (Photo 4).

▶ On bare wood, first put down two coats of an alkyd enamel undercoater. This is a primer specially made to be used with enamels—it sands easily and grips the wood well.

Repair any flaws in the wood with wood putty and latex spackling compound after applying the first layer of undercoater. Sand thoroughly and remove all dust specks and surface blemishes before you put on each coat. Start with 100-grit paper before the first coat, then use 120- or 150-grit between coats. Careful preparation here will make the next step—painting—easy.

Watch Out for Dust

Paint in a well-ventilated but draft-free area. Do not use a fan nearby—it will pull dust onto the paint. Vacuum the room thoroughly. Hang plastic sheeting over an open archway to prevent drafts. Do not use cloths, because it may be a source of lint. If necessary, wedge a door about one-third of the way open. This will admit air for ventilation but will avoid a direct draft into the entire room.

PAINTING CABINETS: PREPARATION

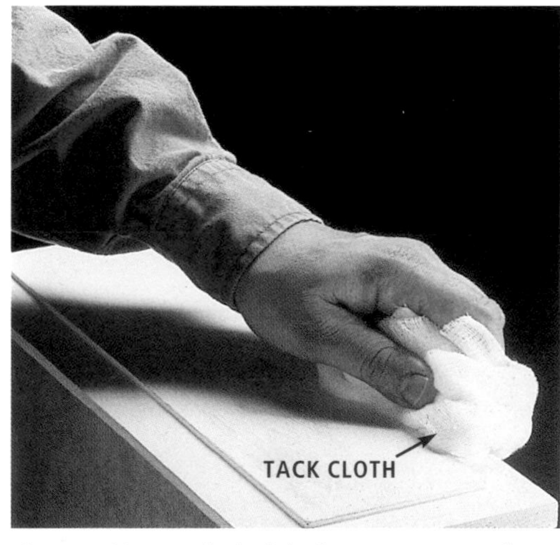

Photo 3. Use a tack cloth before every coat, after sanding thoroughly with 150-grit paper and vacuuming off the dust.

Photo 4. Strain the paint before every coat—even paint that's fresh from the can. Use a nylon stocking or a commercial paint filter.

Painting Over Oak Grain

If you have oak cabinets, you probably won't be able to get as smooth a paint finish as you could on a fine-grained wood like birch. The deep pores of oak grain show through even several coats of paint. This is fine if you like the look of the grain showing through the paint, but if you want a mirror-smooth finish, leave the original finish and sand completely with 150-grit paper.

The idea is to leave the old finish in the pores and sand the finish off the surface. Follow with two coats of undercoater and a coat of enamel.

Before trying to paint an entire oak cabinet, test the finish in an unobtrusive place such as the back of a cabinet door or on the back of the false front of a drawer. Remove the drawer pulls and see if the false front comes off. If not, check inside for additional screws holding the front. If there are none, the front is probably glued in place, and not worth removing. Do not test your finish on the plain wood of the drawer; it probably isn't oak.

Applying Enamel

Apply the gloss or semigloss enamel as the third and final coat.

▶ Paint items horizontally whenever possible. Lay the doors flat on cardboard boxes or sawhorses, and keep the drawer fronts horizontal by standing the drawers on their ends (Photo 5). This allows the paint to flow out evenly, eliminating brush marks and making drips and sags less likely.

▶ Paint the backs of the doors first. Do this with all the coats, but especially with the final coat. If you paint the fronts first, the paint on the front can get marred when the doors are turned face down.

▶ "Tip off" lightly. After every painting step, drag the tip of the brush lightly through the paint (Photo 6) in the direction of the wood grain—a technique called "tipping off." This minimizes brush marks, making it easier for the paint to flow out.

▶ Let each coat dry thoroughly. You can't sand safely if the paint is not completely dry. Sand with 150-grit paper between the first and second coats. Wait at least 24 hours for the final coat to dry before installing new hardware and hanging the doors (Photo 7). In addition, be careful of the enamel finish for a few more days. Even though the paint might feel dry, it's still soft enough to be damaged or scratched by careless handling.

PAINTING CABINETS: APPLYING ENAMEL AND INSTALLING HARDWARE

Photo 5. Lay doors flat and stand the drawers on end for painting. Start with the proper kind of primer or undercoater for your finish paint.

Photo 6. For a smooth finish, gently drag the brush tip through the paint in the direction of the wood grain to "tip off" the final coat of enamel.

Photo 7. Install new hardware to finish off the project and rejuvenate the cabinets. This knob has a backplate to protect the paint finish.

STAINING CABINETS

A white stain finish, also called a "pickled" finish, brightens cabinets while letting the wood grain show through. The white stain, available at any paint store, is applied the same as any other wood stain.

You don't have to stain the cabinets white, though. The basic procedures described here apply to any color stain you might choose.

Begin by stripping off the old finish and stain, as described on page 14. Then proceed according to the following steps.

As with any new finish, it may be a good idea to test the new stain in an inconspicuous place before proceeding.

▶ Bleach the wood using a one- or two-part wood bleach, available at paint stores (Photo 8). One or two bleaching treatments should lighten the wood enough for restaining. Be sure to wear rubber gloves whenever you are working with bleach.

▶ Apply the stain following the manufacturer's directions carefully. Wipe on a first coat of stain so it penetrates down into the pores, then wipe it off the surface (Photo 9). Let this first treatment dry, and then wipe a second coat onto the surface.

You can change the appearance of the stain if you wish. To make it more opaque, add enamel undercoater. To make it more transparent, add sanding sealer. To change the shade slightly, add a small amount of artist's oil paint to the stain.

▶ After the stain has dried, add a finish sealer over the stain unless the manufacturer recommends otherwise.

STAINING CABINETS

Photo 8. Apply bleach with a sponge, rubbing it on uniformly and generously. Rubber gloves are essential for this part of the job.

Photo 9. Apply two coats of stain with a rag or brush. Wipe the first coat off the surface, leaving it only in the pores.

Replace a Countertop

A new kitchen countertop can improve the appearance of an old kitchen virtually overnight. Even a relatively young kitchen may benefit from the fresh look a new countertop can provide.

Installing a new countertop doesn't cost much and is well within the capabilities of even moderately skilled do-it-yourselfers. It can be a stand-alone project, or you might consider installing new cabinets or refurbishing your old ones at the same time, as explained in other chapters.

The countertop is the primary work surface in every kitchen. It's easy to replace a worn or damaged countertop with a stock or a custom-made top. That will make cooking and cleanup easier—and much more pleasant.

COUNTERTOP OPTIONS

For this project, you have two basic choices: a top custom-made to your specifications, or a stock plastic laminate top.

▶ **Custom top.** With a custom-made top you can choose any style, color, and covering material, with a backsplash of any height—or without a backsplash if you prefer to cover the wall behind with ceramic tile, laminate, or some other material. You can have a top made in any size, and with one or two mitered ends to go around a corner, if necessary, which cuts installation work to a minimum. And although a custom top is more expensive, installing it yourself will save several hundred dollars off having a pro do the job.

To order a custom top, check in the phone book under "Countertops" or ask a local kitchen cabinet dealer. The countertop shown in the how-to photographs was made to order without a backsplash; installation is easier without one. If you've done any work requiring careful carpentry, you should be able to install a custom-made countertop without encountering any difficulty.

▶ **Stock top.** Stock, factory-made laminate tops, available at home centers, kitchen design centers, and cabinet shops, cost about a third less than custom-made tops. They have a built-in backsplash (see Countertop Construction, below) of fixed height, and are available in only a limited range of colors and edge styles.

Stock tops usually come in 2-foot increments of length, so you may have a good deal to trim to get down to the size you need, and you may have to finish one or both ends.

The techniques for installing a stock top are much the same as for a custom top, and no more difficult. They are explained on page 23.

Countertop Construction

Almost all stock countertops have a backsplash, with laminate molded continuously from the front to the rear edge. Custom tops can be made with or without a backsplash.

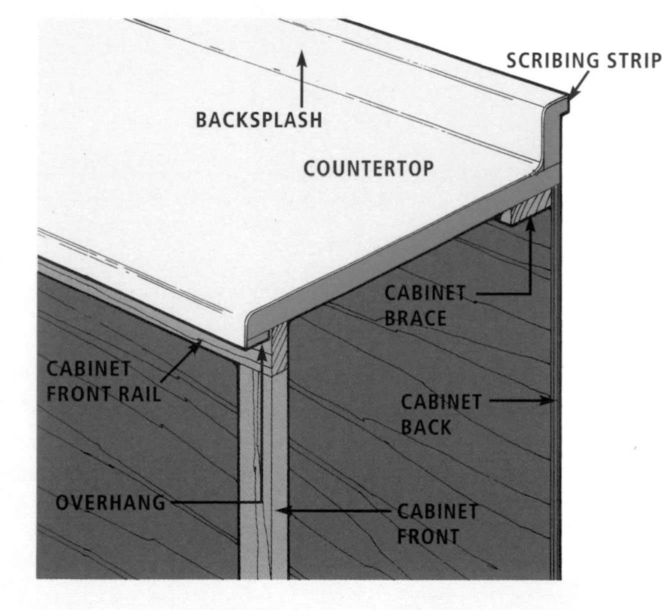

MEASURING FOR A NEW COUNTERTOP

Before ordering a custom-made countertop or selecting a stock top, you need to measure the space where it will fit. In doing that, the most important thing is to measure everything twice. Mistakes are expensive.

▶ Measure the length of the existing top, at both the front and back. Measure the depth from the front edge to the wall behind at both ends. Include the depth of the backsplash if there is one. Also measure the overhang from the countertop edge to the face of the base cabinet that supports it. If one or both ends are exposed, the overhang there is likely to be less than along the front edge.

▶ With this information, make a drawing showing the corners, ends, and the kitchen walls. Mark your measurements on it. Before taking the drawing to a countertop supplier, use a framing square to check whether the walls are square at the corners. You can easily trim the ends of a countertop to fit in most situations, but severely out-of-square corners may require special treatment. Consult your supplier about this problem.

Working from your measurements, the supplier will determine what size countertop sections you need, with allowances so you can trim the edges for an exact fit. If the counter goes around an inside or outside corner, a custom-made top will be in two or more pieces, with ends cut for a mitered joint. If you are buying a stock top for a corner, you will need to get two tops with precut miters on the appropriate ends.

TOOLS

- Carpenter's level
- Framing square
- Belt sander
- Circular saw with steel plywood blade
- Saber saw
- Compass
- Open-end wrenches
- Drill
- Screwdrivers
- Caulking gun
- Iron (optional)
- C-clamps
- File

MATERIALS

- Silicone acrylic caulk
- Scrap lumber
- Construction adhesive
- Liquid hide glue
- 60-grit sandpaper
- Wood shims

Trimming with a Belt Sander

Hold a belt sander so the belt moves downward across the edge of a laminate top. If the belt moves in the other direction it could rip laminate off the board on which it is mounted.

INSTALLING A CUSTOM-MADE COUNTERTOP

Once you have your new countertop, the steps for installing it are:

▶ Prepare the cabinets.
▶ Scribe and trim the top.
▶ Assemble the corner.
▶ Attach the countertop.
▶ Install the sink.

Often installation is somewhat simpler than this because there is no corner to be assembled, or no sink to be installed.

PREPARE THE CABINETS

Remove the old top. It's likely to be screwed to the base cabinets from underneath. Remove the sink at this time also.

▶ Place a carpenter's level along the tops of the base cabinets, both front to back and side to side. If you need to do any leveling, it won't be easy to drive shims under the cabinets, especially with the kitchen flooring, base trim, and the bottom cabinet shelf in place. Instead, glue shims to the top edges of the cabinet to provide level support for the countertop.

SCRIBE AND TRIM THE TOP

Lay the new countertop in place. If there is a wall at just one end, let the top overhang the other end so you can mark the wall end for a proper fit. If the counter fits between two end walls, slide the top into the opening, tipping one end up so it rests on the wall. In either case, adjust the top so it overhangs the front of the cabinets a uniform distance. You will trim the back edge or the backsplash to achieve a 1-1/4 inch or smaller overhang.

Scribing

The technique for marking an edge to fit against a real-life wall—one that curves, bulges, or is out of square—is called scribing.

▶ To scribe a countertop, position it on the base cabinets as described above and push the edge to be marked snugly against its wall. Set a compass to the width of the largest gap between the wall and the edge of the top. Move the compass along the wall with the pencil tip on the countertop (Photo 1). It will trace a line that conforms to the irregularities in the wall. Then you can trim to the line as described below.

▶ Scribe and trim the end or ends of the countertop first, then do the back. If the top fits between two end walls, scribe and trim the lower end first, then do the high end (Photo 2).

Trimming

With a custom-made top, there usually won't be much to remove when you trim an edge to the scribed line.

▶ Use a belt sander with a coarse, 60-grit, abrasive belt (Photo 3), or use a saber saw. The saw is best if you have 1/8 inch or more to remove. To avoid scratches, run a couple of strips of masking tape on the top to protect the surface from the base plate of the saw. Use a sander for fine adjustments after sawing the countertop.

▶ Your goal is an even fit, but not an absolutely tight one. The trimmed edge should leave a consistent gap about 1/16-inch wide when the top is pushed into position against the wall. A bead of latex or silicone acrylic caulk, applied later, will fill this space and accommodate any movement due to changes in temperature and humidity.

SCRIBE AND TRIM THE TOP

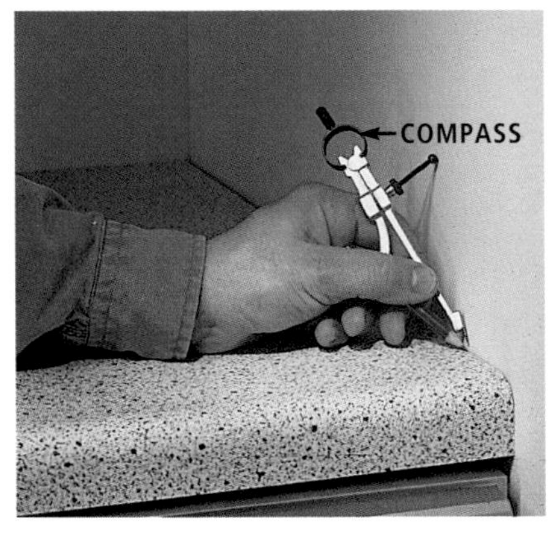

Photo 1. Use a compass to scribe an edge to fit against a wall. Set the compass to the largest gap and move it along the wall, drawing a line on the countertop that matches the wall contour.

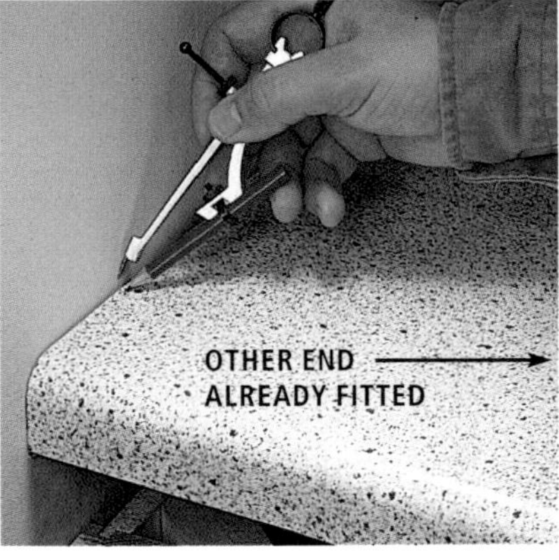

Photo 2. To fit a countertop between two walls, position it with one end high, the other low. Scribe and trim the low end first, then scribe the high end for trimming as shown.

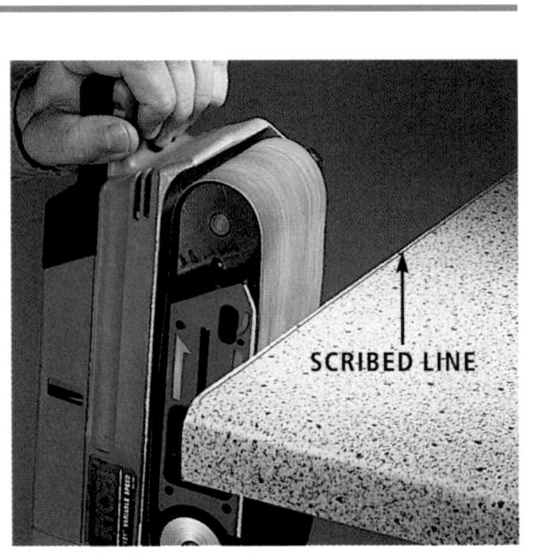

Photo 3. Trim countertop edges with a belt sander and a coarse abrasive belt. For large amounts, use a saber saw. Work up to the scribed line, then check and refine the fit.

ASSEMBLE THE CORNER

If the custom-made countertop turns a corner, it is supplied in two mitered sections that join to form a 90-degree corner. The sections are held together with glue and special toggle fasteners, which are supplied.

▶ If one of the mitered pieces must fit between two walls, fit that section first. Place it on the base cabinets with the mitered end at the corner. First scribe and trim the end opposite the miter against the wall, then scribe and trim the back edge. The point of the mitered end should fit tightly into the corner of the wall (Photo 4). Fit the second mitered piece against the first, scribing it in back so the front edges of the corner are flush (Photo 5).

▶ Apply liquid hide glue along the joint. You can use yellow carpenter's glue instead of liquid hide glue, but you must work quickly because it sets faster. Toggle bolts supplied with the countertop connect the mitered sections. Position each bolt across the joint on the underside of the countertop and slowly tighten it with an open-end wrench (Photo 6).

▶ Check that the two laminate surfaces remain flush along the joint and at the front corner. Use a clamp in front, and pressure sticks wedged between the upper cabinets and the top to hold the joint perfectly flush (Photo 7).

ASSEMBLE THE CORNER

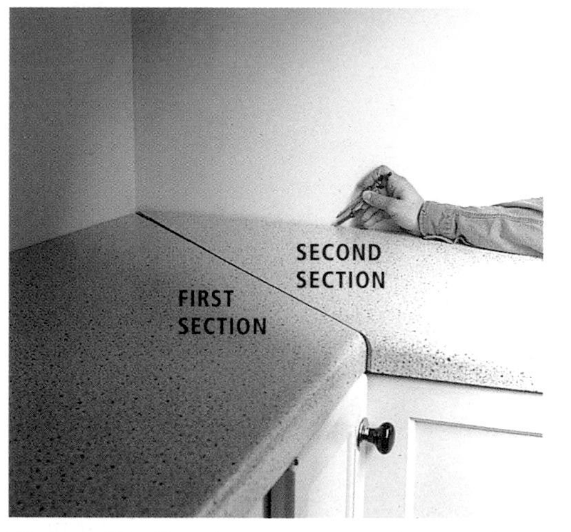

Photo 4. Fit mitered corners one section at a time. Trim the square end and the back edge of the first section so the rear mitered point fits exactly into the wall corner.

Photo 5. Scribe and trim the back edge of the second section in a corner to make the joint fit flush in front. Don't trim the custom-cut mitered edges forming the joint.

Photo 6. The miter joint at a corner is held together with glue and special toggle bolts. Tighten them gradually, checking that the joint remains flush on top.

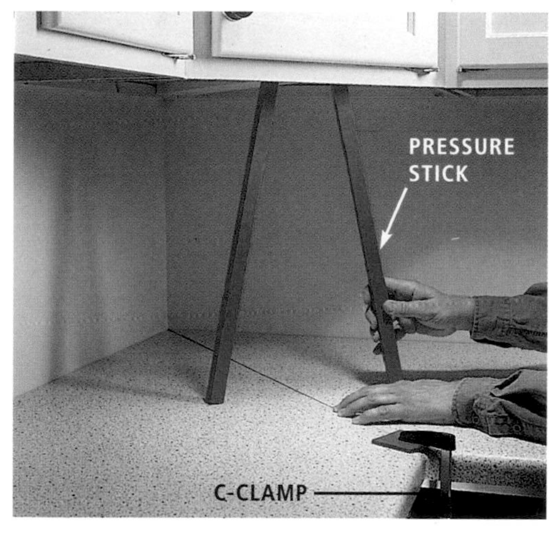

Photo 7. Pressure sticks wedged between upper cabinets and the countertop and a C-clamp keep corner joint surfaces flush as the glue dries. Protect the counter surface.

ATTACH THE COUNTERTOP

After the countertop is fitted to the walls and the mitered corner is snug and the glue has dried, attach it to the base cabinets.

▶ Tip up the countertop and apply silicone caulk or construction adhesive to the top edges of all cabinet parts that support the top. Include the triangular braces if there are any. Then lower the countertop into position.

▶ With the top pushed snugly against the walls, drill pilot holes up through the face frame of the base cabinets at an angle, at least one per cabinet. Then screw into the countertop from underneath (Photo 8). Measure carefully so the screws won't go through the plastic laminate. Use pressure sticks between the countertop and the cabinets above to hold the top down tightly at the rear until the adhesive sets.

▶ Seal the gaps along the ends and the back edge with a clear silicone acrylic caulk.

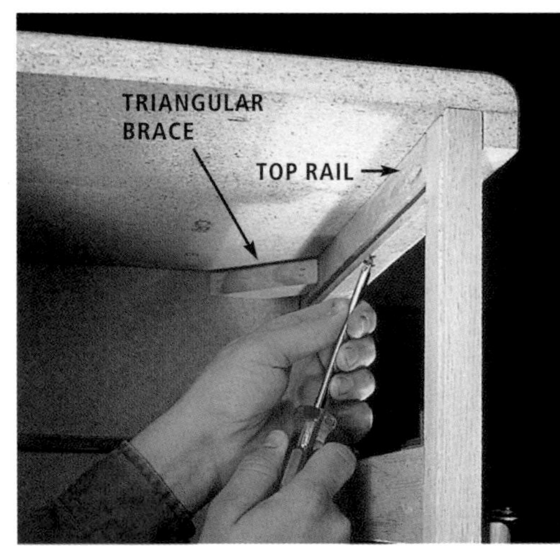

Photo 8. Screw the countertop to the base cabinets from below, through the top rails of the cabinet fronts or through the triangular braces at the corners of the cabinets.

INSTALL THE SINK

Measure carefully before placing the sink. Make sure the drain and fixtures will align with existing plumbing.

▶ Most sinks come with a paper template to help cut the hole in the countertop. If there is no template, place the sink upside down on the countertop and trace its outline.

▶ Measure the lip on the underside of the sink and mark a second outline that far inside the first on the countertop. This will provide a countertop ledge on which the lip of the sink will rest. The exact amount differs with various sinks but is usually 3/8 or 1/2 inch.

Cutting the hole

To cut the hole for the sink, use a saber saw or a circular saw with a steel (not carbide-tip) plywood blade. If you have trouble fitting a power saw along the rear edge of the hole, near the wall or backsplash, use a handsaw there, or cut from underneath.

▶ Drill starting holes for a saber saw blade at diagonally opposite corners, just inside the cutting line for the sink hole. (Photo 9). Make the cut directly on the marked line. Any slight chipping of the laminate at the edges of the cutout will be covered by the lip of the sink.

Photo 9 . Cut the sink opening with a saber saw, leaving enough material to support the edge of the sink. Drill starting holes at opposite corners.

Mounting the sink

Mount the faucet, drain, and spray hose on the sink before installing it in the countertop.

▶ Run a bead of acrylic caulk on the surface around the opening and set the sink down on it. Then run a bead of caulk around the sink edge where it meets the countertop.

▶ Install and tighten the mounting clips supplied with the sink. They fasten to the sink and grip the underside of the countertop.

▶ Finally, make all the plumbing connections.

INSTALLING A STOCK COUNTERTOP

The steps for installing a stock countertop are the same as for a custom-made top. In addition, you must cut the top to length before fitting and trimming it, and you must scribe and trim the backsplash as well as the ends. You may be able to order a stock top with either or both ends finished with laminate. If not, you can add laminate end caps that are factory-coated with hot-melt adhesive.

Cutting a stock countertop

Because most stock countertops are supplied in 2-foot increments of length, you may have several inches to cut in order to obtain the length that you need.

▶ Use a circular saw and a fine-tooth steel (not carbide-tip) plywood blade. Turn the countertop face down for cutting and be sure to cover the support bench or table to protect the laminate surface from scratches. Clamp on a board or other straightedge for a cutting guide (Photo 10). Cut from the rear, through the backsplash, toward the front. Keep the cutoff end supported and complete the cut through the backsplash with a handsaw or sabersaw if you find it necessary.

▶ If you are installing a countertop to go around a corner, use sections with precut 45-degree ends. Cutting countertops for a mitered joint is not a do-it-yourself task. Trim the square-cut ends to get the sections to fit.

Trimming the backsplash

A stock plastic laminate countertop has a laminate backsplash with a scribing strip at the top to help you fit it to the wall.

▶ After scribing and trimming the ends, push the backsplash against the back wall and then scribe along the top.

▶ Trim to the marked line with a sander (Photo 11). It is unlikely you will need to use a saw unless you need to notch the edge to go around an obstruction on the wall.

Adding a laminate end cap

A stock end cap is an L-shaped piece of laminate that matches the countertop surface. The countertop and backsplash edge must be cut in a straight line—not an irregular trimmed line—to receive the cap.

▶Glue a wood strip to the bottom of the countertop flush with the edge, to support the end cap. Make this support strip the same size as the one along the front edge.

▶ Hold the end cap flush with the back of the scribing strip and use a household iron to melt the glue coated on its back (Photo 12). When the glue has cooled, finish the edges carefully. Use a file, always pushing toward the top, or a router and a laminate trimming bit. Be very careful in trimming the curves at the backsplash and at the front edge of the countertop.

INSTALLING A STOCK COUNTERTOP

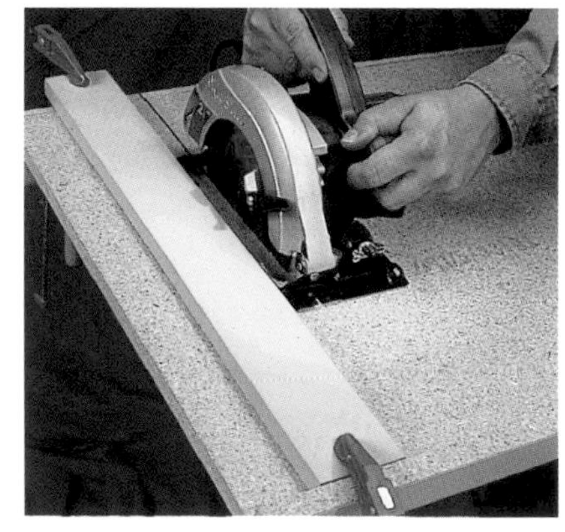

Photo 10. Trim a stock top to length with a circular saw and a straight-edged guide. Use a fine-tooth plywood blade; place the top face down on a padded surface.

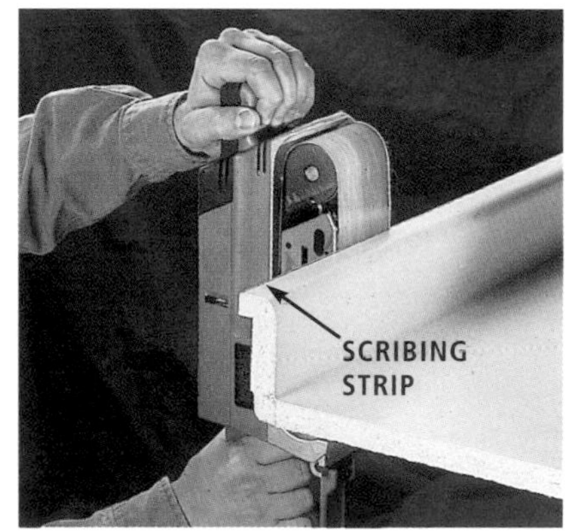

Photo 11. Fit the backsplash to the wall by scribing and sanding. A stock countertop has a scribing strip on the backsplash to make fitting easier.

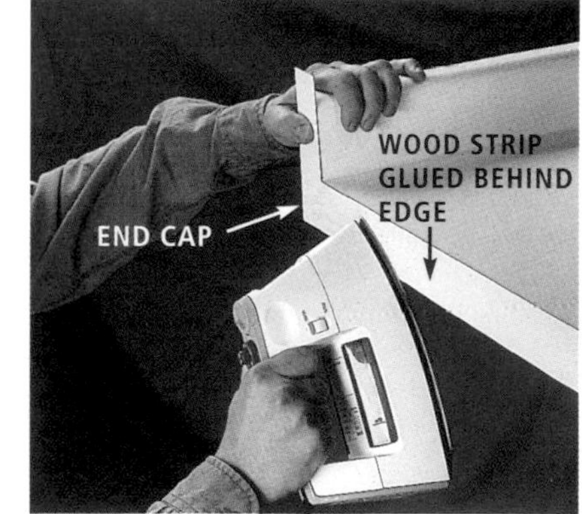

Photo 12. Glue on an end cap using an iron to activate the hot-melt adhesive. Trim the edges carefully with a file or a router and a laminate trimming bit.

Reface Kitchen Cabinets

Here's how to perform magic that will transform the look of your kitchen.

The secret is to reface the cabinets. That can make as big a change as installing new cabinets, but at far less cost, especially when you do the work yourself. If the existing cabinets are basically functional you can easily go from, say, painted pine to natural oak, or from traditional to sleek contemporary. And because only basic handtools and skills are required, this is a remodeling project that even a beginning do-it-yourselfer can handle with ease.

Refacing your old kitchen cabinets can give them a completely new look for half the cost of new cabinets. Pressure-sensitive veneers make simple work of what used to be the trickiest, most difficult part of cabinet renewal.

ABOUT REFACING

Refacing involves replacing the existing cabinet doors and drawer faces and covering the cabinet ends, face framing, and other exterior surfaces with thin plywood and pressure-sensitive wood veneer. The only skills you need are the ability to make precise measurements and to cut thin materials accurately and cleanly. There are many benefits to refacing; the principal question is whether it is the most suitable way to update your kitchen.

Benefits

Compared to many other remodeling techniques, refacing has several advantages:

▶ **Cost saving.** Refacing materials cost less than half what you would pay for new cabinets. In a professional installation, labor may be 50 percent of the total cost. By doing the job yourself, you avoid that expense entirely.

▶ **It's fast and easy.** This project is not much harder than wallpapering. Two people working together can often reface a kitchen over a long weekend.

▶ **You can use the kitchen as you work.** Refacing is a low-mess job that has little effect on the workings of your kitchen. You may create a little sawdust, but the countertops, appliances, and sink stay put, so you can use them throughout the project.

▶ **It's a chance to further update a kitchen.** While refacing the cabinets you can take the opportunity to add special touches like glass doors, a dishwasher front that matches the cabinets, a new countertop, or other features.

Suitability

Should you choose refacing for your kitchen? The answer depends on design and space as well as the condition of the existing cabinets. You may also want to consider doing other kitchen projects at the same time.

▶ **Design and space.** Refacing is a decorative project, not a structural one. If your kitchen is poorly designed, lacks storage space, or is just plain too small, refacing is not enough. This project is for those who are pleased with the existing kitchen layout but not its look.

▶ **Cabinet condition.** Almost any cabinet can be refaced, regardless of age, style, or finish. But the insides of the cabinets must be in good shape. In addition, although you have a tremendous range of door styles to choose from, you must install them with surface-mount hinges. If the stiles (vertical pieces) between adjoining doors are narrow, your choices may be severely limited, or installing new doors may not be possible.

▶ **Other projects.** Since you'll be reducing the cabinets to their basic elements for refacing, this would be the time to install a new countertop (see Replace a Countertop, page 18). And as long as you're replacing drawer faces, consider adding tip-out trays behind the sink fronts for extra storage space (see Improve Kitchen Storage, page 56). The hardware for these items should be available where you buy hinges. You could also add panel fronts to the dishwasher and refrigerator so they match the cabinets. Your cabinet door supplier can find stock sizes or custom-make panels to fit.

▶ **Gaps.** If you find a gap where two cabinets have pulled away from one another, draw them together with bar clamps, drill pilot holes, and drive drywall screws to fasten them together. Where a cabinet has pulled away from the wall or ceiling, anchor it with drywall screws driven into wall studs or with hollow-wall fasteners in the spaces between studs. Drive screws or bolts through the mounting strips attached to the cabinet backs, near the tops. These were used to anchor the cabinets when they were installed. For greatest accuracy, do this corrective work before taking measurements for materials.

CONSTRUCTION DIAGRAM

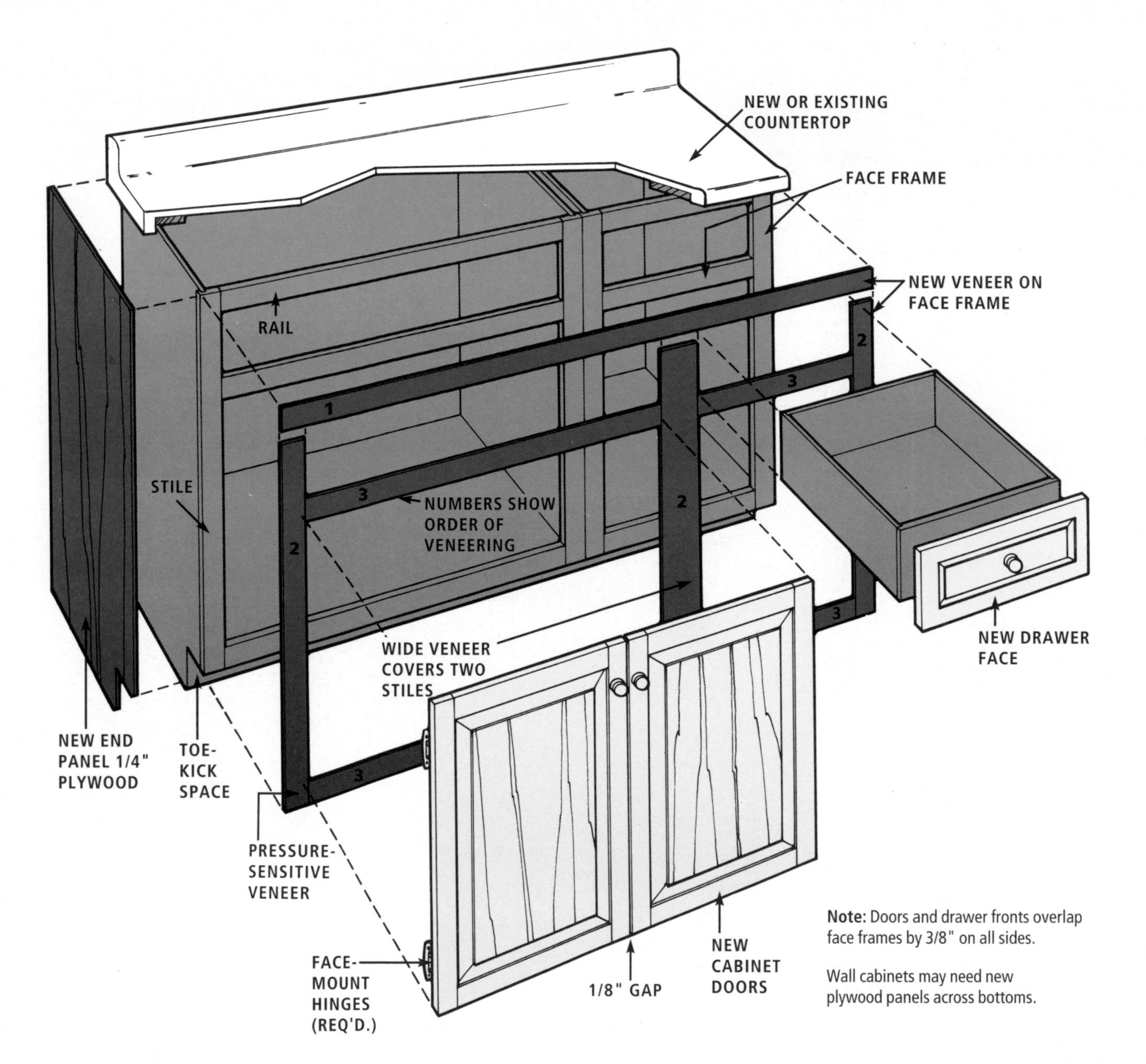

Note: Doors and drawer fronts overlap face frames by 3/8" on all sides.

Wall cabinets may need new plywood panels across bottoms.

BUYING MATERIALS

To reface kitchen cabinets you'll need new doors and drawer fronts, matching plywood and veneer, hinges, door knobs, and drawer pulls (see diagram, opposite).

Ready-made doors and drawer faces are available at some home centers, but the range of sizes and styles is limited. If ready-made components will fit your cabinets exactly, consider using them. However, make sure that you can get veneer for the cabinet facings that will match the doors and drawer faces exactly, and that you can stain plywood to match for end panels and other large surfaces.

Although it is more expensive to order cabinet doors, drawer faces, and other materials from a local cabinetmaker, you'll have far more choices. There is a tremendous array of styles and materials for doors and drawers available, as well as moldings, hardware, and veneers. In addition, when the parts you need are custom-made, you can be sure of a proper fit. If you have a hard time finding a supplier for a particular item, check with refacing contractors—some will sell materials to the do-it-yourselfer.

Measure twice—order once

You must make careful, accurate measurements before ordering (Photo 1). The supplier will usually tell you what measurements are required. Here are some specific points:

▶ Measure the height and width of door openings between the inside faces of the cabinet frame members. Then add 3/4 inch to both measurements. This allows the doors to overlap the cabinet frames 3/8 inch along each edge. When two doors cover a single opening, add 3/4 inch to the width, then divide by 2 to determine the individual door widths.

▶ Measure for drawer faces in the same way and add 3/4 inch to the measurements so they will overlap their openings 3/8 inch all around. However, wherever a drawer is directly above a cabinet door or pair of doors, the drawer face should be the same width as the door(s), even if the drawer opening itself is narrower than usual.

▶ Make a sketch of each row of cabinets and note which measurements are for which opening. If you are ordering veneer, plywood, and moldings from your door and drawer-face supplier, include measurements of the width and height of all the surfaces you intend to reface. If you will get those materials elsewhere, put the relevant measurements on a separate sketch.

Photo 1. Determine new door and drawer-face sizes by measuring the openings and adding 3/4 in. to both width and height. Doors overlap 3/8 in. all around.

Problems to anticipate

The older existing cabinets are, the more likely they are to present certain challenges. Some will affect your measurements and ordering, others require corrective measures. Here's how to deal with the most common problems:

▶ **Crooked or out-of-square cabinets.** Plan to use doors that overlap the edges of the openings 1/2 or 5/8 inch all around, rather than the standard 3/8 inch. Hang the doors to align with a level or chalkline rather than with the lines of the face frame opening (see Hiding Crooked Frames, page 32).

▶ **Irregular surfaces.** Pressure-sensitive veneers will span nail and screw holes, but not gaps, holes, or cracks larger than about 1/4 inch. You'll need to fill such problem spots with wood putty or wedges of wood glued in place; also fill surface dents with wood putty. Sand all patches and repairs level with the adjoining surfaces.

▶ **Narrow stiles.** To avoid having to apply veneer to the narrow, inside edges of framing members, the new cabinet doors must be installed with surface-mount hinges. If the old doors don't have surface-mount hinges, the stiles—the vertical pieces of the face frame—may be too narrow. Stiles must be at least 2-1/4 inches wide where two new hinges meet back to back and 1-1/4 inches wide at inside corners. If necessary, cut strips of wood and nail them to the inside edges of the opening to make the stiles wider. Do this before you measure for new doors, because it narrows the door openings.

TOOLS

- Measuring tape
- Carpenter's square
- Combination square
- Circular saw
- Saber saw
- Electric drill
- Block plane
- Hammer
- Nail set
- Screwdriver
- Orbital sander
- Utility knife
- Metal straightedge
- Veneer roller
- Paintbrush
- Sanding block
- File

MATERIALS

- 1/4" plywood, one surface oak or other finish wood
- Pressure-sensitive wood veneers
- Contact cement (nonflammable)
- Face-mount hinges and matching screws
- Cabinet door knobs
- Drawer pulls
- Clear spray lacquer
- Wood putty
- Stain

GETTING READY

Prepare carefully to make the task of refacing go easily and quickly:

▶ Remove food and utensils from the cabinets before starting. Then unscrew the door hinges and pull the drawers out of their openings.

▶ Scrub, paint, or stain the insides of the old cabinets and drawers, if they need it. They can be drying while you do the refacing.

▶ Remove the range hood, towel rack, spice rack, and all other fixtures that are in the way of the surfaces you want to reface.

▶ Put down a tarp or drop cloth to protect the floor, and hang a shower curtain or plastic sheeting across the doors and openings to confine sawdust and odors to the kitchen.

Consider the countertop

You can reface your cabinets with the countertop in place, but if your cabinets are ripe for change, perhaps the countertop is too.

▶ If a new top is in your plan, install it first (see Replace a Countertop, page 18) or at least loosen and lift the old one. Many old countertops were built in place and are nailed or glued to the cabinet framework; pulling the countertop off after refacing a cabinet could damage your work.

▶ Some older tops have a lip that hangs down over the base cabinet in a way that can block putting new facing on the top rail of the frame. Check for this before starting work, to avoid an unpleasant surprise.

Prefinish the wood

Stain and varnish the materials before installing them (Photo 2). Self-adhesive veneer is often already stained, but you must make the unfinished pieces match. Plywood and solid wood absorb stain at different rates, so test the stain first, using the back of a new drawer face and scraps of veneer and ply-wood. Control color differences by the amount of time you let the stain remain on the wood—longer for a darker appearance, shorter for a lighter effect.

Photo 2. Prefinish the veneers, plywood, doors, and drawer fronts. Touch them up after they have been attached.

REFACING THE CABINETS

When all the materials are at hand and have been prepared, you can start the work of refacing. The project has six major steps. Do them in the following order:

- ▶ Square the cabinet corners.
- ▶ Attach the plywood.
- ▶ Prepare the face frames.
- ▶ Apply the veneer.
- ▶ Install the doors.
- ▶ Attach the drawer faces.

Procedures for each step are explained in the following sections.

SQUARE THE CORNERS

The face frame of a cabinet commonly extends beyond the end panel in a kind of "ear" at an exposed corner. To get finished corners without complex veneering or paneling techniques, you can remove these ears or fill in to bring the cabinet ends flush with them.

▶ **Removing the ears.** This approach uses the least amount of material and doesn't affect kitchen features that must fit next to the cabinets. A block plane works for this task (Photo 3). Use a chisel in spots the plane can't reach. Finish the corner as shown in the diagram for Method A, opposite page.

▶ **Filling in.** If you can't remove the ears, add a filler panel of lauan plywood or other inexpensive material to bring the cabinet end flush with the ear. Finish the end with new facing over the filler and the ear; see the diagram for Method B, opposite page.

Photo 3. Plane off the ears at the cabinet sides so the face frame is flush with the end. Use a chisel to finish the cut at the top of the cabinet.

Squaring Exposed Corners

To square off and reface the end of a cabinet, use the method that best suits the space and working conditions.

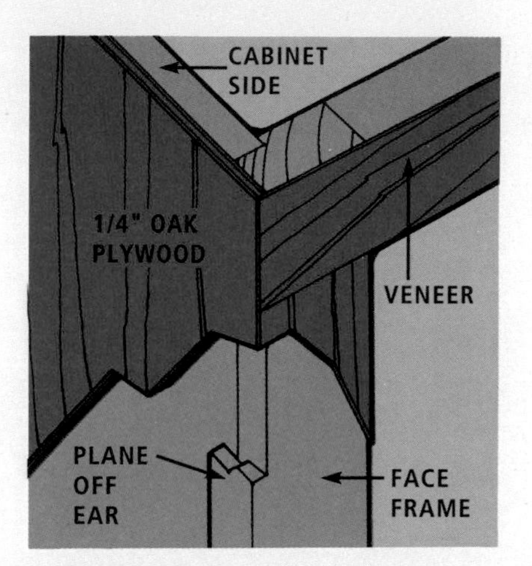

Method A. Plane or chisel off the protruding ear on the face frame. Cover the cabinet end with a 1/4-inch finish panel. Apply face veneer over the panel edge.

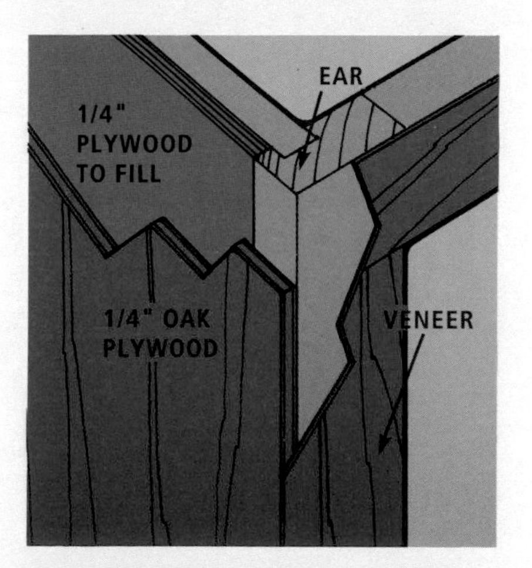

Method B. Add 1/4-inch plywood fill to bring the cabinet end flush with the ear on the face frame. Add a finish panel and face veneer as in Method A.

ATTACH THE PLYWOOD

Some cabinet surfaces are out of sight and can be left as they are or painted. But all visible large surfaces must be covered with plywood that matches the new finish.

▶ Wherever the bottoms of upper cabinets can be seen, cut 1/4-inch plywood to fit over them. Use a plywood blade in a circular saw, and a straightedge to guide the saw. If a cabinet bottom isn't square, cut the plywood a little wide, hold it against the bottom of the cabinet with its edges tight to the wall and adjoining cabinet, and trace the profile of the cabinet front onto the plywood. Cut along this line. When put in place, the front edge of the plywood must be perfectly flush with the face frame so the veneer will cover it smoothly. Apply contact cement to the back of the plywood and the underside of the cabinet; then press the plywood in place. Fasten it in position with brads or finish nails all around the edges (Photo 4).

▶ Cover end panels in the same way. Although you might use large sheets of veneer, 1/4-inch plywood is better, especially if the panels are wavy or otherwise not smooth and flat. Again, keep the plywood flush with the edge of the face frame (Photo 5). If the panel is slightly narrow, leave a small gap where the plywood meets the wall, rather than where it intersects the face frame.

▶ Finally, cut and install strips of plywood to cover the face of the recessed toe-kick area on the base cabinets.

ATTACH THE PLYWOOD

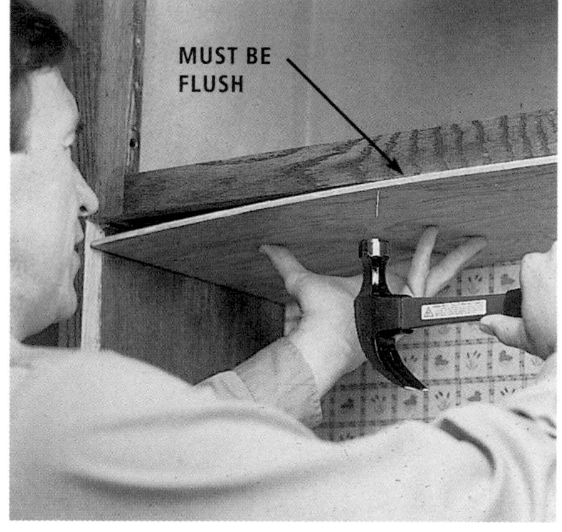

Photo 4. Nail 1/4-in. plywood to any visible cabinet bottoms. Cut it with a circular saw and plywood blade, guided by a straightedge.

Photo 5. Attach plywood to cabinet sides with contact cement and brads. Get the front edge flush with the face frame.

PREPARE THE FACE FRAMES

Proper preparation of the cabinet face frames is crucial if the new veneer facings are to last. Here's what to do:

▶ Sand the face frames to remove built-up deposits and loose finish (Photo 6). Then wash the wood with a mild dishwashing detergent and rinse with clean water.

▶ Smooth any uneven joints between cabinets with a file or sandpaper. Check the edges of any plywood you have installed and sand any protruding edges so they are flush with the faces of the cabinet frames. Fill gouges, cracks, and edge voids with wood putty.

▶ Spray all face frames with a light coat of clear aerosol lacquer (Photo 7). This gives a smooth, stable base for the veneer adhesive. Hold a piece of cardboard inside the cabinet to block overspray, and give the lacquer a few hours to dry.

APPLY THE VENEER

Apply veneer to the face frame of each cabinet in the order shown in the diagram on page 26. The strips must be fitted and trimmed in this order because they butt into one another. Start with a long, continuous strip across the top rails of all adjoining cabinets. Then do the vertical stiles. Finally, cover the lower horizon-tal rails between the stiles.

Basic techniques

Follow the procedures shown in Photos 8–11 for cutting and applying the veneer.

▶ Use light pressure to position a strip of veneer initially; once pressed down, it's very difficult to get off.

▶ Precut the veneers for the stiles a bit wide. Install the veneer on an end stile with its outside edge flush with the corner, covering the edge of the new end panel, and the other edge overlapping the door or drawer opening. Where two cabinets meet, cover both stiles with a single wide strip of veneer, slightly overhanging the openings on both sides. Use the inner edge of the face frame as a guide to cut the veneer to an exact fit (Photo 12). This way, any slight trimming problem will be covered by a door or drawer face.

▶ Install veneer on the lower horizontal rails last. Cut each strip a little long, with one end square. Butt the square end against the veneer on one stile and press the strip in place. Trim the overlap at the other end to an exact fit with a straightedge (Photo 13).

▶ Use a fine-tooth file to smooth all edges and corners as you proceed (Photo 14).

Dealing with mistakes

If you make a mistake, lift one end of the veneer with a sharp chisel or knife blade and try working it up and off. Unfortunately, it will most likely come off in splinters, especially if the adhesive has been allowed to set for long. In that case, use a sander to remove everything you can't pry or peel off the face of the frame and apply a new strip.

PREPARE THE FACE FRAMES

Photo 6. Sand face frames to remove loose finish; you don't need to strip them. Then wash with detergent and rinse clean.

Photo 7. Seal face frames with clear spray lacquer. Pressure-sensitive veneers are designed to adhere to sealed, not bare, wood.

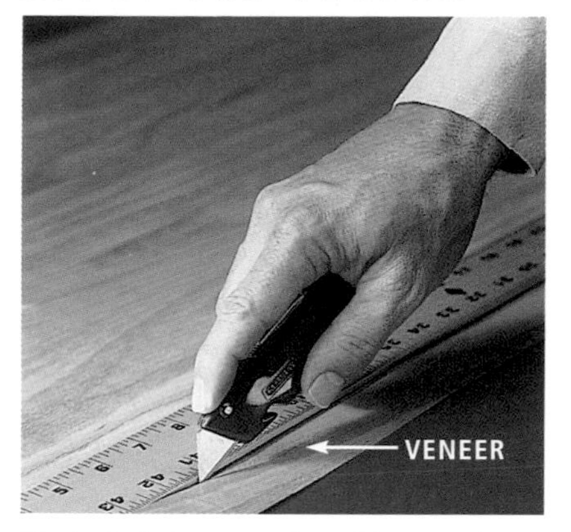

Photo 8. Cut veneers face side up, using a straightedge and a sharp blade in a utility knife. Make the cut on a smooth, hard surface, not cardboard.

Photo 9. After cutting, pull the backing paper off the veneer in a continuous strip to expose the pressure-sensitive adhesive. Keep it clean.

Photo 10. Position the upper strip across a group of cabinets first, using light pressure. Molding will cover the gap along the ceiling or soffit at the top edge.

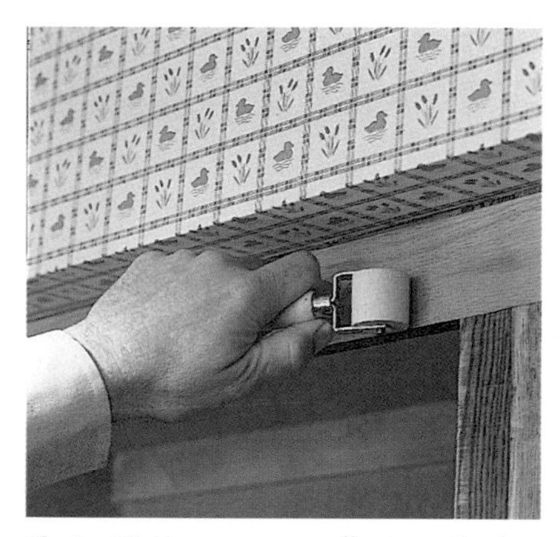

Photo 11. Use a veneer roller to activate the glue. Cut small slits in any bubbles or bulges and then press them down with a warm iron.

Photo 12. Cut pieces for the stile strips slightly wide and apply flush with the outside edge. Trim the inside edges using the face frame as a guide.

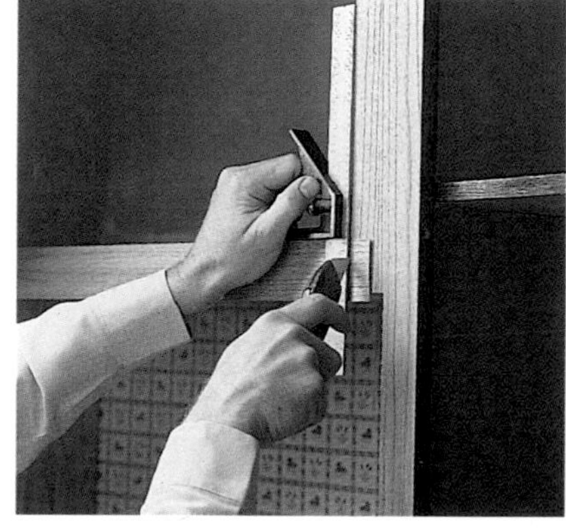

Photo 13. Cover cabinet bottom rails and drawer rails with short horizontal strips. Trim the overlap in place with a straightedge to guide the knife.

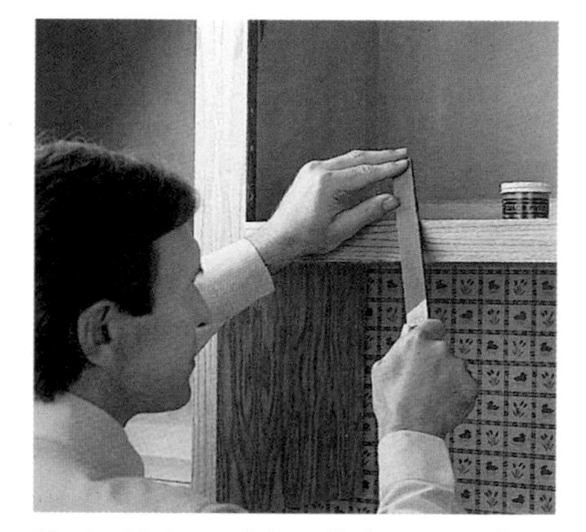

Photo 14. Smooth installed veneer edges and corners with a fine file. Use forward strokes to avoid pulling the veneer away from the frame.

INSTALL THE DOORS

Door placement can make or break the appearance of your refaced cabinets. Work carefully to get all of the door tops level and their edges plumb, and to get consistent spacing between the door edges and the outside edges of the cabinet face frames.

▶ Snap a level chalk line on the face frame 3/8 inch above the tops of the door openings. Hang the doors to this line. This gives cabinets a clean, uniform look even if the door openings are crooked and out of square (see diagram below).

▶ Hang the doors with surface-mount hinges. Attach them first to the backs of the new doors, positioned 3 inches from the top and bottom edges. Then hold the door with its top edge on the chalk line and the side edges overlapping the face frame equally. Drill pilot holes and screw the hinges to the face frame (Photo 15).

▶ Where two doors meet to cover a single opening, allow a 1/8-inch gap between them for closing clearance.

Photo 15. Hang doors with surface-mount hinges. Align the top edges with a chalk line snapped 3/8 in. above the openings.

Hiding Crooked Frames

Hang doors to a level top line whether frames are square or crooked. Where frames are badly out of square, cut doors 1 to 1-1/8 inch (rather than 3/4 inch) larger than the openings.

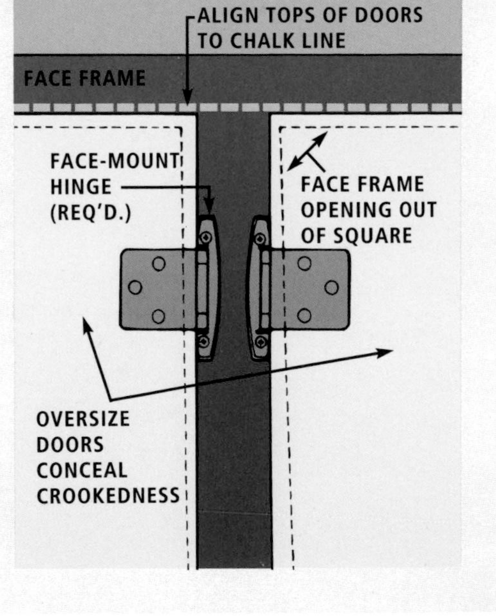

ATTACH THE DRAWER FACES

How you replace the old drawer faces depends upon how the drawers are built. There are three possibilities: a two-piece front with a removable face, a two-piece front with a non-removable face, or a single-piece front.

▶ Examine the drawer. If it is a box with a separate finished face attached to the front, look inside at the back of the drawer front. If you see screw heads, remove the screws and the finished face should come free.

▶ If the front of the drawer is two pieces but there are no screws, the face is probably nailed and glued on. Don't try to pry it free; you are likely to damage the structure of the drawer. Instead, treat it the same as a one-piece front.

▶ A one-piece front is both a structural element and the drawer face. It is attached directly to the sides of the drawer and extends beyond the sides, top, and bottom of the drawer opening. You cannot remove it without having to rebuild the drawer. Instead, cut all the edges of the front flush with the sides, bottom, and top of the drawer (Photo 16).

▶ Attach the new face with screws driven through the front from inside the box. Before drilling holes for the screws, slip each drawer in its opening and use clamps to position the new face so it aligns with the cabinet door below or above it (Photo 17).

ATTACH DRAWER FACES

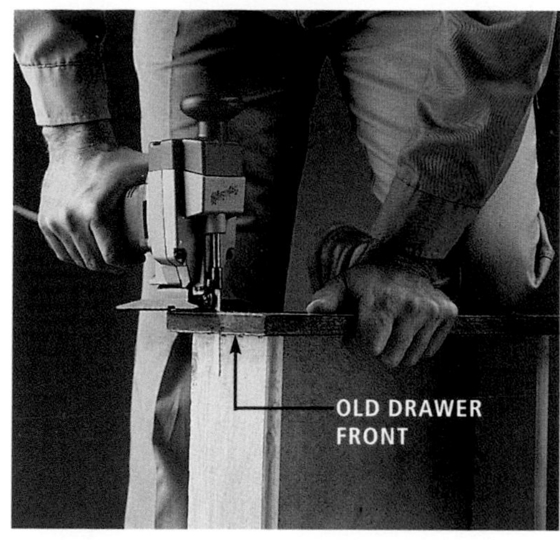

Photo 16. If the old drawer faces cannot be removed, trim them flush with the sides, top, and bottom edges of the drawers.

Photo 17. Attach new drawer faces with glue and screws. Clamp them in position after lining them up with the neighboring cabinet doors.

FINISH THE JOB

Once the doors are hung and the drawer faces are attached, a few details remain.

▶ Attach the knobs and pulls (Photo 18). Make sure cabinet door knobs are all at the same height and centered in their stiles. Make sure drawer pulls are centered left and right and between the top and bottom of the drawer faces.

▶ Touch up the finish and veneer edges wherever required with colored wood putty and stain. Be sure to set all nailheads, fill with putty, and color with stain on a fine-tip artist's brush. If you can't get an exact match, a spot that is darker rather than lighter than the surrounding area is usually least noticeable.

▶ Add prestained cove molding to cover any gaps along the top edge of the face frame, where it meets the ceiling. You can also use cove molding to cover gaps between cabinet sides and uneven walls.

▶ If you ordered matching panels for the front your refrigerator or dishwasher, you should have prefinished them when you prepared the other materials. Install them now to complete your refacing project (Photo 19).

FINISH THE JOB

Photo 18. Install door knobs centered in the stile width. Position drawer pulls carefully in the centers of the drawer faces.

Photo 19. A ready-made raised panel added to a dishwasher or refrigerator door can be stained to match the refaced cabinets.

Install Stock Kitchen Cabinets

If your kitchen cabinets can no longer hold everything you have to put in them, if the doors sag and the drawers stick, it's time to install new cabinets. It's easiest and most economical to use ready-made stock cabinets. With good planning, a moderate cash investment, and plenty of elbow grease, the operation can be a rousing success.

This is an ideal project for the moderately skilled do-it-yourselfer who wants to save money and feel the satisfaction of a job well done. There's another benefit, too: Improving the kitchen is one of the best investments for future resale.

Give your kitchen a great new look and add a lot more storage space by putting in new cabinets. There are styles and finishes to suit any home. Using stock sizes keeps the cost down and makes installation simple.

ABOUT STOCK CABINETS

Stock cabinets are mass-produced units offered in a limited number of styles and finishes, and in standard sizes. They cost about half as much as cabinets that are custom-built to fit your kitchen exactly, and they are readily available through home centers, kitchen design centers, and many lumberyards.

Mass production does not mean that stock cabinets are inferior. Their appearance and functional design have improved greatly over the years. In addition to standard base and wall cabinets, better designed corner, pantry, and specialty cabinets offer many of the conveniences and extra storage capacity of more expensive custom cabinets.

The kitchen "footprint" of many homes is limited; often there is little space to expand. But you can pick up space in a few simple ways—remove an old broom closet for more countertop area with cabinets above and below; remove the boxed soffit near the ceiling to install upper cabinets that are 42 inches tall rather than the standard 30 inches or to install a tall pantry cabinet.

Even if you can't change the size, shape, or overall layout of your kitchen, you can gain extra cabinet and counter space with modern cabinets. And the colors, styles, and accessories available will suit almost anyone's taste.

PLANNING THE PROJECT

Good planning is the key to a successful kitchen makeover. Here's how to organize the project for the least expense and the most effective use of your time and effort. For tips and ideas on layout and design, see pages 36–37.

Basic considerations

You will not have the use of your stove or oven during the time it takes to install the cabinets, so do your planning carefully.

▶ Do everything you can to shorten the project. Solicit professional or volunteer help as needed, and be sure to allow plenty of delivery time so you don't hold up the whole project because of one missing cabinet or appliance.

▶ As soon as the old cabinets have been pulled out, add new outlets you may need for a microwave, dishwasher, or other appliances. Do it yourself if you are qualified; otherwise hire an electrician.

▶ Allow time to scrape, patch, and prime the walls after completing remodeling work but before installing the new cabinets. Those jobs are messy, and it's easier to work on bare walls than between and around new cabinets.

▶ Taking out a wall, installing new floor coverings, adding windows, or including built-in appliances can easily double the length of the project. If you are going to work only on weekends, plan enough time at the end of each session to get the kitchen into usable condition for the rest of the week.

▶ Consider the condition of the existing floor. If it has vent and plumbing holes, stubborn adhesives, old tile, or other flaws, it may be best to install a new layer of 3/8- or 1/2-inch plywood over the entire area. Do this immediately after taking out the old cabinets.

▶ If you intend to put down new finish flooring, plan to do it after the new cabinets have been installed. This will save on materials and prevent damage to the new floor.

Standard dimensions

In order to consider what the possibilities are and to plan what you can do, you need to know the dimensions of the units available.

▶ Most lower cabinets, called base cabinets, are 34-1/2 inches high and 24 inches deep. They range in width from 9 to 48 inches, usually in increments of 3 inches.

▶ Stock upper cabinets are normally 12 inches deep. Pantry cabinets and those for use over a refrigerator measure 24 inches deep. Height ranges from 12 to 42 inches, commonly in 6-inch increments. Like base cabinets, upper cabinet width changes in 3-inch increments.

▶ Almost always, a row of stock-size cabinets will not fill the available wall space exactly. The row is completed with filler strips. Because cabinets come in 3-inch increments, it's rare to need a filler strip wider than 3 inches on any one wall. If you have unusual needs or size requirements, consider having a cabinet custom-made to match the stock cabinets.

TOOLS

- Levels, 2' and 4'
- Chalk line
- Tape measure
- Carpenter's square
- Circular saw
- Saber saw
- Variable-speed drills
- Hammer
- Drawing compass
- Screwdrivers
- Stud finder
- Belt sander
- Block plane
- Pry bar
- Clamps

MATERIALS

- Long 2x4
- 1x4 ledger strips
- 1x4 or 2x4 braces
- Shims
- Construction adhesive
- 2-1/2" drywall screws
- 1-1/2" finish nails

See the design tips at right for additional information about countertop height, adequate work space requirements, and related considerations.

Ordering stock cabinets

Order cabinets through a home center or a specialized kitchen center. In some cases, you can order direct from the manufacturer.

▶ Large home centers often have a staff consultant or designer, whose services are free, to help you with your cabinet selection and purchase. You may or may not pay a design fee when working with a specialized kitchen center. It pays to shop around for a cabinet style, price, and consultant you like.

▶ When you do shop for cabinets, be sure to bring sketches of your kitchen with critical information: the exact dimensions of the room; the exact location of windows, doors, and permanent fixtures; if possible, include the location of wiring, plumbing, and ductwork. Also bring the dimensions of your old appliances and installation instructions and measurements for any new appliances you may be adding.

▶ Accurate measurements are important. Most cabinet dealers have kitchen-design software on a computer that makes the design process much easier and more flexible. They just enter the numbers and the computer lets you test any number of various possibilities. But the computer can't tell how accurate the original information is, so be careful when you make your measurements.

▶ Find out how long it will take for your cabinets to be delivered, then work backward and plan your demolition and installation schedule around that.

Kitchen and Design Details

If you're simply going for a new look—replacing old cabinets with new ones the same size and shape—you won't need to ponder your new layout much. But if you're going through the work and expense of installing cabinets of different sizes than what you now have, with different features, it's a good idea to take a look at the possibilities for an improved layout.

Redesigning a kitchen isn't a 1-2-3-step process. You must work and plan on several fronts all at the same time, then sift and sort features, costs, and schedule in order to arrive at a design that will work for you.

▶ Before making any design or layout decisions, keep a list for a month or two of all the problems you encounter while working in the kitchen or improvements you'd like, such as more counter space next to the refrigerator, cabinets that are too deep, no convenient place for large pots and pans, or too many small appliances taking up counter space. In a few weeks you'll have a pretty good feel for what you want and need in a kitchen.

▶ Consider how your family uses the kitchen. Are you messy, or meticulous? Does more than one person cook at a time? Do the kids use the space for science projects, homework, and talking on the phone? Are there any special needs to be considered, such as wheelchair access?

▶ Keep in mind clean-up tasks and storage needs. A little time spent planning for these requirements can avoid a lot of aggravation later.

▶ Select new appliances before ordering the cabinets. Dishwasher width is usually a standard 24 inches, but ranges, refrigerators, and sinks can vary in depth and width. Check refrigerator height, too, to see if you can put a cabinet above it.

▶ If at all possible, avoid changing the location of the sink, dishwasher, and stove. That will avoid the hassle of moving a lot of wiring and pipes —and the considerable expense if you have to hire it done.

▶ To arrive at the most efficient layout, consider the work triangle—the area bounded by the sink, the refrigerator, and the stove (see figure, opposite). In a poor layout the triangle is long and skinny, putting these major task centers too far apart. In a well laid out kitchen the triangle is short and fat. Try to keep each leg of the triangle between 2 and 8 feet long, and limit the total distance to 12 to 24 feet. This makes work easy and efficient because it's only a step or two from one task center to another.

▶ Design at least 15 inches of counter space next to the handle side of the refrigerator; 2 feet on each side of your sink; 1 foot on each side of the range.

▶ Put the dishwasher next to the sink.

▶ Allow a minimum of 36 inches of space between cabinets that face each other.

▶ Place pantry cabinets or double-decker oven cabinets at the end of a row of cabinets so they don't break up the counter space.

▶ For snack bars or eating areas, allow 21 to 24 inches of room for each person. If the eating area is at the standard base cabinet height, the countertop should overhang the base by 12 to 15 inches. If it is attached to the sides of the cabinets, as in the figure, opposite, it should be 30 inches high. Stools or chairs should be 12 inches below the countertop (for example, you need a 24-inch high stool for a 36-inch top).

▶ Pay attention to the necessary clearance for doors and drawers—especially where knobs and drawers can bump into cabinets or appliances.

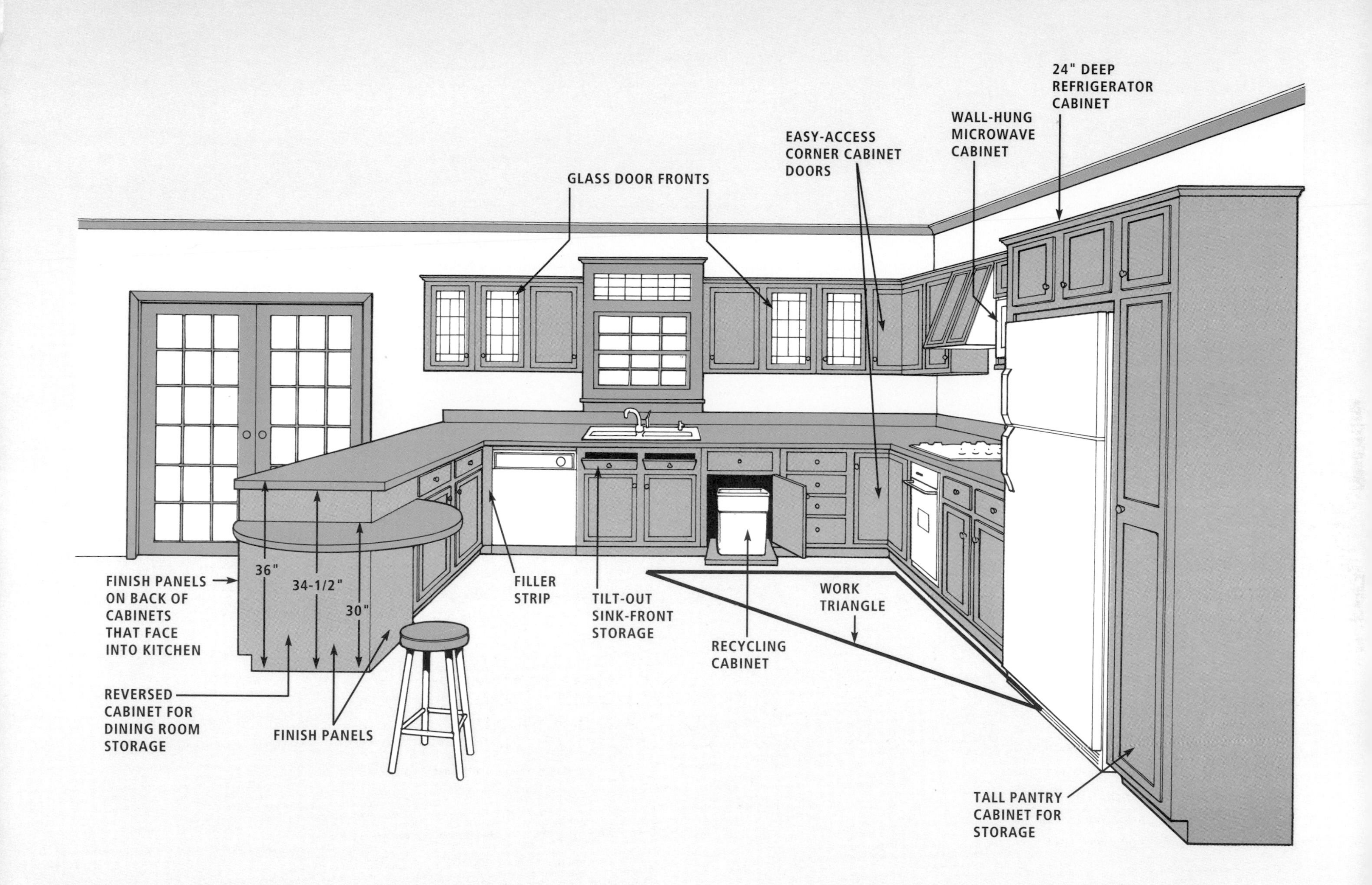

24" DEEP REFRIGERATOR CABINET
WALL-HUNG MICROWAVE CABINET
EASY-ACCESS CORNER CABINET DOORS
GLASS DOOR FRONTS
36"
34-1/2"
30"
FINISH PANELS ON BACK OF CABINETS THAT FACE INTO KITCHEN
FILLER STRIP
TILT-OUT SINK-FRONT STORAGE
WORK TRIANGLE
RECYCLING CABINET
REVERSED CABINET FOR DINING ROOM STORAGE
FINISH PANELS
TALL PANTRY CABINET FOR STORAGE

Reuse Old Cabinets

Remove old cabinets carefully; they can be reused in a laundry room, garage, or workshop.

PREPARATION

Plan your time before starting to work. It will take one weekend to carry out the three stages listed below. You'll need a second, three-day weekend to install the new cabinets, and a third weekend to install countertops, moldings, and appliances. If you need to remove a wall, or plan to install new wall or floor coverings, the entire project will take even longer.

When you are ready to begin, prepare the kitchen for new cabinets in three stages:

Remove the old cabinets

If necessary, turn off the water and disconnect the sink plumbing. Also turn off electricity, and disconnect and remove any appliances that are going to be replaced or relocated. Then tear out the old cabinets.

▶ Upper cabinets are usually held in place by screws driven through hanging strips at the top and bottom.

▶ Many old countertops are both glued and screwed down, so it may take some prying to remove them (Photo 1).

▶ Base cabinets are held by screws driven through a fastening rail at the top that is accessible when the countertop is removed.

▶ Peninsula cabinets are attached to other base cabinets at the top, and to floor blocks at the bottom. Look for screw heads in the toe-kick space or behind base molding at floor level.

Make physical changes and repairs

Once the cabinets have been removed, examine the walls and floor.

▶ Make any extensive wall repairs or changes before removing or repairing the existing floor. If the floor is to be left as it is, protect it adequately during all your work.

▶ Make electrical changes at this time, such as moving outlets and running cable for new circuits (Photo 2). Major appliances require individual circuits; most electrical codes call for 20-amp circuits for all kitchen outlets; outlets within 6 feet of the sink must have ground fault circuit interrupt (GFCI) protection. Check your local electrical code on these points, or rely on a professional electrician.

▶ If you plan to put down new flooring directly over the old, wait until the cabinets are installed to prepare the floor. Otherwise, remove the old flooring now and if necessary put down a proper base for the new flooring. If the new finish flooring will be 3/4-inch wood or tile, use particleboard or plywood to build up the area where the base cabinets will rest in order to maintain the normal 36-inch floor-to-countertop height.

PREPARATION: REMOVE AND REPAIR

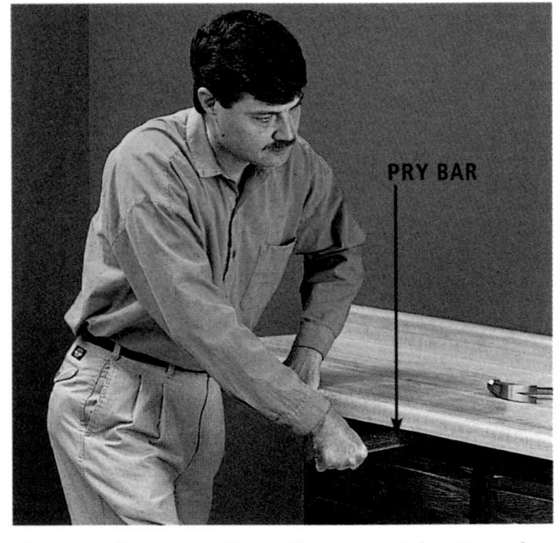

Photo 1. Clear out all appliances and furniture for an unobstructed work area. Then remove the old cabinets and countertop.

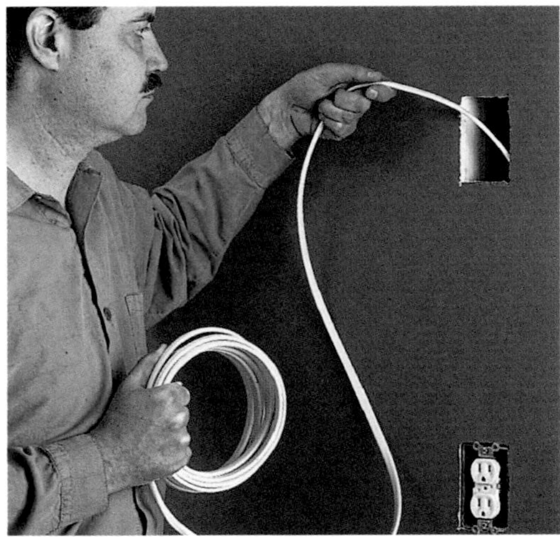

Photo 2. With the old cabinets gone, install new wiring where required, or hire it done, and repair the walls and floor.

PREPARATION: MARK REFERENCE LINES AND MOUNTING LOCATIONS

Photo 3. Check the floor with a 4-ft. level and a long, straight 2x4 to find the highest point. Take readings against the wall and 2 ft. out.

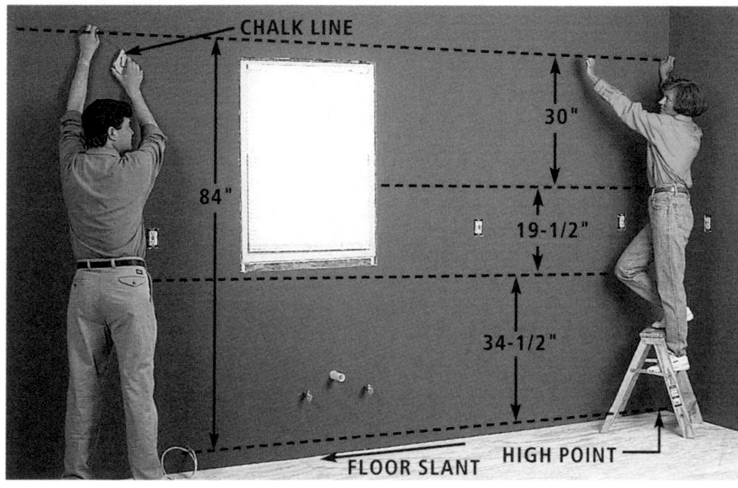

Photo 4. Snap chalk lines to mark the top of base cabinets 34-1/2 in. above the high point, and mark the top and bottom lines of upper cabinets.

Photo 5. Mark the positions of base and upper cabinets along the chalk lines. Mark stud positions, too, for mounting cabinets later.

Mark reference lines and mounting locations

This is a crucial step in installing cabinets. Without accurate reference lines, cabinets are likely to be cockeyed or misaligned.

▶ Use a 4-foot level and a long straight 2x4 to check the floor for level (Photo 3). Do this against the wall and about 2 feet out from the wall, where the front of the base cabinets will be located. Find the highest point and mark the wall 34-1/2 inches above it. This is the height of the top of the base cabinets before a countertop is installed. Draw a level line at this height along all the walls.

▶ From this line, measure up the wall and mark the height of the top and bottom of the upper cabinets. For wall cabinets 30 inches tall, the bottom line is usually 19-1/2 inches above the base cabinet line. Snap chalk lines along these marks (Photo 4).

▶ If you are installing cabinets over a refrigerator, or double-decker cabinets (see Photo 14, page 43), mark just the top line and measure or temporarily set the cabinets in place to make sure they will fit and line up properly.

▶ Measure the width of the cabinet fronts and mark the locations of all base and upper cabinets along your horizontal reference lines (Photo 5). If you have traditional face-frame cabinets, the frames extend in "ears" on each side (see diagram, next page), so the rear edges of the cabinets will fall 1/4 inch off the marks. In either case, be sure upper and lower cabinets line up vertically, especially around appliances.

▶ Check the walls for plumb. If the walls that the cabinet sides butt against lean drastically in or out, you may need to add a thin filler strip to make up for the difference.

▶ Mark the stud positions along each horizontal line. Make the marks in a distinctive color to avoid confusion later when you install the cabinets. Use a stud finder to locate a stud in each wall. Probe with a finish nail to find the exact center of the stud. Then measure in each direction to mark the other studs—their centers should be 16 inches apart. In an old house, probe at each location; stud spacing may differ or be inconsistent.

INSTALLING BASE CABINETS

Unbox the new base cabinets and remove all their doors and drawers. Code each door, drawer, and cabinet with numbered masking tape so you know where to reinstall them.

Join cabinets together

▶ Always start installing cabinets from a corner. Roughly position a corner cabinet and the one abutting it, and clamp them together (Photo 6). Make sure the cabinet tops are even and the face frames flush.

▶ Fasten the cabinets together along their front edges. Starting at the top, predrill holes near the top and bottom and in the middle (Photo 7). For face-frame cabinets, use a countersink bit so the screw heads will be concealed. Lubricate the threads of drywall screws with soap before driving them into the holes with a Phillips head bit (Photo 8). For Euro-style cabinets, use two-piece connector bolts and drill holes to the appropriate size.

▶ Tap in wood shims coated with construction adhesive to raise the top rear edge of the cabinets to the height of the horizontal line on the wall. Then use a 2-foot level and shims to level the front (Photo 9). Take time to do this right—failure to do so means uneven cabinet tops and great trouble making the countertops fit.

Secure cabinets to the wall

▶ When the cabinets are level side to side and front to back, secure them to the wall studs with screws driven through the fastening rail (see diagram at left). Predrill holes in the rail and use 2-1/2 inch bugle-head drywall screws (Photo 10) to fasten.

▶ Install the other base cabinets, fastening them to one another and to the previously installed cabinets as appropriate. Be sure to leave exactly the correct opening in places where the oven, dishwasher, or refrigerator will be installed.

▶ Where you must cut into a cabinet to accommodate fixtures such as plumbing pipes, heat registers, or electrical outlets, make sure to do so *before* screwing it to any adjacent cabinets. Measure carefully, mark the back of the cabinet, and cut out the required holes with either a saber saw or a hole saw (Photo 11).

Base Cabinet Details

Key features of face-frame base cabinet construction include a toe-kick at the bottom front, corner blocks at the top for rigidity, and a fastening rail at the top rear. The face frame extends in 1/4-inch ears on each side, so the cabinet box is 1/2-inch narrower than the overall front width.

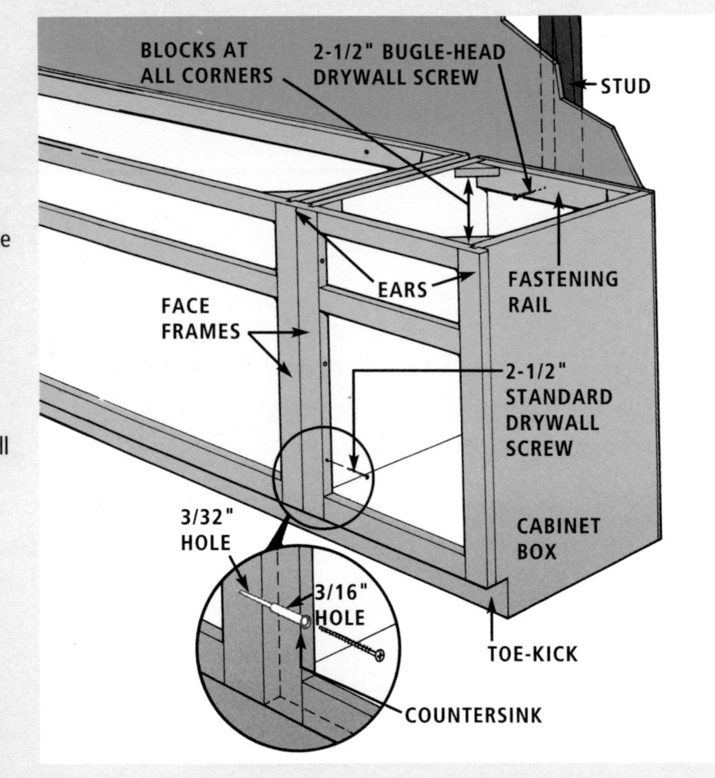

INSTALLING BASE CABINETS: JOIN CABINETS TOGETHER

Photo 6. Position and clamp the base corner cabinet to the one next to it. Be sure the face frames are flush and tight to one another.

Photo 7. Predrill holes for screws. Use a countersink bit in face frames so the screw heads will be hidden once they're installed.

Photo 8. Fasten face-frame cabinets together with at least three drywall screws. Soap the threads for faster, easier work.

Drilling Pilot Holes

Drill the clearance hole in the first cabinet a bit larger than the screw itself. Then drill the pilot hole in the second cabinet slightly undersized. That way the first cabinet is pinched tightly between the head of the screw on one side and the grip of the screw on the other.

INSTALLING BASE CABINETS: SECURE CABINETS TO THE WALL

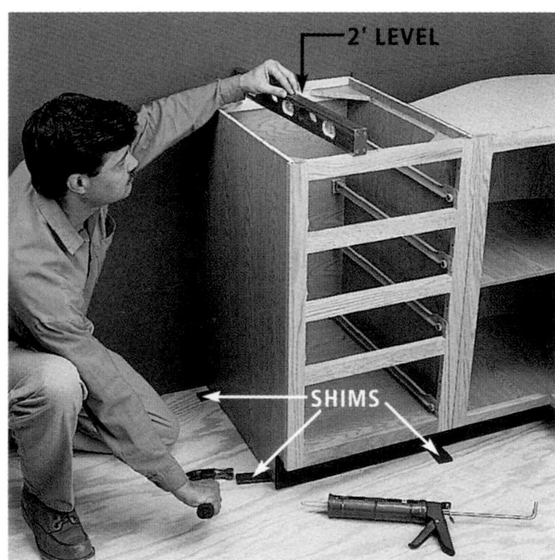

Photo 9. Shim base cabinets so the backs are even with the chalk line and the fronts and sides are level in every direction.

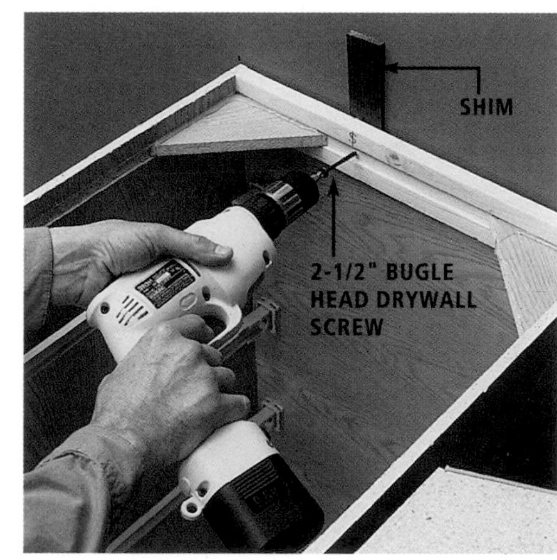

Photo 10. Screw the cabinets to the wall. Use shims at screw points as needed to prevent the screws from twisting or tilting the cabinet.

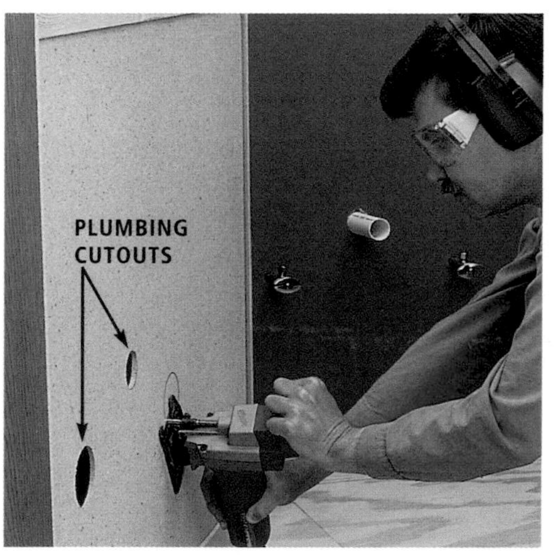

Photo 11. Cut openings in cabinet backs for pipes or other permanent fixtures. Measure twice—expensive mistakes are easy to make.

SECURE PENINSULA CABINETS TO THE FLOOR

Base cabinets that have one long side fastened to the wall at several points do not need to be attached to the floor. But peninsula cabinets, which have only one end at a wall, and island cabinets do require floor attachment.

▶ Put the peninsula or island cabinet in position and draw lines on the floor to mark its end, or ends, and sides (Photo 12).

▶ Tip the cabinets back or move them out of the way so you can measure the thickness of the cabinet panels or frame at the floor level. A panel may be only 1/4 inch thick, or there may be a 1/2- or 3/4-inch rail behind it. Measure the appropriate distance back from each line on the floor and mark positions for floor blocks that will fit snugly behind panels and frames.

▶ Screw wood blocks to the floor at the inner lines (Photo 13). Put the cabinet back in place and secure it to the blocks with drywall screws.

Care with Screws

Don't overtighten drywall screws—they can snap in hard woods.

Upper or Lower First?

Some pros like to install upper cabinets first so they won't have to reach over the base cabinets to work. Others like to install base cabinets first; it allows them to space the uppers an exact height above the base cabinets, which is convenient for appliance or full-height backsplashes.

The installation procedures on these pages begin with the base cabinets. One advantage of this approach is that you can lay scrap plywood over them like a workbench. That gives you a place to spread out tools for installing the upper cabinets. It really doesn't matter whether you do uppers first, lowers first, or do both on one wall before moving on to the next wall. The main thing is to lay out everything precisely and not go on to the next cabinet until the one you're working on is perfectly placed. That kind of care is the key to fine results.

SECURE PENINSULA CABINETS TO THE FLOOR

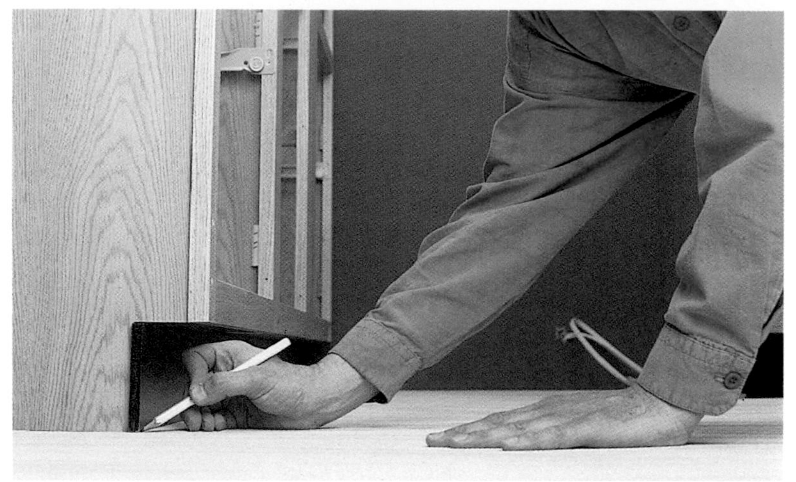

Photo 12. Mark the position of peninsula or island cabinets on the floor after putting them temporarily in position.

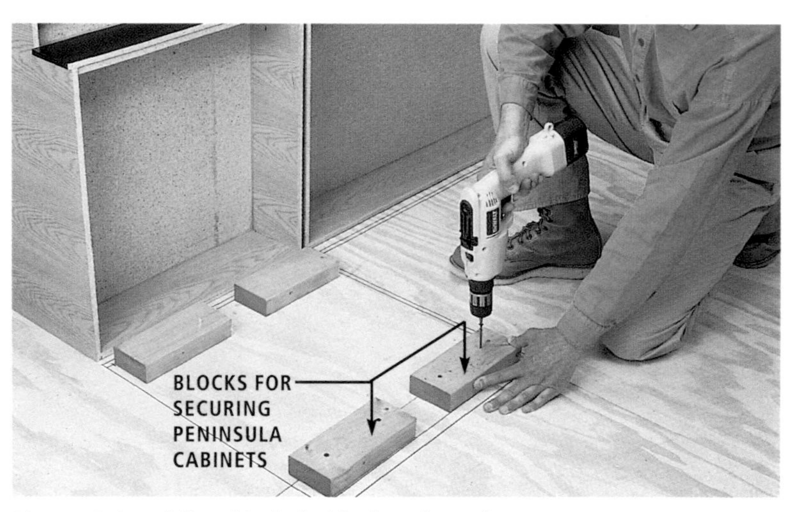

Photo 13. Install floor blocks inside the edges of the cabinet position. Replace the cabinet and secure it to the blocks with drywall screws.

INSTALLING UPPER CABINETS

Unbox the upper cabinets and remove the doors. Identify each cabinet and its doors with numbered masking tape for accurate remounting later. Installation procedures are essentially the same as for base cabinets, but with the added need to support the cabinets while you align and fasten them.

▶ With a stacking unit, such as a pantry cabinet, position the lower section in first, then place the upper section on top of it (Photo 14). Fasten the upper cabinet to the lower one, then screw through the mounting rails of both cabinets into the wall studs behind.

▶ For hanging cabinets, fasten a temporary 1x4 ledger strip to the wall studs to support them during installation. Align the ledger strip with the horizontal reference line on the wall. If you are working without a helper, also cut some lengths of lumber with V-notches in their upper ends to support the front edges of the cabinets. When you use these braces, put cardboard in the notches to protect the cabinets, and butt the bottom ends against temporary blocks tacked to the floor.

▶ Start by carefully positioning and leveling the corner cabinet. Remember that with a face-frame cabinet, the rear edges of the cabinet will be located inside the position lines you made when marking the layout on the wall. The offset will be the amount that the face frame "ear" extends beyond the end panel of the cabinet, usually 1/4 inch.

▶ Often the wall corner isn't square because drywall compound or plaster was applied too thickly there. If this is the case, mark the top and bottom of the cabinet on the wall, then shave away the excess wall material between the marks with a scraper or putty knife. With a face-frame cabinet this may be necessary only on the back wall. For a Euro-style cabinet, do the side wall as well so the corner fits properly.

▶ Before putting a wall cabinet into position, pre-drill holes in the top and bottom hanging rails where they will be fastened to the studs and start screws in the holes. Then lift the cabinet up onto the ledger strip (Photo 15). Either have a helper support the front edge, or put braces in place to support it while you screw the cabinet to the wall.

▶ Put the next cabinet in position and attach it to the wall studs. Then align the front edges of the cabinets and clamp them together; you may need to loosen the wall screws a bit to do this. Drill holes and fasten the cabinet fronts together just as you did with the base cabinets.

▶ A cabinet less than 15 inches wide may fall between studs. If so, fasten it to the adjacent cabinets at both the front and rear.

INSTALLING UPPER CABINETS

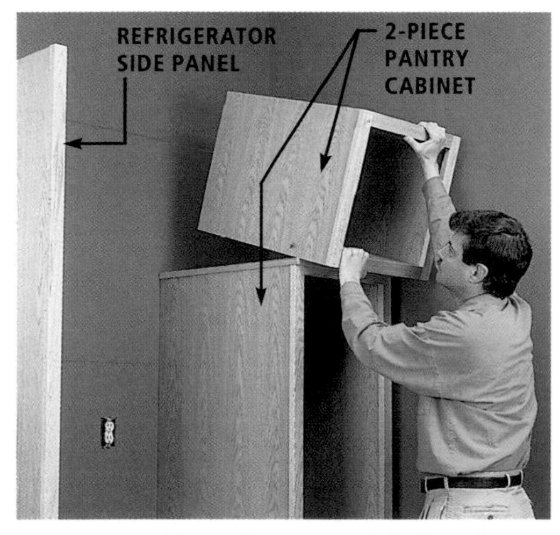

Photo 14. Position tall pantry and similar cabinets so their tops are on the upper reference line. Screw cabinet sections together.

Photo 15. Use a ledger strip to support upper hanging cabinets during installation. Begin with a corner cabinet and work outward.

Alignment

▶ When two or more cabinets have been fastened together, put a level on the face at each end to check for plumb (Photo 16). If they lean in or out more than 1/8 inch, drive in shims where needed before retightening the mounting screws into the wall.

▶ Check repeatedly that the cabinets stay lined up with the layout marks on the wall and have the proper spacing for appliances to fit neatly between them (Photo 17). If you need to gain some space for an appliance, plane off small amounts of the face frame ears . Adding a thin strip of wood is a last-ditch effort for filling in a space that's too wide, but this shouldn't be necessary if you work carefully.

Filler strips

▶ Use filler strips in the spaces between end cabinets and the walls. Scribe each strip with a compass to conform to the contours of the wall (Photo 18), then cut back to this line with a circular saw, block plane, or belt sander. After shaping the strip, screw through the face frame to secure it in place (Photo 19). Also use screws to secure a filler strip to a Euro-style cabinet.

INSTALLING UPPER CABINETS: ALIGNMENT

Photo 16. Use adhesive-coated shims to make upper cabinets plumb as you install them. Make sure they stay level, too.

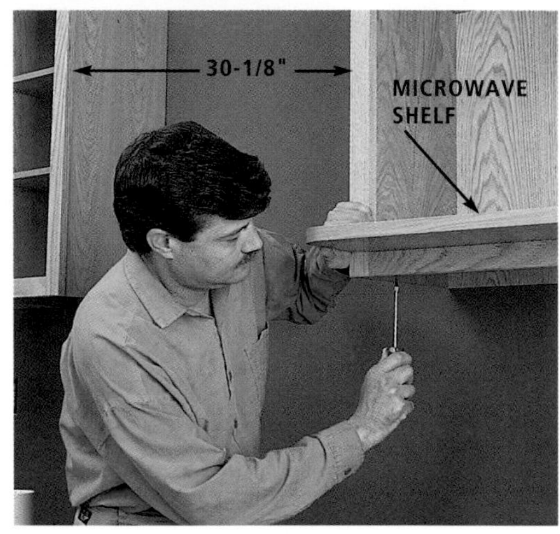

Photo 17. Maintain proper spacing between all cabinets so that ovens, refrigerators, dishwashers, and other appliances will fit.

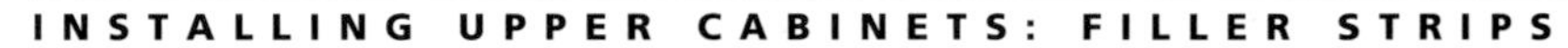

INSTALLING UPPER CABINETS: FILLER STRIPS

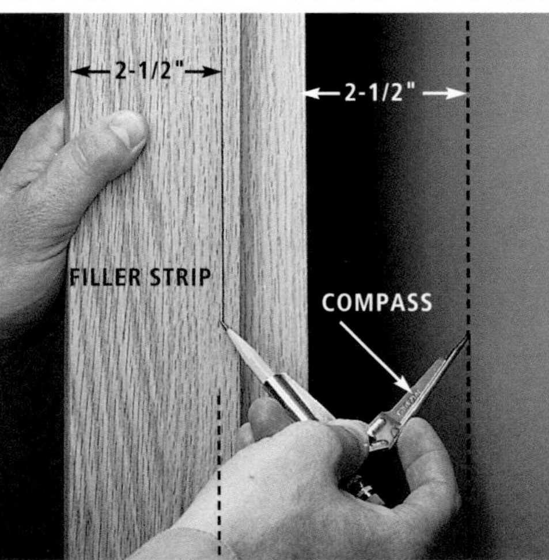

Photo 18. Scribe filler strips to fit gaps between cabinets and walls. Use a compass to transfer the contours of the wall onto the strip.

Photo 19. Secure the filler strip in place with screws after shaping it to the scribed line with a saw, belt sander, or plane.

FINISHING TOUCHES

▶ Glue finish panels to the exposed side or sides of a peninsula or island cabinet (Photo 20).
▶ Cover the toe-kick of base cabinets with strips of plywood cut to width (Photo 21) or with vinyl baseboard.
▶ Rehang the cabinet doors. Some cabinets are shipped with the doors unmounted. After installing the cabinet, drill holes and hang the doors to match those on the other cabinets.
▶ Hang all the doors before adding the knobs. Build a simple homemade jig for drilling the holes for knobs (Photo 22). This will eliminate a lot of repetitive measuring and will ensure that knobs are placed uniformly on all the doors.
▶ Clean out and install the drawers. You may find it easiest to stand the drawers on end to drill holes for the pulls before putting them in place. Center the pulls on the drawer fronts.

Counters, sinks, and appliances

▶ Home centers can supply countertops with built-in rounded edges and backsplashes in stock sizes, or exactly sized, and mitered at the corners to fit an L-shaped layout if needed. You can also opt for a custom-made top (see Replace a Countertop, pages 18–23). Installation is relatively simple: You clamp the top in position, then fasten from below with screws (Photo 23).
▶ After installing the finished floor, you can add quarter-round molding around the cabinet bases. It is pliable enough to conform to irregularities and cover gaps between the cabinet edges and floor. You can also use it along the sides and around upper cabinets to hide gaps at the walls. Stain the molding to match the cabinets before installing. Set and fill the nailheads, and touch up with a fine-tip brush and stain.
▶ Finally, install the dishwasher and other appliances yourself, or hire it done.

FINISHING TOUCHES

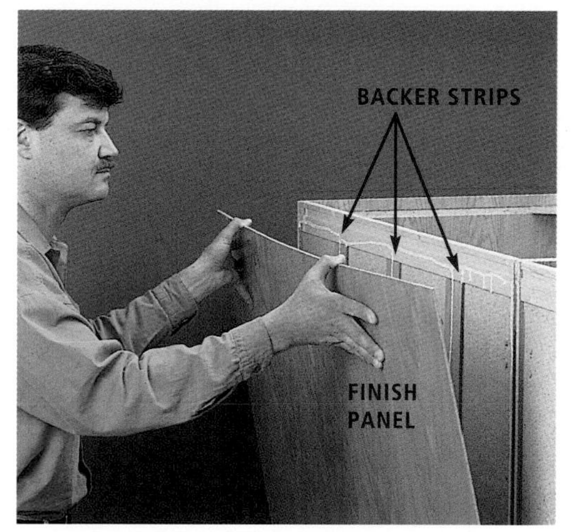

Photo 20. Add finish panels to exposed cabinet sides or backs where they are needed. Use construction adhesive and finish nails, with backer strips along the edge for support.

Photo 21. Nail toe-kick covers in position with 1-1/2 in. finish nails. After flooring is laid, add quarter-round molding to cover the gap where floor and cabinets meet.

Photo 22. Use a jig to drill uniformly positioned holes for door pulls. This jig can be turned over for right or left doors, and used at the top or bottom corner of a door.

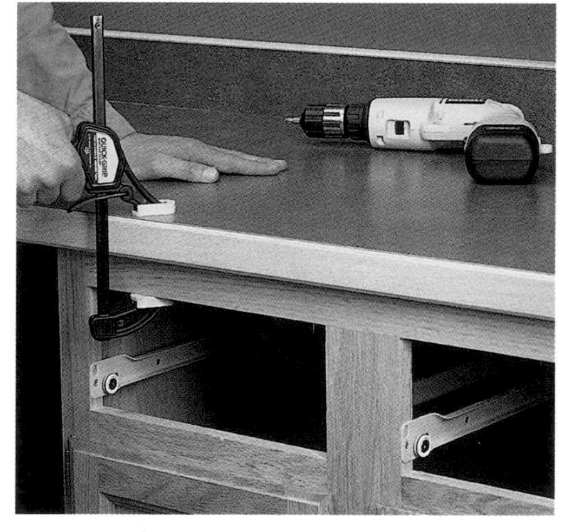

Photo 23. Clamp the countertop to the base cabinets, then secure it from below. Install the sink, the appliances, the floor, and wallcoverings to complete the project.

Build Euro-style Kitchen Cabinets

For a sleek, modern look in your kitchen, nothing can match easy-to-maintain cabinets designed and constructed in the style that is almost universal throughout Europe.

Euro-style cabinets can be very expensive if you order them custom-made to fit your kitchen. But you can build them yourself, to the exact sizes you need, at great savings.

This is not a quick-and-easy weekend project for a beginner, but if you have moderate carpentry skills and some power tools it is a very practical undertaking. The instructions and illustrations here describe what to do. If you can measure accurately, and cut, fit, and assemble parts with care and patience, you can build a first-rate set of cabinets.

European-style cabinets give a kitchen a clean, efficient appearance. They are very convenient to use, and easy to maintain. Best of all, they are not very difficult to build if you follow the instructions for modular construction on these pages.

GUIDELINES

With the information given on these pages you can build efficient, modern Euro-style cabinets for your kitchen no matter what size it is or what kind of layout it has.

Because no two kitchens are the same, the instructions here do not tell you how to build a specific set of cabinets in a specific arrangement. Instead, they explain how to build cabinets for any situation. The plan and detail drawings show you how Euro-style base and upper cabinets are constructed. Using these plans for typical cabinets as points of reference, you can adapt the dimensions given to build cabinets of any size you choose. And you can add some ingenuity and imagination to work out the details as they apply to your own particular kitchen and taste.

The text and photos supplement and expand upon the drawings. They explain the steps in assembling the cabinets and show you techniques for making the work easy and efficient. All you have to supply are the materials and elbow grease.

Basic construction and techniques

Euro-style cabinets are essentially simple boxes without face frames around the openings where doors and drawers fit. The boxes, called cases, are usually constructed of pieces of particleboard precoated with white plastic melamine, a low-pressure plastic laminate. The basic material is available in 4x8-foot sheets that can be cut and routed like plywood. Techniques for cutting and drilling the cabinet material are shown on page 49. The cases are assembled with butt joints and drywall screws. The doors hang on European-style concealed hinges, which can be easily adjusted both vertically and horizontally after the doors are mounted.

Choosing a cabinet style

You have many choices of color and material to use for the cases, the doors and drawer faces, and for the style of visible trim and hardware. The casework shown in these pages can accommodate doors and drawer faces of any style—raised panel, flush, plastic laminate, or a combination of wood and laminate. The cabinets feature finished end panels in the same style as the doors, for all visible sides. This eliminates the need for finishing work on the melamine-coated cases.

To get ideas for style, visit kitchen showrooms, page through design magazines, pick up some cabinet manufacturers' literature—or simply invent your own style. The models built here—with doors, drawer faces, and end panels of rift-cut oak veneer plywood edged with walnut—were chosen for their simple appearance and their ease of construction.

Cabinet sizes

While you have plenty of leeway in designing cabinets, two dimensions are standard; if you deviate from them you almost certainly will have problems elsewhere in the kitchen, especially when you try to integrate appliances into the layout. The two standard dimensions apply to base cabinets:

▶ Base cabinet height is always 34-1/2 inches from the floor to the underside of the countertop. All appliances that fit within or under the counter are made to fit in this space.

▶ Base cabinet depth is 24 inches from front to back to accommodate the depth of these same appliances and the standard countertop depth of 25 inches, which allows for a 1-inch overhang at the front.

There are no set rules for other dimensions, although there are some practical considerations. Wall cabinets are usually 12 inches deep and 30 inches high, but you can vary that to meet your needs. A wall cabinet over a refrigerator, a wall oven, or a microwave should be deep enough to bring the doors close to or flush with the face of the appliance.

In most cases, the width of each cabinet will be determined by the overall layout of your kitchen. In general, a run of wall cabinets should match the width of the base cabinets and built-in features below. If you are planning to change your present kitchen layout, be sure to measure the width of each appliance and the distance between end walls precisely before planning the size of each cabinet.

Within the limits of your ideal layout, try to keep in mind these points about cabinet size:

▶ Avoid cabinets less than 12 inches wide or deep; they provide very little storage.

▶ Use two doors on cabinets that are wider than 21 inches, and avoid cabinets wider than 42 inches. A door 21 inches or more wide takes up a lot of space when it swings open, and is likely to sag on its hinges.

▶ Try to keep door sizes consistent in width and height. If you must have a cabinet with doors noticeably different from the others, put it at the end of a run or in a corner.

Choosing materials

Cabinet sides, tops, bottoms, shelves, stringers, and hanging strips are cut from 3/4-inch white melamine-coated particleboard (page 48). Case backs are 1/4-inch melamine particleboard. Use material with melamine on both sides for shelves and the bottom of upper cabinets; use one-sided material for other parts.

TOOLS

- Measuring tape
- Carpenter's square
- Table saw or radial arm saw
- Router with slot-cutting, round-over, and trimming bits
- Straightedge
- Bar clamps
- Rubber mallet
- Drill with drill guide, twist bits, and 1-3/8" Forstner bit
- Hammer
- Screwdrivers
- Chisel

MATERIALS

- 13/16" plastic T-molding
- 3/4" particleboard, melamine coated one and two sides
- 1/4" plywood, melamine coated one side
- 3/4" fir plywood
- 3/4" oak veneer plywood
- 13/16" walnut edging strips
- 1/2" birch plywood
- Euro-style hinges, 95° and 176°
- Shelf clips
- Drawer glides
- 4d finish nails
- No. 6 x 1-3/4" drywall screws
- 1-1/2" flathead wood screws
- 1-1/2" round-head wood screws and matching washers

OVERALL ASSEMBLY

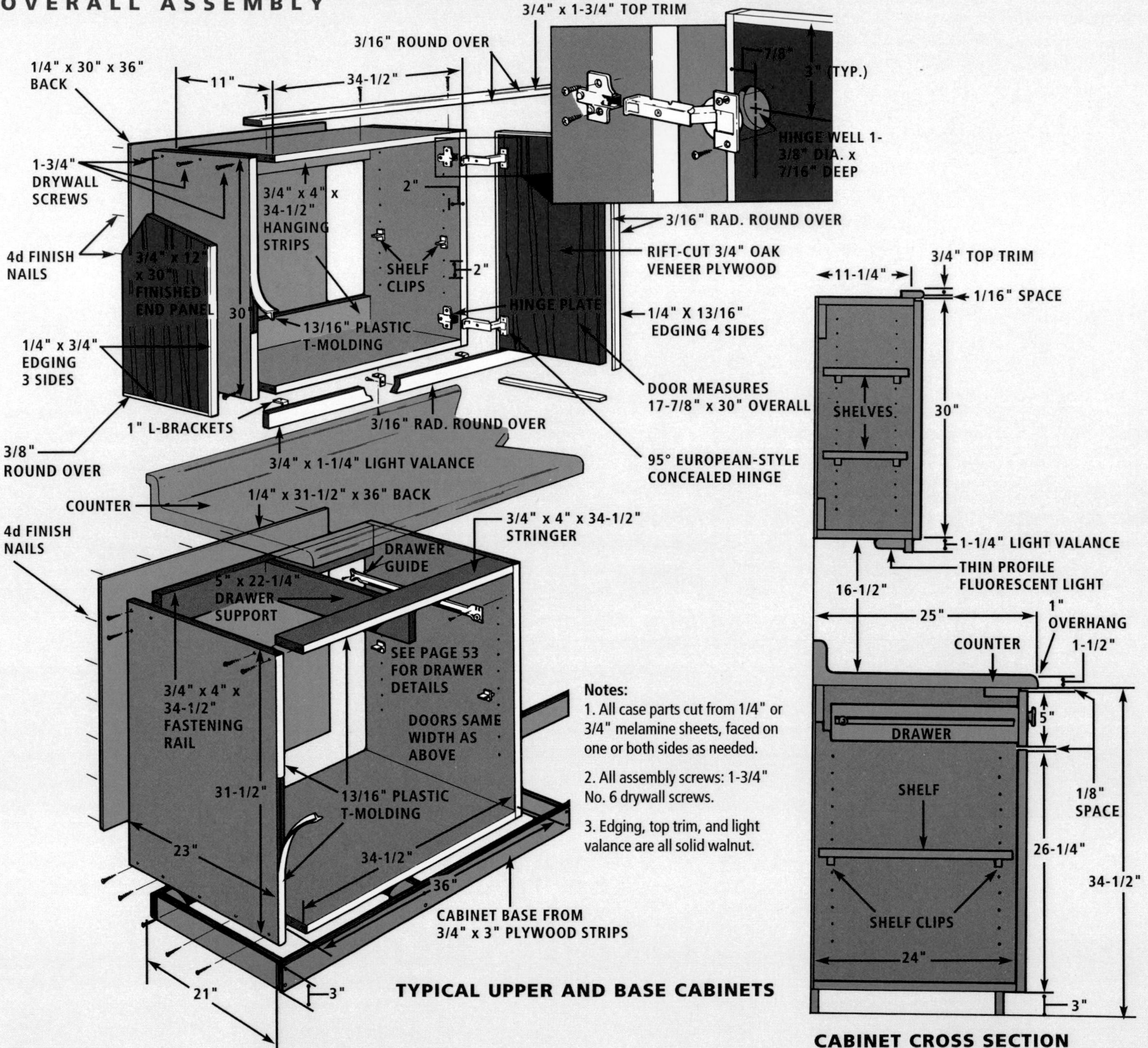

SCOPE OF THE PROJECT

There are several stages to this project:

▶ Cut and drill the parts.
▶ Assemble all the cabinet cases.
▶ Make doors, drawer faces, and end panels.
▶ Trim the edges.
▶ Build the drawers.
▶ Install the drawers.
▶ Finish the drawer faces, doors, and end panels.
▶ Attach the drawer faces.
▶ Hang the doors.
▶ Install the cabinets.
▶ Finish the cabinets.

Each stage is explained step by step in the following sections.

CUTTING AND DRILLING

Proper planning and careful work are required to cut the parts and predrill holes for shelf clips cleanly and accurately.

▶ Lay out the parts carefully to minimize waste. Start with the largest parts—base cabinet sides and bottoms—then proceed to the smaller parts. To reduce error and get consistent sizes, cut as many similar-sized parts as possible with one saw setting before changing to the next setting.

▶ Use a sharp, fine-tooth carbide saw blade in a radial arm saw (Photo 1), table saw, or circular saw. Or use a carbide straight bit in a router. Whatever you use, the blade or bit must pass through the material very slowly to minimize splintering or chipping. Be sure to clamp a straightedge to the work to guide a circular saw or router for cutting.

▶ Identify the edges that will be exposed—all front edges, the bottom edges of wall cabinet sides, and one long edge of each hanging strip. Use a router with a 1/16-inch slot-cutting bit to cut a centered groove the length of each exposed edge (Photo 2).

▶ Tap 13/16-inch wide plastic T-molding into the edge slots (Photo 3). Trim the molding flush by running a sharp chisel along the melamine surfaces of the case parts.

▶ Before assembling the cases, drill holes for the plug-in shelf clips. Use a drill guide to ensure that holes are perpendicular (Photo 4). For even spacing, make a drilling template from 1/4-inch plywood or hardboard.

CUTTING AND DRILLING

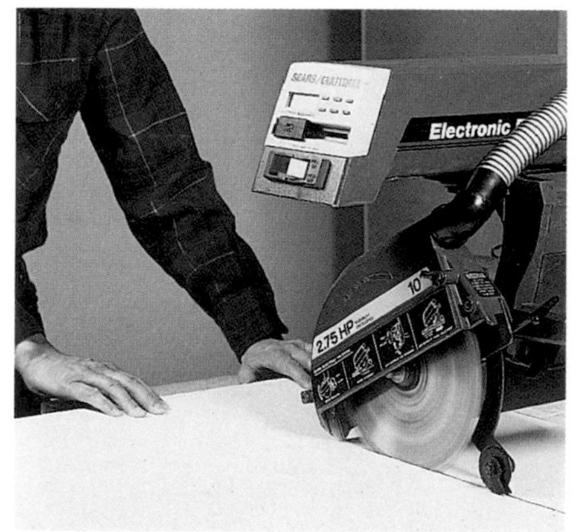

Photo 1. Cut case parts from 3/4-in. melamine-coated panels. Use any power saw with a fine-tooth carbide blade, or a router with a straight carbide bit.

Photo 2. Rout a 1/16-in. slot along the center of all case front edges, the bottom edges of upper cabinet sides, and one long edge of the cabinet hanging strips.

Photo 3. Tap plastic T-molding into the edge slots with a rubber mallet. Trim off excess plastic with a sharp chisel, running it flush along the melamine surface.

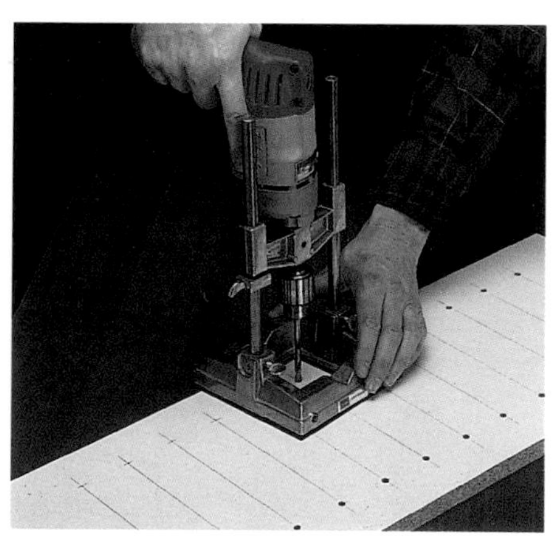

Photo 4. Drill holes for shelf clips using a drill guide with the depth set to avoid drilling all the way through. Make a template to ensure even hole spacing.

UPPER CORNER CABINET

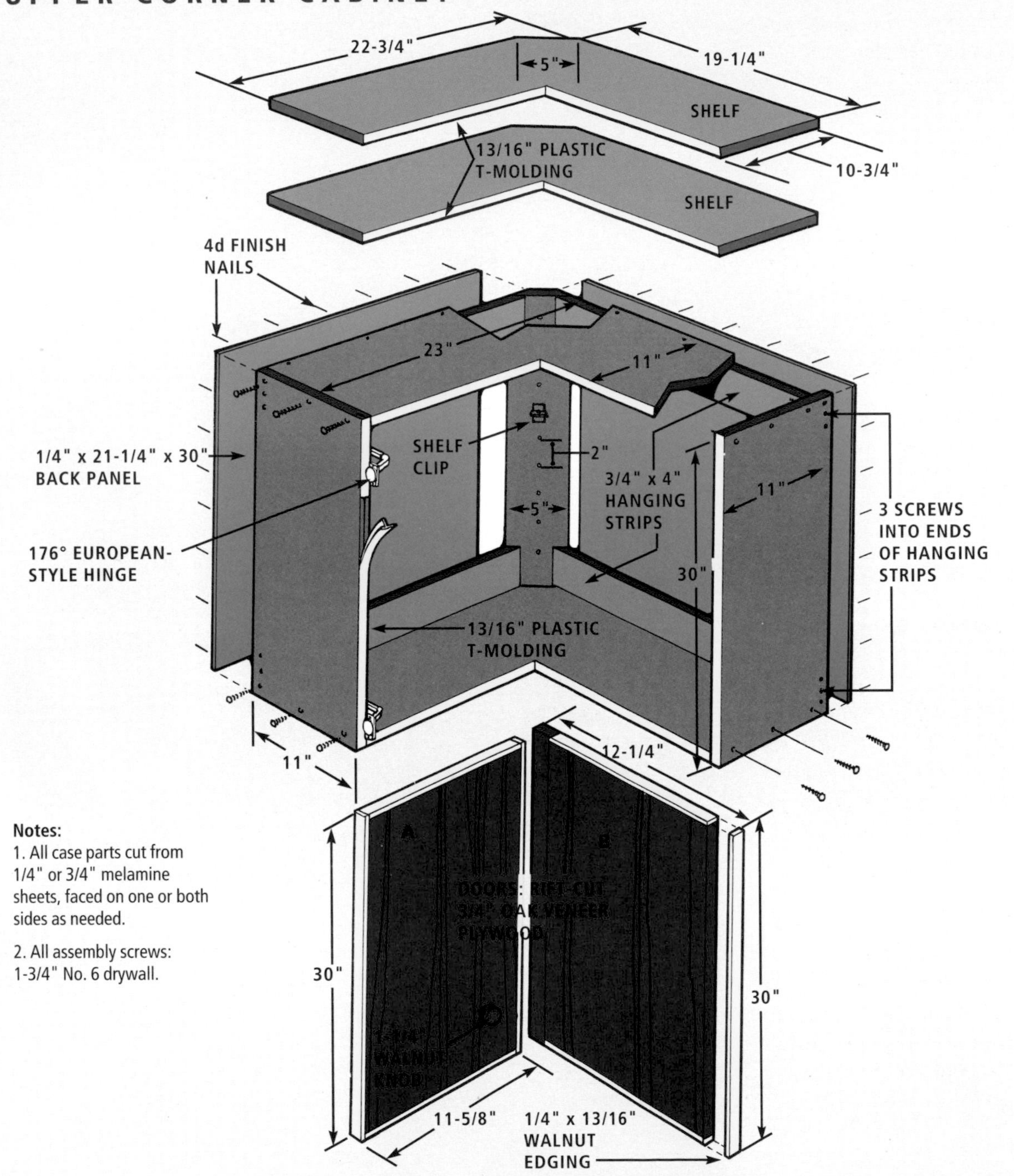

ASSEMBLE THE CASES

The cabinet cases are held together with 1-3/4 inch No. 6 drywall screws. There's no need for glue; it won't stick to the melamine.

▶ Clamp a case top, bottom, and sides together with pipe clamps, with the case lying on its back on a level work surface. Position the clamps so they don't interfere with drilling pilot holes (Photo 5).

▶ Before drilling any holes, make sure the case is square by measuring from corner to corner; the distances should be the same. If not, loosen the clamps slightly and push on one corner or the other until the diagonals are equal.

▶ Drill holes properly to avoid splitting the particleboard. Drill a pilot hole through both pieces clamped together in alignment, then drill the hole in the outside piece larger as a clearance hole. The easiest way to do this is

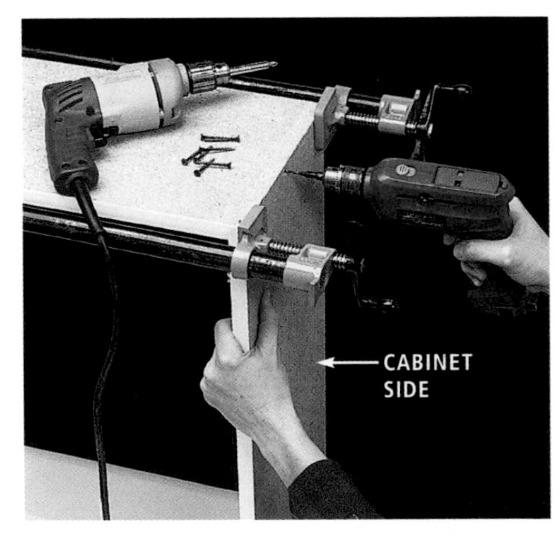

Photo 5. Clamp case pieces together, butting the sides to the tops and bottoms. To save time, predrill and countersink with one drill, and drive screws with another.

with a combination bit, which drills a pilot hole and clearance hole and countersinks for the screw head all in one pass. The pilot hole should be about half the diameter of the drywall screw. Hold a drill bit up against the shank of a screw; you should be able to see the screw threads but not the center shank. The clearance hole through the outside piece should be the full diameter of the screw, allowing it to pass through freely.

▶ Save time by using two variable-speed drills—one for drilling holes, the other with a Phillips head bit for driving the drywall screws. Drill all the holes along a single edge, then drive screws in them before moving to the other side and doing the same. Do not loosen the clamps until both ends of a piece have been secured.

▶ When assembling wall cabinets, don't neglect to drive screws into both the ends, and the top or bottom of each hanging strip (see plans, opposite). These strips are essential for holding a heavily laden cabinet together and securely on the wall. Similarly, drive screws into the ends of the fastening rails at the top rear of base cabinets.

▶ When the sides, top, bottom, and hanging strips or mounting rail and stringers have been assembled, add the cabinet back. Set the cabinet on its bottom, make sure it is square, and attach the back with 4d finish nails spaced about 5 inches apart along all edges. Drill pilot holes for the nails in the back, and be sure that the melamine-coated side of the back faces the interior of the cabinet.

MAKE DOORS, DRAWER FACES, AND END PANELS

You can make these pieces of melamine-coated particleboard to match the cabinet cases if you wish. However, every corner of these pieces is exposed, and it is very difficult to get neat corner joints using T-molding as edge trim. Using a finish plywood for these parts presents a striking visual contrast to the cabinet cases and makes it far easier to trim the edges.

The doors and drawer faces shown in the photographs are cut from 3/4-inch white oak veneer plywood and trimmed with 1/4-inch thick walnut edging. The finish surface of the plywood is a rift-cut veneer; its straight, regular graining looks better than the irregular looping grain of less expensive rotary-cut oak veneer.

Measuring, layout, and cutting

Accurate measurements are critical in making doors, drawer faces, and end panels. Proper layout ensures good appearance and economical use of materials. Careful cutting provides pieces of consistent size, with clean edges.

▶ Begin by measuring for the doors. Measure the outside height and width of the case opening and subtract 3/4 inch from each dimension. When you cut the door to that size and add a 1/4-inch edging all around, it will have a 1/8-inch setback from the case edges.

▶ For a corner cabinet in which one door overlaps another when closed (door A in plans at left), there must be a 1/4-inch space between that door and the adjoining one (door B). To get the cutting width of door A, measure the case from the outside face of the end to the edge that will be behind door B. Subtract 3/4 inch for the thickness of door B, 1/2 inch for the trim of both edges of door A, and 1/8 inch for the setback of A from the case edge.

▶ To measure for drawer faces, figure the width of each face by subtracting 3/4 inch from the case width. To figure the heights of several drawer faces one above another, measure the case height and then divide it into as many drawer spaces as you wish. The drawers do not all have to be the same height; the height of each drawer box will be 1 inch less than its finish face (see text and Cabinet Cross Section plan, page 53). From each drawer face, subtract 1/16 inch face height to provide 1/8 inch space between adjoining faces, and 1/2 inch for the 1/4-inch edge trim on the top and bottom. Subtract 1/8 inch more from the top and bottom drawer faces so they will have the proper setback from the top and bottom edges of the case.

▶ Wherever doors and drawer faces adjoin, allow for a 1/8 inch space between their overall, edge-trimmed sizes. Where two cabinets meet, figure door and drawer face widths for a 1/16-inch setback at the case edges, to give a consistent 1/8-inch space.

▶ For a cabinet end panel, measure the outside dimensions of the case. Subtract 1/2 inch from the height and 1/4 inch from the depth to get the panel size. When edging is added to the top, bottom, and front of the panel, it will be flush with the case dimensions.

▶ Lay out the pieces on the plywood so that the grain of the finish surface runs vertically on each piece. Mark out pieces that will be installed side by side on adjacent areas of a plywood panel, so the grain pattern will match. Make the cuts with a plywood finish blade.

TRIM THE EDGES

There are several ways to cover the exposed plywood edges. The easiest is to simply hide the plies by staining the edges with an opaque stain the same color as the surface. This method is appropriate only for a basic utility cabinet. An alternative method is to use an iron-on veneer tape. However, because you cannot then round over the edges, this gives doors and drawer faces a thick, boxy look. The most durable and attractive edging is 1/4-inch thick hardwood, which can be shaped. You can use the same kind of wood as the plywood veneer, or a contrasting variety.

▶ Attach hardwood edging to the plywood pieces with carpenter's glue and clamps; use strips of scrap wood to equalize the clamping pressure (Photo 6). Put edging on both narrow ends of a piece first. Keep glue off the face of the plywood to avoid blotches when staining later. Remove squeezed-out glue with a chisel after it has started to harden. When the glue has cured, trim the edging to length and then add edging to the sides of the piece. Make either butt or mitered joints at the corners.

▶ When the piece has been completely trimmed, shape the outside edges—those that do not fit against the cabinet case—with a 3/16-inch round-over bit in a router (Photo 7).

TRIM THE EDGES

Photo 6. Use hardwood strips for edge trim on plywood doors, drawer faces, and end panels. Glue and clamp the edging in place. Sand edging flush with the surface.

Photo 7. Shape the hardwood edging along its outside edge after a piece has been completely trimmed. Use a round-over bit in a router. Make smooth, continuous passes along the edges.

BUILD THE DRAWERS

The drawers are simply boxes with fronts, backs, and sides of 1/2-inch birch plywood and bottoms of 1/4-inch hardboard or birch veneer plywood (see plans at right). The edge-trimmed finish faces are attached after the drawers are mounted on glides in the cabinets.

▶ Measure and mark out pieces for the drawers you need. The height of each drawer box is 1 inch less than its finish face, which you have already made. The width of the drawer box depends on the glides that support it. Almost all metal drawer glides require 1/2 inch of space between the drawer and the case on each side. Check the clearance requirements in the installation directions supplied with the drawer glides you plan to use. Drawer depth from front to rear is 2 inches less than the outside measurement of the case depth.

▶ Cut all the drawer pieces to size—two sides, a front, back, and bottom for each drawer. Then cut a 1/4 x 1/4-inch groove located 3/8 inch from the bottom edges of the fronts, backs, and sides. The grooves will hold the drawer bottoms. Also cut 1/8 x 1/2-inch wide rabbets in the sides to receive the fronts and backs of the drawers.

▶ Assemble the drawers with glue and 4d finish nails (Photo 8). Make sure each box is square as you nail it together. Countersink the nailheads. Don't mount the finished drawer faces until after the drawer boxes have been installed on glides within the cabinet.

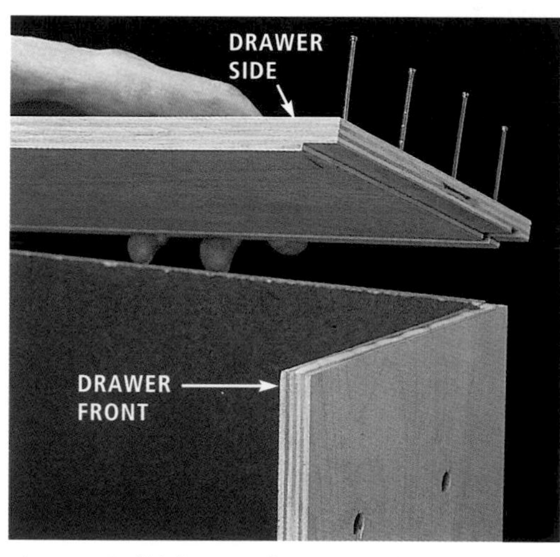

Photo 8. Build drawers from 1/2-in. birch plywood. Cut rabbets in sides for the front and back, 1/4-in. dadoes for bottom. Assemble with glue and 4d nails.

BASE CABINET WITH DRAWERS

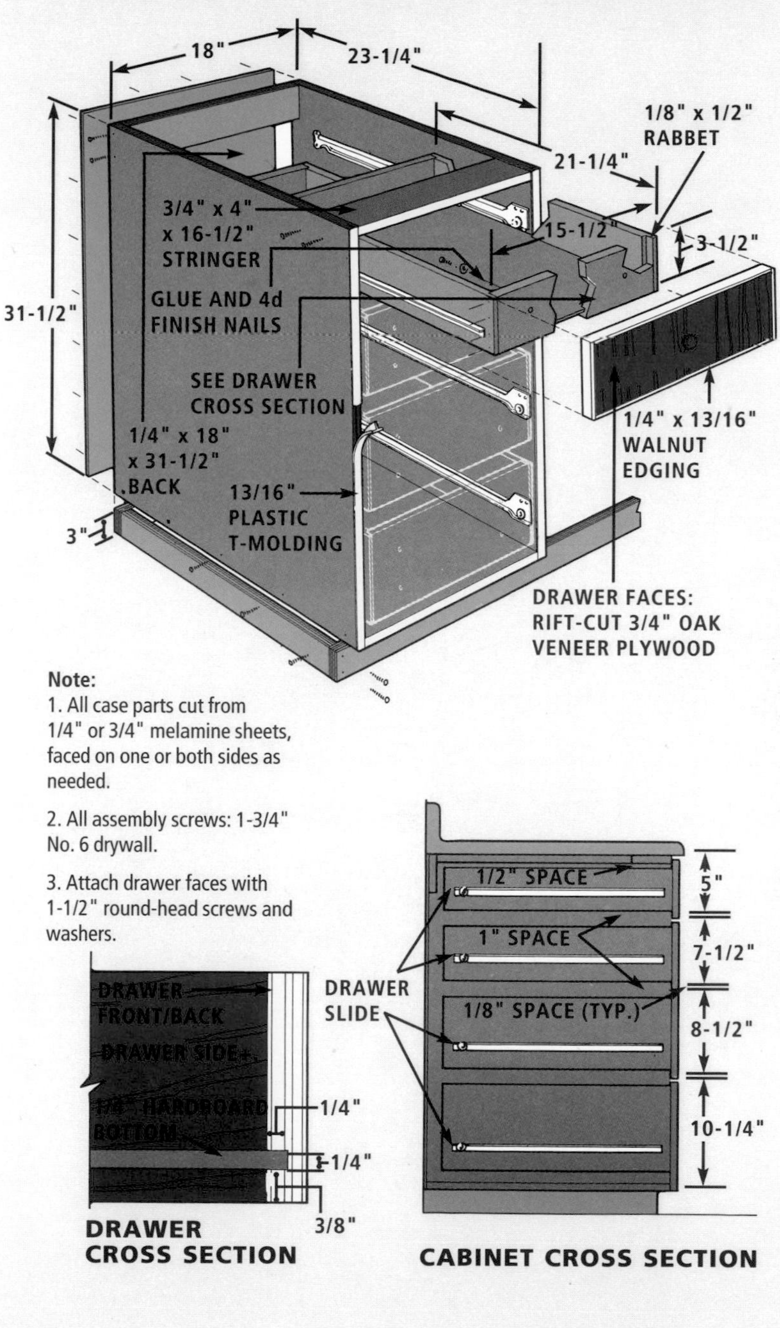

Note:

1. All case parts cut from 1/4" or 3/4" melamine sheets, faced on one or both sides as needed.
2. All assembly screws: 1-3/4" No. 6 drywall.
3. Attach drawer faces with 1-1/2" round-head screws and washers.

INSTALL THE DRAWERS

Drawers are mounted on metal or plastic slides, which are supplied in pairs; each slide has one fixed and one movable runner.

▶ Screw the fixed runners of the drawer slides inside the cabinet cases and attach the movable runners to the drawer boxes (Photo 9).

▶ Put the drawers in position on their slides. Check that each box is level from side to side and front to back and that it slides in and out smoothly. Also check that the spaces between the bottom of one drawer and the top of the next are equal in a stack of drawers. To make adjustments, remove the drawer and loosen the screws in the case-mounted runner.

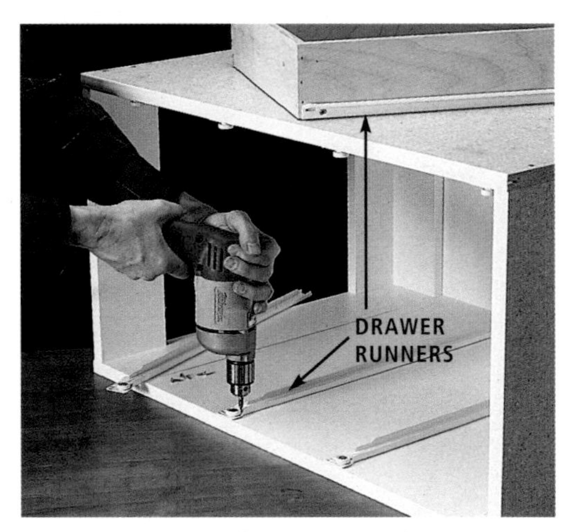

Photo 9. Attach the fixed runners of drawer slides to the insides of the case. Space opposite pairs precisely. Attach the movable runners to the drawer boxes.

FINISH THE DRAWER FACES, DOORS, AND END PANELS

▶ Thoroughly sand the wood surfaces of these pieces with 100-grit paper, then 120-grit, and finally 160-grit. Also sand a few sample pieces of the plywood and the edging to test the stain and finish, to ensure that you will get the desired color and gloss.

▶ For a natural tone, do not use stain but apply a varnish or polyurethane finish directly to the raw wood. Allow each coat to dry thoroughly, then sand lightly and wipe clean before applying the next coat. Whether you use stain or not, for really smooth results apply the final coat with finish from a spray can.

ATTACH THE DRAWER FACES

▶ Drill two 1/4-inch holes in the front of each drawer box, centered from top to bottom and about one-quarter of the drawer width from each side (see plans, page 53).

▶ Center a finished drawer face on the front of its drawer, mark the hole positions on its back, and drill pilot holes for screws.

▶ Attach the face with 1-1/2 inch round-head screws and washers driven from the inside of the drawer.

▶ Insert the finished drawer in the cabinet and check the alignment of the face. It should be 1/8 inch from the cabinet edges and 1/8 inch from any adjoining drawer face. To make adjustments, loosen the screws holding the face; the 1/4-inch holes in the drawer fronts will permit the necessary movement.

HANG THE DOORS

Use two Euro-style hinges on each door. The hinge body fits into a recess on the back of the door and its arm attaches to a plate that mounts inside the case, flat on the side. Follow the directions supplied with the hinges.

▶ Drill recesses in the door backs with a 1-3/8 inch Forstner bit. The center of each recess must be precisely 7/8 inch from the side edge, and typically 3 inches from the top or bottom edge, although that can vary if necessary (see plan detail, page 48). Use either a drill press or a portable drill guide (Photo 10). Set the depth stop so the hole is just deep enough for the hinge body and its mounting flange lies flat against the back of the door. Attach the hinge to the door with the screws supplied (Photo 11).

▶ When both hinges have been attached to a door, slip a mounting plate onto the arm of each hinge—without screws—and hold the door in position. Mark the screw hole positions for the mounting plates on the side of the case. Remove the door, drill holes, and attach the mounting plates (Photo 12).

▶ Insert the hinge arms into their mounting plates on the case and drive the screws that fasten them together. Close and open the door to check that it swings freely and is properly aligned. The hinge mounting plates permit you to adjust the alignment if necessary.

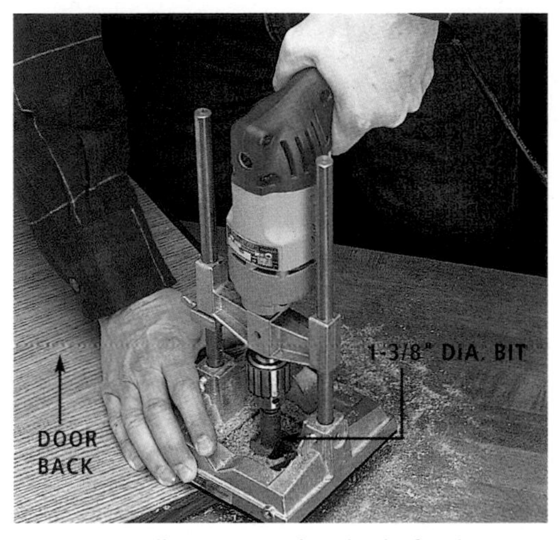

Photo 10. Drill recesses in door backs for the hinge bodies. Hole setbacks must be precise. Set the depth stop on the drill guide so the hinge exactly fits the hole.

Photo 11. Press the hinge body into the recess and secure it with supplied screws. Make sure each hinge arm is at a right angle to the door edge.

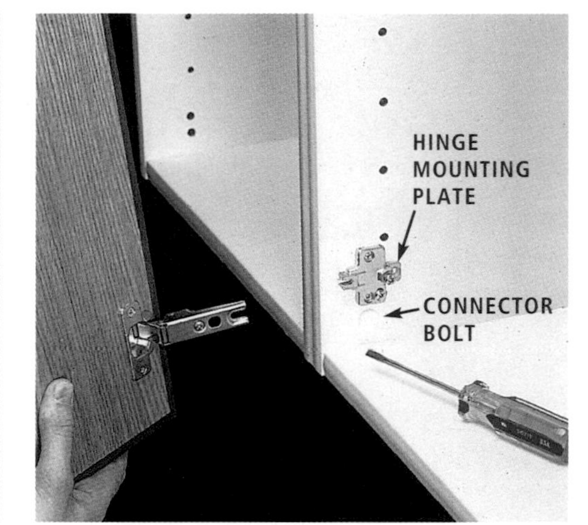

Photo 12. Mount hinge plates inside the cases, then secure the hinge arms to the plates. Most Euro-style hinges allow 1/8-in. adjustments up, down, forward, and back.

INSTALL THE CABINETS

To install your new cabinets, follow the procedures described for installing stock cabinets on pages 34–45, with the following exceptions:

▶ Because Euro-style cabinets have no face frames, their rear edges will fall exactly on the lines marking cabinet locations on the wall.

▶ Adjacent cabinets must be fastened together through their case sides with two-piece connector bolts. Clamp wall cabinets together on a level surface and drill holes for the bolts just above and below the hinges and midway between. After hanging the cabinets individually, install the connector bolts in the predrilled holes (Photo 12).

▶ Drill holes and install connector bolts in base cabinets after they have been fastened in place.

FINISH THE CABINETS

▶ Clamp the cabinet end panels in place, making sure that they are properly aligned with the cabinet edges and fit well against the wall. Drill holes from inside the cabinet and fasten the panel using flathead screws. Touch up the screw heads with paint to match the melamine coating.

▶ Add a filler strip where needed to close the space between a cabinet side and an adjoining wall or appliance (see page 44). Use wood that matches the doors and drawer faces. Install it flush with the surface of the adjacent door or drawer faces.

The photo on page 46 and the plans on page 48 show two optional finishing details—a trim strip across the top of a run of the wall cabinets, and a light valance across the bottom.

▶ Make the top trim of 1x2 stock that is the same as the door, or glue edging to a pine 1x2. Round over the exposed top edge to match the door trim. Attach the top trim flush with the face of the cabinet doors and extend a return piece to the wall at the top of the end cabinets. Drive screws from above or below, or glue the trim in place.

▶ The light valance conceals undercabinet light fixtures. It also helps prevent the bottoms of wide upper cabinets from sagging under heavy loads. Cut it from wood that matches the door edging. Screw it to the bottoms of the cabinets with L-brackets and screws (see plans). Include returns to the walls at the end cabinets. If you don't plan to use a light valance, limit the width of upper cabinets to 36 inches.

Improve Kitchen Storage

A modern kitchen requires better storage space than your parents' required. Today we expect cabinets to accommodate what they always have—plus several small appliances, recycling bins, a great variety of cleaning materials, and of course cartloads of prepackaged supermarket foods. In most cases existing cabinets can handle the load, but they need to be better organized and the space within made more accessible.

Using easily found items and a few specialty kits, you can increase the capacity and efficiency of your kitchen storage space for a small investment in time and money—and without any complex or difficult construction.

Every kitchen has both unused and underused cabinet storage space. Among the improvements you can add to a sink cabinet are tilt-down fronts, a slide-out tray, a roll-out basket for trash or recycling, and a glide-out towel rack.

PROJECT REQUIREMENTS

There are four storage projects on these pages as well as suggestions for additional improvements. The four projects are:

- ▶ Tilt-down sink front.
- ▶ Slide-out tray.
- ▶ Swing-out spice racks.
- ▶ Pivot-and-glide corner shelves.

Each project requires a bit of construction, but ready-made hardware makes installation easy. You'll need basic tools and skills, and for two of the projects a power saw and a router. Look at all the projects and consider the following information before deciding which one to do first.

▶ Frameless Euro-style cabinets, built-in custom cabinets, and modular, stock-size cabinets like those shown on these pages differ considerably in construction. Before going too far into a project with specialty hardware or fittings, determine if you need to modify either the product instructions or the instructions given here to suit your situation.

▶ These projects make your cabinets more accessible and better organized, but not all of them create more space. For instance, pivot-and-glide shelves (Photo 1 and page 61) provide excellent access to the back reaches of corner cabinets, but you may actually wind up with less total shelf space. So weigh the increase in convenience and efficiency against other factors before deciding on a project.

▶ Watch out for overloading the cabinets. You can modify the spice rack (Photo 2 and page 60) to hold soup cans, but hanging an extra 20 pounds from the outer frame of an upper cabinet may cause the frame or the entire cabinet to sag.

▶ These projects are described for use in a kitchen, but every one will work just as well in the bathroom and laundry room. Consider making all the cabinets in your home more space efficient.

▶ You can find the commercial items described here in home centers, kitchen specialty stores, and many full-service hardware stores. When shopping, keep your eye out for other products that are easy to install. Two examples are a glide-out towel rack and a roll-out basket (see photo, opposite page). Each is self-contained and is installed simply by driving screws in the mounting flanges.

Photo 1. Pivot-and-glide shelves—available in kit form—provide access to items that would otherwise be lost in the depths of a blind corner cabinet.

Photo 2. Hanging spice racks can be fitted behind existing cabinet doors. You can build and install the racks with only basic materials and skills.

TOOLS

- Tape measure
- Drill
- Offset screwdriver
- Hammer
- Router
- Miter box or power miter saw
- Screwdrivers

MATERIALS

- 1x3 pine
- 3/8" plywood
- 1/4" plywood
- 1/4" perforated hardboard
- 8d box or common nails
- 6d finish nails
- 1" brads
- Carpenter's glue

TILT-DOWN SINK FRONT

Most kitchen sink base cabinets have a fixed false front that masks the depth of the sink. The space behind the false front is wasted. Altering the front so that it tilts out will give you storage space for pot scrubbers, soap pads, rubber gloves and other items that you'd like to have at hand, right at sink height.

You can make the conversion with four "fall front" spring-loaded hinges, a 36-inch cut-to-length plastic tray, and end caps for the tray. Kits with these components are available, or you can purchase them separately. Here's what to do:

▶ Remove the false front panels carefully (Photo 3); often there are two, the same width as the cabinet doors below. They are usually held by back clips or screw blocks that you can reach from below. Measure the distance between the front of the sink basin and the outer surface of the cabinet face frame. Some sinks are too large or mounted too close to the front of the counter to accommodate tilt-down trays. If that is the case, replace the panels and choose another project.

▶ Assuming you can proceed, drill holes for mounting a handle on each front panel. Use the same style as the handles on the adjacent cabinet drawers, and position it to match them.

▶ Predrill holes for the hinges inside the cabinet and screw the hinges in place (Photo 4). Hold each panel in position and mark the location of the hinge holes on its back. Remove the panels and predrill the hinge holes.

▶ Cut the trays to the required length, fit on the end caps, and hold each section in position against the back of its panel to mark holes for mounting screws. Then drill the holes.

▶ Attach the handles to the panels. Then screw each front panel to the hinges in the cabinet (Photo 5). Finally, mount the accessories tray. You'll need an offset screwdriver to work in the awkward space between the panel and the cabinet frame.

TILT-DOWN SINK FRONT

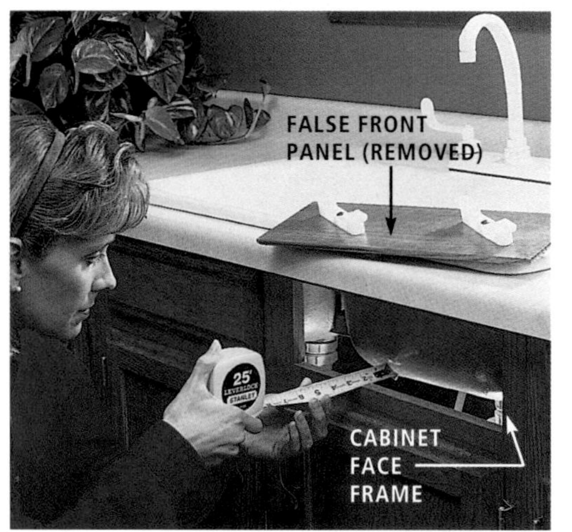

Photo 3. Measure the space between the sink and the front of the face frame. To remove a false front panel, twist its brackets or loosen the screws on the back of the panel.

Photo 4. To install a false front panel, first mount hinges on the edges of the cabinet opening. Then hold the panel in place to mark the back for drilling hinge holes.

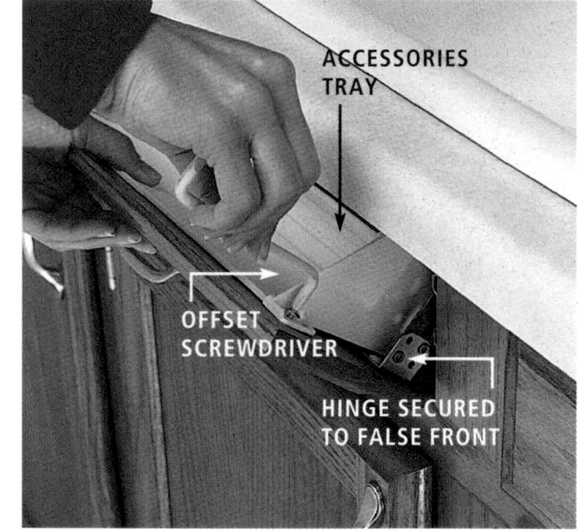

Photo 5. Attach the handle to the front panel, then mount the panel on the hinge and add the accessories tray. An offset screwdriver fits into the tight space.

SLIDE-OUT TRAY

A slide-out tray brings its contents out of the cabinet, so you don't have to stoop and search inside. It can be a simple box-frame tray, or you can add bins, dividers, or racks to customize it.

▶ Measure the cabinet space and cut pieces of 1x3 pine for a tray frame that is 1 inch narrower than the cabinet opening and 1 inch shallower than the cabinet depth.

▶ Miter the corners of the frame; use a miter box and a handsaw or a power miter saw (Photo 6). If you plan to make spice racks also (page 60), consider renting a power miter saw and cut those pieces at the same time.

▶ Assemble the frame with carpenter's glue and nails (Photo 7). Drive the lower nails 1/2 inch from the bottom edge to stay clear of the bottom of the tray.

▶ Turn the assembled frame face down and rout a 3/8 x 3/8-inch rabbet all around the inside bottom edge to receive the bottom drawer panel (Photo 8).

▶ Cut the bottom panel from 3/8-inch plywood. If the cabinet has moisture or ventilation problems, use perforated hardboard and paint it. Angle-cut the corners of the bottom panel to fit the rounded corners of the rabbet in the frame.

▶ Glue and nail the bottom in place, then attach a metal slide (Photo 9). A single, center-mounted slide is sufficient for most installations, but for heavy loads use two slides, one at each side. If the tray must be raised to pass over the lip of the cabinet face frame, mount the fixed channel of the metal slide on a strip of plywood on the cabinet shelf.

SLIDE-OUT TRAY

Photo 6. Cut the corners of the 1x3 frame pieces to make mitered joints for strength and rigidity. Use a miter box or power miter saw.

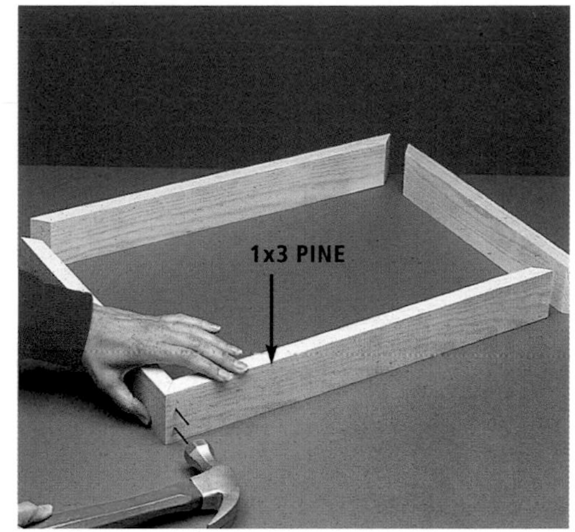

Photo 7. Assemble the frame with carpenter's glue and 8d nails. Keep the lower nail 1/2 in. above the bottom and make sure that all the corners are square.

Photo 8. Rout a 3/8 x 3/8-in. rabbet around the inside of the back edges of the frame. Cut, fit, and glue and nail the bottom panel into the rabbet. Trim the bottom corners to fit the rabbet.

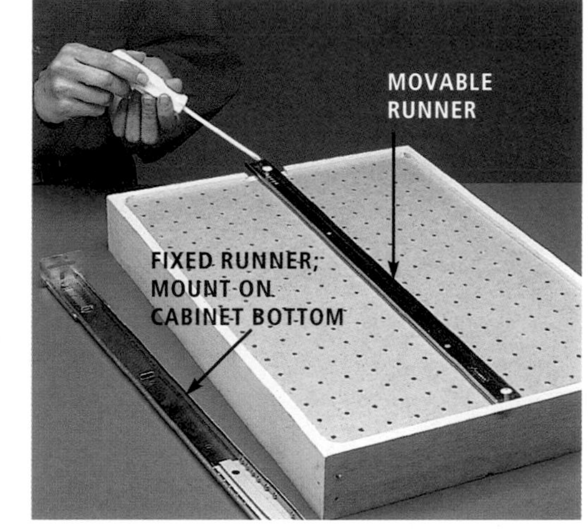

Photo 9. Screw the movable runner of the slide to the tray bottom and the fixed runner to the bottom of the cabinet. Use two slides if the tray will have heavy loads.

SWING-OUT SPICE RACKS

In cabinets that hold packaged foods, air often takes up more space than the food. That's because a 2-inch high jar of paprika takes up just as much shelf space as an 8-inch tall jar of olives. The result is a lot of wasted space. A good solution to this problem is to build swing-out racks to organize and store short boxes and jars such as spice containers.

Swing-out racks can be used in any type of cabinet—base or upper, short or tall. They can be tailored to hold everything from spices to cleaning supplies. Just don't overload the cabinet or the racks won't swing freely.

You may need to cut 2 inches off the depth of the existing shelves so the cabinet can accommodate the racks. In that case, you'll probably have to drill new holes for the clips or pegs that support the front edges of the shelves.

▶ Build a frame for each rack from 1x3 stock, with glued and nailed miter joints at the corners, as described for the slide-out tray frame (page 59).

▶ Rout a rabbet in the back edge of the frame 3/8 inch wide by 1/4 inch deep. Cut a back from 1/4-inch plywood (Photo 10). Angle-cut the corners to fit the rabbet corners, and fasten the back in place with finish nails.

▶ Shelves must be narrower than the frame, because the back is inset 1/4 inch. Rip 1x3 stock to width on a table saw, or use 1x8 stock and a circular saw with a rip guide. The wider stock will support the circular saw better for making rip cuts.

▶ Use the thin strips left over from ripping the shelves for guard slats. Or use 1/4-inch lattice or similar stock. Cut the guard rails to reach across the full width of the frame and nail them to the face of the rack with 1-inch brads (Photo 11).

▶ Use a hacksaw to cut a strip of piano hinge to fit between the existing cabinet door hinges. Drill pilot holes and screw it to the rack. Then mark, drill holes, and screw it to the cabinet frame (Photo 12). You must set the piano hinge back far enough on the edge of the cabinet frame so the spice rack does not interfere with the swing of the cabinet door.

Photo 10. Cut a plywood back for each spice rack. Construct the frame of 1x3's with mitered corners. Glue and nail the back into a rabbet that is routed in the frame.

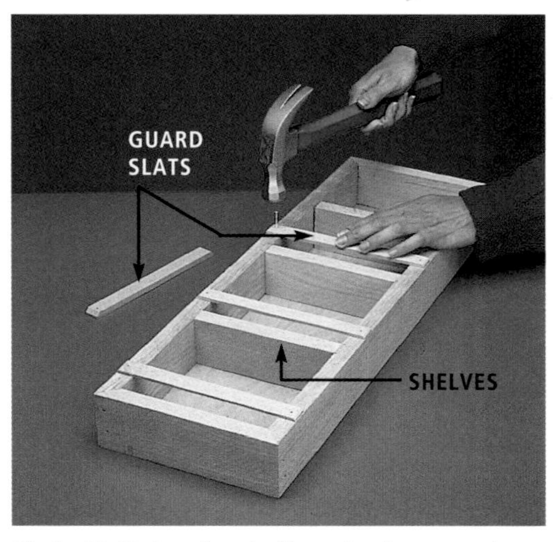

Photo 11. Determine shelf spacing by measuring items you'll keep on the rack. Fasten the shelves with finish nails; use 1-in. brads for the guard slats on the front.

Photo 12. Mount the spice rack on piano hinges. You may have to reduce the depth of the existing shelves to fit the rack.

PIVOT-AND-GLIDE SHELVES

To cope with the dark, inaccessible area where cabinets meet at a corner, install pivot-and-glide shelves to bring stored items out to you.

You have two choices for pivoted shelves: pivot-only, which allows you to swing the shelf halfway out of the cabinet; and pivot-and-glide, like the installation shown here. It allows you to swing the shelf out of the cabinet, then glide it another 10 to 12 inches toward you for even greater accessibility. Both kinds are available in kits that include half-moon shaped tray-shelves, a post, pivots, and shelf support assemblies. Installation is easy:

▶ Measure the cabinet door opening carefully before buying a kit. There is a minimum door width required for the shelves to fit through. Consult the kit specifications for size requirements. Most kits can be adapted to either right- or left-hand blind corners.

▶ Unpack the parts and rough-assemble them to get a picture of how the components fit together and the unit operates.

▶ Drill mounting holes for the lower and upper post pivots. They mount on the back of the cabinet face frame. Use the template supplied in the kit (Photo 13), or follow the instructions to make precise measurements for laying out the holes.

▶ Screw the pivots in position on the cabinet frame (Photo 14). Put the lower pivot-and-glide assembly in place and install the metal post. It sits in the bottom pivot and extends up through the upper pivot. Tighten the screws in both the pivots.

▶ Place the upper pivot-and-glide assembly over the top of the post; it rests on the upper post pivot (Photo 15).

▶ Finally, screw the plastic tray-shelves to the pivot-and-glide assemblies (Photo 16).

PIVOT-AND-GLIDE SHELVES

Photo 13. Drill holes for the post pivots using the kit template as a guide. The upper pivot position determines the height of the upper movable shelf.

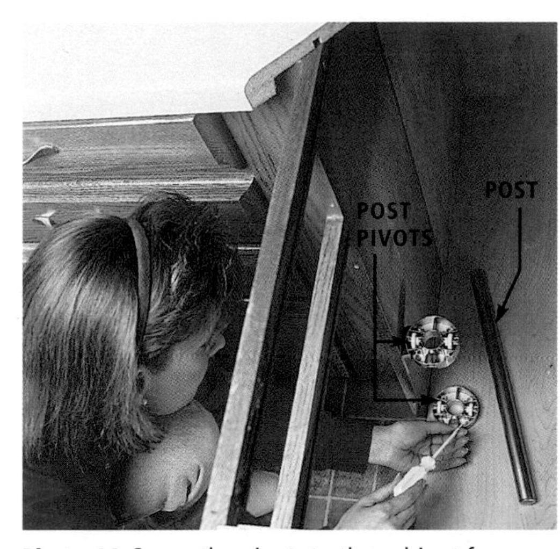

Photo 14. Screw the pivots to the cabinet frame. Put the lower pivot-and-glide assembly in place, then insert the post and tighten the setscrews.

Photo 15. Place the upper pivot-and-glide assembly over the end of the post that extends up through the pivot. The assembly rests on the pivot.

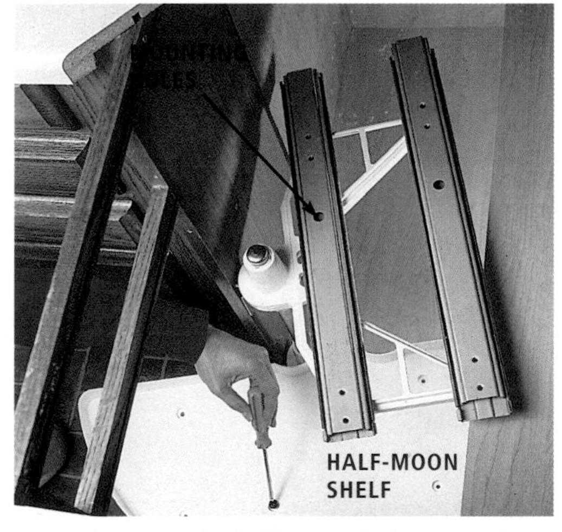

Photo 16. Screw the half-moon shelves to both the top and bottom pivot-and-glide assemblies. Plug the holes with the plastic screw covers that are provided in the kit.

Hardware Source

Hardware for these kitchen storage projects is available from The Woodworker's Store, 21801 Industrial Blvd., Rogers, MN 55374-9514.

Lighting Your Kitchen

The right lighting is the third major element in a kitchen that is an inviting, easy place to work. A good layout and modern fixtures are important, but without proper lighting, kitchen activities can be a chore rather than a pleasure.

Today, modern kitchens use a variety of fixtures to provide three specific kinds of lighting—general, task, and accent. When well placed and properly balanced, they transform a kitchen into a good-looking, well-lit room.

The best kitchen lighting is not only highly functional but also adds grace and visual interest. These two factors can make the kitchen both an easy and a pleasant place to work. The secret lies in using the right kinds of light, in the right combination.

GENERAL LIGHTING

General lighting is the base on which all other lighting is built. Its function is to provide bright, even illumination for the entire kitchen. Task lighting is then added to provide additional light in work areas, and accent lighting where visual interest is to be heightened.

In evaluating general lighting for your kitchen the major considerations are how much you need, the kind of light, and the arrangement of the fixtures. Here are some guidelines (if you are not familiar with the usual types and sources of light, see Lighting Basics, page 65):

▶ Consider the colors of the cabinets, counters, walls, and floors. Dark areas absorb light and therefore more is required for proper illumination. Light colors reflect, and may reduce the amount of light needed. In general, for a kitchen from 75 to 120 square feet in size you need 150 to 200 watts of incandescent light, or 60 to 80 watts of fluorescent light.

▶ Either fluorescent or incandescent light is quite suitable for general lighting, but because the color of their light is different, they should not be mixed for this purpose. Also, consider comfort; fluorescent tubes remain cool, even with extended operation. Incandescent bulbs begin radiating noticeable amounts of heat as soon as they are turned on. That may be welcome in winter, but unwanted in summer.

▶ For general lighting, fixtures must be positioned to provide even illumination throughout the room. A single fluorescent fixture typically can be placed in the center of the ceiling, because the tubes radiate light evenly along their full length (Photo 1). To get an equivalent spread of incandescent light—especially in a large kitchen—you can position two to four ceiling-mounted, domed fixtures so their light blends to form a uniform spread of illumination at upper cabinet level and all areas below. You can also use incandescent recessed fixtures (Photo 2), or track lights perhaps fitted with diffusers or globe bulbs (Photo 3). They too must be spaced so that their individual light paths blend uniformly.

GENERAL LIGHTING

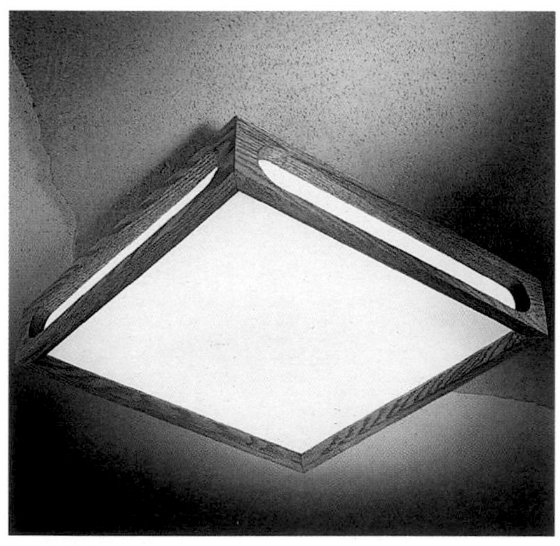

Photo 1. Fluorescent ceiling fixtures come in many different styles. A surface-mount fixture is best for most kitchens, but there are also recessed models. Many sizes are available.

Photo 2. Incandescent recessed lights are the least obtrusive way to obtain general lighting. Position them so that the light they cast overlaps to provide even illumination throughout the kitchen.

Photo 3. Track lights can provide general lighting when mounted close together and aimed to wash over the ceiling or downward, with their beams overlapping for even coverage.

TASK LIGHTING

Good general lighting brightly illuminates the kitchen, but it is not always adequate for specific work areas. As you work at the counter, the stove, or other locations, your back usually faces the general light source and you cast a shadow on the work you are doing.

Light directed at individual work areas is called task lighting. It is produced by fixtures placed above the counters, the sink, the stove, and the other places food is prepared, as well as over islands and tables.

Task lighting is even illumination concentrated in a specific area and is intended to make the work there both easier and safer. It should be soft (diffused) and placed to avoid work-surface glare.

Which kinds of lights work best and how much illumination is needed depends on conditions in the task area—chiefly whether the adjacent wall and cabinet surfaces are light or dark, and the distance from the fixtures to the work surface. Follow these guidelines:

▶ For lighting counters, install lights on the underside of the overhead cabinets, close to their front edges. Shallow fixtures designed to mount in such locations without obstructing the work space are called minilights; some are only an inch or so thick. There is a wide variety of both incandescent and fluorescent minilights from which you can choose to fit your needs (Photos 4, 5). You'll need 8 watts of undercabinet fluorescent light for every foot of counter workspace, or 15 to 20 watts of incandescent light.

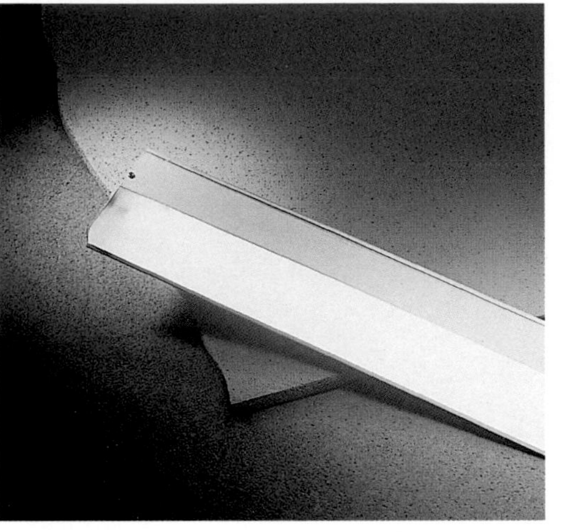

Photo 4. Miniature fluorescent lights are shallow enough to be virtually hidden when they are mounted, while providing plenty of bright illumination for counter-level work.

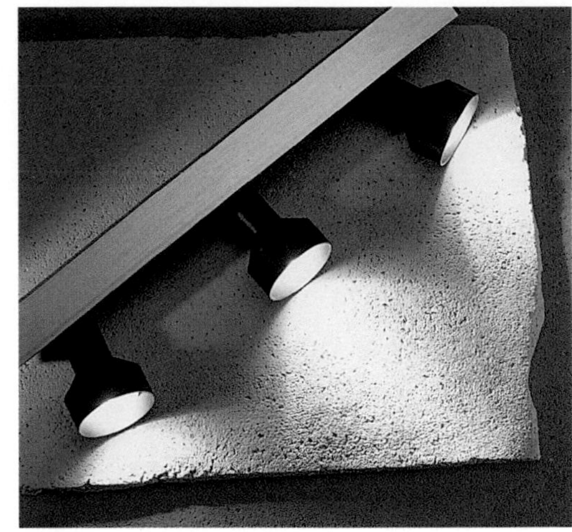

Photo 5. Miniature track lights attached to the bottom of cabinets can be adjusted to aim their beams where needed. They are useful for both task and accent lighting.

▶ To illuminate a sink, place a light directly above, recessed in or mounted on the ceiling or soffit. (A soffit is the box created by dropping the ceiling a bit along the wall—usually to the tops of the upper cabinets.) A recessed fixture or a small fluorescent unit works best. Be sure that the lightbeam covers the entire sink. The proper amount is about 75 watts of incandescent light or 40 to 60 watts of fluorescent light. You may need two fixtures to illuminate a double sink and the adjacent area evenly.

▶ For task lighting at a stove, consider installing an exhaust hood with a built-in light fixture above the burners. Some existing hoods can be retrofitted with a light fixture. Otherwise, follow the suggestion given for sinks. You should have 40 to 60 watts of incandescent light or 15 to 20 watts of fluorescent light.

▶ To light islands or eating areas, place recessed, track, or hanging lights above the area. The amount required depends on how far above the area the fixtures are mounted. If you use incandescent fixtures, you can adjust the amount of illumination by changing bulbs.

ACCENT LIGHTING

Accent lights are primarily decorative. They are optional in a kitchen lighting scheme, but can add drama and interest to the room. Generally, the same types of undercabinet lights used in countertop task lighting can be used as accent lights (Photo 6).

▶ Place accent lights on top of upper cabinets that are not flush with the ceiling or a soffit. Direct the lights toward the ceiling and back wall to give a sense of height to the room.

▶ Place accent lights in the toe-kick space of base cabinets. Besides emphasizing the cabinet-to-floor transition, toe-kick installations make good night-lights.

▶ Place accent lights along the inside upper or lower edge of a glass-door cabinet to highlight the cabinet's contents.

▶ As a general rule, keep accent lighting less bright than task lighting. A little of it draws a great deal of attention, so don't overuse it.

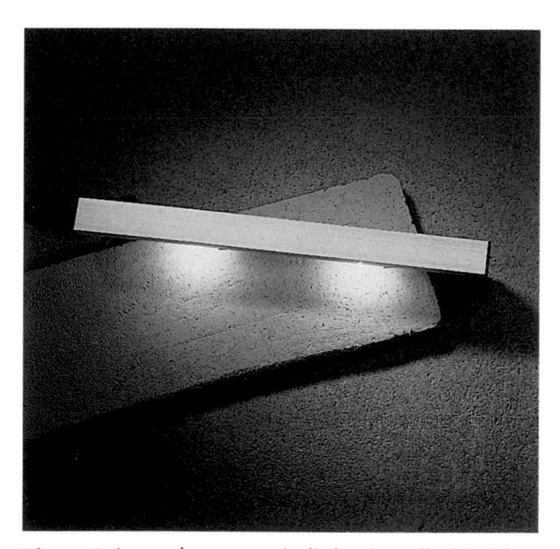

Photo 6. Incandescent strip lights installed inside or under cabinets or in the kick space are usually so small they cannot be seen from the room.

Lighting Basics

There are two major types of illumination used in residential lighting, incandescent and fluorescent. A third kind, halogen, is a special variety of incandescent light.

▶ Incandescent. This kind of light is provided by screw-base bulbs. They include the familiar pear-shaped bulbs and spherical globe bulbs, as well as cone-shaped reflector bulbs used in recessed and track lights. Pear-shaped and globe bulbs have various interior coatings to diffuse (soften) the light they emit, so as to reduce glare and soften shadows. All types of incandescent bulbs are available in various strengths, roughly indicated by their power demand, which is expressed in watts. For overall illumination and work-area lighting, bulbs from 40 to 200 watts are most useful. Bulbs of 20 watts or less are useful for accent lighting; they are also used in appliances, such as inside a refrigerator. Incandescent bulbs produce a significant amount of heat, which may make them unsuitable in some cases—for instance, close to a task area. The color of the light they produce is pleasantly "warm"—red-yellow—compared to fluorescent illumination and natural daylight.

▶ Fluorescent. Fluorescent light is provided by straight or circular tubes with buttons or protruding pins on each end that make electric contact with sockets in their fixtures. Light output depends on the length and diameter of the tube, as well as the interior coating. Energy-efficient fluorescent tubes use less electricity than incandescent bulbs, so a lower wattage will produce the same amount of light. Tube power demands are typically only 20 to 80 watts. Fluorescent tubes do not generate a noticeable amount of heat, which makes them especially suitable for close-range installations, and for lighting where air conditioning is required a good deal of the time. Tubes are commonly described as "warm white," "cool white," "daylight," or by other terms describing the color quality of the light they produce. In all cases it is "cooler"—bluer or more blue-white—than incandescent light.

▶ Halogen. Halogen bulbs have a tungsten filament, like standard incandescent bulbs, but are filled with a different gas at higher pressure and operate at a higher temperature than conventional bulbs. Their tubelike glass enclosures are much thicker and smaller. The glass is uncoated and the light emitted is much whiter—closer to natural daylight—than either incandescent or fluorescent light. As a result, colors illuminated by halogen bulbs look truer. Household and kitchen halogen fixtures are becoming increasingly available for a variety of applications. The bulbs have a longer life than equivalent incandescent bulbs but are more costly than either incandescent or fluorescent lights. When operating, halogen bulbs are hot enough to cause an instant second-degree burn if touched. However, because they are so small, the amount of heat they radiate is not usually a significant comfort factor. The bulbs have a pin-type plug-in base. Never touch the glass envelope when installing or removing a halogen bulb. Any trace of moisture, dirt, or skin oil on the surface can cause the bulb to shatter when it is turned on.

The Bathroom

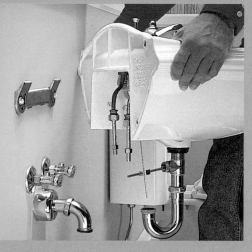

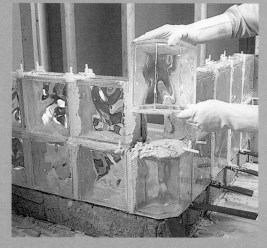

Give Your Bathroom a Makeover

It's easy to give a tired-looking bathroom a facelift by installing a new vanity, sink, medicine cabinet, and light.

The project requires only the most basic skills, and it shouldn't take the bathroom out of action for more than a weekend. As for expense, you can spend a lot or a little, depending on how fancy you want the new fixtures to be.

A new vanity, sink, medicine cabinet, and light can transform a tired-looking bathroom into a showcase. Best of all, it's not a difficult improvement to make, and won't take a long time.

FIRST CONSIDERATIONS

The basic project explained on these pages—replacing the bathroom sink, vanity, and mirror—is a quick and easy makeover. But evaluate both work and cost factors carefully so it won't grow into a major undertaking.

Work involved

Don't do more than is necessary. If the walls, floor, and tub are in good shape, leave them alone. Painting or covering the walls, replacing the tub, or tiling the floor will increase both the scope and the cost of the job.

Consider the age and condition of your plumbing. Any time you tinker with an old installation, unexpected problems can throw your project off budget and off schedule. Old valves might not close, or rusted pipe threads might break. Consider what you can and can't cope with. If yours is an old house, you may need a plumber for part of the work.

Also consider the lighting. If you now have a single, center-mounted light over the medicine cabinet, you'll want to replace it with another center-mounted unit. To spread the light over a larger area, use a light bar like the one in the photograph, opposite. Trying to split the old wiring to serve outlets on each side of the mirror will involve breaking into the wall, running new cable, and installing new boxes, which is a great deal of work.

Cost

The project shown in the photographs was fairly expensive because of the fixtures chosen. They include a traditional-style cherry vanity with matching medicine cabinet and lights, a custom-made "solid surface" countertop, and a fancy faucet.

You don't have to spend nearly as much to give your bathroom new life. Vanities come in many styles in standard widths of 24, 30, 36, 42, and 48 inches, costing about $100 and up. The standard depth, front to back, is 21 inches, but you can buy 18- and 16-inch deep vanities to save space. If you buy a shallower unit, be sure to get a correspondingly smaller sink top.

Vanity tops with integral molded sinks are both practical and reasonably priced. A top of solid-surface material is more expensive. Similarly, plain but excellent faucet sets are available at moderate prices, although some fittings can be very expensive. Whichever you choose, be sure to buy a sink top or sink with holes properly spaced to accept the new faucet.

The price of bathroom light fixtures also varies widely. Many people consider it ideal to have a light on each side of the mirror for balanced illumination. If that is not practical or to your taste, a moderately priced light bar is by far the best choice.

Finally, if your original plumbing is more than eight or ten years old, plan to install new sink connections: flexible water supply tubes, shutoff valves, and a P-trap drain. They don't cost much, and it's well worth the investment to bring your bathroom up to date.

REMOVE OLD FIXTURES

Disconnect the old sink and remove both the sink and the vanity cabinet.

▶ First, turn off the water at the shutoff valves under the sink (Photo 1) or at the main house valve. Replace faulty or missing valves.

▶ With a wrench, unscrew the nuts that hold the supply tubes to the valves.

▶ Put a bucket under the sink trap, loosen the slip nuts, and remove the trap. Unscrew the nut at the wall stub carefully; a rusty or weak drainpipe could break.

▶ Turn off the electricity at the circuit panel before removing the old lighting. If you can't use the existing electrical box, install a new box now. If the fixture requires wiring suitable for 90°C (194°F), install cable with the proper heat-rated insulation. Patch the wall before starting to install the new fixture.

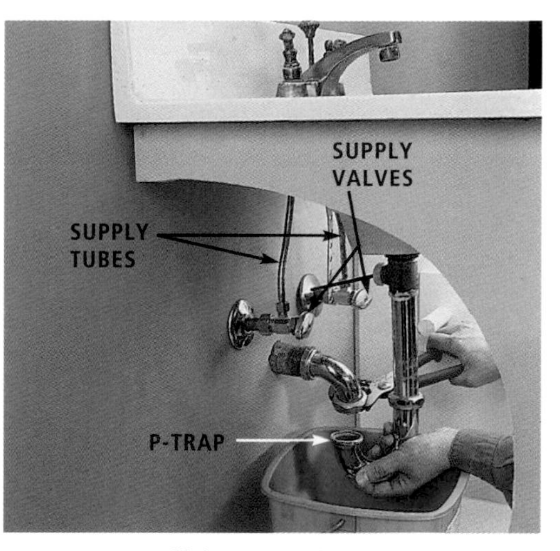

Photo 1. Turn off the water, disconnect the supply tubes, and remove the sink drain trap. Then you can remove the sink, top, and faucet all together.

TOOLS

- Adjustable wrench
- Slip-joint pliers
- Drill with Phillips bit
- Saber saw
- 2' level
- Bucket
- Block plane
- Belt sander

MATERIALS

- Shims
- Adhesive caulk
- Silicone caulk
- Teflon plumbing tape
- 2" drywall screws
- Electrical cable and fittings as needed

INSTALL THE VANITY AND SINK

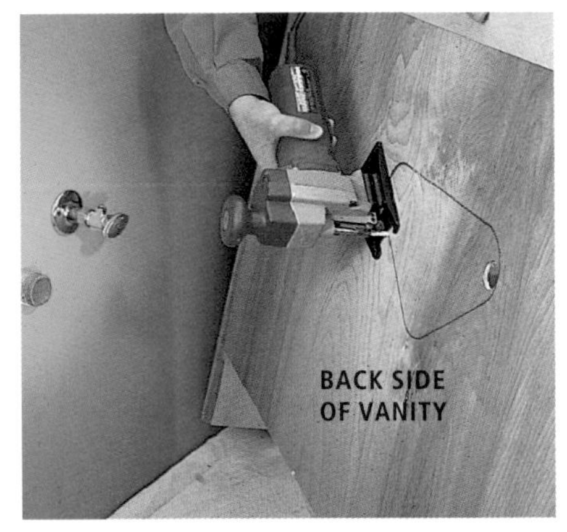

Photo 2. Mark an opening for the supply valves and drain on the back side of the vanity, and cut it out with a saber saw.

Photo 3. Position the vanity against the wall and shim under the bottom to level it front to back and side to side.

Photo 4. Scribe the bottom edge of the vanity with a marker and trim to the line so the cabinet rests level on the floor.

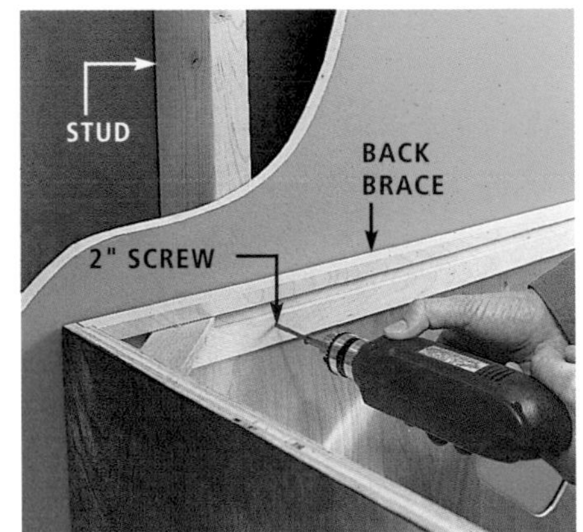

Photo 5. Drive 2-in. drywall screws through the vanity's back brace into wall studs near both sides of the cabinet.

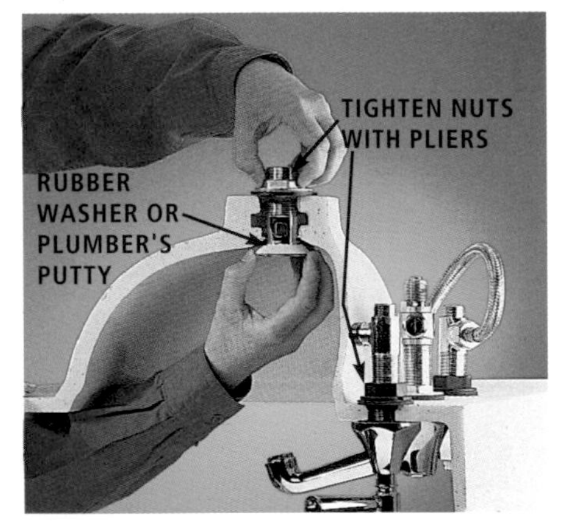

Photo 6. Mount the faucet, handles, and drain on the sink according to the directions and attach new water supply tubes.

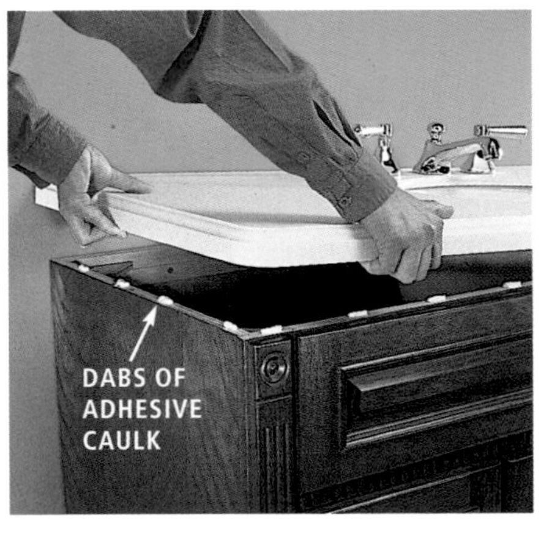

Photo 7. Apply adhesive caulk every 4 inches around the cabinet's upper edges and center the top on the vanity.

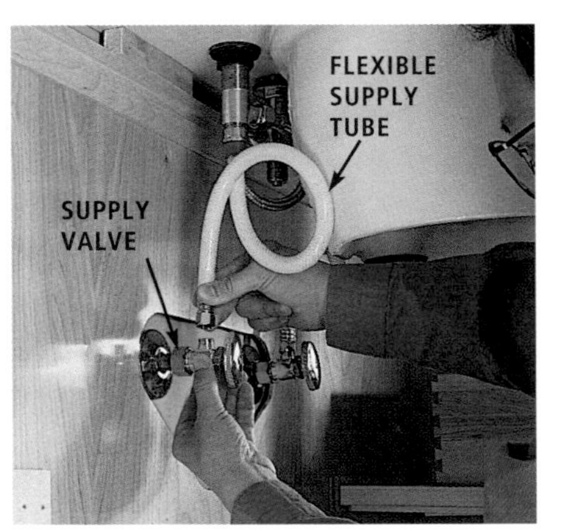

Photo 8. Attach the flexible supply tubes to the shutoff valves. Tighten the final quarter turn with an adjustable wrench.

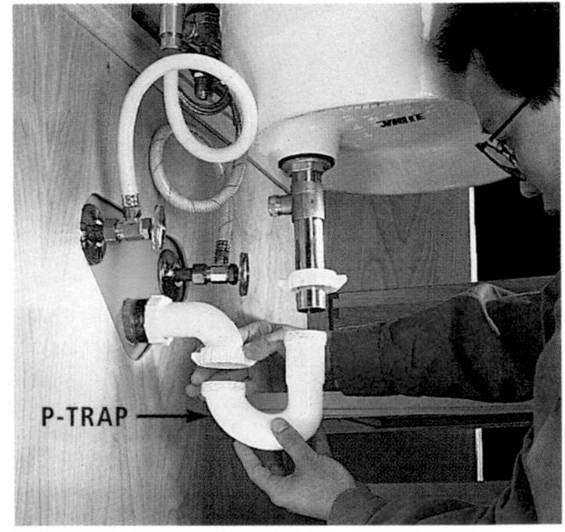

Photo 9. Slide the P-trap into the wall drain-pipe and over the sink tailpiece. Secure it with slip nuts and washers.

INSTALL THE VANITY AND SINK

Proceed as follows to install and connect the new vanity and sink:

▶ Mark the positions of the shutoff valves and drainpipe on the back of the new vanity. Cut an opening for them using a saber saw (Photo 2).

▶ Position the vanity against the wall and level it front to back and side to side (Photo 3). Tap in shims to achieve level, then scribe the bottom edge (Photo 4). Trim to that line with a saber saw, plane, or sander. Seal the cut edges with two coats of varnish.

▶ Fasten the vanity to the wall studs with 2-inch drywall screws (Photo 5). Use an electronic stud finder, or probe through a small hole in the wall with a stiff wire. Studs are usually spaced 16 inches on center.

▶ Install the new faucet and faucet handles, then turn the sink over and install the sink drain (Photo 6). Seal the drain collar inside the sink with plumber's putty if it isn't supplied with a rubber washer. Attach flexible water supply tubes to the faucet extensions.

▶ Apply dabs of adhesive caulk along the top edges of the vanity and lower the top into position (Photo 7).

▶ Connect the water supply tubes to the shutoff valves (Photo 8).

▶ Screw the drain tail piece to the sink drain, and the outlet section to the drain stub in the wall. Then connect the P-trap with the slip nuts provided with the trap (Photo 9).

▶ Turn on the water and check for leaks.

INSTALL THE MEDICINE CABINET AND LIGHT

Center the medicine cabinet over the vanity and fasten it to the wall studs. Then install a light above it.

▶ Mark the position of the bottom corners and top side edges of the medicine cabinet on the wall with masking tape .

▶ Support the medicine cabinet on 2x4 blocks or have a helper hold it in position as you drive 2-inch drywall screws through the cabinet's back into the wall studs (Photo 10). Keep the cabinet level as you drive the screws.

▶ Be sure the electrical circuit is off before hooking up your new light fixtures. Follow the fixture instructions. In most cases, simply connect the colored fixture leads to like-colored wires in the electrical box. Use twist connectors to fasten the wires together.

If the fixture has a wooden backplate and frame, like the one shown (Photo 11), proceed as follows for fire safety:

▶ Add an extension collar to the electrical box to extend it through the wood into the interior of the fixture. Mount the backplate of the fixture on the wall with the box collar protruding through it.

▶ Connect a new section of cable to the old cable inside the electrical box. Run it through a cable clamp in the center of a metal cover plate for the box; tighten the clamp to secure the cover plate.

▶ Fasten the end of the cable in the clamp on the fixture, strip the wire ends, and make connections with the fixture leads.

▶ Be sure to attach a ground clip to the electrical box cover plate and connect it to the green or bare wire ground in the cable.

Making Plumbing Connections

For a tight seal, wrap Teflon plumber's tape around the threads of the sink faucets and the shutoff valves before attaching the water supply tubes. Tighten the supply tube nuts firmly by hand, then use an adjustable wrench to turn them a quarter turn more. Do not overtighten them, to avoid cracking the fittings.

INSTALL THE MEDICINE CABINET AND LIGHT

Photo 10. Center the medicine cabinet over the sink and screw it to the studs through its back. Use masking tape to mark its position and 2x4 blocks for support.

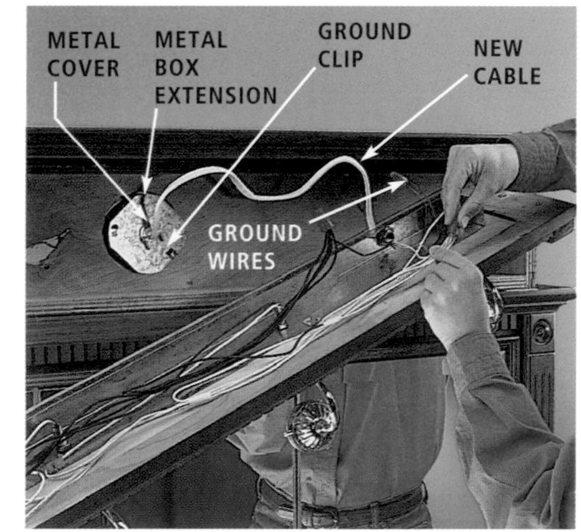

Photo 11. Install the light fixture according to the manufacturer's directions. If necessary, extend the electrical box with a metal extension collar; ground the box cover plate.

Plumb a Small Half Bath

Additional bathroom space is not a luxury; if there are more than three in your family, or if you have guests often, it is a necessity.

In many cases, a half bath equipped with a toilet and sink, but no shower or tub, will be enough to eliminate morning lineups at the bathroom door and to serve as a guest washroom for visitors.

As the name implies, a half bath needs only about half the space of a full bathroom, so it can usually be fitted into the existing plan of a house. There's no more economical way to get the convenience of a second bathroom.

Permit Required

You must apply for a building permit for this project. Building, plumbing, and electrical inspectors will approve your plans and will check the work in progress and when it's finished to make sure all is correct.

WHAT'S INVOLVED

This project involves plumbing, wiring, wall construction, and wall and floor finishing. If you have remodeling experience and well-developed tool and plumbing skills, it should be within your capabilities. If you feel insecure in some of these areas, you probably will need professional help at some point. If you are a beginner, you'll need to hire someone to do almost all of the work.

The most challenging part of the job is running the new drains and water supply lines and connecting them to the existing plumbing system. The work described on these pages focuses on preparing the space and doing the fundamental plumbing. The instructions also cover installing the sink and toilet in general detail, but do not deal with wiring, framing the walls, hanging drywall, or setting tile.

You will have to adapt the general principles described here to the specifics of your house and local building and plumbing codes. If necessary, you can hire a professional plumber to help you design the system and assist you through the tough parts of the job. You may want to consult a professional electrician about wiring problems. Often, plumbing, building, and electrical inspectors can give you helpful advice, but their job is to approve your plans and work, not give home-improvement lessons. Sales personnel at home centers and other suppliers are almost always very willing to explain how to use or install the items you are buying, but again you can't expect them to coach you through the entire project.

FINDING SPACE

Look at your closets, pantry, and portions of bedrooms to find space for a new half bath. The basement is a possibility, too.

Most building codes have the following minimum requirements:

- ▶ A ceiling height of at least 7 feet.
- ▶ A space at least 30 inches wide for the toilet, and at least 24 inches of open space in front of the toilet (see diagram, below).
- ▶ A window that can open or a ventilating fan ducted to the outside.
- ▶ A light, and an outlet with ground fault circuit interrupt (GFCI) protection.

Begin with these requirements, and add the fixture dimensions to determine the space you need. Toilets measure 24 to 28 inches from front to back, and sinks 13 to 24 inches. You can position the sink in front of the toilet, to one side, or in a nook of its own. Smaller fixtures are available; check the catalogs at a plumbing store or home center, or consult a professional kitchen and bath designer.

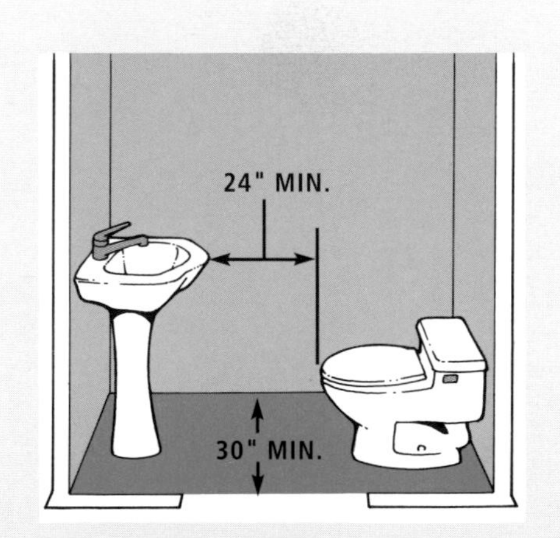

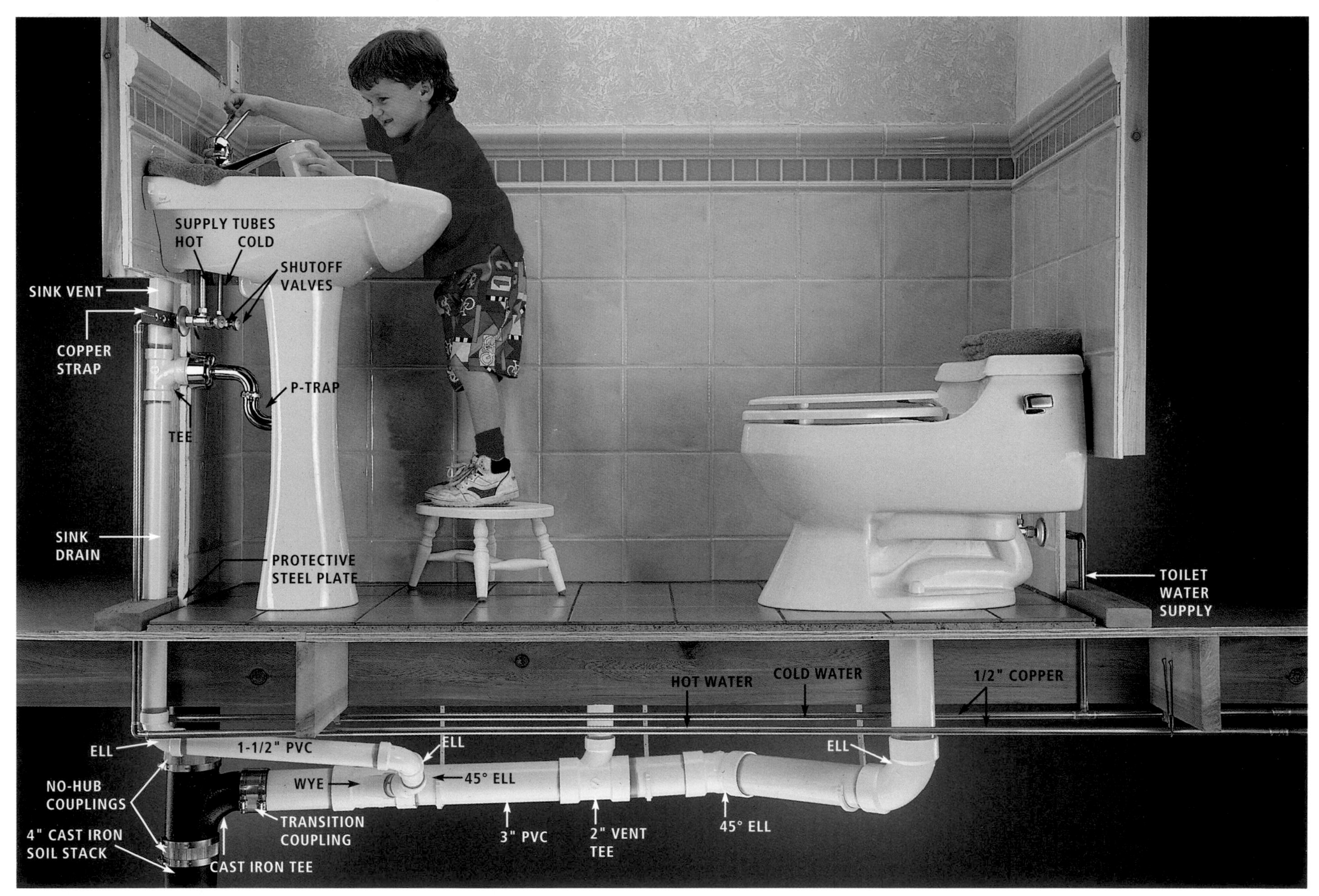

A new half bath can make life easier in any household, and will definitely increase the value of a home. However, installing one is not a project for beginners. The photo above shows the major components used in plumbing a new toilet and sink.

Half Bath Drains and Vents

This cutaway plumbing diagram provides an overall view of the drain and vent installations used for a half bath. Note that the sink drain joins the toilet drain but each drain is individually vented. The offset in the sink vent is not necessary if there is nothing in the way of a straight vertical run. The vents do join just below the roof, allowing only one new opening to be cut.

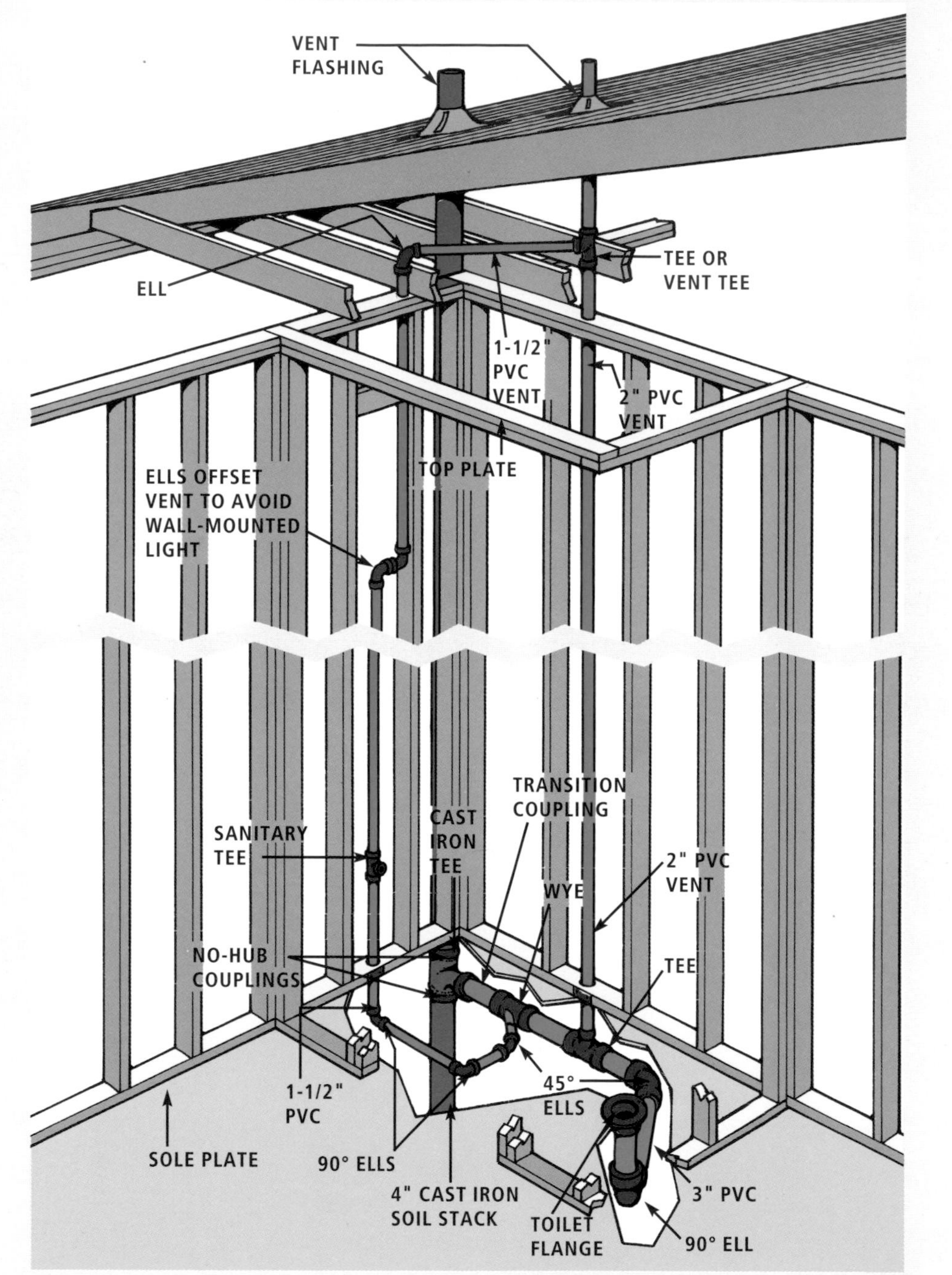

PLAN THE PLUMBING

Your new fixtures must be connected to water supply lines and to the drain-waste-vent (DWV) system of your house. There are few limitations on making water-supply connections, but significant matters to consider when planning DWV piping. In addition, your planned installation must be approved by both building and plumbing inspectors before you begin work.

A common material for the DWV system is a white plastic pipe called Schedule 40 PVC (polyvinyl chloride). In some regions, you can install black plastic pipe ABS (acrylonitrile-butadiene-styrene) pipe. Techniques for working with plastic pipe are explained in the box on page 79.

Routing DWV pipes

The main waste line in your house is a 4-inch (sometimes 3-inch) diameter pipe to which all fixture drains are connected. The vertical portion of the main waste line, between the topmost drain and the lowest point of the line, is called the soil stack. The portion above that, which runs through the roof, is the main vent or stack vent. The horizontal portion in the basement that runs underground to the sewer pipe or the septic tank is the building drain. Here are some points to consider:

▶ The farther you locate the bathroom from the soil stack, the more plumbing problems you could encounter. You will have to attach a 3-inch soil (waste) line from the toilet and a 1-1/2 inch waste line from the sink to the main waste line. The shorter the runs are, the better.

▶ To simplify installation, the sink waste line can connect to the toilet soil line before they join the main waste line (see diagram at left). In addition, it usually is easier to tie into the

vertical soil stack than to the horizontal building drain, which may be underneath the basement floor.

▶ Codes require that each fixture waste line have a trap, and that each trap be vented by a pipe that leads to the outside above the highest fixture in the system. For that reason, vents almost always exit through the roof. Their purpose is to equalize air pressure in the drains so the traps—the U- or P-shaped bends in the fixture drain pipes—remain filled with water to prevent noxious sewer gases from entering the house.

▶ A vent must rise vertically, or at no less than 45 degrees, until it is 6 inches or more above the "spill height" of its fixture—the top edge of the toilet bowl or the sink. After that it can run horizontally if necessary, with a slight uphill slope. The sink waste line must have a 1-1/2 inch vent connected no closer than 3 inches nor farther than 3-1/2 feet from the trap. The toilet soil line must have a 2-inch vent that is no more than 4 feet from the flange under the center of the bowl.

▶ Vents must extend through the roof or be tied to an existing vent that leads to the open air. Unless you want it running exposed up through the rooms, be sure to find space to run the vent piping inside the walls. In the installation shown in the diagram, the toilet soil line runs at an angle—instead of directly to the soil stack—so its vent pipe can extend straight up through the wall.

Approval

Before you start this project, sketch the half-bath floor plan on paper, make sure the toilet and sink dimensions fit, and then sketch in the proposed routes of the drains and vents.

▶ Label the pipe sizes you will need and the necessary fittings—ells (90-degree elbows, to turn corners), 45-degree or half-ells, tees (for connecting with branches at 90 degrees to the main line), wyes (for connecting with branches at 45 degrees), and couplings (for joining pipes in a straight line). In soil and waste lines you must use sanitary tees, which direct the flow from a 90-degree branch line into the main line at a slight angle, rather than exactly head on. Both sanitary tees and wye fittings must be installed so the direction of flow is toward the main stack, never back toward a fixture. Direction arrows are stamped on or molded into sanitary tees; the direction of flow in a wye fitting is obvious.

▶ Show your sketch to the local building inspector, who will make sure it meets community codes and will tell you what permits to obtain and what inspections to schedule.

▶ Also show your sketch to the plumbing inspector, who will check the sizes of the pipes and fittings, trap-to-vent distances, and other specifications. Codes vary around the country, so this step is crucial. The plumbing inspector can also tell you what method to use to test the drain and vent system for leaks (see Test the DWV System, page 80).

PREPARE THE SPACE

Begin the bathroom by framing the walls and door opening with 2x4's. Then clear away the old flooring in the new bathroom area.

▶ You may have to move an existing wall. If you cut into or move a bearing wall—one that supports part of the weight of the house—you must install a beam in its place to provide structural support. The building inspector who checks your plans can help you determine if a bearing wall is involved and can recommend methods to brace it.

▶ In a minimum-size half bath the door might have to open outward into the hall. If that's awkward or not possible, build framing for a pocket door, which slides back into the wall.

▶ Pry up and discard the old floor covering, down to the subfloor. You will put down new underlayment and install the finish tile before putting the toilet and sink in place.

With the walls framed and open, you can proceed to install the plumbing, electrical wiring and outlets, and exhaust fan, along with 2x4 or other backing for mounting the sink, towel racks, and shelves.

TOOLS

- Measuring tape
- Level
- Saber saw
- Torpedo level
- Keyhole saw
- Respirator with organic vapor filter
- Drill with 3/4" spade bit
- Propane torch (optional)
- Air compressor and pressure gauge
- Soil pipe cutter (optional)
- Torque wrench
- Adjustable wrench

INSTALL THE TOILET SOIL PIPE AND VENT

The toilet soil pipe is 3-inch PVC; and the vent is 2-inch pipe.

▶ Cut an opening for the toilet flange that is centered between the side walls and 12 inches on center from the finished wall surface behind the toilet (Photo 1). If you measure from the framing, allow space for drywall and any tile or wainscoting.

▶ Install underlayment; 1/2-inch cement backer board is best. Cut out the hole for the toilet and screw the flange in place, using floor tiles as spacers to put it at the proper height (Photo 2). The flange has slots for the closet bolts that hold down the toilet bowl. Make sure the slots are parallel with the wall that runs behind the toilet.

▶ Assemble the toilet soil pipe beginning at the flange. Include tee and wye fittings at appropriate points (Photo 3). Support the pipe with a plastic hanger at least every 32 inches, and make sure it slopes down toward the main stack 1/4 inch per foot. Stop a bit short of the stack; you'll make the connection there after the system is pressure tested.

▶ Cut holes in the wall plates for the 2-inch vent (Photo 4), and cement the vent pipe into the tee in the toilet soil pipe.

MATERIALS

- PVC DWV pipe: 3", 2", 1-1/2"
- Assorted DWV pipe fittings, toilet trap, sink P-trap
- 1/2" copper or CPVC supply pipe
- Assorted supply line fittings
- Plastic pipe primer and cement
- Toilet floor flange
- Shutoff valves
- 1/2" escutcheon plates
- 3/8" water supply tubes
- Lead-free solder
- Wax toilet ring

INSTALL THE TOILET SOIL PIPE AND VENT

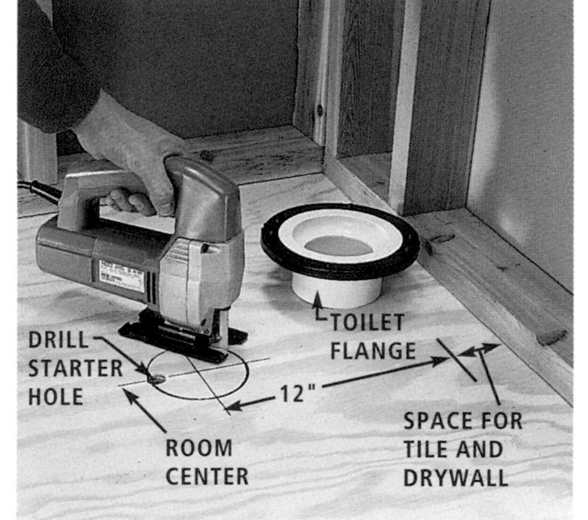

Photo 1. Use a saber saw to cut a hole in the subfloor for the 3-in. toilet flange. Center it 12 in. from the finished wall, allowing space for the wallboard and tile.

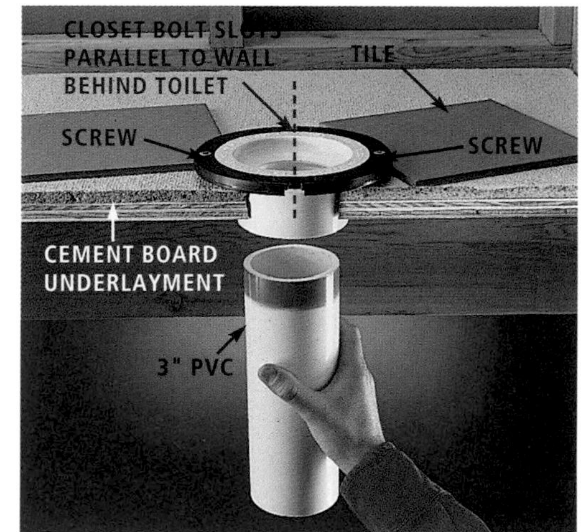

Photo 2. Anchor the flange with screws at the height of the finished floor. Begin assembling the soil pipe from this point. Use primer before cementing plastic pipe into fittings.

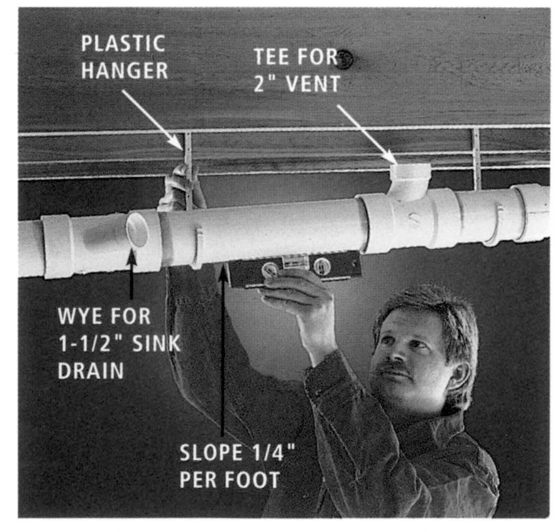

Photo 3. Maintain a minimum slope of 1/4 inch per foot in drainpipes. Assemble the run without glue to test the fit. Space plastic pipe hangers no more than 32 in. apart.

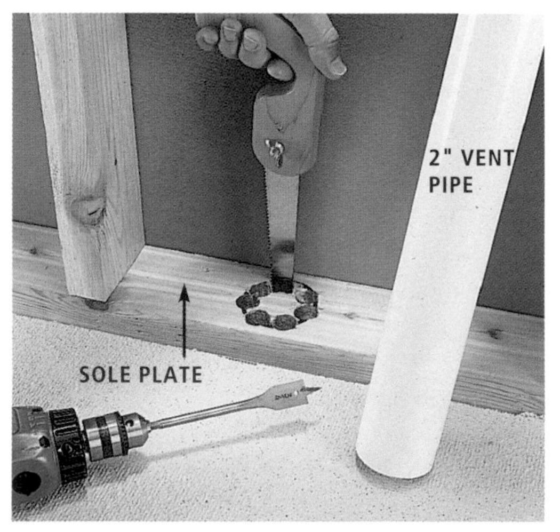

Photo 4. Cut holes for the vents in the wall plates. A handy method is to drill a series of holes with a 3/4-in. spade bit and then cut out the center section with a keyhole saw.

RUN THE SINK WASTE LINE AND VENT

Assemble the sink waste line and vent from 1-1/2 inch pipe and fittings.

▶ Mark and cut a hole for the drainpipe line through the sole plate and floor in the wall directly behind the center of the sink location.

▶ Start at the wye fitting on the toilet soil line and work toward the hole in the floor for the sink drain. As before, install pipe hangers at least every 32 inches. Make sure the horizontal run maintains a slope of 1/4 inch per foot down toward the wye at the soil line (Photo 5).

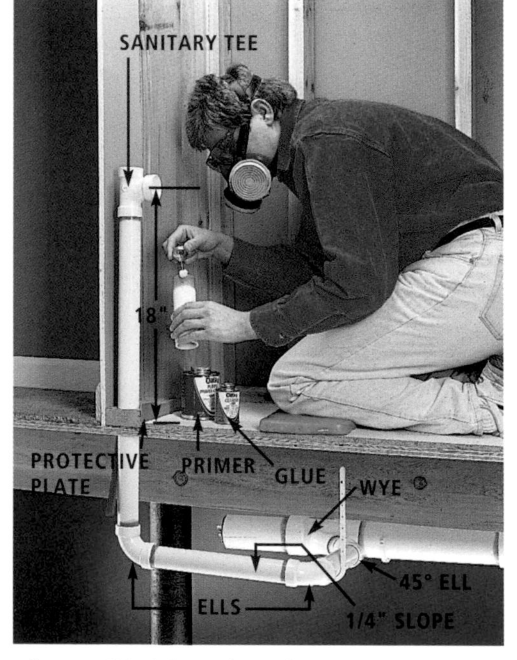

Photo 5. Work from the soil pipe wye back to the sink position to install the sink drain. Glue the assembly together only after dry-fitting and marking the pieces.

▶ Extend the waste line straight up through the floor. Measure and cut this piece of pipe so it is long enough to put the center of a sanitary tee on its top end 18 inches above the floor. Install the tee on the pipe with its branch hub pointing straight out of the wall, and oriented so the flow direction in the hub is downward.

▶ Continue with vent piping out the top of the sanitary tee. Keep in mind that once the vent is 6 inches or more above the spill height of the sink, you can install ells to offset its path around a light fixture or other obstruction in the wall, if necessary (see diagram, page 74). You can also route it to join the toilet vent or any other existing vent. Whenever a vent runs horizontally, it must slope slightly down toward the drain line where it originates.

EXTEND THE VENTS

Try to run both the sink and toilet vents up to the attic and connect them to an existing vent, to avoid cutting into the roof.

▶ If you must cut through the roof, first join the 1-1/2 inch sink vent to the 2-inch toilet vent, so you need to make only one hole.

▶ Carefully remove some shingles, saw a hole in the roof with a saber saw or reciprocating saw, and extend the 2-inch vent at least 12 inches above the roof (Photo 6).

▶ Replace the shingles on the downhill side of the vent. Slip vent flashing—a ready-made collar—over the top of the pipe, and replace the uphill shingles so that they overlap the flashing. Seal the flashing with roofing cement to make the installation leakproof.

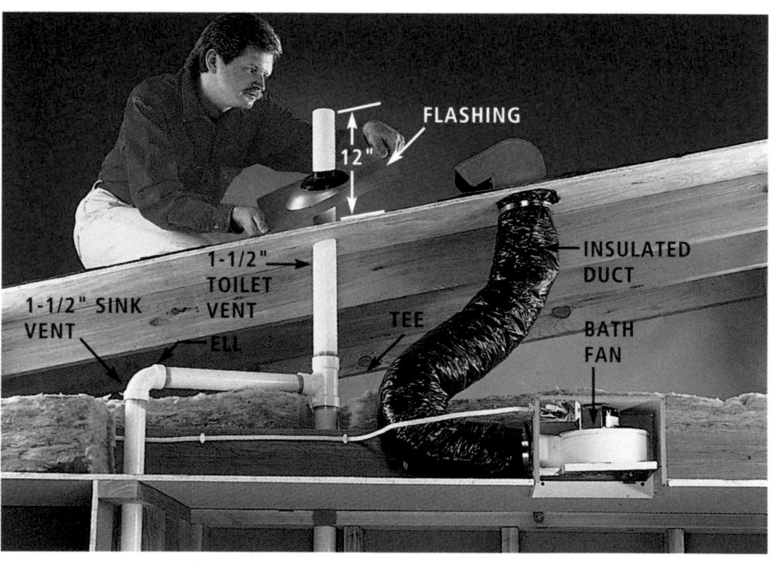

Photo 6. Connect the vents in the attic and run a pipe through the roof. Add flashing. Also install a vent for the bath fan if it exhausts through the roof rather than a side wall.

Running Pipes in Walls

Cut holes through the floor and 2x4's slightly larger than the pipes that run through them. A pipe that fits tightly will generally squeak as it expands and contracts.

Mount a protective steel plate wherever a pipe passes through a 2x4 within 1-1/4 inch of the edge. The plate will prevent nails and screws from piercing the pipe when wallboard is installed.

Water Supply Lines and Electrical Wiring

These are the water and electrical connections for this project. Details will vary in your half bath. Often the fan can be vented directly through a side wall.

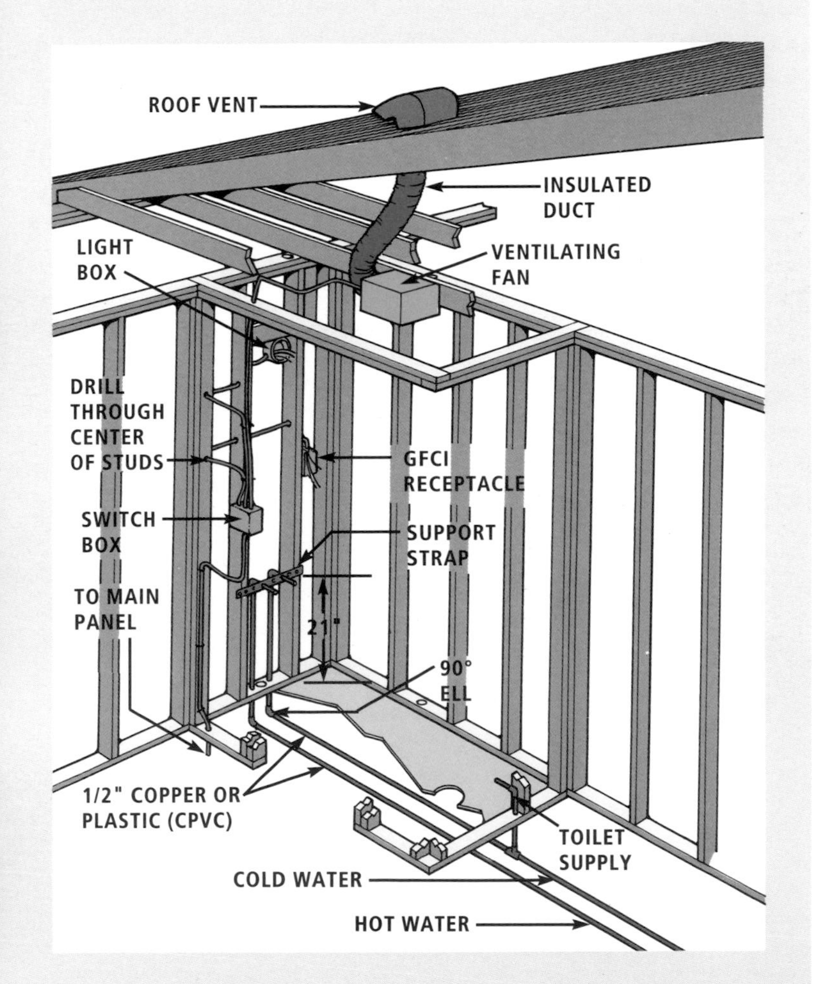

INSTALL WATER SUPPLY LINES

You need to run hot and cold water lines to the sink location, and a cold water branch to the toilet (see diagram at left). Running water lines is much easier than running drains; you can route the pipes around obstacles to fit almost anywhere. Copper pipe or tubing is the most common material for water supply lines, but many jurisdictions allow CPVC (chlorinated polyvinyl chloride) to be used as well. PVC pipe is rated only to carry cold water; CPVC pipe can carry hot water. Check your local code for the kind and sizes of pipe you can use.

Copper pipe is joined by soldering it into copper fittings (see Working with Copper Pipe, page 111). CPVC is joined with cement in the same way as PVC (see box, opposite page), but may require a different primer and cement. Check this carefully when you buy materials for the project.

▶ To begin, turn off the water at the main valve where it enters the house. Then cut into existing hot and cold water lines and run 1/2-inch copper or CPVC pipe to the toilet and sink.

▶ Half-inch pipe can serve only two or three fixtures, depending on the code in your region. Because both the sink and the toilet require cold water, be sure to tap into a 3/4-inch cold water pipe to feed your half bath.

▶ Support copper pipe every 6 feet with copper or plastic hangers; other metals can cause corrosion. Support CPVC pipe every 32 inches with plastic hangers.

▶ When soldering copper pipe, use a steel plate as a heat shield in front of flammable material (Photo 7).

▶ Bring the water lines up through holes drilled in the sole plates of the walls. At the top use 90-degree ells and 6- or 8-inch lengths of pipe to form stubouts. Shutoff valves will mount on the stubouts.

Standard wall locations for most sink stubouts are 21 inches above the floor and 4 inches to the left and right of center, but check the specifications that come with your sink. (Locations vary for pedestal sinks; see Install a Pedestal Sink, pages 104–111.) The standard wall location for a toilet stubout is 6 inches up from the floor and 6 inches to the left of center as you face the toilet. But again, toilets vary, so check the model you plan to install.

▶ Anchor the sink supply pipes just below the stubouts to prevent vibration in the wall. Use wood blocks and pipe strap, or solder copper stubouts to a special copper strap that is nailed into notches in the studs (Photo 8).

▶ Finally, solder or cement caps on the ends of the stubouts to seal the system. Then turn on the water and look for leaks. Drain the lines and resolder joints that leak in copper pipe. With CPVC, cut apart a leaking joint, dry it out, and then reglue it.

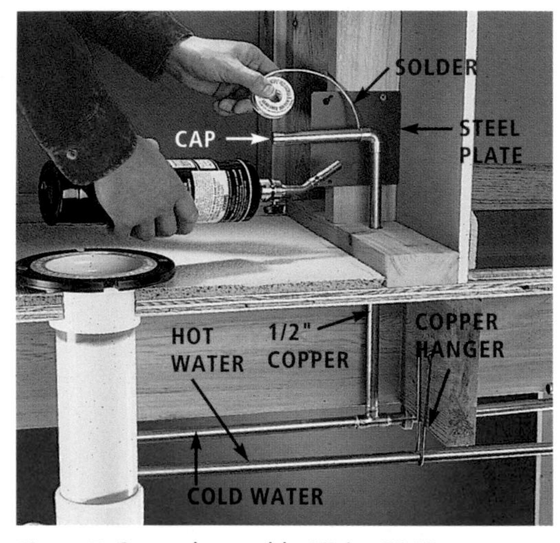

Photo 7. Cut and assemble 1/2-in. CPVC or copper water supply lines. Solder copper and support it every 6 ft. Protect nearby flammable material while soldering.

Photo 8. Support the sink supply lines where they stub out from the wall. Use wood blocks and pipe strap, or a special copper support strap like the one shown here.

Working with Plastic Pipe

The end of a plastic pipe simply slips into a fitting and butts against a shoulder in the collar or hub of the fitting. When final assembly is made, the fitting and pipe are fused together with a special plastic cement. Working techniques are the same for drain, vent, and water supply pipes:

▶ Before starting, seat the end of a piece of pipe in a fitting and mark the pipe at the edge of the fitting. Remove the pipe and measure the marked depth of the insert. You must add this much for each fitting when measuring pipe for cutting.

▶ To determine the length of pipe required along a section of run, put the fittings at each end in place—you may need a helper to hold one in position—and measure between their face edges. Then add the insert depth for each fitting.

▶ Cut plastic pipe with a handsaw. Make sure the cut is at right angles to the pipe, so the cut end is square. A wood miter box is very helpful. Remove any burrs on the cut end with sandpaper or a file.

▶ Test-assemble an entire installation by fitting the pieces together in position, but without cement. When everything is properly aligned, mark each joint before disassembling it. Draw a pencil line across the fitting hub onto the pipe. When you reassemble the joint, simply align the marks. If a test joint sticks, tap it with a hammer and block of wood to separate the parts.

▶ To cement a joint you need a special solvent primer—it is purple—and either PVC or CPVC cement, to match the pipe material. Paint primer on the outside of the pipe and the inside of the fitting hub. Then coat both surfaces with cement. Immediately insert the pipe into the fitting with the pencil marks out of alignment no more than a quarter turn. Twist the pipe to line up the marks and hold the joint until the cement sets, typically about 10 seconds.

▶ If you make a mistake, cut the joint apart and remake it. New fittings are not expensive.

▶ **For Your Safety:** Wear a mask with an organic vapor filter when using PVC/CPVC primer and cement. These compounds both contain powerful solvents that give off harmful fumes.

Avoid a Mess

When you cut into the soil stack to connect the half-bath soil pipe, all the drains above that level must stay out of action. Post signs so no one flushes the toilet or uses a sink located above the break.

TEST THE DWV SYSTEM

Before connecting the new DWV system to the main stack, test it for leaks with a small air compressor and a pressure gauge assembly, which you can rent from a plumbing store.

▶ Insert airtight plugs in all open ends of the system—the vent on the roof, the toilet flange, and the end of the toilet soil line.

▶ Attach the gauge and compressor to a drain stub at the sink position (Photo 9). Pump the air up to 5 pounds of pressure; it should remain there for 15 minutes.

▶ If the pressure drops, pump it up to 5 pounds again and brush a mixture of dish-washing soap and water on the joints. Look for bubbles to spot the leaks; remake the joints where necessary to stop the leaks.

▶ Some codes permit testing by plugging all the lower openings and filling the system with water. Check with your plumbing inspector about the required method.

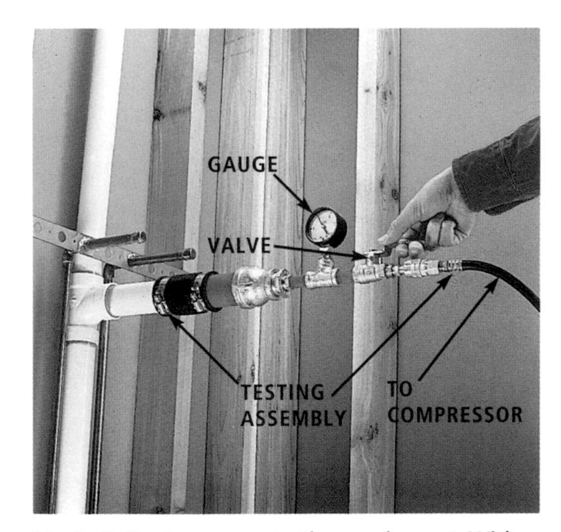

Photo 9. Rent pressure-testing equipment. With the open ends temporarily plugged, the DWV system should hold 5 pounds of pressure for at least 15 minutes.

CONNECT TO THE SOIL STACK

With the DWV system tested, connect the toilet soil pipe to the main soil stack. That's not much work if the stack is plastic—simply saw out a section and splice in the proper-sized sanitary tee fitting with approved transition couplings. If yours is an older house, it probably has a cast-iron stack; connecting to that is a good deal more work. Before cutting into the stack, stuff a rag into the sink drain and the toilet flange to block sewer gases after you connect to the soil stack. The fixture traps will not be filled with water until later.

Cracking the stack

You can't cut cast iron easily; you must use a "soil pipe cutter," which you can rent. Be sure to ask for instructions when you get it.

▶ To prevent the heavy stack from dropping down when you remove a section, bolt a 4-inch riser clamp to the stack and support each end with 2x4's nailed betweeen the joists (Photo 10).

▶ Measure the cast-iron hubless tee you plan to insert in the stack and add 1/4 inch for clear-ance. Mark a section that length on the stack opposite the end of the soil pipe from the toilet.

▶ Wrap the cutter chain around the pipe so the cutting wheels in the chain sit on the mark. This tool weighs about 50 pounds, so you may need a helper here. Put on safety goggles, tighten the latch, and work the handle of the cutter until the pipe cracks in a neat line.

▶ Move the cutter to the other mark and repeat. Remove the cutout section using a hammer and block of wood.

Connecting the soil pipe

▶ The hubless tee will be secured with couplings that consist of neoprene collar gaskets surrounded by metal clamps much like oversize automobile hose clamps. Slip a coupling onto each end of the soil stack and push it out of the way; also slip a special metal–plastic transition coupling onto the plastic soil pipe from the toilet.

▶ Lever the cast-iron tee into position, then work the couplings into place across each of the joints (Photo 11).

▶ There are two hex-head bolts on each coupling clamp, one on each side of the joint line. Tighten them with a torque wrench set at 60 inch-pounds. At this torque, the neoprene gaskets should be crimped firmly, but not so tightly that they bulge.

CONNECT TO THE SOIL STACK

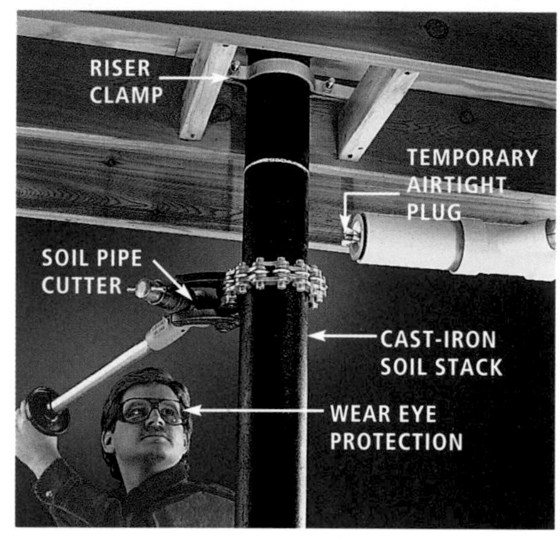

Photo 10. Support the upper soil stack with a riser clamp on 2x4's. Then use a soil pipe cutter to remove a section for a sanitary tee to connect with the toilet soil pipe.

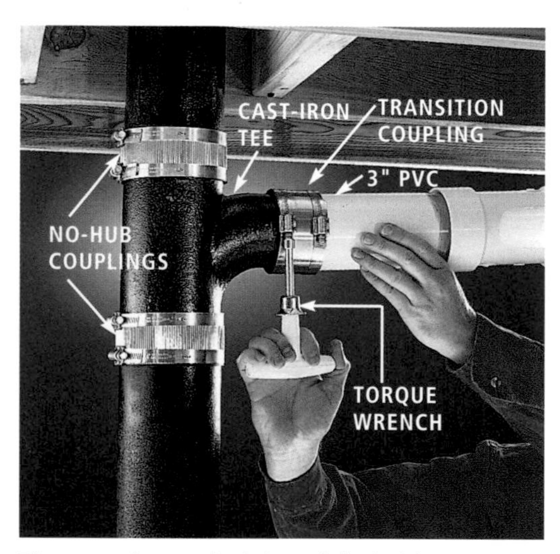

Photo 11. Secure the joints of the hubless tee in place with neoprene-and-steel couplings. Use a torque wrench to avoid overtightening the coupling clamps.

FINISH THE PROJECT

With the plumbing roughed in, proceed to the electrical work. Install the bathroom fan and duct, and electrical boxes for the switches, light, and GFCI-protected receptacle.

Once the plumbing, electrical, and building inspectors approve the roughed-in work, close up the walls with drywall, install tile, hang the door, and complete other finish work. Finally, install the toilet and sink.

▶ Turn off the water at the house's main valve again, then cut off the capped ends of the water supply stubouts. Install escutcheon plates and shutoff valves on each one.

▶ Put closet bolts in place in the toilet flange and fit a wax ring around the horn on the bottom of the toilet bowl. Take the rag out of the flange and set the bowl in place (Photo 12). Twist the bowl slightly back and forth to help the wax ring form a seal. Put nuts and caps on the closet bolts, install the tank on the bowl, and connect the water supply to the tank.

▶ Bolt the sink in place and connect the faucets to the water shutoff valves with 3/8-inch supply tubes. Remove the rag from the drain and connect the P-trap between the sink and the wall stub (Photo 13).

▶ Open the water shutoffs at both fixtures, turn on the water, and check for leaks.

FINISH THE PROJECT

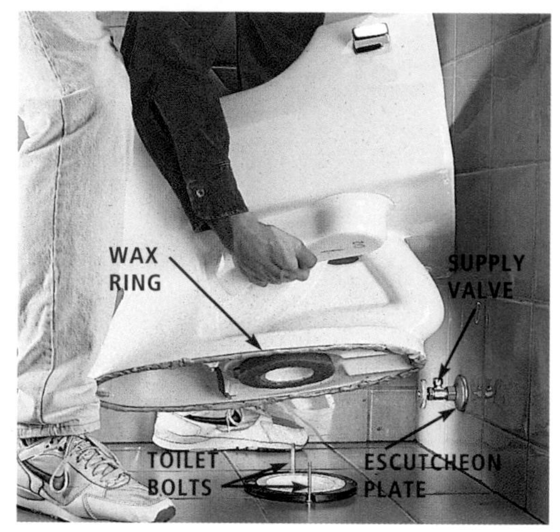

Photo 12. Set the toilet bowl on the flange with a wax ring to make a seal. Then mount the tank and connect a 3/8-in. water supply tube from the shutoff valve.

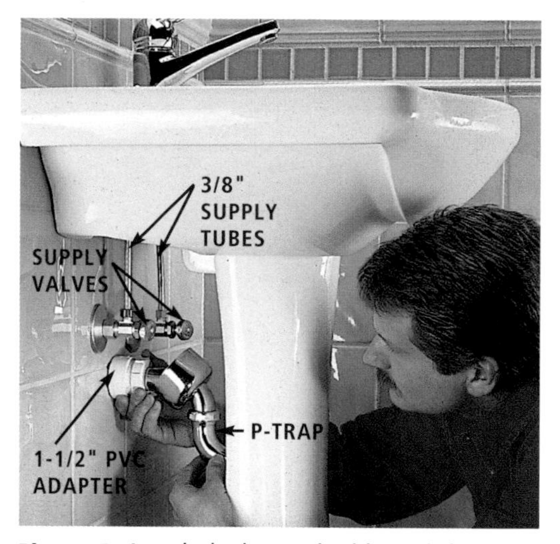

Photo 13. Attach the hot and cold supply lines to the sink faucets, then install a P-trap to the drain. Use an adapter fitting between a PVC drain and a metal sink trap.

Build a Glass-Block Shower

A shower that offers both a lot of light and low maintenance is a rare, great pleasure. The secret lies in building the shower out of glass blocks.

Glass block walls admit light over their entire area; they are strong, waterproof, and easy to keep clean. Their transparency makes them less obtrusive than solid walls and adds sparkle to a room.

Building a glass block shower is not a beginner's project. If your DIY experience is limited, you can hire professional help for the difficult parts. However you do it, you're sure to enjoy the results.

Glass block is versatile, bright, and impervious to moisture—just the right qualities for a custom-made shower. A corner location saves work and makes the most efficient use of bathroom space.

BASIC REQUIREMENTS

The ideal shower should be both simple in design and watertight. Glass blocks and a molded fiberglass shower base make it easy to attain both objectives.

Glass blocks have standard shapes and sizes:

▶ **Wall blocks** are 6 or 8 inches square, and either 3-1/2 or 3-7/8 inches thick.

▶ **Corner blocks** make 90-degree turns without a joint and come in two sizes to match the size and thickness of wall blocks.

▶ **End blocks** have one finished edge, and are used wherever the thickness of the wall is exposed, as in the entrance of the shower shown here. End blocks are 8 inches square and 3-7/8 inches thick, so you must use wall and corner blocks of the same size in order to have the horizontal joints aligned. If you want to use other sizes, add trim to finish the wall edge or install jambs for a shower door.

Molded shower bases come in stock sizes. You can't cut glass blocks to partial widths, so the shower base dimension of the glass block end must be close to a multiple of full-size block widths, although it is possible to differ by an inch or two. The dimension along the entrance wall is not critical; you can vary the width of the entry as necessary.

In addition to glass blocks, you will need plastic spacers, metal anchors, wire reinforcement mesh, expansion strips, white mortar for block joints, and prepackaged concrete mix.

Other materials include 2x4's and joist lumber, plumbing materials, and fiberglass panels or tile, mastic, and grout to finish the other walls in the shower.

TOOLS

- Carpenter's square
- Tape measure
- Saw
- Drill
- Hammer
- Level
- Wood trowel
- Metal mason's trowel
- Joint striking tool
- Caulking gun

MATERIALS

- Glass blocks
- Plastic spacers
- Packaged concrete mix
- Fiberglass shower pan
- White mortar
- 2x4 and 2x10 boards
- Asphalt roofing material
- Shims
- 1/2" expansion strips
- Wire reinforcement rods
- Metal anchor straps
- Silicone caulk
- Tiles, mastic, and grout

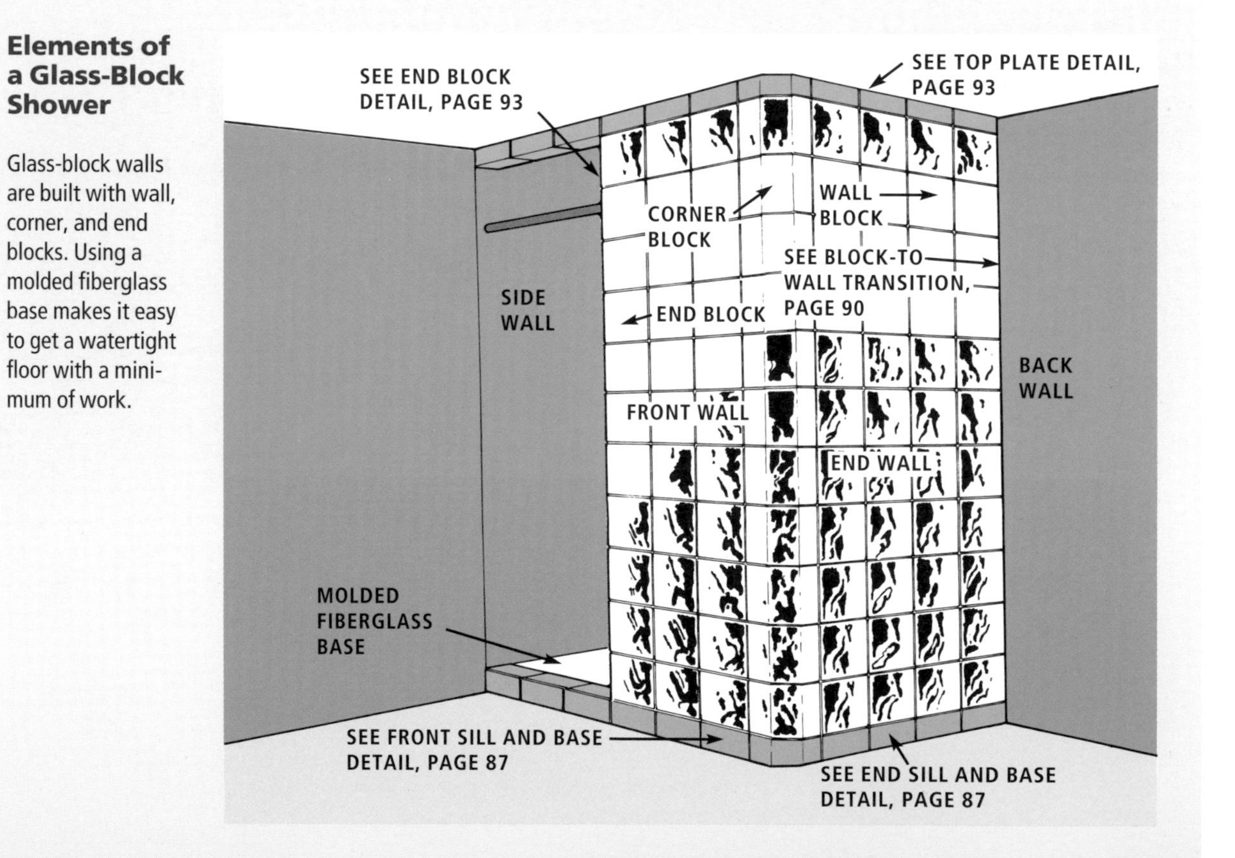

Elements of a Glass-Block Shower

Glass-block walls are built with wall, corner, and end blocks. Using a molded fiberglass base makes it easy to get a watertight floor with a minimum of work.

SCOPE OF THE PROJECT

Before you can build the glass-block walls you must:

- ▶ Clear and mark the area.
- ▶ Reinforce the floor.
- ▶ Install a drain and water lines.
- ▶ Add wall studs and lay out top plates.

Actual construction of the shower includes the following steps:

- ▶ Build the sill.
- ▶ Install top plates.
- ▶ Lay the first course.
- ▶ Lay subsequent courses.
- ▶ Finish the joints.
- ▶ Finish the walls.

In the following instructions, the walls are identified as in the drawing on page 83.

CLEAR AND MARK THE AREA

Assuming that you are building the shower in an existing corner—to minimize work and materials—strip the existing side and back walls to the studs. Then remove the old flooring, down to the subfloor.

▶ The shower base has an upturned wall flange on two or three sides, and a sill with a finished return to the floor on one side. The flange and return must be removed on the sides where the glass-block walls will be built. With a saber saw, trim off the finished face of the sill, leaving just a horizontal lip that will cover a concrete sill on the entrance side of the base. Also cut off the vertical wall flange on the side where the glass-block end wall will be at the level of the sill-lip.

▶ Make a trial layout of blocks extending straight outward from the back wall stud nearest the glass-block end wall of the shower. Allow 1/2 inch for an expansion strip on the studs, and 1/2 inch between blocks for mortar joints (nominal 8-inch blocks are actually 7-3/4 inches square), and add a corner block at the end. Mark the front or face edge of the corner block on the floor and extend the line to the existing side wall. This shows where the face of the front wall will be (Photo 1).

▶ Place the shower base in position against the side wall studs and set back from the front wall line so the inside edges of the glass blocks will overlap its trimmed-off front flange (see Front Sill and Base diagram, page 87). There will probably be extra space between the base and the back wall studs; add furring on the stud edges to bring them forward as far as necessary.

▶ Now measure and mark the location of the face of the end wall, again allowing for the inside block edges to overlap the shower base (see End Sill and Base diagram, page 87).

▶ With the shower base in position, mark the drain position. If the floor joists are open from the basement below and you will not have to take up the subfloor for any reinforcement work (see next section), simply cut a 2-inch hole for the drain when you lift the shower base out of the way. Otherwise mark reference points on the walls and on the floor outside the shower area so you can locate the center of the drain strings when the subfloor is taken up.

CLEAR AND MARK THE AREA

Photo 1. Strip the walls and floor, then mark the outside faces of the walls on the floor. Trial-fit glass blocks with proper spacing to establish the front and end wall locations.

REINFORCE THE FLOOR

Each of the 88 glass blocks in the shower described here weighs 6 pounds; with mortar joints, that is a total weight of about 530 pounds. In addition, the walls are built on a concrete sill. Weight is a significant factor in building this shower.

A standard 4-inch concrete floor will support the shower, but a wood floor must be reinforced in almost all cases. The preferred way is to double the joists beneath the shower. You should double at least two, those that support the most weight. If that is not possible, you may be able to put in a short beam running at right angles below the joists at a critical support point. Consult a local building inspector to make sure that you are providing enough support. Otherwise the floor will sag or bounce enough to cause the walls to crack or leak.

▶ If you do not have access to the joists from below, cut and remove the subfloor in the shower area. Without access from below, you must do this anyway to run the drain and water lines. One wall of the shower will run parallel with the joists. If it falls directly over a joist, open up just that far; if it falls between two joists, open to the joist just beyond. Open the floor as far as necessary in the other direction to install the plumbing.

▶ Double at least the outermost two parallel joists: the one directly under the shower wall and the next one in, or the two that the shower wall lies between (see Front Sill and Base diagram, page 87). Cut each new joist from the same size lumber as the one it doubles, and full length. Position the new joist tightly against the existing joist with their top edges flush.

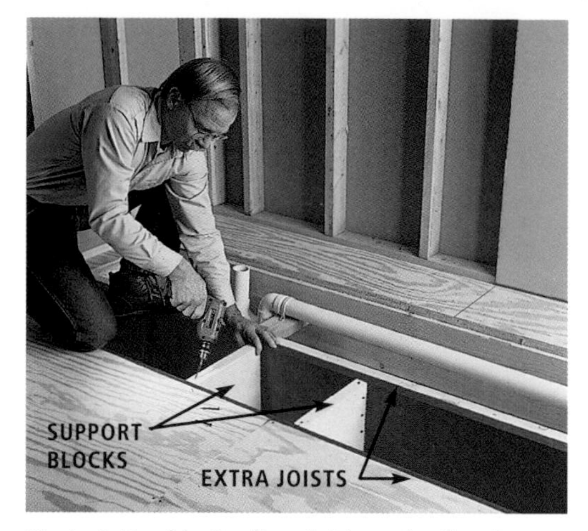

Photo 2. Double the floor joists under the glass-block wall before running the drain line. Add support blocks where a glass-block wall runs parallel to the joists.

Fasten it with three 16d nails staggered between the top and bottom edges every 24 inches. Each end should have strong support, like the existing joist.

▶ Add support blocks at right angles between the two doubled joists every 16 inches in the shower area (diagram and Photo 2). Cut the blocks from joist-size lumber, drill pilot holes, and drive toenails in their sides and top edges.

▶ If you can't double key joists because pipes, wiring, or ducts are in the way, put support blocks 16 inches on center between all joists in the shower area.

▶ If you took up part of the subfloor, replace it now. Fasten it to the joists every 16 inches with 2-inch drywall screws.

INSTALL A DRAIN AND WATER LINES

If they will not be in the way, you can install the shower drain and water lines before completing reinforcement work; that was the case in Photo 2. Or you can put them in after the reinforcement work is done.

The drain can be 2-inch diameter PVC (polyvinyl chloride) plastic pipe, with a trap directly under the shower base. The waste line from the trap must slope downhill at least 1/4 inch per foot toward its connection to the main drain, and it must be vented within 4 feet of the trap. Be sure to check with your local plumbing inspector about the required pipe sizes, locations, and connections for the shower drain and vent.

The preferred pipe for carrying hot and cold water to the shower control is copper tubing, but many localities also permit CPVC (chlorinated polyvinyl chloride) pipe. Each supply line should have a shutoff valve for servicing. Follow the directions supplied with the shower control for making connections with the water supply and the shower head.

For some basic information about installing vented drains and water supply lines, see Plumb a Small Half Bath, pages 72–81. Techniques of working with plastic pipe are described in the box on page 79; working with copper tubing is described on page 111.

ADD WALL STUDS AND LAY OUT TOP PLATES

You must add studs in the back wall where the glass-block wall ends. You must also provide for top plates at the ceiling above both the end and front walls of the shower. You can mark the top plate positions now; you will install them later, after making a trial layout of the first course of glass blocks.

▶ On the floor, mark lines 1/4 inch inside and parallel to the front and end wall lines. This is where the concrete sill will begin, and the top plates on the ceiling must be exactly above the sill. The face of the glass blocks will extend 1/4-inch beyond the sill and top plates; the space is filled with finish tile (see diagrams, pages 87 and 93).

▶ In the back wall, install metal drywall bead over the cut edge of the drywall, where the glass blocks will meet the wall. You will use the bead as a marking and alignment guide when laying the glass block, and then to finish the corner after the shower walls are up.

▶ Next, install a double stud in the back wall where the glass block wall will end (see Block-to-Wall Transition detail, page 90). Place two studs side by side with their edges facing out and nail them to the sole plate and top plate of the wall. The front corner of the outer stud should be directly on the sill line. That will put the center seam of the 3-inch thick double stud directly on the centerline of the 3-7/8 in thick glass-block wall. Make sure the studs are absolutely plumb (Photo 3) and that they align with the faces of the other studs in the back wall (before any furring is added for the adjusted shower base location).

▶ Use a plumb bob to project the outside sill corner, where the sill lines intersect, from the floor up to the ceiling. Also project the sill line at the existing side wall up to the ceiling. Snap a chalk line between the corner mark and the side-wall point to mark the outside edge of the front wall top plate. Then snap a line between the corner and the outside edge of the double stud in the back wall to mark the edge of the end wall top plate.

▶ Add furring strips to adjust the depth of the corner wall studs if necessary.

Photo 3. Insert two studs to back up the end of the glass-block end wall. Align them with the faces of the existing studs and get them plumb.

BUILD THE SILL

The sill supports the fiberglass base and the glass blocks in the front and end walls (see diagrams, opposite page). A concrete sill is better than wood, because dampness won't cause the concrete to swell and open gaps. In addition, by putting the concrete between an outer or face form board and the shower base on the inside, you can get the concrete to fit the shape of the shower base exactly. For this job, use dry premixed concrete mix in sacks.

▶ Nail 2x4 boards to the floor with their inner faces exactly on the sill line. Level their top edges with the top edge of the shower base, even if the floor dips. Put a diagonal filler across the inside corner so the sill corner will match the angle of the glass corner blocks.

▶ Put the shower base in position with its edges firmly against the existing studs and furring. Line the channel between the outer form board and the shower base with plastic to keep moisture out of the subfloor.

▶ Mix prepackaged concrete according to the directions; it must be thoroughly wet but not runny or sloppy. Fill the form with concrete,

forcing it down with the end of a short piece of 2x4 (Photo 4). Be sure the concrete doesn't lift the shower pan as you pack it into place. Use a wooden trowel to smooth off the top of the sill. It must be level and flush with the edges of the form boards and the shower base edges. Cover the exposed top edge with plastic and let the concrete harden for two days.

▶ When the sill has hardened, lift the pan out. Trim off the plastic at the floor level, spread a thick layer of asphalt roof patching material on the top of the sill, and reset the pan, embedding it in the asphalt (Photo 5). When the asphalt is dry to the touch, you're just about ready to lay the glass blocks.

BUILD THE SILL

Photo 4. Pack concrete between outside form boards and the walls of the shower base to form the sill. Trowel the top level and flush with the shower base edges.

Photo 5. Leave the shower base in place until the sill has cured. Then lift it out and spread a thick asphalt layer over the top of the sill. Reset the base, embedding the edges in the asphalt.

Sill and Base Details

The concrete sill supports the front and end edges of the shower base and the glass-block walls. The width should allow the glass blocks to overhang 1/4 inch on the outside, allowing room to set tile trim below. Floor reinforcement is essential to avoid flexing and cracked joints later.

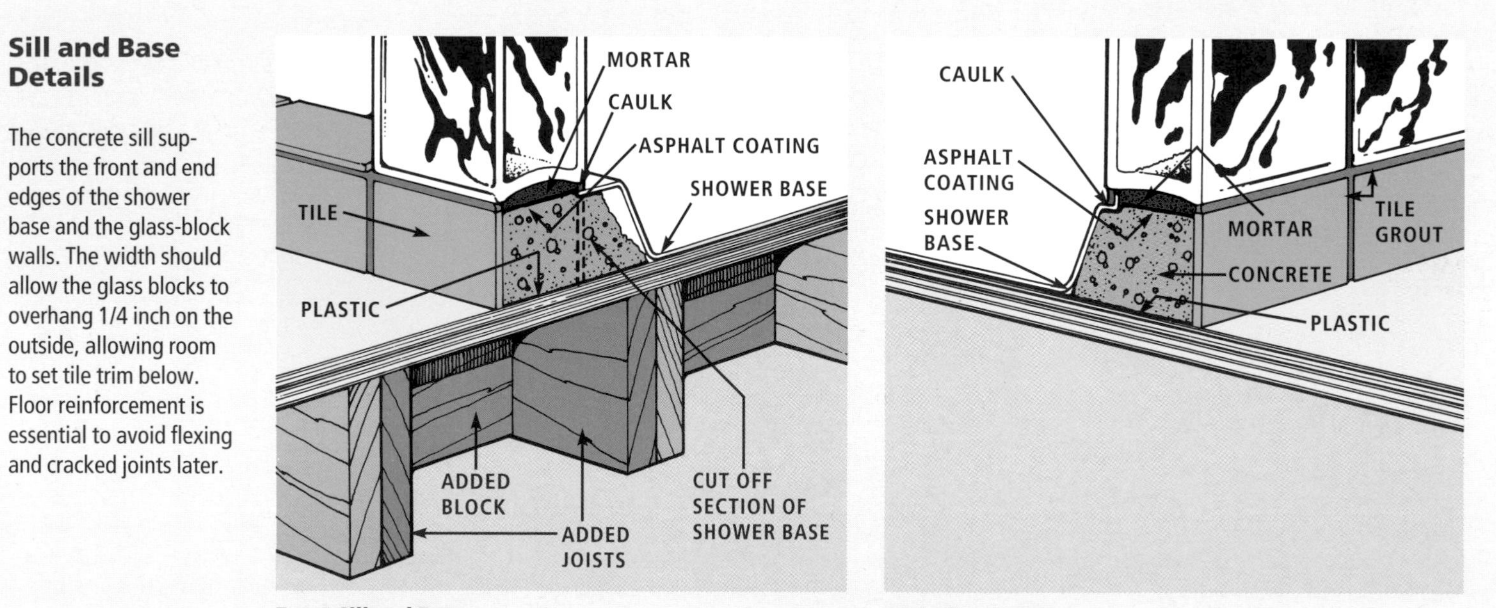

Front Sill and Base

End Sill and Base

INSTALL TOP PLATES

You need three reference lines to build walls that are straight and vertical. One is the line of the sill on the floor. The second lies along the double stud and drywall bead in the back wall. The third is a top plate fastened to the ceiling. It must be located exactly in line with the sill, and just deep enough to allow a 1/2-inch thick expansion strip to be placed across the topmost course of glass blocks.

▶ When you marked the sill lines on the floor, you also marked lines for the top plates on the ceiling. Check their alignment with the finished sill by hanging a plumb bob from two or three points on each ceiling line. If the bob does not point precisely to the face of the sill, shift the ceiling line until it does.

▶ To determine the depth of the top plates, you must mark out the height of each course of glass blocks, to see where the top will be. Begin by dry-laying the first course of glass blocks along the top of the sill. Insert 1/2-inch shims under the blocks to allow for the bed of mortar that will be there (Photo 6). Adjust the shims as necessary to keep the top of the course level. Insert plastic spacers to align the block faces and maintain uniform joints between blocks. You can't use spacers with corner blocks. Space them freehand or with shims.

▶ Now add a partial dry-laid second course on top of the first. Again, use plastic spacers for uniform placement. Unlike a brick wall, where vertical joints are staggered, joints in the glass-block wall must be aligned exactly.

▶ Mark the top edges of the first course and second courses on the drywall bead on the back wall (Photo 7). Continue upward, marking up the bead at 8-inch intervals. These marks represent the height of the top edge of each course of blocks. When they reach a point less than a full block from the ceiling, make a final mark 1/2 inch above the topmost course mark. This marks the depth of the top plate and allows 1/2 inch for an expansion strip.

▶ Fasten 2x4's flat to the ceiling along the top plate lines, driving nails into the ceiling joists. If there are no ceiling joists to nail to, secure the 2x4's with construction adhesives and long hollow wall anchors. Add a second 2x4 board or strips of plywood thick enough to bring the bottom of the top plate to the marked depth (Photo 8). Trim the outside corner so the ceiling plates follow the angle of the corner blocks.

INSTALL TOP PLATES

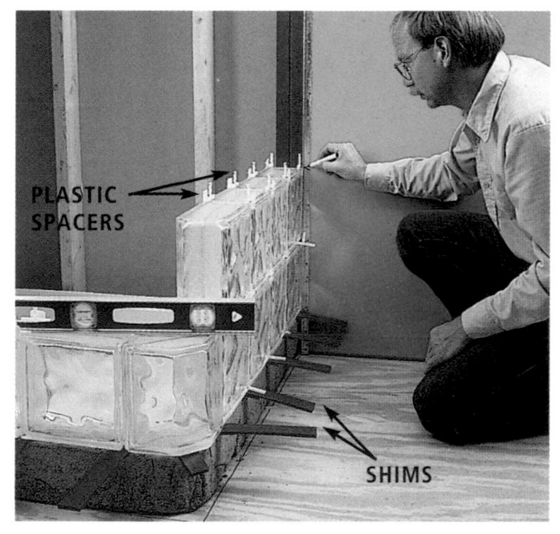

Photo 6. Dry-lay the first course and part of the second course to establish the vertical intervals. Use shims and plastic spacers for level placement and uniform spacing.

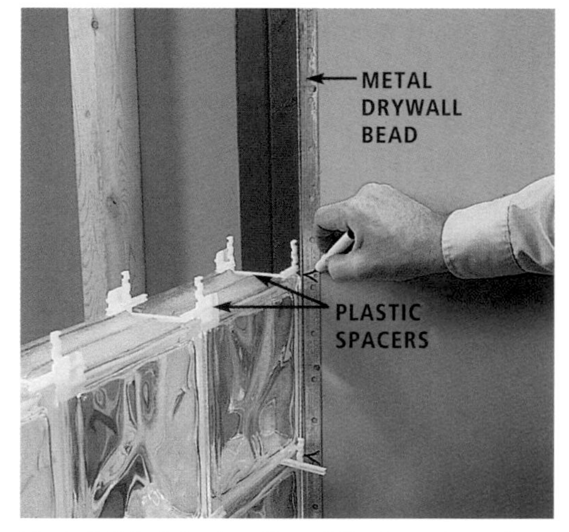

Photo 7. Mark the location of the top edges of the first two courses on the drywall bead on the back wall. Continue marking at 8-in. intervals up to the top of the wall.

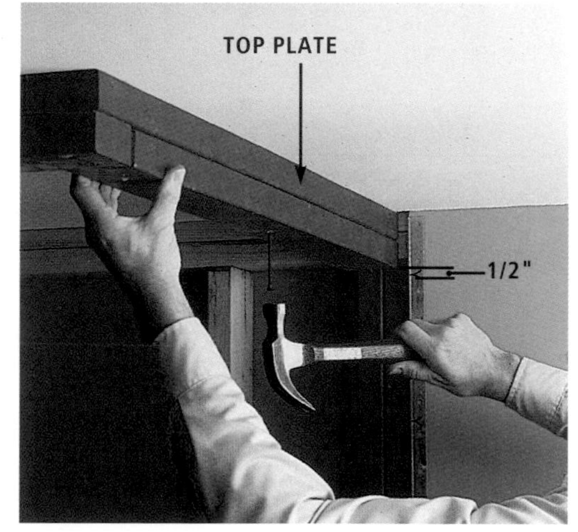

Photo 8. Nail a top plate to the ceiling precisely above the concrete sill below. The plate bottom should be 1/2 in. above the mark for the top course of glass blocks.

LAY THE FIRST COURSE

Plan to lay the blocks in just the lower half of the wall on one day. Let the mortar in this section harden overnight before proceeding. That will make the wall more stable when you climb a ladder to lay the upper blocks.

Wear rubber gloves to mix and handle the mortar, and work carefully. Laying the first course in particular isn't easy, so take your time. The following steps will help your wall-building go smoothly.

▶ Use a white, prepackaged mortar mix from a glass-block dealer, because the white will show through the insides of the blocks and brighten the wall.

▶ Prepare about a third of a 50-pound sack of the mortar for the first row, mixing it to the consistency of soft, sticky pudding. The mortar should stick to the trowel.

▶ Spread a 1/2-inch layer of mortar on the sill for the end wall and set the first course of blocks, beginning with the corner block and working toward the back wall. Make sure the blocks overhang the face of the sill by 1/4 inch, so they will be flush with the finish tile.

▶ As you place each block, tap it down into the mortar with the handle of the trowel. Level the blocks perfectly with the first wall mark, using wood shims beneath and plastic spacers above (Photo 9). The shims prevent the blocks from compressing the mortar; they can be snapped when finishing the joints.

▶ When you reach the back wall, insert a soft, plastic expansion strip between the block and the double studs to maintain a 1/2-inch flexible gap between the wall and glass blocks.

▶ Spread mortar on the sill for the front wall. Lay the blocks, again starting from the corner block. Maintain uniform spacing and keep the tops level. Finish with an end block when you reach the shower entrance.

▶ Scrape off excess mortar and let the blocks sit until the mortar stiffens—one to two hours. This course must be firmly anchored to provide a solid base and an accurate starting point for the rest of the wall.

▶ Mix another batch of mortar from the remainder of the sack, and fill the joints in the first course (Photo 10). Be sure to fill space between the blocks and the outer edges of the joints completely.

LAY THE FIRST COURSE

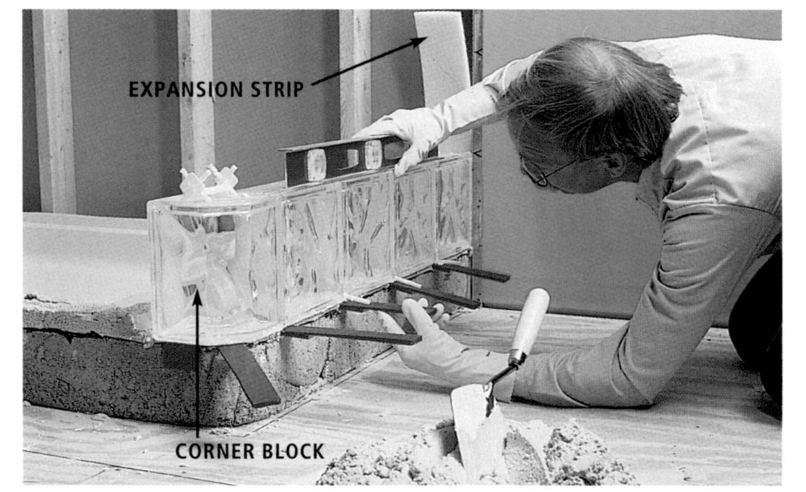

Photo 9. Spread a mortar bed on the sill and lay the first course, beginning at the corner. Use spacers, and shim the blocks to level them. Let this course set for up to two hours.

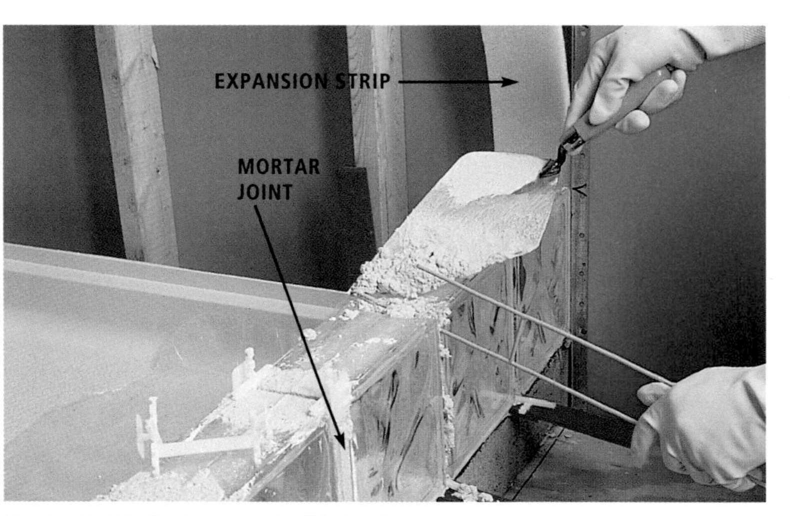

Photo 10. Mix fresh mortar to fill the first course joints. Use a trowel and a piece of wire reinforcement to pack the vertical joints completely with the mortar.

LAY SUBSEQUENT COURSES

There are three very important concerns in laying the second and succeeding courses of glass blocks. One is to maintain the alignment of the joints and the faces of the blocks from course to course. The second is to insert reinforcement and anchors at the required locations. The third, explained on page 92, is to shape and finish the mortar joints correctly.

▶ Cut a length of wire reinforcement to reach from the corner block to the back wall. With the spacers in place, spread a 1/2-inch bed of mortar across the top of the first course of blocks and lay the wire into the bed (Photo 11). Insert wire reinforcement every second row as you build.

▶ Lay the second course of blocks working from each end toward the corner. Start at the back wall and put a block against the expansion strip. Butter the exposed vertical edges with mortar, fill the concave space between, then place the next block against the strip. Do this each time before putting the next block in place (Photo 12). Add spacers at the top, and tap the blocks together and down to seat them in the mortar and on the spacers below. Make sure the tops of the blocks remain level. Stop at the corner block.

▶ Lay second-course blocks from the entrance toward the corner in the same way. When you get to the corner, butter the edges of the wall blocks on each side and set the corner block into position (Photo 13).

▶ Before laying the third course, run a special metal anchor—available from glass-block suppliers—along the top of the second course of blocks and fasten it to the studs in the back wall with two 1-1/4 inch screws (Photo 14 and Block-to-Wall Transition diagram, below left). Insert an anchor like this every other row, alternating with the wire reinforcement.

▶ Spread mortar and lay the third course. Continue laying the next courses, using a 2- or 4-foot level to make sure each row is level. To help keep the wall perfectly vertical as you work, use a straightedge long enough to reach from the sill to the top plate (Photo 15). Because the block faces protrude 1/4 inch beyond the sill and the top plate, add 1/4-inch spacers to the top and bottom of the straightedge (Photo 16). Use the trowel handle to tap the blocks into alignment.

Block-to-Wall Transition

An expansion strip is required between the glass blocks and the double studs in the back wall. Steel anchors are also required in every other course, beginning with the second course at the bottom.

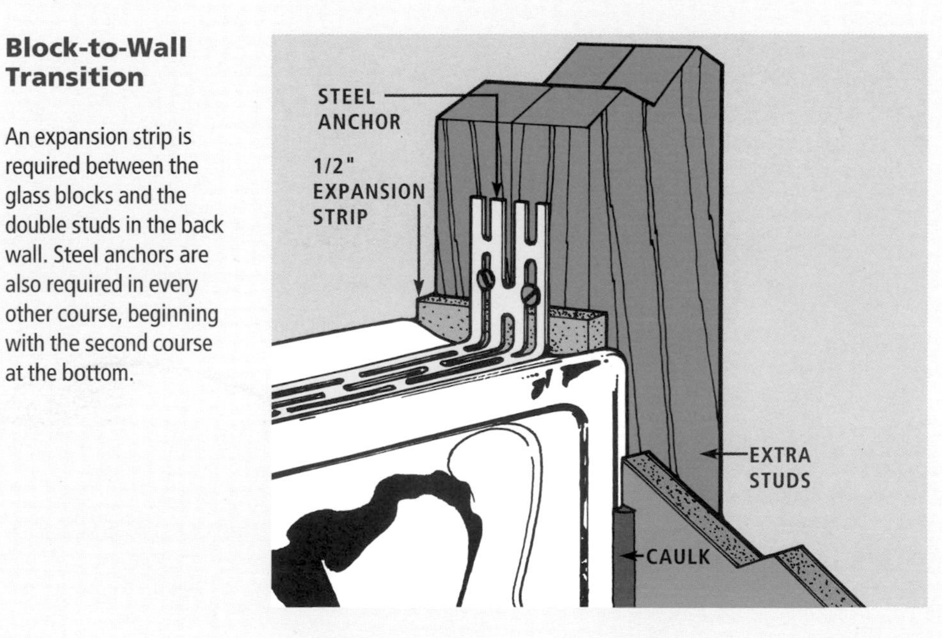

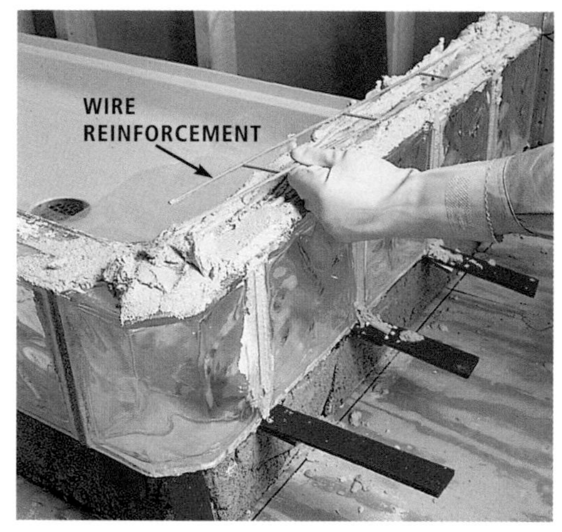

Photo 11. Spread a bed of mortar over the first row and lay wire reinforcement into it. Repeat every other row. The plastic spacers remain in place and are clipped off later.

Photo 12. Butter the side of each set block and press the next block against it so mortar squeezes out. Make sure the block fits tightly against the plastic spacers.

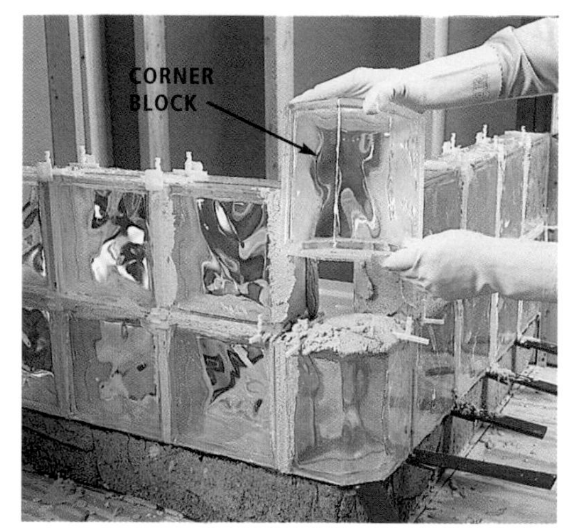

Photo 13. Set the corner block last in each course. Spacers won't fit it, so be sure it's level and plumb. Adjust the entire row as needed to set the corner correctly.

Photo 14. Screw a steel anchor to the studs just above the second course. The mortar bed for the third course will hide the anchor. Repeat this process every other row.

Photo 15. Use a straightedge that reaches from the concrete sill to the top plate to keep the wall plumb. Tap blocks with the trowel handle to adjust their alignment.

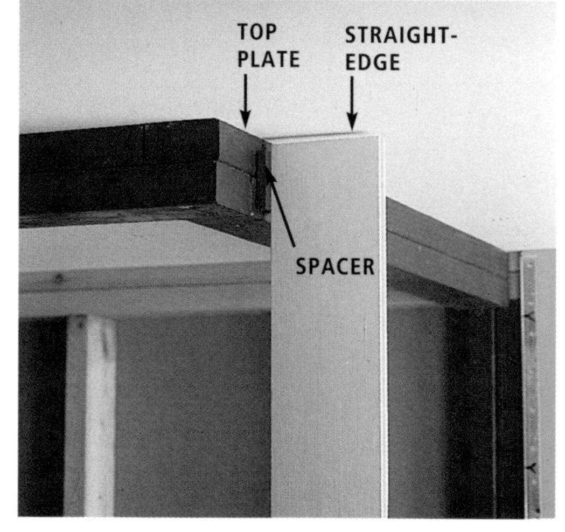

Photo 16. Add a 1/4 in. thick spacer to the face of the straightedge at the top and bottom. This allows for the distance the glass blocks overhang the sill and top plate.

FINISH THE JOINTS

By the time you get to about the fourth course, the mortar in the lower courses will be starting to set. Go back and shape the joints—a process called "striking"—before the mortar hardens.

▶ First, break off the ends of each plastic spacer by grasping them with a wire cutter or pliers and twisting. Leave the body of the spacer in place.

▶ Fill the resulting holes with mortar, then pack and smooth the joints with a 1/2-inch concave striking tool, available from the block supplier or a well-stocked home center (Photo 17). Run the tool along the vertical and horizontal joints with smooth, steady pressure.

▶ After striking the joints, brush excess mortar off the blocks with a soft brush and buff off the cement residue with a towel (Photo 18). The mortar will be getting hard at this point, but don't scrub too hard yet, since you could break a block loose. Use a dry, nonmetallic abrasive pad if necessary.

FINISH THE JOINTS

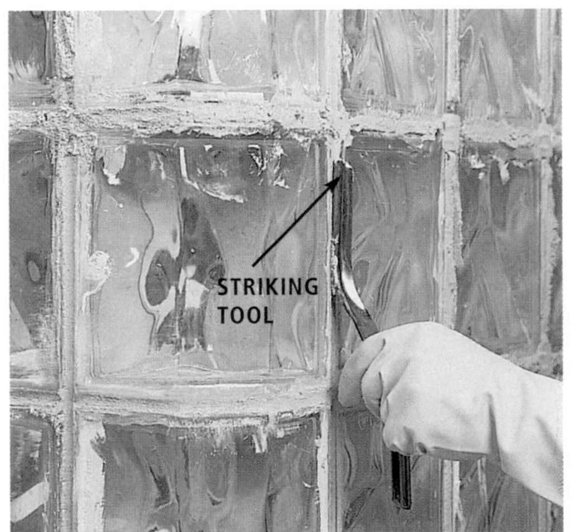

Photo 17. Use a striking tool to shape the mortar in the joints when it stiffens but before it hardens. Break off the plastic spacer ends first.

Photo 18. Brush off remaining lumps of mortar, then buff back faces with a dry towel. Scrub off stubborn residue with a plastic abrasive pad.

FINISH THE WALLS

After letting the first section harden overnight, continue on to the top. Insert wire reinforcement and metal anchors as you did in the lower courses, checking frequently in order to keep the courses level and the faces of the blocks properly aligned.

▶ When you lay the top course, insert a 1/2-inch expansion strip between the blocks and the top plate (see Top Plate diagram, opposite page). Also install metal anchors vertically between every second block, securing them to the top plate (Photo 19). These anchors are the only solid connections between the ceiling and shower wall. They'll flex slightly so the rigid glass-block wall can "float," or move, as the wood floor dips slightly when you walk on it.

▶ Add finish tile to all the exposed faces of the top plates and the sill, and fill the joints between them with tile grout. Do not grout the joints between the tiles and the glass blocks. Instead, use silicone caulk (Photo 20). These joints at the ceiling will move slightly, and will crack if you fill them with mortar or grout.

▶ Also use silicone caulk in the joints between the glass blocks and the back wall, both inside and outside the shower.

▶ If you do not install a door, add a rod to hang a shower curtain across the entrance. Support the end at the existing side wall with a screw-mounted flange; use silicone caulk at the end against the glass block (see End Block diagram, right).

▶ Finally, seal the mortar joints on the inside of the shower after giving them about a week to dry. The sealer, also used on tile grout, is available from tile dealers.

FINISH THE WALLS

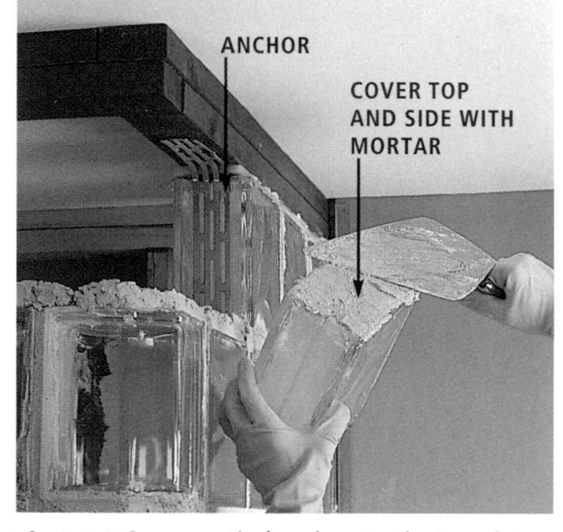

Photo 19. Screw vertical anchors to the top plate at every other block in the top course. Butter the tops of the blocks with mortar as well as the sides.

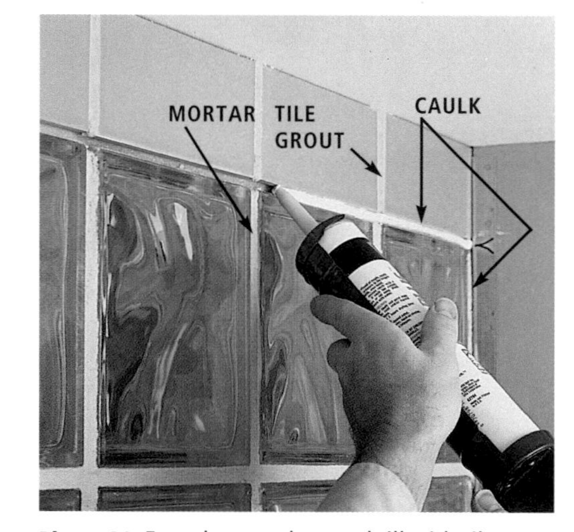

Photo 20. Face the top plate and sill with tiles. Use grout in the tile joints and silicone caulk around the glass-block edges.

Finishing Details

Once the glass blocks have been laid, finishing touches include tiling and scaling the top plate and securing a door or curtain rod to the end block.

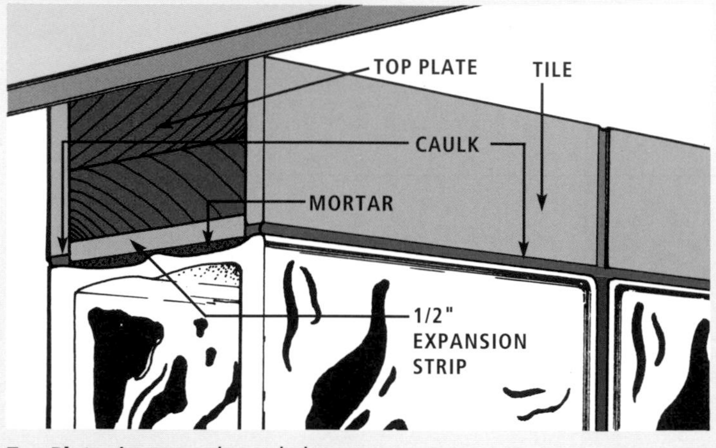

Top Plate. An expansion strip is essential between the top plate and the top course of glass blocks.

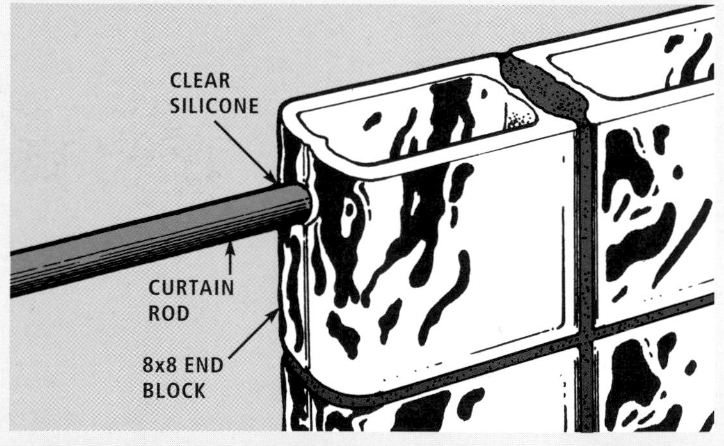

End Block. Secure the end of the shower curtain rod directly to a glass block as shown, or use silicone caulk to adhere a flange to the block.

Build-in a Whirlpool Tub

Few things are more relaxing than the swirling water of a whirlpool tub to help you forget the stress and strain of everyday life.

At one time whirlpool tubs were found only in luxury hotels, health clubs, and very expensive private residences. Today anyone can enjoy such a tub at home. No matter how small the bathroom, there's almost sure to be a tub that will fit.

Relaxation is better than ever when you have a whirlpool tub. You can install one in place of an existing tub, or in a new bath. There are models for all budgets, and a drop-in tub like this can be built into any style of bathroom.

PROJECT SCOPE

The project described here involved removing an existing tub and moving a closet wall to make additional space. The new tub was a drop-in model supported on short kneewalls and a narrow deck. If you can't create space for a 6-foot tub, consider installing a 5-foot whirlpool tub that will fit in the place of a standard size bathtub.

This is not a project for a beginner. Installing the tub is only a small part of the work. It also requires carpentry, and installing drywall, plumbing, wiring, and ceramic tile. You may also need a larger water heater. Most tub manufacturers recommend a minimum water heater capacity of 40 gallons.

If you do not have all the necessary skills, do what you feel capable of handling and hire professional help for the other tasks.

PLANNING

A project of this size requires several permits from local building authorities. In most cases, you'll need permits for carpentry and framing, plumbing, and electrical work.

Basic considerations

This project takes many days. If you intend to replace an existing tub with a whirlpool model, the tub will be out of commission for a long time. Deal with that problem before beginning any demolition work.

Make sure the space is suitable. It's a good idea to have a building inspector check the existing floor joists to make sure they are sufficient to support the new tub when it's full of water. Whirlpool tubs can hold 50 to 60 gallons of water, which weigh 400 to 500 pounds.

Will you try to gain some room around the tub for a tiled deck, as shown in this project? That will affect the size of the tub you order and the location of the pump motor. Many full bathrooms share one or two walls with closets; this offers a way to gain some space for the tub. In most cases, you won't lose very much if you move the walls 6 or 8 inches.

Before moving an interior wall, make sure it's not load-bearing—one that supports the weight of the floors or roof above. If you're not sure how to determine whether a wall is load-bearing, check with a building inspector.

Shopping for a whirlpool tub

As you plan this project, be sure to answer several important questions: What size tub should you buy? Where should the pump go? Where is the drain located? And how much do you want to spend?

▶ Tub size will be determined by the available space. Are you going to slip the new whirlpool into the same space as the old one? Or can you find enough extra space to add a tiled area around the sides of the tub?

▶ Pump location is a critical consideration in selecting a whirlpool tub. You need easy access to the pump for service and to meet building codes. If the tub you like has the pump at a rear corner that will be inaccessible, check with the dealer to see if it can be moved. Many tub manufacturers offer this option. If not, choose a different model.

▶ The location of the drain is known as the "hand" of a tub. A left-hand tub has the drain at the left end as you face the tub from the room side; a right-hand tub has the drain at the right end. Which hand you need depends on where you can make drain connections and which way you want to face when using the tub. If you special-order a tub of the wrong hand, replacing it could be very expensive.

▶ Whirlpool tub prices range widely. Some single-person, simple retrofit tubs sell for a few hundred dollars; a drop-in, multiperson tub can cost more than $5,000. The average cost for a good-quality, drop-in whirlpool tub is about $2,000. Whirlpool tubs are available in fiberglass, enameled cast iron, and plastic. They are sold at home centers, plumbing supply stores, and through kitchen and bath design centers.

ORGANIZE THE WORK

Once you have chosen the tub size and style, get the precise installation or "rough in" dimensions from the dealer. Use those dimensions to draw up work plans and order materials. The best approach is to take the project in five major steps:

- ▶ Remove the existing fixtures.
- ▶ Adjust existing walls.
- ▶ Build the kneewalls and deck.
- ▶ Install plumbing and pump wiring.
- ▶ Install the tub and faucet.

That's the way the information on the following pages is organized.

TOOLS

Mini-hacksaw
Drywall saw
Pry bar
Hammer
Saber saw or reciprocating saw
Circular saw or table saw
3-lb. maul
Handsaw
Screwdriver
Drill
Notched trowel
Grout float
Tile nippers
Caulking gun
Plumbing tools

MATERIALS

- Tile adhesive
- Tile grout
- Mortar mix
- Silicone caulk
- Tiles
- 2x4 lumber for framing
- 3/4" exterior-grade plywood
- 1/2" cement board
- PVC drainpipe and fittings
- 1/2" copper pipe and fittings
- 20-amp electrical receptacle
- No. 12, 2-conductor NM-C cable
- Electrical boxes
- 8d nails
- 16d nails
- 1-1/2" roofing nails
- 2" drywall screws

REMOVE THE EXISTING FIXTURES

Whatever the scope of your project, the old tub must first be removed.

▶ Shut off the water at the main valve in the house, then remove the individual faucets or the tub–shower control (Photo 1). Cut copper or plastic pipes with a mini-hacksaw; use pipe wrenches to disassemble steel water pipes.

▶ Disconnect the tub drain. It's usually accessible through a wall panel at the end of the tub, or from the basement or crawl space below.

▶ If the existing tub is made of cast iron, break it with a sledgehammer into manageable pieces. Wear protective goggles and work gloves. If the tub is enameled steel, pry away the tiles and drywall around the edges, remove the screws in the mounting flange, and pry the tub loose. With a helper, lift it out in one piece.

▶ If the tub is a one-piece fiberglass unit with integral wall panels, cut away a 4-inch wide strip of drywall all around so you can remove the nails or screws that secure the unit to the wall studs (Photo 2).

▶ Slide a pry bar under the front edge of the tub, push down, and pull the tub away from the back wall (Photo 3). If the tub was installed before the subfloor was laid, you must raise the tub to get it over the floor edge. Move the unit at least 4 inches from the back wall. Note the positions of any plumbing lines, heating ducts, and cables in the walls.

▶ Use a saber saw or a reciprocating saw to cut the unit into easy-to-remove sections (Photo 4). Wear gloves, a dust mask, and hearing and eye protection when cutting the fiberglass.

REMOVE THE EXISTING FIXTURES

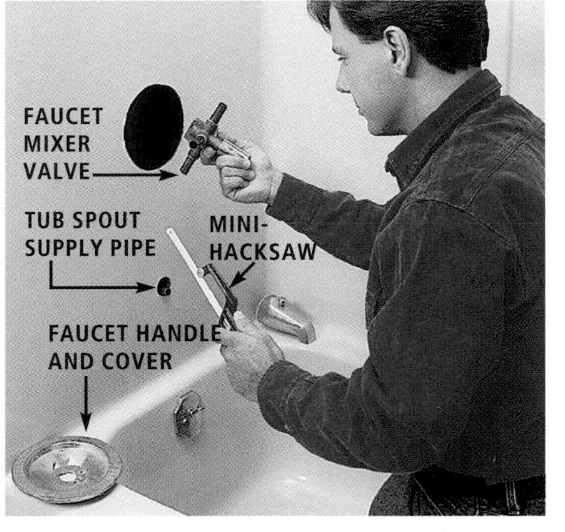

Photo 1. Remove the existing plumbing fixtures. If the pipes are plastic or copper, cut them with a mini-hacksaw. If they are galvanized steel, unscrew the fittings.

Photo 2. Cut a 4-in. wide strip of drywall along the sides and top of a tub-and-wall unit. Remove the nails or screws that fasten the flange.

Photo 3. Use a pry bar under the front edge of the tub to lift and slide it forward. Check the walls around the tub for electrical wires, pipes, and heating or ventilating ducts.

Photo 4. Cut a fiberglass tub unit into sections with a saber saw or reciprocating saw. Wear safety goggles, a dust mask, hearing protection, and work gloves.

ADJUST EXISTING WALLS

If you have to move or remove an existing wall or two, as in this project (see diagram at right), start by pulling off the wallboard from the far side of the shared walls, then remove the wall covering on the bathroom side.

▶ Loosen the wall studs by hitting them with a 3-pound maul or hand sledge where they join the bottom plate (Photo 5). Be careful not to damage the water supply lines when you are removing the wall studs.

▶ Remove the sole plates by cutting them into smaller sections. In a wall with plumbing, first cut and remove the sections on each side of the pipes (Photo 6). Then split the remaining section with a pry bar and hammer (Photo 7) so you can remove the pieces without bending the water supply pipes.

▶ Now construct walls in the new positions. The exact size and location of the walls will depend on the dimensions of the new tub and the thickness of the materials used to cover the wall—drywall and cement board, each usually 1/2 inch thick. An 18-inch high piece of cement board is required where the walls and deck surface meet (see diagram, page 98).

Wall Changes

An adjoining closet was made shorter but deeper to gain enough space to build the new tub.

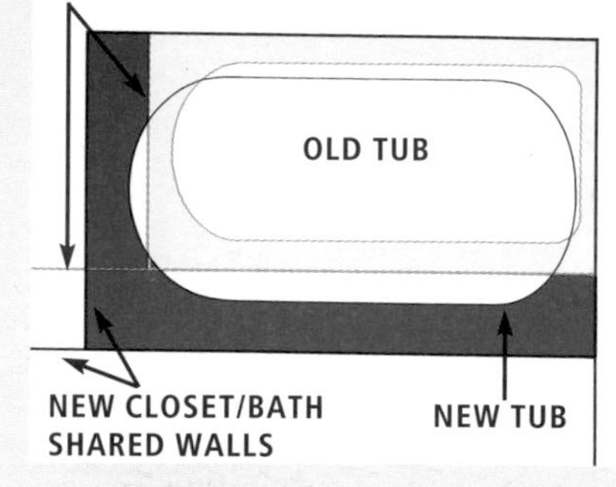

ADJUST EXISTING WALLS

Photo 5. Remove old wall studs with a 3-lb. maul. Knock them free where they're nailed to the bottom plate. Avoid hitting the water pipes.

Photo 6. Cut through the sole plate on each side of the pipes, then use a pry bar to remove the outer sections. Leave the center section in place.

Photo 7. Split the center section with a pry bar and hammer. Remove the split sections carefully to avoid bending the water pipes.

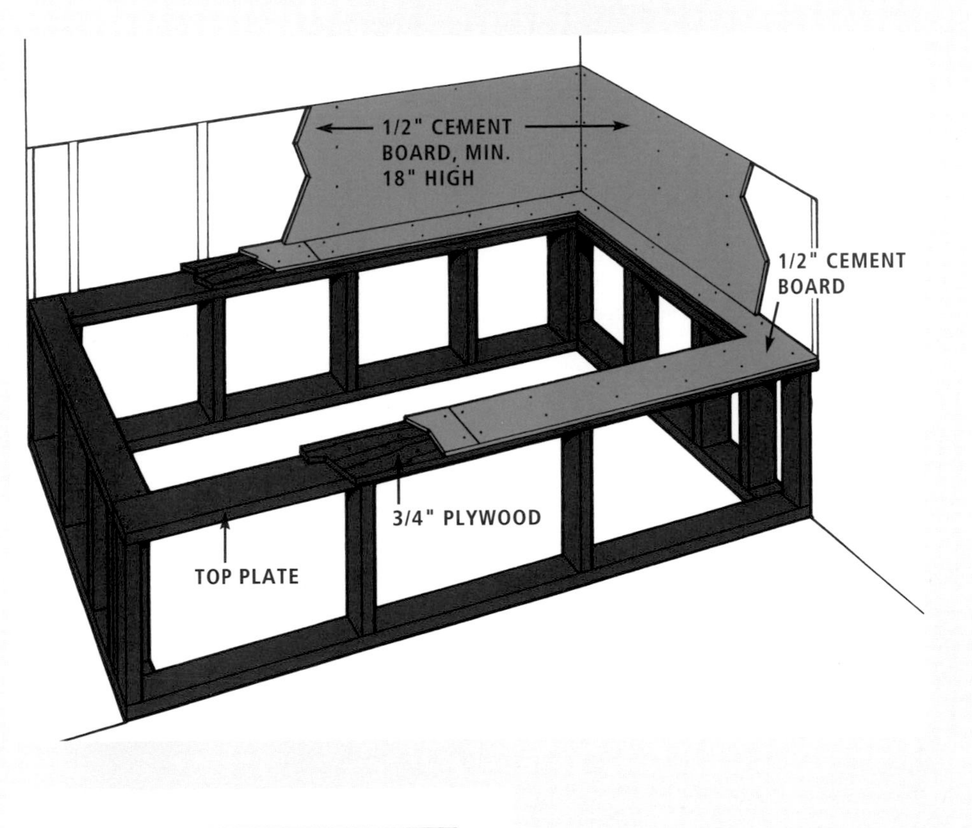

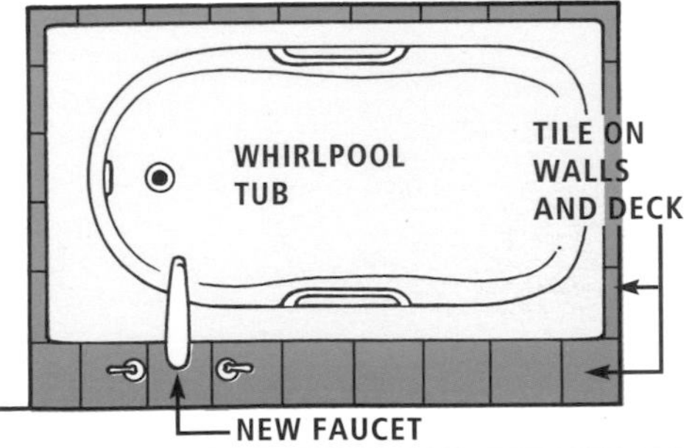

BUILD THE TUB KNEEWALLS AND DECK

You'll need to build kneewalls that extend all around the tub. You can build them in place, but it is easier to build the frames separately and then nail them in position. The deck should be cut from a single 3/4-inch plywood panel if possible, and nailed to the installed frames. The deck and walls must be covered with cement board (see diagram at left).

Construct the kneewalls

The kneewalls are usually less than 20 inches high, but building them requires very accurate measurements. Determine the height from the rough-in specifications for the tub, or measure from the floor to the underside of the tub rim. Then add in the depth of the subfloor and a mortar bed under the tub.

The finished height of the support structure includes the kneewall, a layer of 3/4-inch exterior-grade plywood, a layer of 1/2-inch cement board, ceramic tile, plus a 1/8-inch to 3/16-inch caulking gap between the tub and the tile. The tub will sit on a bed of mortar 1 to 2 inches thick (see page 102). If the outer kneewall will sit on the subfloor, put filler pieces the same thickness under the other kneewalls.

▶ Build the kneewall frames like any other 2x4 stud wall, with top and sole plates and vertical studs. For a wide tiled area along the front or ends of the tub, use 2x6's or 2x8's as plates and add filler pieces to the width of the 2x4 studs.

▶ Install the kneewall frames with their tops absolutely level (Photo 8). Nail them to the floor and existing wall framing with 16d nails; toenail at the corners with 8d nails.

Construct the deck

The deck is 3/4-inch exterior-grade plywood, which is made with waterproof glue between the various plies.

▶ Cut a piece of plywood to the same dimensions as the outside edges of the frame formed by the top plates of the kneewalls.

▶ Mark and cut out the tub opening in the center of the plywood. The size of the center cutout depends on the style of the tub, so check the rough-in specifications carefully. Be sure to locate the opening accurately if one or more edges of the deck is wider than the others.

▶ Fit the deck into place on top of the kneewalls (Photo 9). Secure it with 2-inch drywall screws spaced 8 inches apart.

▶ Install a layer of 1/2-inch thick cement board over the plywood to provide a solid surface for the tiles. Cement board is available in sheets 3 feet wide and 3, 4, or 5 feet long. To minimize the number of joints, choose sheet sizes that let you cut two U-shaped sections to exactly cover the deck outline. Plan to use the cutout material for the 18-inch high strip around the walls (see diagram).

▶ Secure the cement board with 1-1/2 inch roofing nails spaced 8 inches apart (Photo 10). Cover each joint with reinforced fiberglass tape and a coat of mortar over the tape. The tape and mortar are available where you buy the cement board.

Cutting Cement Board

Use a masonry blade in a circular saw to cut cement board. Work outdoors, because the sawing produces a great deal of dust. Wear eye and hearing protection, a dust mask, and heavy work gloves. A more time-consuming but less messy method is to score the cement board several times with a sharp utility knife, then snap the board in two.

BUILD THE TUB KNEEWALLS AND DECK

Photo 8. Prebuild the kneewall frames, then install them in the tub area. Secure them to the floor with 16d nails. Toenail the frames with 8d nails at the corners.

Photo 9. Cut the deck from 3/4-in. plywood. Get dimensions from the tub installation instructions. Secure it to the kneewall top plates with 2-in. drywall screws every 8 in.

Photo 10. Attach 1/2-in. cement board to the plywood deck with 1-1/2 in. roofing nails. Seal each of the joints with self-adhesive fiberglass tape and ready-mix mortar.

INSTALL THE PLUMBING AND PUMP WIRING

The plumbing work involves extending or rerouting the water supply lines and the tub drain. The diagram below shows the changes this project required. The electrical work involves providing a properly protected power supply for the whirlpool pump and bonding metal parts together with a permanent grounding connection.

Water supply lines

Because the tub will have a tiled surround, a conventional wall-mounted faucet and fill spout won't be long enough to reach into it. It's usually best to mount both the faucets and spout on the end or side deck at the drain end.

▶ Extend the hot and cold water supply lines to the new faucet locations. Identify the lines so you can orient them in standard arrangement: cold water controlled by the right-hand faucet, hot water by the left. The added pipe lengths do not need to be exact at this point. You will cut them to length when installing the faucet valves after the tub is in place.

▶ If the existing pipes are copper, simply solder on elbows and the necessary lengths of pipe (see Working with Copper Pipe, page 111). If the pipes are galvanized steel, use adapter fittings to run CPVC (chlorinated polyvinyl chloride) plastic pipe if allowed in your community, or copper pipe. Adapters for steel-to-copper connections must provide dielectric isolation between the two metals to prevent corrosion.

Drain

More than likely, you will have to move the drain and P-trap, since they probably won't line up with the connections on the new tub. Even if the drain is accessible from below—as in an open basement ceiling—complete as much of the drain work as possible now, before the tub is in place.

▶ If the drain is PVC plastic, cut it with a handsaw (Photo 11). Add fittings and a new trap at the new drain location. For more information, see the instructions for running a bathroom sink drain on page 77, and the box Working with Plastic Pipe on page 79.

▶ If the drain is cast iron, call a plumber to rework the drain line. This is a difficult job for anyone but a pro.

Water Supply and Drain Location

Extend the water supply lines to the new faucet locations. Shorten or extend the drain in order to position a trap in line with the waste outlet of the new tub.

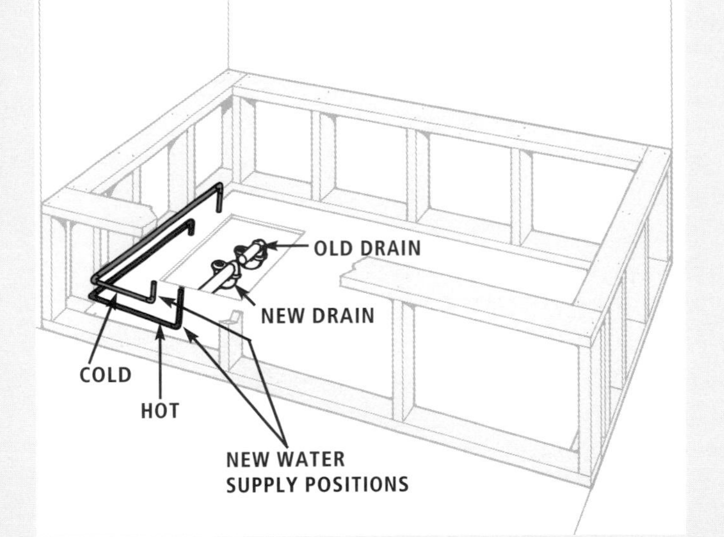

Pump wiring

A whirlpool tub has a built-in electric pump that circulates the water. The pump must be supplied by a dedicated 20-amp circuit protected by a ground fault circuit interrupt (GFCI) breaker at the main electric service panel. In addition to proper grounding for the pump wiring, all metal parts and surfaces in the whirlpool tub and within 5 feet of it must be grounded by connecting them with a minimum of No. 8 solid copper wire. If you are unsure of any part of this work, hire a licensed master electrician— required in many communities for this kind of installation.

▶ Run 12-gauge, 2-conductor type NM-C cable with ground from the service panel to an electrical outlet box located under the deck near the front wall at the pump end of the tub, often at the rear end. NM-C cable is designed to be used in damp areas.

▶ If the pump has a plug attached to its electric cord, connect and install a 20-amp receptacle in the box. A 20-amp receptacle has a horizontal prong opening on one of the two vertical openings (Photo 12); a 15-amp receptacle doesn't. If the pump has no plug it must be connected directly—hard-wired—to the cable in the box after the tub is in place. In that case, just strip insulation from the ends of the cable wires in the box at this time.

▶ After installing a receptacle, connect the other end of the cable to a 20-amp, GFCI breaker at the service panel. If you are intending to make a hard-wired connection to the pump later, DO NOT connect the cable to the service panel at this time. Again, this is often a task best left to a certified electrician.

▶ Add ground bonding between all metal parts in the tub area as required and specified by your local electrical code.

Electrical Tip

The tub pump must have its own 20-amp circuit. To provide ground-fault protection you can use a GFCI circuit breaker at the service panel or you can install a GFCI receptacle at the tub and plug the pump into it.

INSTALL THE PLUMBING AND PUMP WIRING

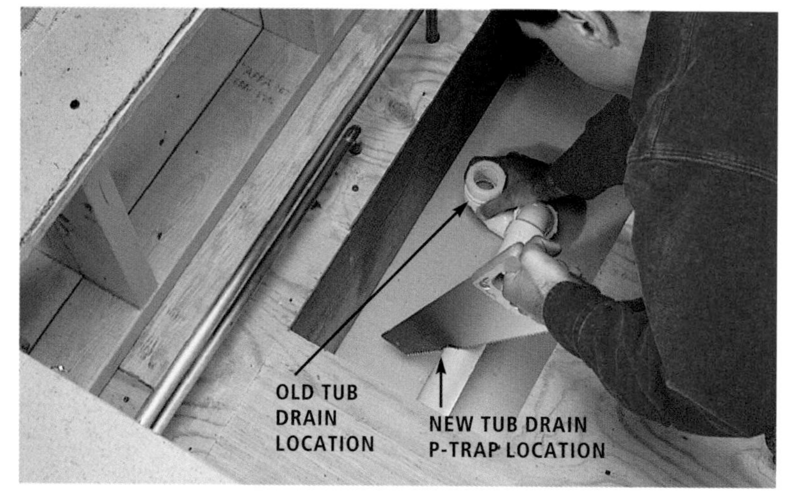

Photo 11. Alter the drain line as required to position a P-trap for the new tub. Cut PVC drain pipe with a handsaw. If the drain line is cast iron, contact a plumber.

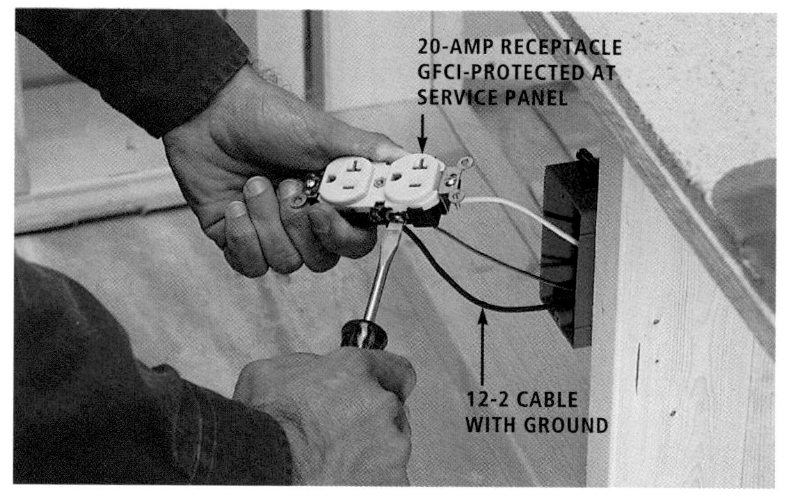

Photo 12. Install a dedicated, GFCI-protected 20-amp circuit for the tub pump. If you're unsure about running this circuit, hire a licensed electrician to do the work.

INSTALL THE TUB AND FAUCETS

You need to prepare the walls, deck, and floor before installing the tub. You'll need to prepare some spacers ahead of time for putting the tub in position, as explained below. When the tub is in place and properly caulked, you can install the faucets and connect the drain.

Walls, deck, and floor

▶ Install a strip of 1/2-inch cement board extending at least 18 inches upward from the deck all around the tub (see diagram, page 98). Use 1-1/2 inch roofing nails to fasten the cement board directly to the wall studs. Seal the joints with fiberglass tape and mortar as you did on the tub deck.

▶ Cover the area above the cement board with 1/2-inch water-resistant drywall.

▶ To reduce noise and conserve water heat, insulate the kneewall with R-11 (3-1/2 inches thick) paper-faced fiberglass insulation.

▶ Cover the deck with equally spaced ceramic tile (Photo 13). If the long walls do not work out to an exact number of tiles, install a partial tile at each end to split the difference equally. Put partial tiles at the back corners of the end walls unless that requires a piece less than one-third of a tile width. In that case, divide the difference between both ends. Install the tiles with mastic and grout the joints.

▶ Tile the walls after the deck tiles are in place. Leaving the job until later is almost sure to result in some damage to the tub.

▶ Seal the floor with a coat of thinned shellac. Then spread a bed of mortar 1 to 2 inches thick in the tub area. (Photo 14). Use prepackaged mortar mix of the type used with concrete block. There is no need to fill the entire floor area between the kneewalls, two or three 60-pound bags of mortar mix should do. Mix the mortar with water according to the package instructions and dump it into the center of the tub floor area. Use a 2x4 to smooth it out.

After leveling the mortar, you have about 30 to 40 minutes to get the tub in place before the mortar mixture starts to harden.

Install the tub

▶ Before putting the tub in place, lay three or four wooden spacers at equal intervals along each side of the opening. The spacers should all be the same thickness, 1/8 to 3/16 inch. They will create a gap between the tub and the tile on the deck, to avoid noise, prevent damage from vibration, and provide some "give" as the tub settles slightly when it is filled

INSTALL THE TUB AND FAUCETS

Photo 13. Cover the deck surface with ceramic tile first, then do the walls. Make sure the tile mastic has set and the grout has cured before setting the tub in place.

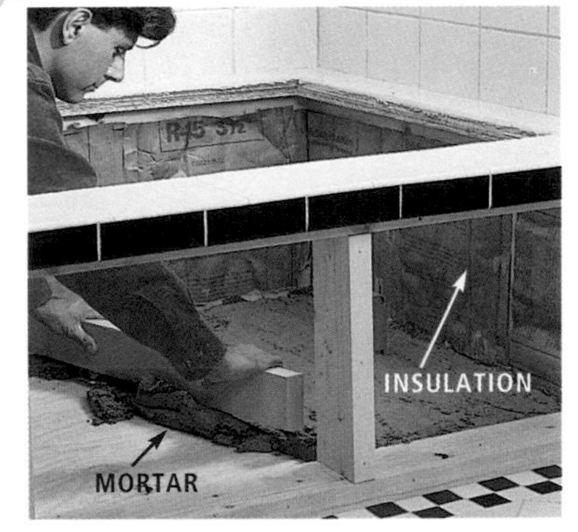

Photo 14. Lay a 1- to 2-in. thick bed of mortar on the floor where the tub bottom will rest. Insulate the kneewalls with R-11 paper-faced fiberglass insulation.

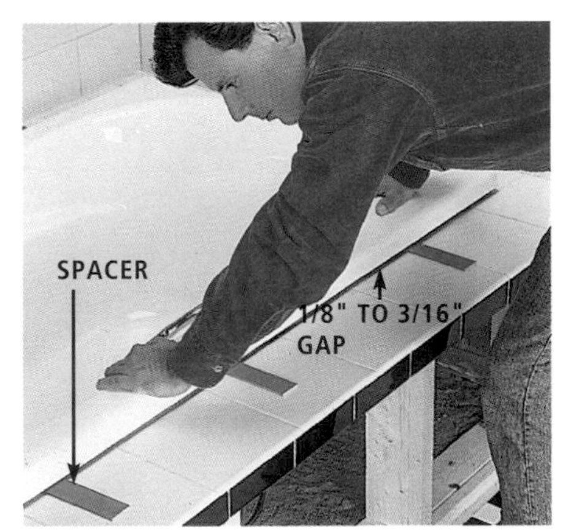

Photo 15. Use spacers to maintain a caulking gap when you set the tub into position. Center the tub and push it firmly down into the mortar bed.

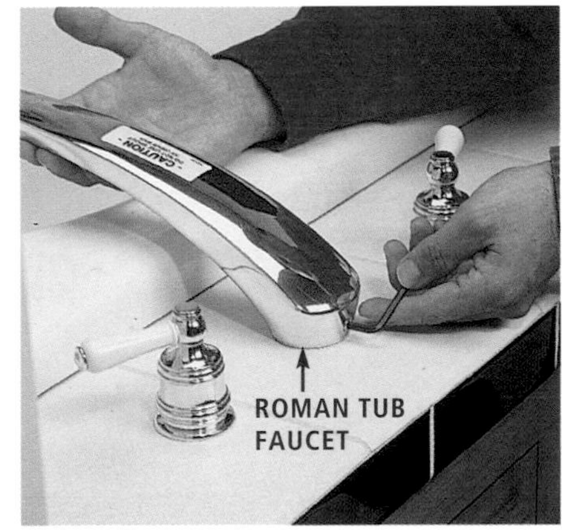

Photo 16. Follow the instructions carefully when installing the faucet. Buy a faucet with a fill spout long enough to clear the inside edge of the tub.

with water. This gap is made watertight with silicone caulk.

▶ With a helper or two, lift and set the tub into place. Make sure the pump cord does not get trapped under or behind the tub. You must be able to reach it through the front kneewall or other access panel. When the tub is centered in the opening, push down along the edges and on the floor of the tub to set it firmly in the mortar (Photo 15). You may need to get into the tub to push down on the back edge. Remove your shoes or put a blanket in the tub to avoid scratching the surface.

▶ Pull out the spacers. The mortar will hold the tub just above the deck; you don't have to wait for it to harden. Fill the gap between the tub edges and the deck tile with 100-percent silicone caulk. Let the tub sit undisturbed overnight for the mortar and caulk to cure.

Faucets and drain

When shopping for the whirlpool tub faucet, sometimes called a Roman tub faucet, you must know where the spout will be positioned; faucet spouts vary in length, so you need one that's long enough to reach into the tub (Photo 16). The whirlpool spout shown is 10 inches long; a conventional spout is only 6 inches long.

Not all tub faucets are installed the same way. A deck-mounted installation often involves cutting the supply tubes on the faucets to length, so read the instructions for the faucets and make necessary cuts and adjustments carefully for a proper installation.

▶ Mark the positions for the faucet spout and the handles on the tiled deck. Use a ceramic tile hole saw blade and a 1/2-inch electric drill to cut through the tiled deck surface. Cutting through ceramic tile is difficult—most smaller size drills are not up to the job. You'll also have to do some cutting or drilling into the top plate of the kneewall.

▶ Install shutoff valves on the water supply lines below the deck level. Although not required by most plumbing codes, they're convenient because they allow you to shut off the tub water supply without affecting the rest of the house. You can gain access to them by removing a front panel of the kneewall.

▶ Connect risers from the water supply shutoff valves to the tub faucets. Make sure the cold water supply goes to the right-hand faucet, viewed from inside the tub, and the hot water supply goes to the left-hand faucet.

▶ Hook up the drain assembly. It is the same as in a conventional tub. You can get at it through the side or front kneewall. Most whirlpools come with a drain, and some come with the drain already fitted to the tub. If a drain isn't included, ask the dealer for one that is suitable for your model tub.

▶ Connect the new P-trap to the tub drain and to the plumbing system drain line. Follow the instructions that come with the whirlpool.

FINISH THE PROJECT

▶ Plug the pump cord into the receptacle under the deck, or complete the hard-wiring connections and cover the electrical box with a plate. After hard-wiring is done, turn off the power at the main circuit panel and connect the cable to its GFCI circuit breaker in the main electric service panel.

▶ Cover the exposed kneewalls, but be sure to provide access to the pump. A small access door in the side of the kneewall facing is the best idea. The treatment shown here (Photo 17) used three panels installed with hinges, providing access to the entire length of the tub. Alternatively, you could face the kneewall with plywood panels covered with tile that matches the deck and walls. One or more of the panels can be held by magnetic or spring catches so they can be removed.

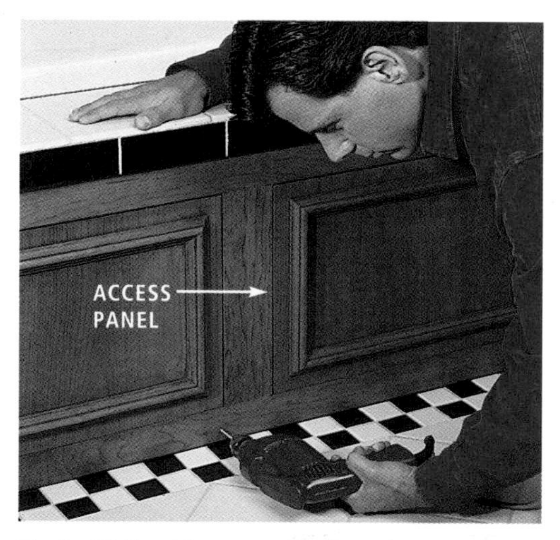

Photo 17. Provide easy and adequate access to the pump for repairs. A hinged or removable panel in the front kneewall is usually the most feasible solution.

Install a Pedestal Sink

A pedestal sink can make a small bathroom look larger and any bathroom look better. It is ideal for a small half bathroom because it frees floor and wall space that would normally be occupied by a vanity. In a large bathroom, a pedestal sink lends a touch of elegance.

One of the best things about this project is that the skills required are well within the range of the intermediate do-it-yourselfer. So look it over; a pedestal sink may be just what you want for your bathroom.

A pedestal sink frees up floor space in a bathroom and adds a definite air of elegance. Models are available in classic, functional, and streamlined or modern styles, in a variety of colors and prices.

FIRST CONSIDERATIONS

Before deciding to replace an old vanity-style sink with a pedestal sink, you'll want to investigate the styles available and their prices. You should consider the amount of work involved; examine the existing installation to make sure that a replacement is really feasible, without major plumbing or remodeling changes.

Style and price

A pedestal sink consists of a bowl resting on a center column (see diagram below). A hanger bracket on the wall supports the rear of the bowl, and the bowl is also bolted to the wall at the lower rear corners for stability. The pedestal is bolted to the floor.

The size and shape of the bowl can vary widely, as can the quality, color, and decoration. The style of the pedestal can make a sink look light and elegant, or solid and substantial.

Pedestal sinks are sold at most home centers and at plumbing supply stores. Prices range widely, with the number of choices of design, color, and quality increasing with price.

Differences in quality may be most noticeable in the appearance of the sink's ceramic finish. Like clothing marked "irregular," cheap models are likely to have visible imperfections. Although surface flaws won't affect the sink's functioning, they may be obvious enough to detract from the overall appearance of the bathroom. This might be insignificant in a family bathroom, but a matter of more concern in a guestroom bath or a half bath intended primarily for visitors.

A surface flaw may indicate a structural defect, although this is seldom the case with the economy-priced line of established manufacturers. More often, a surface flaw signals a thin protective glaze, and therefore perhaps a shorter life expectancy than a more expensive model. Don't be afraid of low-priced sinks if your budget is limited; just be sure to inspect them carefully to make sure any imperfections are cosmetic, not evidence of deeper flaws.

Work required

This project involves more than just replacing an old, outdated vanity and sink. A pedestal sink installation, by its nature, often involves a larger bathroom renovation. You'll need to make drywall repairs, since you'll probably be moving the water supply lines, which are inside the wall. And when you take out a vanity or other old installation, you will uncover areas that are unfinished: floor tiles may be missing beneath the old vanity. More than likely, you will want to replace the old flooring and the wallcovering.

Feasibility

With a pedestal sink, all the plumbing connections at the wall—the shutoff valves and drain—will be exposed, although the drain trap will be concealed in the pedestal. Examine the existing connections. Measure and record their locations, then compare the measurements with the installation requirements of various new sinks before you decide on one.

A critical measurement is the height at which the existing metal or plastic drain enters the wall. If the distance from the floor to the center of the drain opening does not match the requirement for the new sink within about an inch, consider a different model sink. It is unlikely that you would have to move the drain, but it is a difficult job if necessary.

TOOLS

- Utility knife
- Drywall saw
- Tape measure
- Torpedo level
- Drill
- Stud finder
- Tube cutter
- Hacksaw
- Propane torch
- Adjustable wrench
- Socket wrench
- Bucket

Pedestal Sink Components

The bowl is supported by a concealed hanger bracket on the wall. Lag bolts at the lower corners also support and stabilize the bowl. The pedestal, while providing some support, is primarily cosmetic.

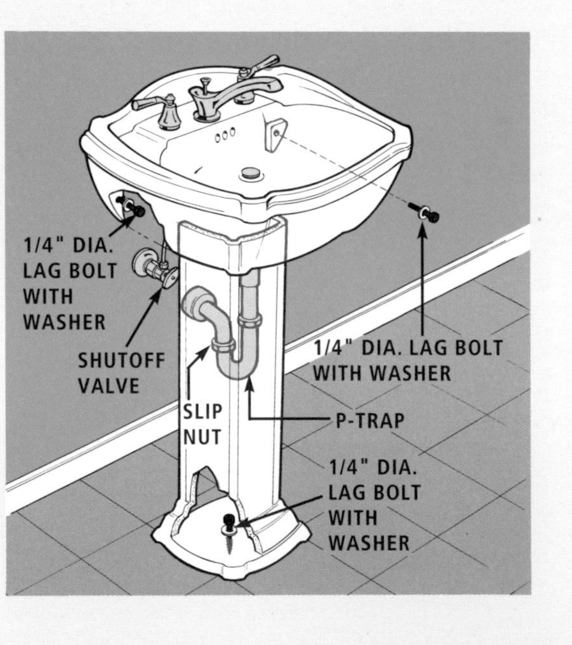

MATERIALS

- 2x8 board, about 16"
- 2-1/2" drywall screws
- 10' of 1/2" rigid copper pipe
- 1/2" copper couplings and ells
- Dielectric unions if necessary
- Lead-free solder
- Flux
- Emery cloth
- 2 shutoff valves
- Drain P-trap
- Water supply tubes

REMOVE THE OLD FIXTURES

If the old sink has shutoff valves in the water supply lines, turn them off. Turn off the water at the main house valve also, because you will remove the individual shutoff valves as soon as the sink is out of the way. The main valve is almost always located where the water line enters the house, just past the water meter; often in the basement or the crawl space, or in a laundry room or attached garage if the house is built directly on a slab. Wait until you have everything organized and are ready to go to work—the entire house will be without water while the main valve is turned off.

▶ Disconnect the water supply lines, drain arm, and trap from the sink. Remove the vanity top and sink together, if possible. Then remove the vanity cabinet (Photo 1). It is probably screwed to the wall and may need some effort to break it free from the floor, too.

▶ Whether the water supply lines that come out of the wall—called stubouts, or simply stubs—have shutoff valves or soldered-on fittings, they must be replaced. Use a mini tube cutter (Photo 2) to cut off the stubouts behind the valves or elbows, then remove their escutcheon plates. Also measure and mark the location of the new stubouts. You'll remove that section of drywall next, and the marks will be a guide to cut a big enough opening.

REMOVE THE OLD FIXTURES

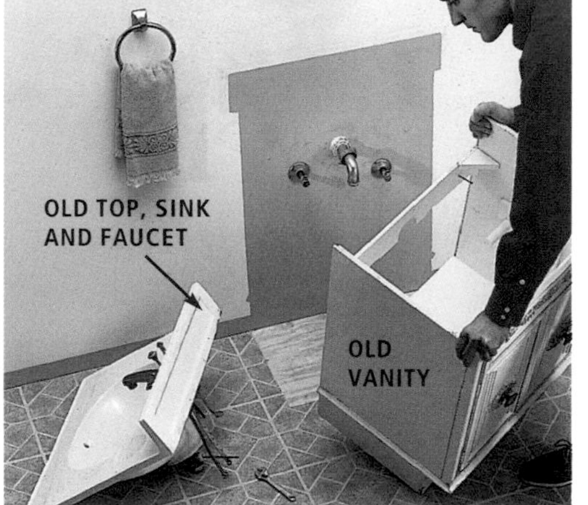

Photo 1. Make sure the water is shut off. Disconnect the faucets and drain and remove the old cabinet top and sink. Then remove the vanity. It may be screwed to the wall or floor, or both.

Photo 2. Cut off the water supply pipes and remove the escutcheon plates. Then open the wall to a point above the location of the new water shutoff valves.

INSTALL A BACKER BOARD

You need to get into the wall behind the sink position to install a backer board that will support the hanger bracket and mounting bolts for the bowl. While the wall is open you can also extend the water supply lines to their new positions (see diagram, opposite page).

▶ Use a utility knife to cut the drywall in clean, straight lines. Make the opening slightly wider than the space between wall studs to expose a 1/2- to 3/4-inch lip on each 2x4 stud. This lip will help you to secure the new drywall patch. Check the installation instructions for the sink to determine the height of the opening.

▶ Cut a length of 2x8 to fit between the wall studs as a backer board, usually a span of 14-1/2 inches. Consult the sink instructions for the installation height of the board. Fasten it in place with drywall screws at the four corners, toe-screwed through the face of the backer board into the wall studs. Set its face flush with the front edges of the studs.

If a 2x8 board is too thick—which may well be the case if the drain vent pipe is in the way—use a 1x8. Support it by notching the front edges of the wall studs and setting the backer board into the notches. Secure it to the studs with drywall screws.

EXTEND WATER SUPPLY LINES

The sink installation instructions indicate how high and far apart the new shutoff valves should be placed. In most cases they will be closer together than in a vanity installation so they will be largely hidden by the pedestal. In the project shown in the photos, the old valves were 10 inches apart and the new ones were spaced only 4 inches apart.

Another option is to install the valves farther apart—8 inches is a standard spacing. That would make the shutoff valves and supply tubes fully visible and more easily accessible. If they are chrome, they may be in keeping with the style of the sink.

▶ Cut off the existing vertical water supply lines inside the wall (Photo 3). You'll probably need to use a mini tube cutter in the limited workspace. Cut off both lines at the same height. This will make it easy to add the same length pipes so the new shutoff valves will be level and evenly spaced.

▶ Extend the lines using the fewest possible number of elbows. As shown in the diagram, this project used a straight coupling, two 90-degree elbows, and three lengths of pipe to extend each supply line to its new stubout position. Measure carefully before cutting each length of pipe. For techniques of joining copper pipe and fittings, see Working with Copper Pipe, page 111.

▶ If the water supply pipes are galvanized steel, you can still make the changes with copper pipe, but be sure to install dielectric unions between the galvanized and copper pipes. A dielectric union has a plastic spacer that prevents the corrosion produced by contact between two dissimilar metals. The galvanized steel end of the union is threaded; the copper end can be soldered onto the copper supply pipe. Dielectric unions are available at home centers and any plumbing supply store.

▶ As soon as the stubouts are in place, solder a cap over the end of each one so you can turn the water back on for the rest of the house.

▶ With this plumbing work done, close the opening with a drywall patch, paint or cover the walls, put in new flooring, and do all other cosmetic repairs so you won't have to work around the new sink.

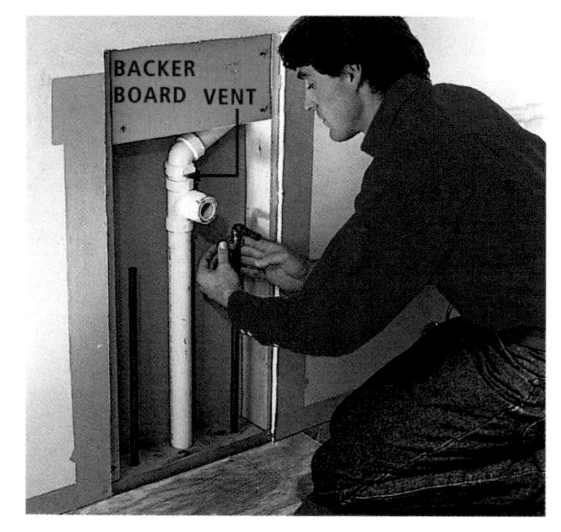

Photo 3. After installing a backer board to support the sink hanger bracket, cut off the water supply pipes so you can extend them to install the new shutoffs.

Backer Board and Water Supply Lines

Set a backer board flush with the front edges of the joists. Extend water lines to their new locations with the minimum possible number of joints.

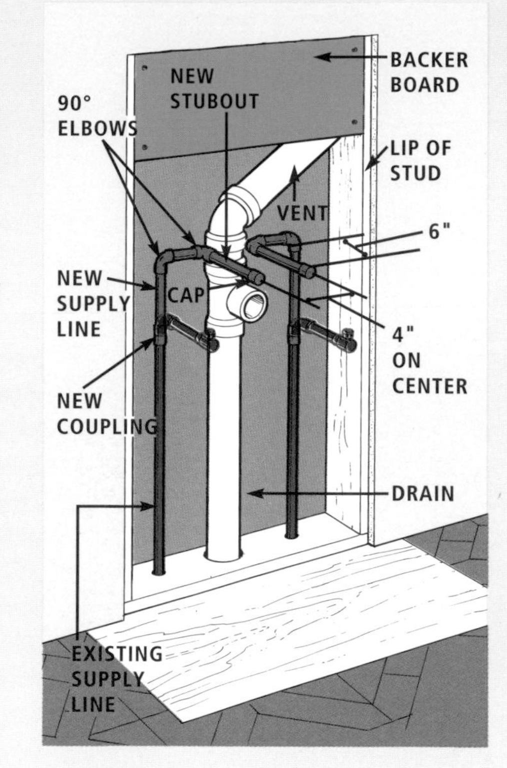

PREPARE THE SINK CONNECTIONS AND SUPPORT

Shut off the water at the main shutoff once again so that you can install compression-fit (solderless) shutoff valves on the water supply stubouts. Then you can install the hanger bracket for the sink.

▶ Measure out from the wall between 1-1/8 and 1-3/8 inches, depending on the thickness of the escutcheon plates, and mark each stubout (Photo 4). You want just enough length to attach the valve in front of the escutcheon plate without leaving any pipe exposed. Cut off each stubout with a tube cutter. You'll need rags and a bucket to deal with the water in the stubouts.

▶ Install each shutoff valve as follows: Place the escutcheon plate on the stubout in the wall, followed by the valve compression nut and then the brass compression ring. Make sure the threads in the nut face outward, toward the cut end of the stubout. Slide the valve as far onto the stubout as it will go and screw the compression nut onto the threads of the valve collar. As the nut is tightened, it forces the compression ring onto the copper supply pipe and against the inside of the valve collar to form a leak-free joint.

▶ Make sure the shutoff valves are closed—turned clockwise until tight. Have a helper turn the water back on at the main shutoff as you check the new valves for leaks. Tighten the compression nuts further if there are any drips at the connection points.

▶ Secure the hanger bracket to the wall with 1/4-inch diameter lag bolts screwed into the backer board (Photo 5). Place a torpedo level across the top of the bracket to make sure it is level. Drive the lag bolts through the slotted mounting holes so you can adjust the bracket to exactly the height specified in the instructions supplied with the sink.

PREPARE THE SINK CONNECTIONS AND SUPPORT

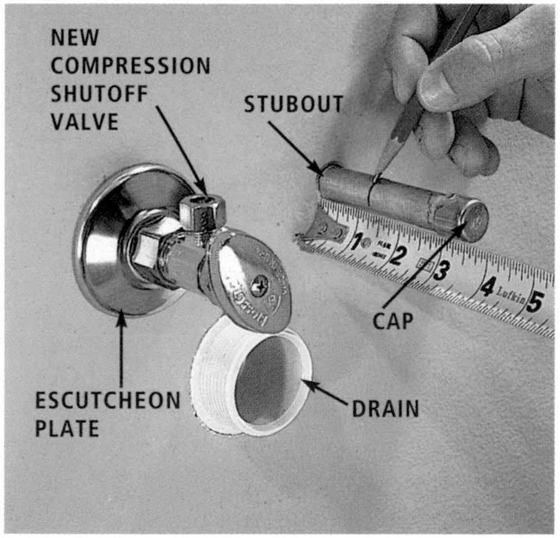

Photo 4. Install the water supply shutoff valves on stubouts just long enough to be concealed by the escutcheon plates and the nuts and collars on the valves.

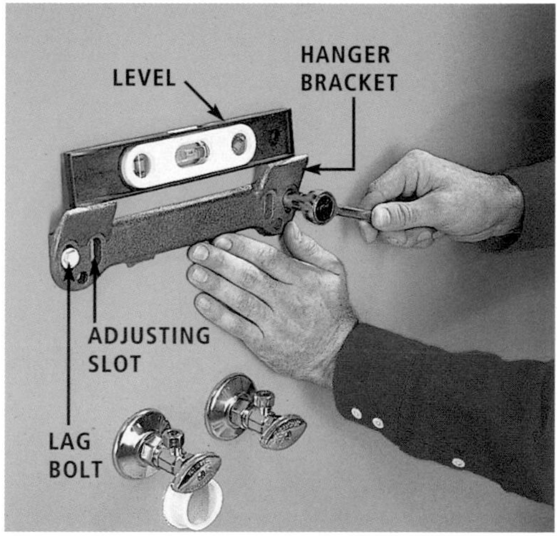

Photo 5. Fasten the hanger bracket to the backer board with 1/4-in. diameter lag bolts. Slotted mounting holes permit adjusting the level and height of the bracket.

MOUNT THE FAUCET AND DRAIN

Attach the new faucet to the sink according to the manufacturer's directions, since the installation steps vary widely among brands. Most drains mount in the same way, however.

▶ Turn the sink upside down and install the handle or handles in their mounting holes (Photo 6). Use the supplied gaskets or some plumber's putty and tighten the mounting nuts as the directions instruct.

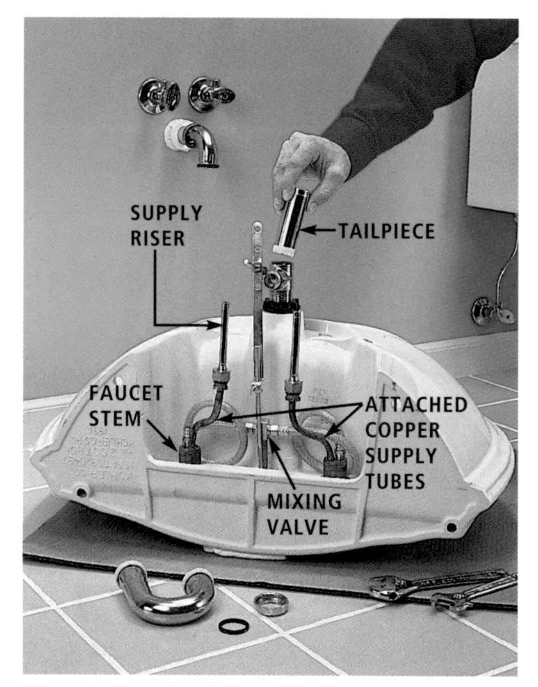

Photo 6. Turn the sink upside down to attach the faucets and drain. Be careful to avoid crimping the copper tubes attached to the faucets if you need to bend them.

▶ Next, bend the supply tubes extending from the faucet stems if necessary. The faucet assembly in this project had separate handles and a spout. Because the handle positions on the sink were 8 inches apart, their copper supply tubes had to be bent to match the 4-inch spacing between the shutoff valves on the stubouts.

▶ Use a coiled-spring tubing bender to bend small-diameter copper tubes. That is the only way to avoid getting a crimp or flat spot that will restrict the water flow. Slip the spring over the length of the tube and gently bend it with your hands. Work carefully. If you crimp or split the tubes, you'll probably have to buy another faucet—you won't be able to fix it.

▶ Now attach supply tubes, called risers, from the connecting nuts on the faucet tubes to the shutoff valves. There are three kinds of tubes: smooth chrome, flexible chrome, and braided metal (see box at right). The type to use really depends on how much bending is required to get the tubes to the shutoff valves. Smooth chrome supply tubes look best; you can bend them with a spring tubing bender. The corrugated section of flexible chrome risers can be bent by hand without a bender. Both types can be cut to length with a tubing cutter. If space is really cramped or extreme bends are required, use braided metal supply tubes. They can't be cut, but are much more flexible.

▶ Insert the sink drain in its mounting hole and secure it in place. Most installations call for a bead of plumber's putty under the ring inside the sink. The mounting nut on the underside screws against a rubber gasket so you can tighten it for a leakproof seal without cracking the bowl. A separate tailpiece extends from the sink drain stub into the P-trap that connects to the drain arm in the wall.

Water Supply Tubes

Riser tubes have shaped tops or fittings for compression joints with the faucet stems. There are also compression fittings at the bottom ends to make connections with the shut-off valves.

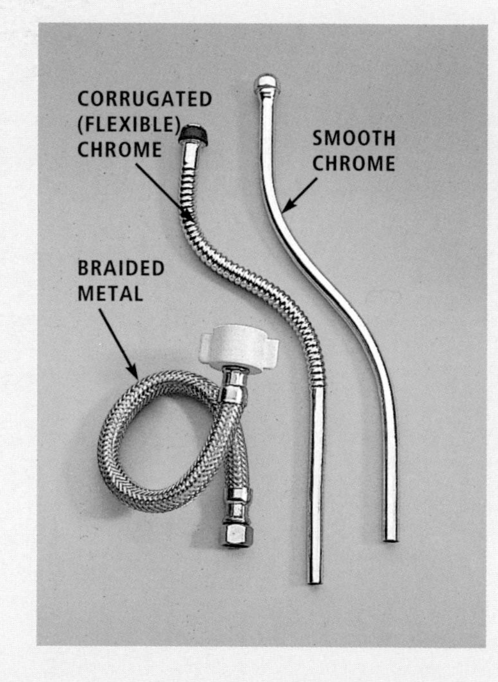

HANG AND CONNECT THE SINK

Pedestal sinks are heavy and hard to handle, so it's best to have a helper for this step. You may be able to do it alone, but it's much easier to position the sink on the hanger bracket and then line up all of the plumbing connections with two people working together.

▶ Lift the sink onto the hanger bracket to check the alignment of the drain, trap, and water supply risers (Photo 7). Be sure the compression nuts and rings needed to make connections with the shutoff valves are on the riser tubes. The photo below shows the P-trap connected to the sink drain at this point, but it is easier to position the sink without the trap in place. Then you can slip it onto the tailpiece to see if it matches up with the drain arm in the wall. While the sink is in position, mark the position of the holes for lag bolts at the rear corners of the sink (see diagram, page 105).

▶ Remove the sink and drill pilot holes for the lag bolts. If necessary, cut the drain tailpiece to final length with a hacksaw or bend the supply risers a bit more. Then rehang the sink.

▶ With the sink on its bracket, tighten the compression nuts that connect the water supply risers to the shutoff valves. Put the trap in position and tighten the slip nuts that connect it to the sink tailpiece and the drain arm in the wall.

▶ Put the pedestal on a thin piece of cardboard, to prevent scratching the floor, and slide it into place under the sink. Lift the bowl slightly—only about 1/8 inch—to move the pedestal into position (Photo 8).

▶ Most pedestals are secured by a lag bolt driven through a hole in the base. Reach in from behind and mark the center of the hole with a nail pushed through the cardboard.

▶ Remove the pedestal and drill a pilot hole for the lag bolt. Do not attempt to drill the hole with the pedestal in place; the space is too crowded, and you risk cracking the base. Cut a center hole larger than the bolt in the cardboard and slit the cardboard from its rear edge all the way to the hole.

Place the pedestal on the cardboard and slide it back into place under the sink. Start the lag bolt with a washer under the head, then pull the cardboard out; the slit will clear the bolt. Finish driving the bolt until it is tight. You will find that ratcheting socket wrench is the best tool to use for this.

▶ Drive lag bolts with washers through the back corners of the sink into the pilot holes you drilled previously.

▶ Apply a bead of clear silicone caulk along the top edge of the bowl where it meets the wall. Also caulk the bottom edge of the pedestal where it touches the floor.

▶ Turn the water shutoff valves on. If there are drip leaks at the riser tubes, tighten the compression nuts. Fill the sink bowl completely with water, then let it out. The sudden rush of water is the best way to check the drain assembly and P-trap. If a joint leaks, tighten the slip nut at that point.

HANG AND CONNECT THE SINK

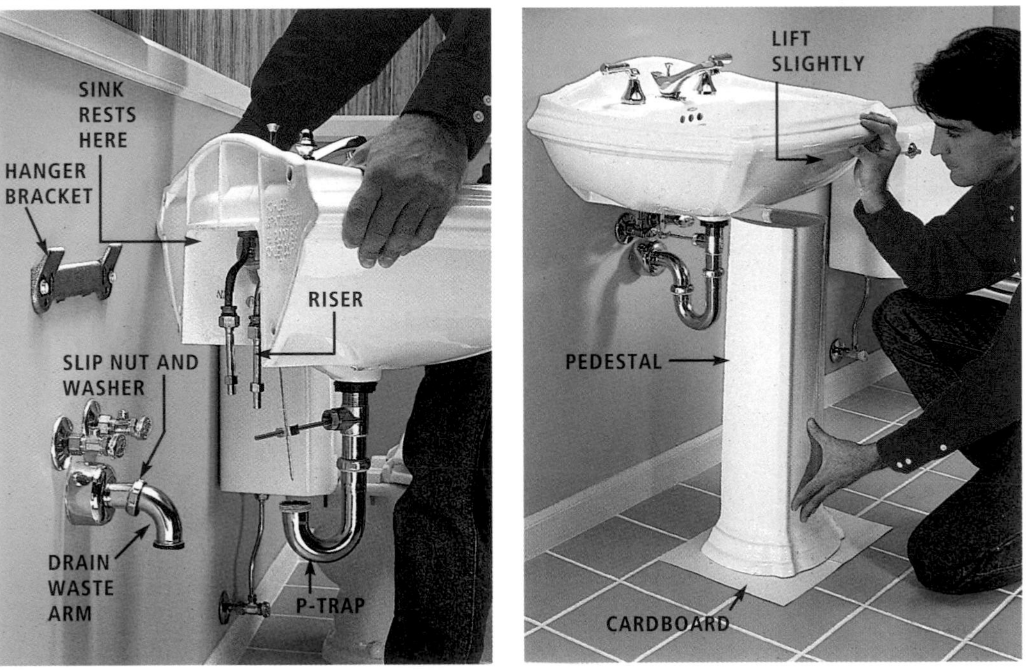

Photo 7. Hang the sink on the hanger bracket to check alignment of the fittings. Then connect the water supply risers to the shutoff valves and the P-trap to the drain.

Photo 8. Protect the floor with thin cardboard as you slide the pedestal in and out of position. Lift up slightly on the sink to move the pedestal.

Working with Copper Pipe

Copper pipe for residential plumbing, such as water supply lines, is joined with soldered, threadless fittings. Here are a few ideas for working with these plumbing materials.

▶Cut pipe ends clean and square. You can use a hacksaw, but a tube cutter does a better job. Place the pipe in the cutter, tighten the knob, and revolve the cutter around the pipe. Tighten the knob with each revolution until the cutting wheel severs the pipe wall.

▶Ream the interior edges of the newly cut end to remove any burrs. Use the fold-away reaming tool built into the tube cutter or a separate hand reamer.

▶Clean the outside surface where a fitting will be soldered on with abrasive emery cloth (Figure A).

▶ Clean the inside of the fitting with a fitting brush (Figure B). Brushes are available in various sizes and do a better job on inside surfaces than emery cloth.

▶ Spread flux on the outside pipe surface and the inside fitting surface (Figure C). The flux provides chemical cleaning in addition to the abrasive cleaning with emery cloth or a brush. Both are essential for leakproof joints.

▶ Place a fitting on the pipe and heat the fitting with the flame of a propane torch (Figure D). The tip of the flame is the hottest part. Hold lead-free solder at the joint; do not direct the flame at the solder. When the fitting is hot enough, it will melt the solder and capillary action will draw the solder into the joint. This is called "sweating" the joint. For 1/2-in. diameter pipe, use about a 1/2 in. length of solder; for 3/4-in. pipe use 3/4 in. of solder.

▶ Wipe away excess solder with a wet rag. There should be a solid shoulder of solder all the way around the joint, with no gaps.

▶ When soldering a transition fitting or an adapter with interior threads, raise the end of the pipe so that the solder will not be drawn into the threads (Figure E).

▶ Work safely. Wear a long-sleeve shirt, heavy gloves, and safety goggles. Use a fireproof cloth or board to protect nearby flammable materials. Keep a small fire extinguisher close at hand.

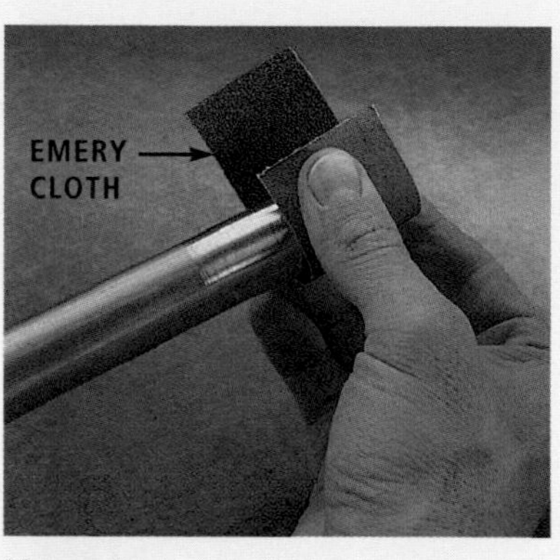

Figure A.

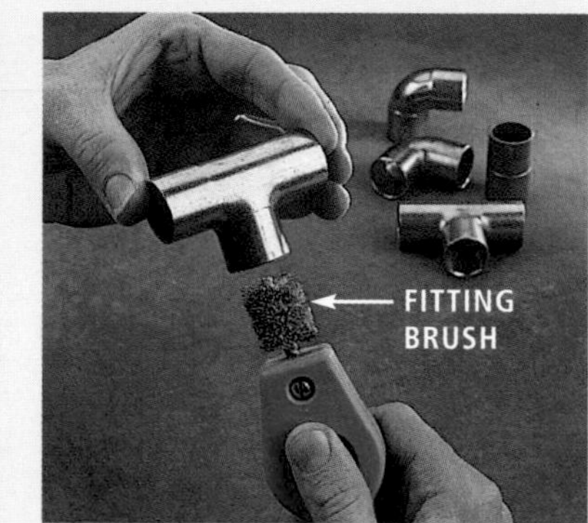

Figure B.

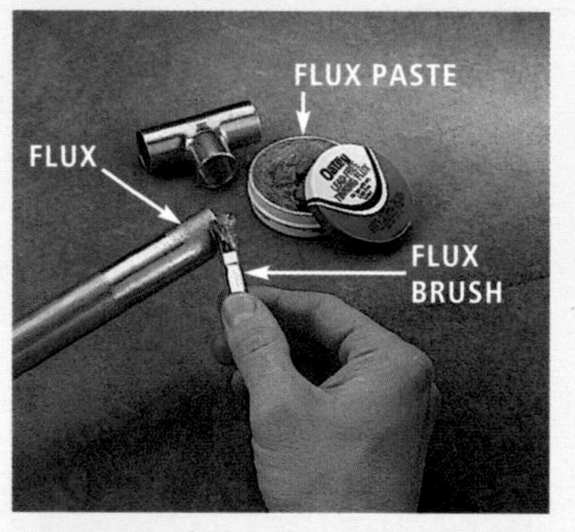

Figure C.

Figure D.

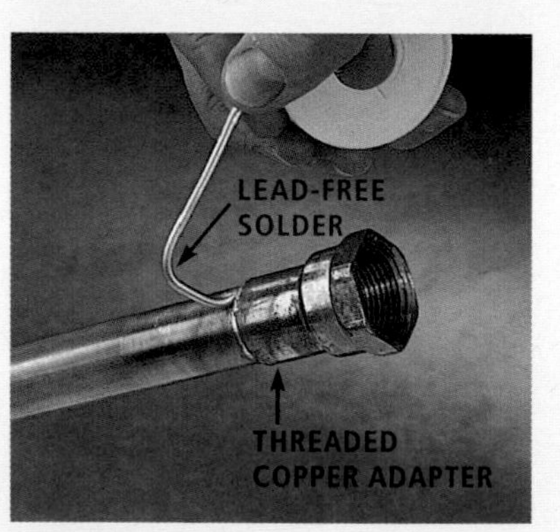

Figure E.

The Bedroom

Improve Closet Storage

This easy-to-build system of drawers, shelves, and hanging rods can almost double storage capacity. You can adapt it to any size clothes closet.

114

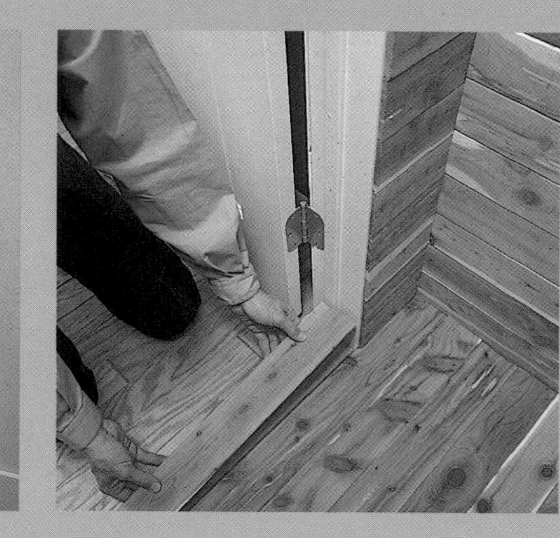

Line a Closet with Cedar

The aroma of Eastern Red Cedar is both pleasing and protective. Kits of prepackaged strips make it easy to line a closet in a day.

122

Build Storage Cabinets and a Window Seat

This versatile cabinet design can be built in any size. Two cabinets flanking a window seat form a furniture unit with great storage capacity.

126

Improve Closet Storage

When chaos overwhelms your closets, it's time to organize! A simple closet system can make a great improvement. A combination of clothes rods, shelves, and drawers puts everything at your fingertips.

This closet system is an easy, straightforward project even for a beginning DIYer. You don't need advanced woodworking tools or expensive materials. The system shown here is sized for a 12-foot walk-in closet, but you can adapt the overall design or individual parts to fit the space in your own closet.

A well-designed organizing system can almost double the storage capacity of a closet without requiring an actual increase in space. The system shown here can be adapted to any size closet; plans are on the opposite page.

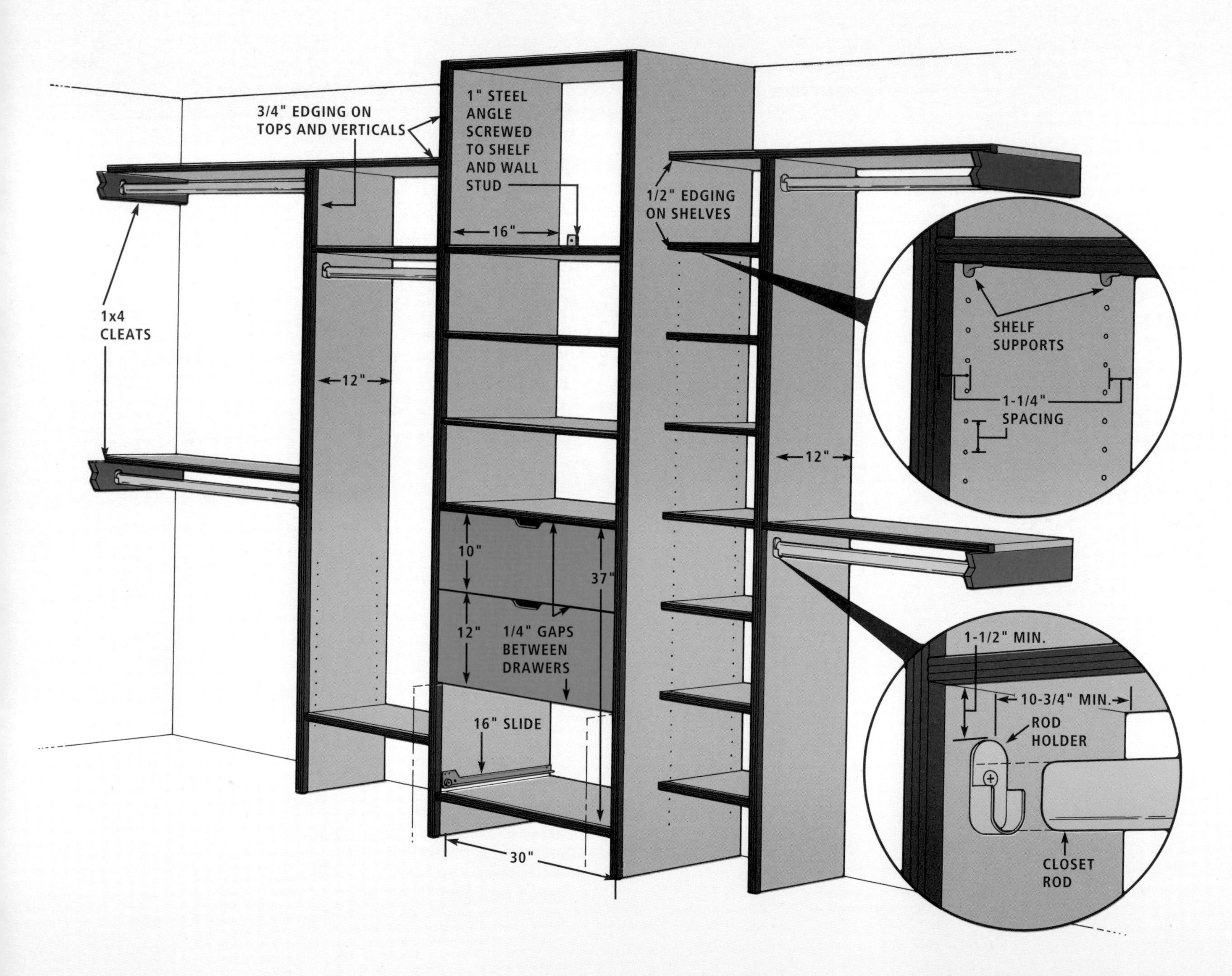

3/4" EDGING ON TOPS AND VERTICALS
1" STEEL ANGLE SCREWED TO SHELF AND WALL STUD
16"
1/2" EDGING ON SHELVES
1x4 CLEATS
12"
SHELF SUPPORTS
1-1/4" SPACING
12"
10"
37"
12"
1/4" GAPS BETWEEN DRAWERS
16" SLIDE
30"
1-1/2" MIN.
10-3/4" MIN.
ROD HOLDER
CLOSET ROD

TOOLS

Circular saw
Framing square
Stud finder
Hammer
Carpenter's level
Drill
Torpedo level
Router and bead-forming bit (optional)
2' or 4' level
Spring clamps

PLANNING THE CLOSET

You can plan closet storage around just two elements: drawers, and rods for hanging garments. Add adjustable shelves to make the best use of the remaining space. As you plan, keep these key elements in mind:

▶ Make the drawers spacious: at least 16 inches front to back, 24 to 30 inches wide, and 10 to 14 inches deep.

▶ To plan rod space, count your long garments first and allow about 1-1/2 inches of rod length for each one. The rod will be mounted about shoulder height, with one or two shelves above and perhaps one near the floor to hold shoes.

▶ Next count shorter items, those that need hanging space less than 40 inches high. Allow 1 inch of rod for thin blouses and skirts, and 1-1/2 inches for jackets. For maximum capacity put in one rod about waist height for short items and another about 42 inches higher.

▶ With these key dimensions in mind, measure your closet walls and draw a rough sketch to figure out the best position for the drawers and long clothes.

▶ Locate drawers below eye level so you can see their contents. The best spot is usually as part of a center tower that supports elements on either side. Plan to put shelves above the drawers. That is not a convenient place to install a hanging rod.

▶ Next decide where to put the rod for long hanging clothes. Because long garments need plenty of access room, directly next to the central core is probably the best place.

▶ Now divide the remaining space between shelves and rods for short clothes. Also establish the depth of each section. The tower can be deeper than the adjacent rod and shelf spaces. This minimizes the amount of material you need to build the units and makes it easy to remove items hanging on the rods and stored on the shelves.

▶ You can extend the core all the way to the ceiling, but that is not necessary. In the installation shown on page 114 the core stops below the cornice molding. It is not unstable, however, because the various elements are anchored to the wall when they are installed.

▶ You may be building around existing closet lighting or may install new lights. In either case, consult the box Closet Lights and Electrical Codes on page 121.

▶ When your planning is complete, draw a final plan on graph paper to determine the exact dimensions of the various parts. Use that plan to formulate a buying list for materials and a cutting guide for assembly.

MATERIALS

The closet system shown on these pages is built from 3/4-inch birch plywood, but you could use any other wood that fits your taste and budget. Plywood is flat, straight, and easy to nail. Shelves of 3/4-inch plywood can span about 3 feet without sagging or needing reinforcement. For finishing, the birch veneer provides a smooth surface for easy painting.

If you use plywood, cover the exposed edges, both for appearance and to avoid snagging clothes on unfinished edges. Solid-wood edging is far better than iron-on or self-adhesive veneer. You can buy 3/4-inch wide edge molding, or you can make your own (see box below). Cutting triple-bead edging puts a good deal of strain on a bit and router—use a bit with a 1/2-inch shank and a router of at least 1-1/4 hp size, rather than a bit with a 1/4-inch shank.

Making Edging

Rout an edging profile on both long edges of a 1x6 or wider board. Use a router table and fence to guide the boards past the bit, then rip off the edges as 1/2- or 3/4-inch molding and repeat. When the board is reduced to about a 4-inch width, use it for cleats in the closet.

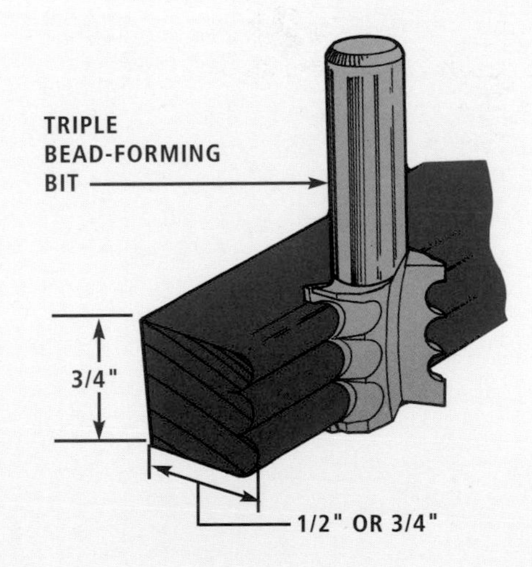

WORKING METHODS

Plywood must be cut cleanly, without splintering or tearing the face veneers. Edging, too, must be cut cleanly. Assembly is simple and straightforward. Following are some helpful working techniques.

Cutting plywood and edging

▶ To cut plywood, use a sharp plywood blade in a circular saw and turn the workpiece with its best face down. Make sure the panel is adequately supported on sawhorses, or place it on the floor with a scrap panel or long boards underneath for support.

▶ To cut shelves and uprights, clamp on a guide strip with a factory-cut edge or use a commercial metal straightedge to guide the side of the saw base. One model has two sections that can be joined with a collar and setscrews for a total length of a bit more than 8 feet. This allows you to clamp it on a full-length panel with enough overhang at each end to guide the saw before the blade enters the wood and as it exits.

▶ Splintering is not usually a problem when cutting along the length of a panel, in the same direction as the grain on the face veneers. Cutting across the grain is a problem, however. To avoid tearing the veneer, score the cut line deeply with a utility knife. Do this on both faces, and then cut just to the outside—the waste side—of the visible scored line.

▶ For a cut across a piece up to about 20 inches wide, hold the short tongue of a carpenter's square against the far edge of the workpiece and use the long tongue of the square to guide the saw (Photo 1). Make sure the cut starts at the front edge of the piece and exits at the back, so if there is any corner tearout it will be concealed after assembly.

▶ You may want to attach the edging to some scrap pieces before cutting them to length. In other cases you will need to cut the edging separately with a fine-tooth handsaw. For clean, square cuts use a backsaw in a miter box.

Assembly

▶ After cutting pieces for sides, shelves, edging, and drawers, stain or paint them before assembly. You'll have to do a bit of touch-up later, but prefinishing the pieces will save a great deal of time.

▶ Attach edging with glue and nails (Photo 2). Use 4d finish nails with edging that is 3/4 or 1/2 inch thick; use 1-inch brads with thinner edging. Test with a scrap piece of edging. If it shows any tendency to split, drill tiny pilot holes in the edging. Pilot holes are not needed in the edge of the wood being trimmed. Wipe off any glue squeeze-out with a damp rag immediately after nailing the edging.

▶ You do not need to cut grooves (dadoes) in the sides for the ends of permanently attached shelves. Instead, cut the pieces to length for butt joints and nail through the side of one piece into the end of the other. Space nails going into the edge of plywood about 3 inches apart; the core veneers do not have as much gripping power as the end grain of a solid wood board. Check frequently with a carpenter's square to make sure that assembled pieces are square with one another.

MATERIALS

- 3/4" plywood
- 1/2" plywood
- 1/4" plywood
- 8d finish nails
- 6d finish nails
- 4d finish nails
- Carpenter's glue
- Drawer glides
- 1" steel angles

WORKING METHODS

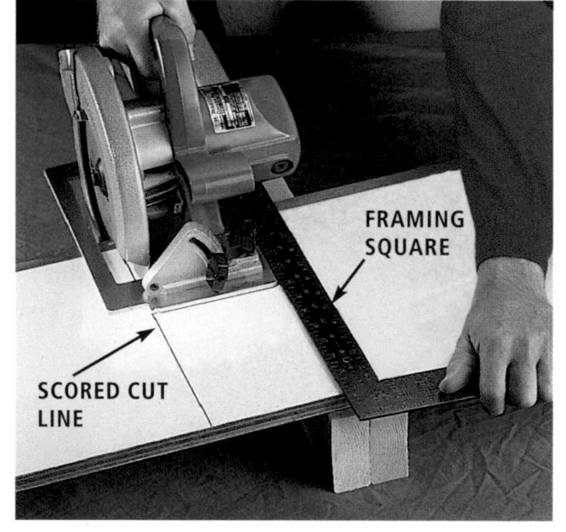

Photo 1. Use a framing square or other straightedge as a guide for straight cuts. Score the cut line with a utility knife to avoid tearing the face veneers in cross-grain cuts.

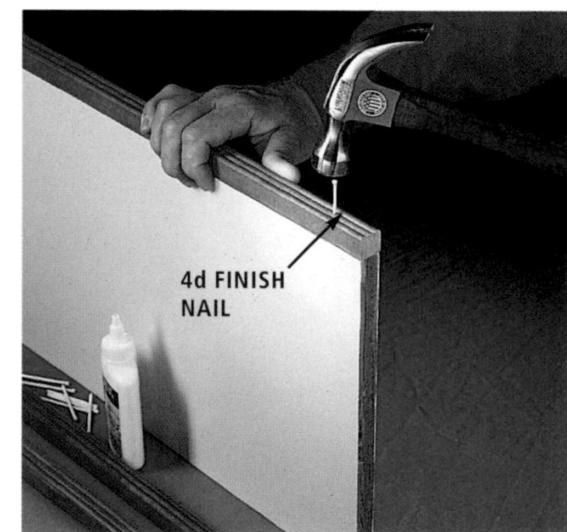

Photo 2. Glue and nail trim to the unfinished plywood edges. Paint or stain the edging and the boards before assembly. Fill nail holes and do touch-up work later.

BUILD THE CENTER TOWER

The fundamental section of this storage system is the center tower, which contains drawers and shelves and supports elements on either side. Build and erect this unit first, making sure the permanent shelves are square. When you install the unit, make sure the shelves are level and that the sides are plumb both side to side and front to back. Otherwise, when you build the drawers later they won't fit squarely. If your floor isn't flat and level, plane or sand the bottom edges of the side pieces until the unit stands both level and plumb when you put it in place.

▶ Cut all the tower parts to size using your plan as a guide. Cut at least three permanent shelves to fit between the sides: one to go at the bottom, one directly above the top drawer, and one that will be the top usable shelf. If you put a top on the unit, cut it to fit between the sides of the tower also, as shown in the plans. If you place it across the tower's top edges, its untrimmed ends will show.

▶ Assemble the tower on the floor, with the finished (front) edges facing up. Nail through the sides into the ends of the permanent shelves (Photo 3). Use 8d finish nails spaced 3 inches apart. Put the bottom shelf about 4 inches above the floor, or higher if there is a baseboard on the wall that it must clear. You may also have to notch the rear corners of the side pieces to fit around the baseboard, so their rear edges will be against the wall.

▶ Mark a layout line on the wall for one side of the tower. Move the tower into position and use a level to get the sides plumb (Photo 4).

▶ Anchor the tower to the floor with two 6d finish nails in each side. Toenail the sides near the front and rear corners. Check plumb again near the top and fasten a steel angle brace to the top permanent shelf and a stud in the wall (Photo 5). If you put the angle brace on the top of the shelf as shown in the photo, it will not be visible. If you attach it to the underside of the shelf it will not interfere with anything pushed all the way to the rear of the shelf. The angle brace preserves plumb until other elements of the system have been added. More important, it is a safety measure that will keep the unit from tumbling forward.

BUILD THE CENTER TOWER

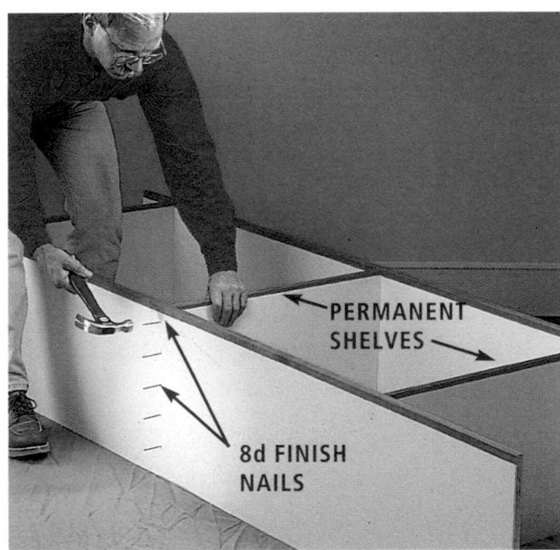

Photo 3. Nail the permanent shelves in place in the central tower with 8d finish nails. Make sure they are at right angles to the sides. Space the nails about 3 in. apart.

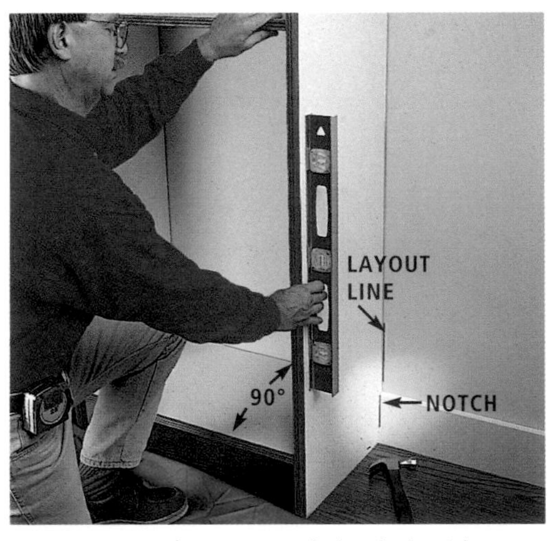

Photo 4. Erect the tower and plumb the sides. Notch the rear corners for the baseboard if necessary. Toenail the sides to the floor with 6d finish nails front and rear.

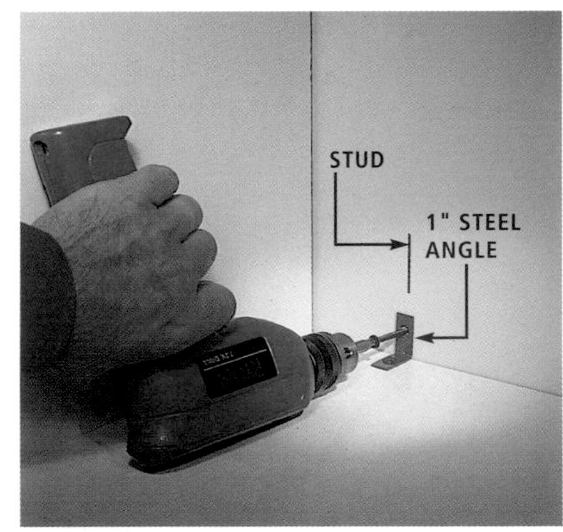

Photo 5. Screw a 1-in. steel angle to a permanent shelf and to a wall stud to hold the tower upright and plumb. The angle can fit on either the shelf top or the shelf bottom.

INSTALL PERMANENT SHELVES

The other sections of the closet system consist of rods and adjustable shelves attached to vertical dividers with permanent shelves across the top and perhaps midway. Put in the permanent elements first.

▶ On the end walls of the closet, install 1x4 cleats to support each permanent shelf and closet rod. Nail each cleat to the wall studs near each end and in the middle, using three 8d finish nails at each point (Photo 6).

▶ Draw a level line from the top of the upper cleat to the side of the core tower. Then install a shelf along that line; it will be the top of the elements on that side of the tower (Photo 7). Nail through the side of the tower into the end of the shelf, and nail through the shelf into the top edge of the wall cleat.

▶ Cut the vertical dividers for the various sections. Space the dividers as indicated in your detailed plan. Nail through the top shelf into the top edge of each divider, make the divider plumb, and anchor it to the floor with 6d toenails at the front and rear as you did with the center tower.

▶ Cut and install the shorter permanent shelves that run between the vertical dividers and the end walls or the tower.

INSTALL CLOSET RODS

Clothes hangers have become fairly standardized. You can center closet rod brackets 10-3/4 inches or more from the back wall. Attach them as recommended in the installation instructions. Be sure that a rod is at least 1-1/2 inches below any shelf above so you can easily slip the hangers up over the rod (Assembly Plans and Photo 8). Oval metal rods like the one shown are more expensive than other choices but won't bend under a weight of clothes that would cause a lightweight round metal rod or a wood rod to sag.

INSTALL PERMANENT SHELVES

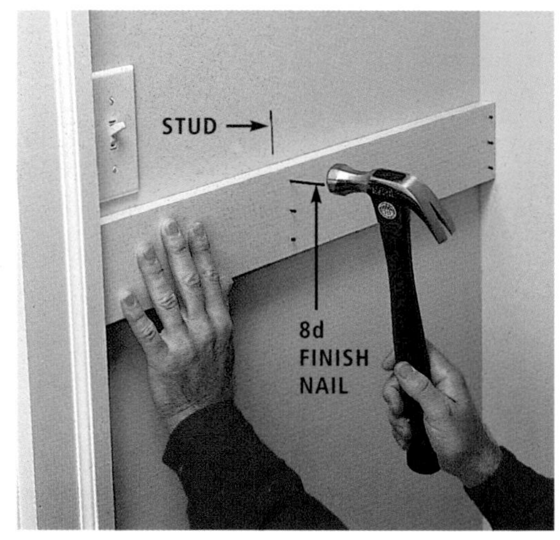

Photo 6. Nail a 1x4 cleat to at least two studs in the walls to support each shelf and closet rod. Make sure all the cleats are level so the shelves will not tip or rock.

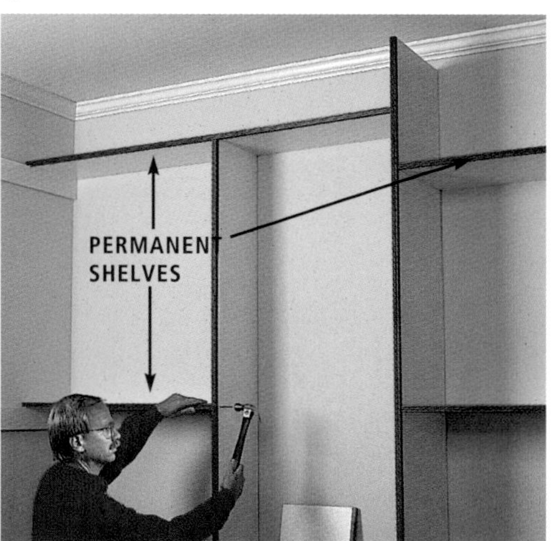

Photo 7. Assemble the permanent shelves and vertical dividers to divide the storage system into sections. Drive 8d finish nails through upright members into shelf ends.

INSTALL CLOSET RODS

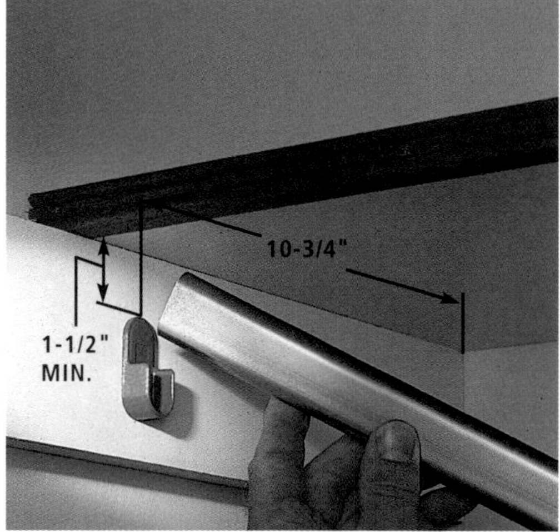

Photo 8. Screw closet rod brackets in position on the cleats and the vertical dividers. Cut rods to length and drop them in. Oval metal rods are the strongest type.

ADD ADJUSTABLE SHELVES

The adjustable shelves rest on four supports inserted into holes in the vertical sides of the closet system (see plans, page 115). The more holes, the more you can move the supports up or down to change the shelf spacing as needed. Don't get carried away, however. Drill equally spaced holes in the most likely area of adjustment, but stop there; you can always drill additional holes later if you need them.

▶ Use a template to make hole-drilling easier and more accurate (Photo 9). Cut a piece of 1/4-inch board the same width as the vertical sides and about 14 inches long. Lay out and drill two lines of holes directly opposite one another, set back an equal amount from the edges of the template. The spacing shown in the photo at right is to support shelves that are 12 inches deep.

▶ Clamp the template in place flush with the rear edge of a vertical divider or a side of the center tower. Drill the holes with a 1/4-inch brad-point bit to avoid chipping the plywood veneer. Mark the bit with a felt-tip pen or wrap a strip of masking tape around it as a depth gauge to avoid drilling all the way through the vertical support piece.

▶ Before moving the template out of its first position, use a level to extend a line to the opposite divider or tower side and mark a reference line there, so you can set the template accurately when you drill there.

▶ When you move the template down to continue the lines of holes on a vertical support, put a nail or short piece of 1/4-inch dowel through the top hole of each line in the template. Insert these in the bottom holes that you have just drilled, so the spacing between groups of holes will be constant.

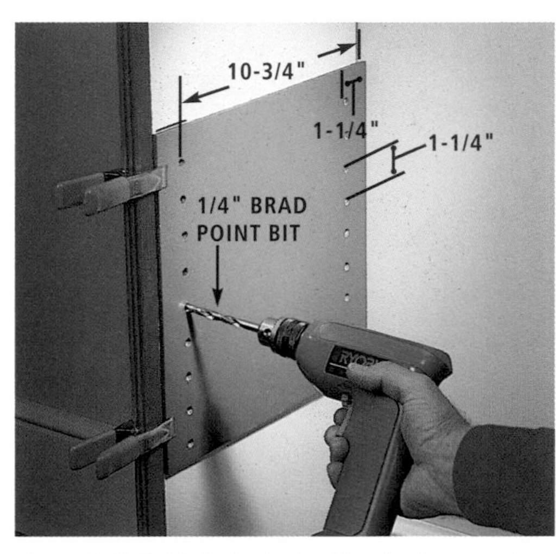

Photo 9. Drill 1/4-in. holes for the shelf supports using a template and a sharp brad-point bit. For consistent spacing, overlap the holes as described in the text when you shift the template.

BUILD AND INSTALL THE DRAWERS

You need to be more accurate in building the drawers than with any other part of the storage system. The drawers must be square, which means the sides and bottom must be cut precisely square. A table saw, though not essential, makes this job easier. The drawers may have different heights, but they are all constructed in the same way (see diagram below). Each drawer is a box with a finished face. The sides and back are 1/2-inch shorter than the finished face. The front of the box is 2 inches shorter.

▶ Cut the drawer sides, backs, and fronts from 1/2-inch plywood and the bottoms from 1/4-inch plywood. Cut the drawer faces from higher grade 3/4-inch plywood.

▶ Assemble the drawers with glue and 4d finish nails. Nail through the drawer sides into the edges of the front and back. Then turn the box upside down, apply a bead of glue to the edges, and nail the bottom in place (Photo 10). If you have cut the bottom square, it will square up the box.

Closet Drawers

Build the drawers as boxes with finished faces. Dimensions here are for a bottom drawer, which is deepest. See the Assembly Plans (page 115) for other suggested sizes.

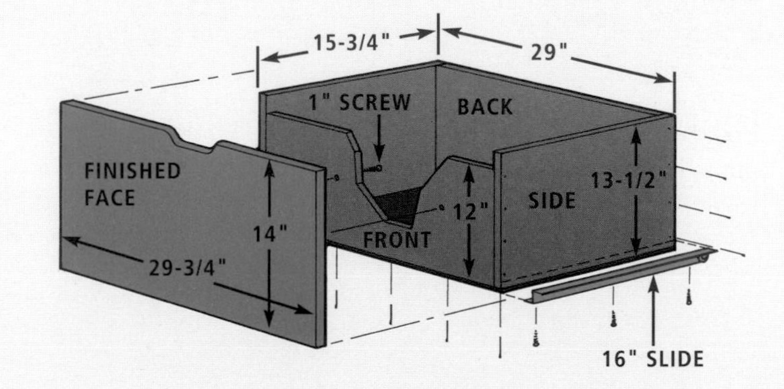

▶ Turn the drawer right side up and attach the finish face with two screws. Drill pilot holes through the front of the box and into the back of the finish face for the screws. Set the bottom edge of the finished front flush with the bottom of the drawer. Do not use glue; you might want to make adjustments later.

▶ The drawers are supported on two-piece slides. Screw one half of the drawer slides to the drawer, along the sides (Photo 11).

▶ Attach the other half of the slides to the sides of the tower (Photo 12). This requires careful work. First, measure and mark their positions carefully so there is a consistent 1/4-inch gap between adjacent drawer faces (see plan, page 115). Use a torpedo level to make sure opposite pairs of channels are at the same level, then mark, drill pilot holes through the oblong holes in the channels and drive screws only through these holes at this time.

▶ Install the drawers. If they do not fit precisely, loosen the screws and adjust the channels as necessary. After the drawers are all aligned, remove them, drill pilot holes through the round mounting holes, and drive screws to lock the channels in position.

Closet Lights and Electrical Codes

To reduce fire hazards, the National Electrical Code restricts the type and location of closet lighting. No hanging fixtures or open or partly enclosed incandescent lights are allowed. Fluorescent lights and certain incandescents may be used, but with restrictions intended to protect an officially defined *storage space*. This is defined as an area 24 inches deep (the usual depth of hanging clothes) up to the height of the clothes bar or 6 feet, whichever is higher. From there to the ceiling, the storage space is 12 inches deep (the normal depth of a closet shelf).

All fluorescents and recessed incandescents must be at least 6 inches from storage space. Surface-mounted, fully enclosed incandescents must be at least 12 inches from storage. If in doubt consult a building inspector. Adding lights may require a permit.

BUILD AND INSTALL THE DRAWERS

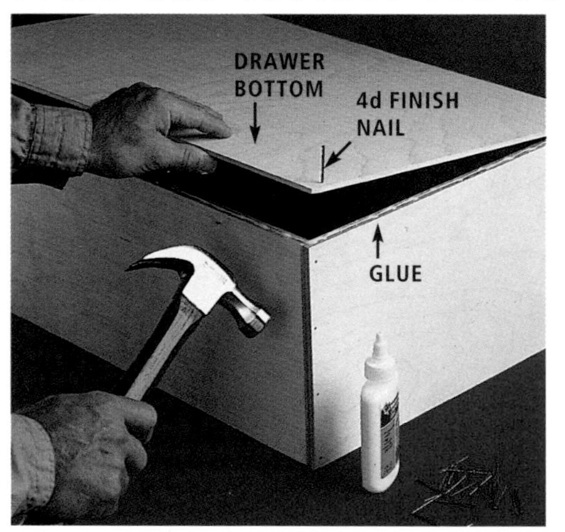

Photo 10. Glue and nail the edges of the drawers together with 4d finish nails. Take care to cut the pieces square so the drawer will be self-squaring when assembled.

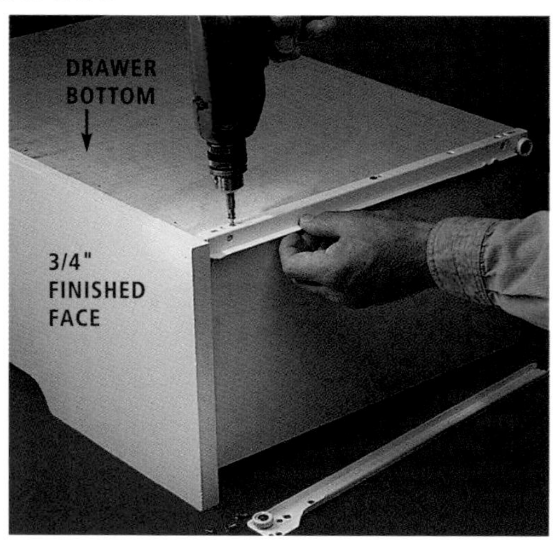

Photo 11. Screw on the finished drawer face from the inside, flush with the bottom of the drawer. Then attach one half of the drawer slides to the bottom edges.

Photo 12. Screw the fixed channels of the drawer slides to the tower sides. Make sure they are level and equally spaced. Slotted mounting holes permit adjustments.

Line a Closet with Cedar

Almost everyone loves the aroma of a cedar closet. The oils and resins in the wood repel moths, and the fragrance prevents clothing from developing the musty smell that long-time storage often produces.

Lining a closet with cedar is easy on the budget, and the project is perfect for a rainy day; all you need is a few hand tools and basic carpentry skills.

The exotic, woodsy smell of a cedar closet helps repel moths and prevents clothes from taking on a musty smell. Not only does the closet look and smell great, but the cedar lining is easy to install.

CLOSET CONSIDERATIONS

Eastern red cedar, more often called aromatic cedar, is used to line closets. It is available at most home centers. For the cedar to be effective, line the entire closet and make sure the door seals fairly tightly. If you plan to use the closet primarily for off-season storage, consider adding weatherstripping around the inside door edges.

Keep in mind that this project is permanent. Unlike moth balls, aromatic cedar will not completely lose its distinctive fragrance, but once the wood is installed, you can't pull it down again without ruining the closet. Never paint, stain, or finish the cedar; that would seal in its protective aroma.

To calculate how much cedar you need to line an entire closet, measure the surface of the back wall, one side wall, and the floor and determine the square footage of each. Double each figure to include the opposite walls—including the back of the door—the ceiling, and the floor.

Look for prepackaged closet-lining kits at a home center. A kit usually contains about 16 square feet of 1/4-inch thick cedar strips per package. In most cases, the strips are of two lengths: about half are 48 inches long, and the rest are either 32 or 16 inches long. Each board is about 3-1/2 inches wide, with either shiplap or tongue-and-groove edges. When assembled, there's a small V-groove at each joint.

PREPARATION

Before starting to work on the closet, open all the packages and sort the strips according to size. Note that each board has a rough back side and a smooth, finished face.

▶ Separate out about a dozen strips that are straight-grained and knot-free. Save these for last; they are easier to rip to width for the final pieces on the walls, floor, or ceiling.

▶ In the closet, start by removing the shelves, hanger bars, baseboard, and moldings (Photo 1). Although you will be covering all the surfaces, work carefully to damage them as little as possible.

▶ Use a stud finder to locate and mark the center of each stud near the top and the bottom of the walls (Photo 2). Snap a chalk line between each pair of marks to give you guides for driving nails. If you don't have a stud finder, drill a small hole and probe with a wire to find the side of one stud. Then tap a small nail into the wall until you find the other edge—a stud is 1-1/2 inches wide—and mark the center. The remaining stud centers should be located at 16-inch intervals from this point.

▶ Locate the joists in the ceiling and snap guidelines along their centers just as you did with the wall studs.

TOOLS

- Level
- Chalk line
- Stud finder
- Trim saw
- Miter box
- Hammer
- Nail set
- Contour gauge
- Tape measure
- Caulking gun

MATERIALS

- Cedar strips
- Construction adhesive
- 1-1/2" colored paneling nails
- Sandpaper

PREPARATION

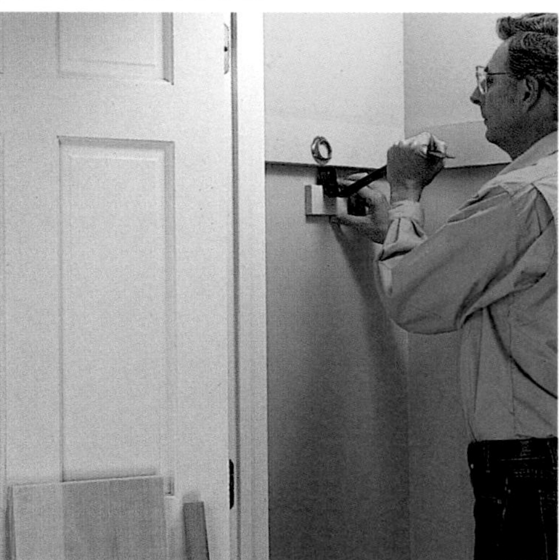

Photo 1. Remove the fittings and trim from the closet interior: shelf, closet rod, supports, and any door and floor molding.

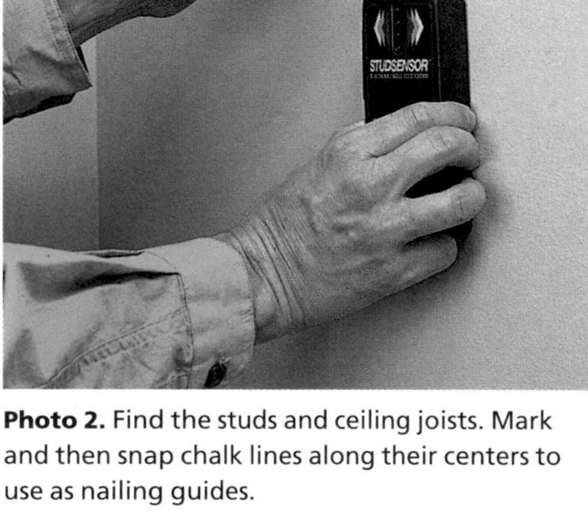

Photo 2. Find the studs and ceiling joists. Mark and then snap chalk lines along their centers to use as nailing guides.

LEVEL THE FIRST STRIP

Cut a cedar strip (or strips) to 1/4 inch less than the width of the back wall. Install it with the grooved side facing downward and toward the wall. The side wall strips will cover the gaps at the ends. Get this strip level (Photo 3) and drive two 1-1/2 inch paneling nails into each stud. Use colored nails that closely match the cedar. Drive the heads flush with the surface with a nail set; don't make hammer dents in the wood.

LEVEL THE FIRST STRIP

Photo 3. Level the first strip carefully so later courses will also be level. Use shims if necessary; strip molding will cover any gap.

COVER THE WALLS

Precut strips to length and complete the back wall first, then do the other walls.

▶ Place construction adhesive on the back of each strip (Photo 4) and press it firmly against the wall, butted against the course below.

▶ Drive a paneling nail through the center of the strip into each stud (Photo 5). Use two nails on either side of a joint between the ends of two strips. Check the level every few rows. At the top, rip strips to fit against the ceiling.

▶ Line the side walls in the same way, from bottom to top (Photo 6). Cut the strips 1/8 inch short and butt them tightly against the strips on the back wall. Use adhesive and nails.

▶ Do the front wall last. Cut the strips to fit between the side walls and overlap the jamb. Nail them into the jamb edge (Photo 7).

COVER THE WALLS

Photo 4. Apply construction adhesive to the backs of the strips. Press each strip against the wall and the course below.

Photo 5. Drive colored paneling nails into the studs, marked by the chalk lines. Use two nails on either side of end joints.

Photo 6. Cut and mount strips on the side walls in the same way. Butt the back edges tight against the back wall.

Photo 7. Butt strips around the door against the side walls and the door trim, or overlap the jamb edges and nail them.

FINISH LINING THE CLOSET

After all the walls are covered, apply strips first to the ceiling, then the floor, and finally to the back of the door.

▶ Install strips on the ceiling at right angles across the joists (Photo 8), using both adhesive and paneling nails.

▶ Cover the floor beginning at the back of the closet. At the doorway, use a contour gauge or make a paper cutout to get the shape of the door jambs. Trace the contour on the ends of the doorway piece and cut it to fit neatly between the jambs (Photo 9). If necessary, rip this strip to width so it does not interfere with closing the door. Round over the front edge of the strip with sandpaper, and then glue and nail it in place.

▶ If the ceiling and floor linings do not meet the walls precisely, cut 1-1/2 inch strips of cedar and install them as molding to cover the gaps (Photo 10).

▶ Close the closet door. From inside, run a pencil along the stop moldings on the side and top jambs to mark the door. Mark the bottom, too, if the door butts against the cedar strip on the floor.

▶ Remove the door. Cut cedar strips 1/4 inch shorter than the distance between the marked side lines. Starting at the bottom, glue and nail the strips in place, leaving a 1/8-inch gap along each marked line (Photo 11). Rip the top strip so its top edge is 1/8 inch below the upper door stop line.

▶ Finally, reinstall the closet rod and shelves. You'll have to cut 1/2 inch off them and their supporting cleats to allow for the thickness of the cedar strips added to the side walls.

FINISH LINING THE CLOSET

Photo 8. Mount ceiling strips with adhesive and nails. Run them at right angles to the chalk lines marking the joist locations.

Photo 9. Cover the floor from back to front. Cut the doorway piece to fit around the jambs; round over the top front edge with sandpaper.

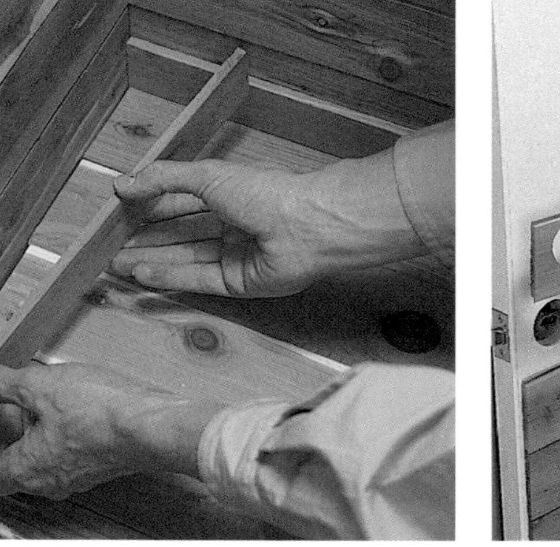

Photo 10. Cut floor and ceiling trim strips about 1-1/2 in. wide. Sand the edges smooth, and install to cover gaps.

Photo 11. Glue and nail strips to the inside of the door. Space them evenly between the lines marked on the sides.

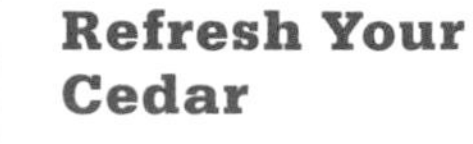

Refresh Your Cedar

Cedar will lose some of its pungency after 10 to 20 years. To restore the aroma, give the surface a light sanding with a medium- or fine-grit abrasive paper.

Build Storage Cabinets and a Window Seat

These cabinets combine simple style with elegant appearance. The design can be adapted to any number of uses, from wall cabinets with a window seat to children's toy boxes or bathroom storage.

Building these units requires only basic tools and no fussy precision woodworking—the perfect project for a DIYer putting together cabinets for the first time.

Handsome storage cabinets like these are easy to make, especially when you use ready-made doors. Adding a window seat between two cabinets is just one of many possibilities with this versatile design.

AN EASY, VERSATILE DESIGN

These cabinets are strong, attractive, and easy to build. The components and the joinery used to assemble them are simple, and there are many design options.

Components

The cabinets have just five basic components (see diagram below right, and Assembly Plan, page 129); they are:

▶ **Doors.** The design shown here uses ready-made frame-and-panel cabinet doors, sold at home centers as replacement doors for kitchen cabinets. You could build similar doors, but that's one of the trickiest tasks in cabinetry.

▶ **Base.** The base under each cabinet is simply a box, made by nailing together 2x4's, with a finished plywood face. The cabinet is screwed to the base from inside. The base can be attached to the floor, or equipped with floor glides or casters.

▶ **Box.** The basic part of the cabinet is a box of 3/4-inch plywood with a 1x4 brace at the top back for attaching the cabinet to the wall. Any screwheads on the sides are covered with 1/4-inch plywood panels, held on with brads and glue, if the cabinet will not be painted.

▶ **Face Frame.** A frame of 1x2, 1x3, or 1x4 boards, joined with screws and plugs, is fastened to the front of the box to cover the edges of the plywood. The doors are mounted on the face frame.

▶ **Top.** A top of finished plywood or other material, with edging, is attached to the box to give it a clean, finished look. If the cabinet is wall mounted, a finished top is not necessary unless the top of the box is below eye level.

Joinery

The cabinets are held together with screws, not glue. Modern hardened drywall-type screws make cabinets assembled in this way very strong, and there's no messy glue cleanup during construction.

Working with screw joinery means you don't have to cut any dadoes, rabbets, or bevels—so you don't need a table saw or router to complete this project. If you make a mistake, just unscrew the parts and try again. Because all the cabinet parts are rectangular, if one piece is a bit too large or out of square you can trim it down without spoiling a joint.

Design options

Because these cabinets are designed around manufactured doors, the doors largely determine the size of the cabinets. You can vary the cabinet height and width to some extent by choosing 1x2's, 1x3's, or 1x4's to make the face frames. For a significant change in height, choose taller or shorter doors. For a significant change in width, use two doors on a cabinet, as in the photo on the opposite page. You can vary the size to accommodate whatever space you have available.

The plans and instructions show the cabinets mounted on a simple base, but there are other possibilities. You can design a different base, stack one cabinet on top of another, or hang individual cabinets from the wall.

The basic design can be adapted to any number of storage situations. Using this same approach, you can build a kitchen island, an entertainment center, a bathroom vanity, cabinets for a den or bedroom, or toy storage for a child's room. Add a suitable top and you could even produce a desk.

Storage Cabinet

The cabinet is a plywood box screwed to a base (1) and covered with a finished top (2). A ready-made door (3) is hinged to a solid wood face frame (4). Finished side panels (5) are optional, depending on installation and kind of finish.

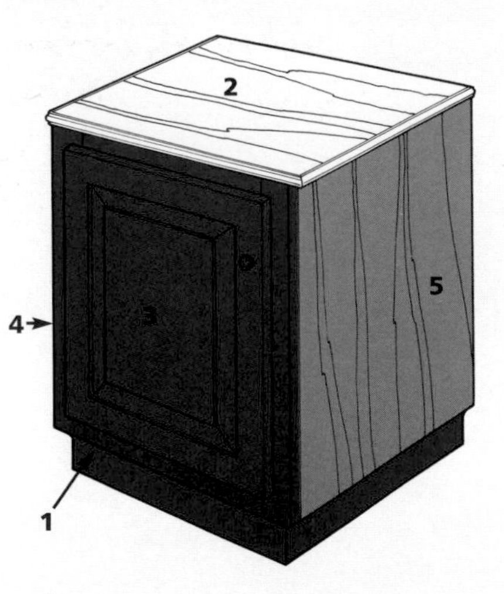

TOOLS

Circular saw with plywood blade

Bar clamps

Drill with combination and Vix bits

Miter box

Handsaw

Hammer

Right-angle clamp

Level

Screwdrivers

Stud finder

MATERIALS

3/4" plywood

1/4" plywood

2x4 lumber

1x2 boards

1x4 boards

Cabinet doors

False drawer fronts (optional)

No. 6 drywall screws

3" drywall screws

6d and 4d finish nails

Wood glue

Adjustable pivot hinges

Piano hinge

Toy chest lid support

TOOLS AND MATERIALS

To build these cabinets you need basic tools plus three specialized ones (Photo 1):

▶ A fine-tooth plywood and paneling blade for your circular saw.

▶ A right-angle or framing clamp.

▶ A self-centering Vix bit for your drill.

Choose wood according to the kind of finish you want. If you plan to paint, AC grade fir plywood is least expensive, but the grain will be hard to conceal. More expensive birch plywood paints beautifully. For a varnish finish, with or without stain, use 3/4-inch hardwood veneer plywood. Or use a less expensive wood and cover it with 1/4-inch hardwood veneer panels.

Use solid hardwood for the face frames. It is attractive and more durable than a softwood such as pine or fir.

Photo 1. These three accessories will make it easy to get clean-edged cuts in plywood, square face-frame joints, and accurately centered hinge holes.

DRAW A PLAN

The Assembly Plan on the opposite page shows how the cabinet parts fit together, but you need a more detailed plan for marking and cutting the parts.

First, draw the overall installation. For simplicity, avoid trying to fit the cabinets tightly between walls, which may require some sophisticated fitting techniques. Next, draw a plan of each unit, showing the individual parts and their dimensions. Here are important points to consider:

▶ When planning specific cabinet sizes, begin with the doors. Select the size and style that best fits your space.

▶ The overall height of a standing cabinet includes the base under it and the thickness of the finished top.

▶ The base under a standing cabinet is usually set back 3 to 4 inches from the front—and sometimes from exposed sides—to provide toe-kick space when standing next to it.

▶ Plan face frames from the door sizes. To use the kind of hinges shown in the photos, make the frame opening 1-1/2 inches smaller than the door's height and width, because the door will overlap the frame 3/4 inch all around. With surface-mount hinges, a 3/8-inch overlap is standard, so the frame opening should be 3/4 inch smaller than the door dimensions.

▶ The outside dimensions of the face frame will depend on the size of the stock you use. Some hardwoods are supplied in exactly the named size—1x2, 1x3, or 1x4, for example—but the finished sizes of other woods are 1/4 inch thinner and 1/2 inch narrower than the nominal sizes.

▶ Determine the width of the cabinet box from the face frame. Construction is easier if the box is a bit narrower, so the face frame overlaps the sides by 1/8 to 1/4 inch. Be sure to allow for any 1/4-inch finished panels on the outside when you are figuring out the size of the basic box. Note that the top and bottom pieces fit between the sides. For a face frame that is flush with the box sides, make the box a bit smaller and plane or sand the frame to size after the cabinet is assembled. That is much easier than trying to construct an exact match.

▶ For a standing cabinet, make the box height the same as the face frame, so the finished top will sit flat and the bottom edges of the box sides will be flush with the bottom of the frame. For a hanging cabinet, size the box for the frame to overlap the edges the same amount all around.

▶ When figuring part dimensions, add up all relevant widths and thicknesses. For instance, to determine the depth of the finished top of a cabinet with sides 12 inches wide, add together 1/4 inch for the back thickness, 12 inches for the side, 3/4 inch for the face frame thickness, and 3/4 inch for the door thickness to get 13-3/4 inches. If the top is to overhang the doors by 1/2 inch, add that for a final measurement of 14-1/4 inches.

▶ Finally, draw out on graph paper a plan showing how the cabinet parts can be laid out on sheets of plywood. Make sure the long dimension of each part is parallel with the face grain of the plywood. Use these graph-paper plans to determine how many sheets of plywood to buy, and later to mark out the parts for cutting.

ASSEMBLY PLAN

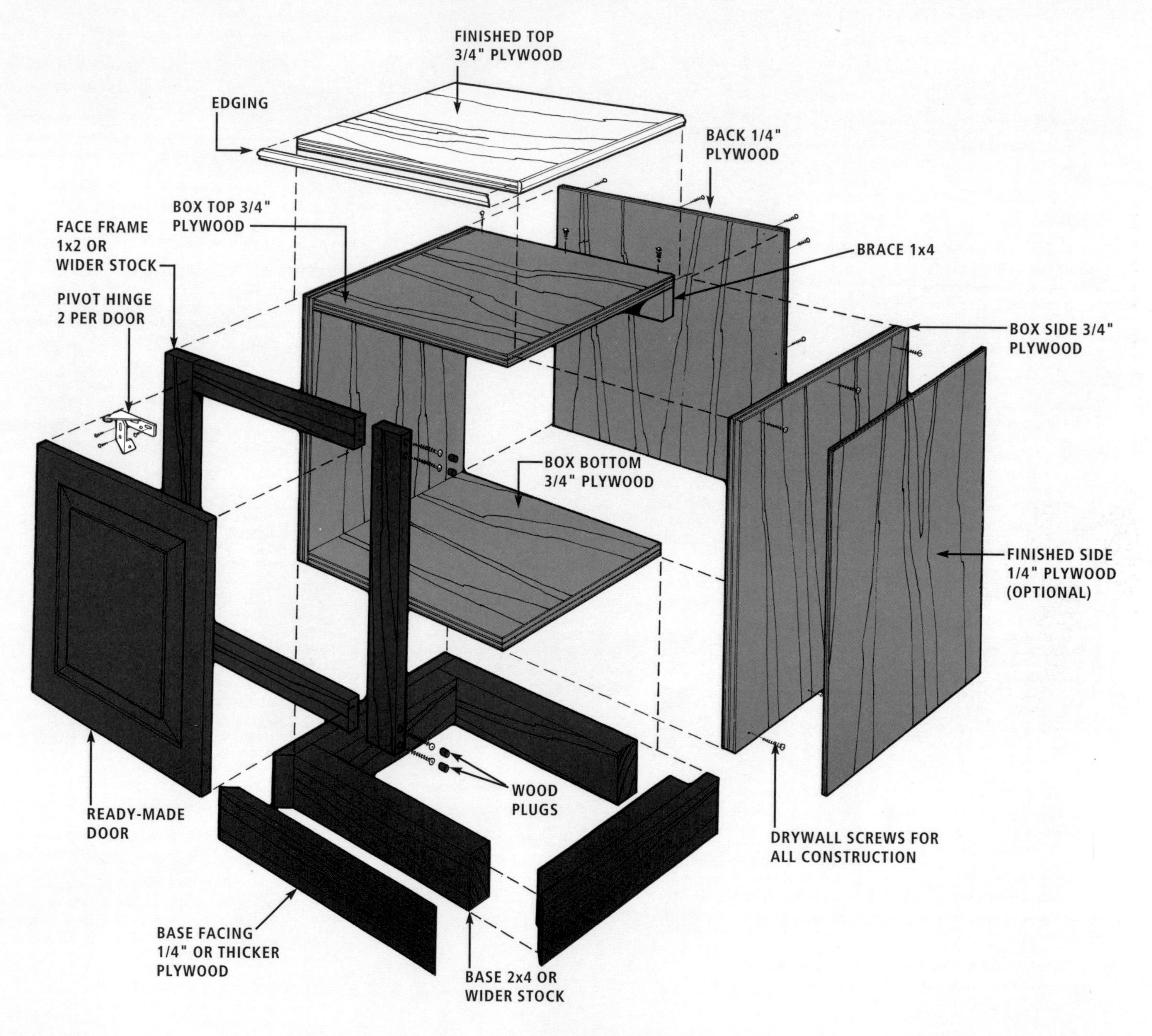

Adapting the Design

If you adapt this design for other kinds of cabinets, use these standard heights to conform with standard chair, sink, and appliance sizes:

- Desks, 29 to 30 in.
- Kitchen base cabinets, 36 in.
- Bathroom vanities, 30–34 in.

Kitchen base cabinets are normally 24 in. deep, wall cabinets at least 12 in. deep.

BUILD THE BASE

The base for each cabinet is made of 2x4's, or wider stock if you prefer. For a finished installation, cover the exposed faces with plywood.

▶ Cut pieces of base stock to length according to your plan. The base sides are butted inside the front and back pieces. Be sure to allow for the thickness of the plywood facing if you plan to use one, so that you get the proper amount of toe-kick space under the cabinet.

▶ Nail the base pieces together using 10d common nails (Photo 2). Make sure the corners are square and the top edges flush so that the cabinet will not rock when mounted on the base. The long base shown in the photos is for two cabinets with a window seat in between (see page 126).

▶ Cut plywood to cover all the exposed faces of the base. You can use 1/4-, 1/2-, or 3/4-inch thick plywood. Miter the corners at the visible joints to conceal the inner plies. Attach the plywood to the base with glue and finish nails. Set and fill the nailheads whether you plan to use paint or varnish for a finish.

▶ If you plan to install the cabinets permanently or to attach them to the wall, remove any carpeting from where the base will go. Use shims whenever necessary to level the base (Photo 3). Toenail the base to the floor, driving the nails from the inside. Or use metal angle braces and screws. The cabinet box will be screwed to the base.

BUILD THE BASE

Photo 2. Build the base from straight 2x stock nailed together. Make it 3 to 4 in. narrower than the cabinets on the exposed sides to provide sufficient toe-kick space.

Photo 3. Level the base, front to back and end to end, using shims. Secure it by toenailing to the floor or using metal angle braces and screws.

BUILD THE BOXES

You can build each cabinet box quickly if you take the time to cut the parts to exact size, with square corners. For information about cutting plywood, see Working Methods, page 117.

▶ Start by attaching the brace that runs across the back edge of the top. Clamp the brace to the cabinet top flush with the back edge (Photo 4).

▶ Drill pilot holes for screws in two stages. First, use a combination bit to drill clearance holes and countersinks for the screwheads simultaneously (Photo 5). Second, extend the pilot holes for the screws into the edge of the brace. For No. 6 drywall screws, use a 7/64-inch diameter bit (Photo 6). Drive the screws before removing the clamps. The easiest way is to use a magnetic bit holder in your drill and a hardened driver bit.

▶ Assemble the rest of the box in the same way (Photo 7). If you do not plan to add finished side panels, drill pilot holes with a combination bit that also drills holes for 3/8-inch plugs to cover the screwheads.

▶ When you attach the bottom, raise it enough so its inside face will lie flush with the top edge of the face frame at the bottom of the box opening; the frame is installed later.

▶ Turn the assembled box face down and attach the back (Photo 8). Space the screws about 4 inches apart.

▶ If your cabinet design calls for finished 1/4-inch thick panels on the sides, glue and nail them on with finishing nails. The cabinet face frame will hide the front edges; the finished top will hide the top edges.

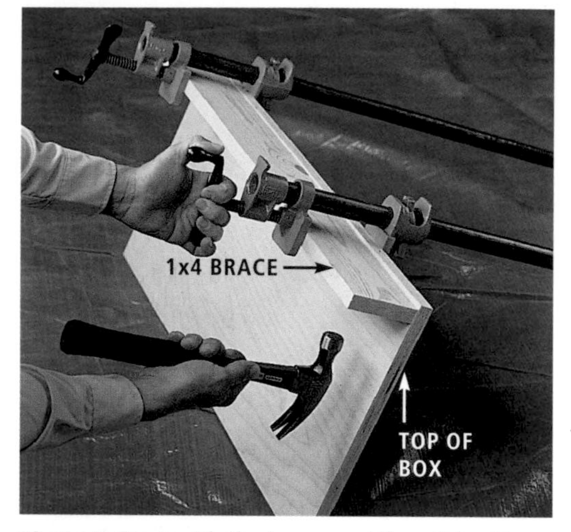

Photo 4. Start with the brace and the cabinet box top. Clamp the parts together and adjust their alignment to bring the back edges flush by tapping with a hammer.

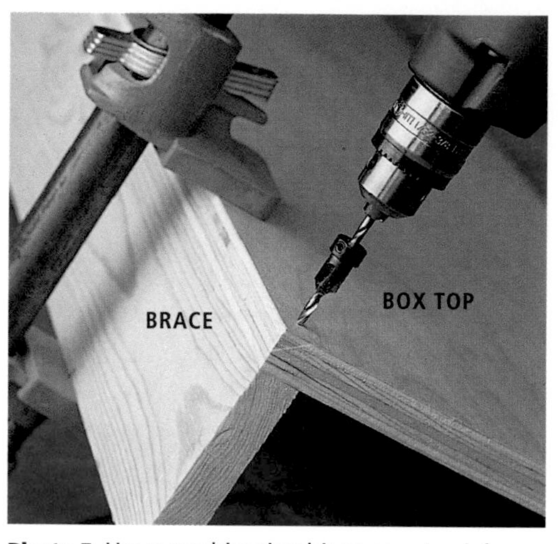

Photo 5. Use a combination bit to countersink clearance holes in the box top. Where needed, use a bit that also drills a 3/8-in. hole for a wood plug to hide the screwhead.

Photo 6. With the pieces still clamped together, use a straight bit to extend each pilot hole into the brace edge. For No. 6 drywall screws use a 7/64-in. diameter bit.

Photo 7. Screw the box sides to the top and bottom. Drill pilot holes; do not use glue. Position the bottom so it will be flush with the top edge of the face frame.

Photo 8. Attach the back with screws spaced about 4 in. apart. Be sure to cut it full size and square—when you align the edges precisely, it will keep the entire box square.

BUILD AND ATTACH THE FACE FRAMES

Make the face frames with care—they and the doors largely determine the appearance of the finished cabinets. The actual construction of the face frames is easy, because butt joints are used at the corners, instead of mitered joints.

▶ Cut the pieces of the face frames in a miter box to ensure perfectly square cuts (Photo 9). Otherwise the frames will be cockeyed or show gaps at one or more corners. Make sure your measurements are precise and clearly marked on the wood. The top and bottom pieces, called the rails, go between the side pieces or stiles of the frames. When setting up for the cut, align the saw so that the kerf is on the waste side of the marked cutting line.

▶ Assemble a frame one corner at a time. Use a right-angle clamp to hold a rail and a stile together with their ends precisely aligned (Photo 10). Drill pilot holes as described in the instructions for building the box. In the face frames you will need to counterbore holes for wood plugs to conceal the screwheads.

▶ Drive the screws before removing the clamp. Because this is finish work, play it safe and drive the screws by hand. A slip with a power bit could scar the wood surface beyond repair.

▶ Attach the assembled face frame to the cabinet box with glue and nails (Photo 11). Run a bead of glue along the box edges and put the face frame in place. If it overlaps the sides, be sure it does so equally. Drill pilot holes and drive 6d finish nails. To avoid denting the wood, use a nailset to drive the heads 1/16-inch below the surface.

▶ Cut plugs or short lengths of dowel to cover the screwheads and insert them in their holes with glue. When the glue is dry, cut off the plugs as close as possible to the surface with a very sharp chisel, then plane or sand them flush with the face frame.

BUILD AND ATTACH THE FACE FRAMES

Photo 9. Cut the face frame pieces in a miter box to ensure square ends. This is essential for getting square corner joints.

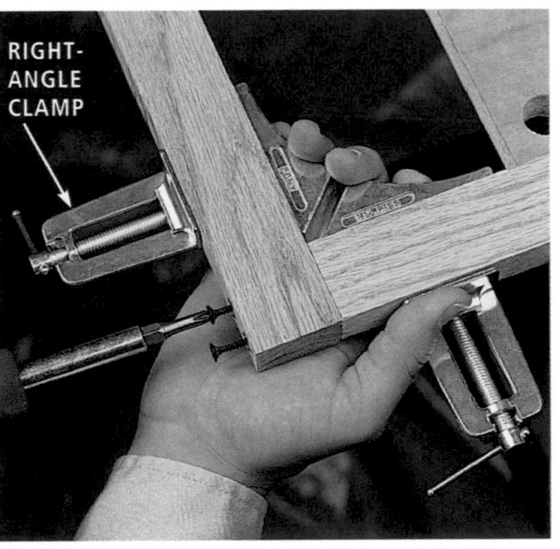

Photo 10. Assemble the face frames using a right-angle clamp. Drill clearance, pilot, and counter-bore holes, then screw.

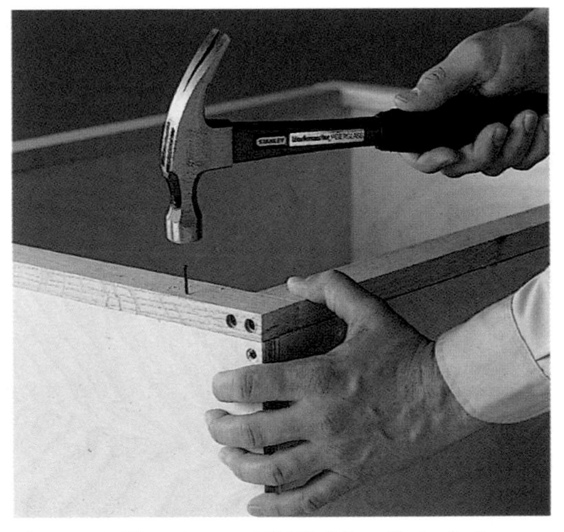

Photo 11. Use glue and 6d finish nails to fasten the face frames to the cabinet box fronts. Predrill holes for the nails.

INSTALL SHELF SUPPORTS

If you are going to have adjustable shelves in your cabinets, the easiest way to support them is with metal standards and support clips.

▶ Attach the standards to the inside walls of the cabinet with screws, two on each side (Photo 12). You can do this before or after attaching the face frame.

▶ For full-depth shelves install standards 1-1/2 to 2 inches from the inside back edge and an equal distance from the front of the face frame. For partial-depth shelves, mark where the front edges will be and place the front standards 1 inch in back of that line.

▶ Make sure that all four standards are vertical and that their slots are aligned.

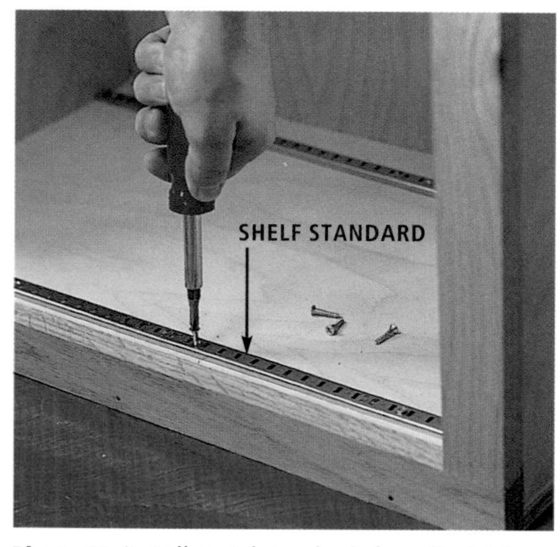

Photo 12. Install metal standards for adjustable shelves in the cabinets. Make sure the slots line up at the same level.

ATTACH THE TOPS

Before installing a plywood finish top, add edging to hide the core plies.

▶ For edging, the simplest solution is to use 3/4-inch wide panel-cap molding or other ready-made edging. An alternate solution is to make your own edging with a router and an edging bit (see box, page 116). Miter the corners and attach the edging with glue and short finish nails or brads.

▶ Position the finish top on the cabinet with the proper amount of overhang at the sides and front. If the cabinet will be mounted against a wall, set the rear edge flush with the back of the box. Drill pilot holes from inside the cabinet, up into the bottom of the finish top, then drive screws to secure it in place. One screw near each corner is enough.

▶ Add 1/2-inch cove molding under the overhanging edges for an additional touch of style and more finished look if you wish.

INSTALL THE CABINETS

Before attaching the cabinets to the base, locate and mark the studs in the walls behind them. Use a stud finder, or drill a small hole and probe with a stiff wire; the cabinet will conceal the patched hole.

▶ Position each cabinet on the base with its back snugly against the wall. Drill countersunk pilot holes in the bottom, then drive drywall screws to fasten the cabinet to the base. Two screws in the front stringer of the base and two in the back stringer are sufficient.

▶ Drill pilot holes through the top brace at the rear of the cabinet and drive screws into the wall studs (Photo 13). Use 3-inch screws, one for each stud.

Photo 13. Screw the cabinets to the base and the wall, keeping them level. Use 3-in. drywall screws to reach into the studs.

HANG THE DOORS

The cabinets shown here use full-overlay doors. They are the easiest type of door to install, because they do not have to fit precisely into the face-frame opening; instead, they overlap the frame on all four sides. You can hang this kind of door with surface-mount hinges of the sort used in many kitchen cabinets. However, pivot hinges like those shown in the photos are virtually invisible and present a much more finished appearance. In addition, they are adjustable, which makes it easy to get the doors plumb.

▶ Use a self-centering Vix bit to drill pilot holes for the hinges. First, position the hinges on each door and drill pilot holes through the elongated mounting holes (Photo 14), but do not drive screws in the holes yet.

▶ Remove the hinges, hold them in place on the face frame, drill pilot holes, and attach them with the supplied screws.

▶ Position the door in the hinges, align the pilot holes with the elongated holes in the hinge leaf, and drive the screws (Photo 15).

▶ Check the swing of the doors and their alignment on the face frame. If an opening has two doors, their tops must align and the gap between their edges must be uniform. Use a level to make sure the vertical edge is plumb. To make adjustments, loosen the hinge screws and shift the door as necessary.

▶ When everything is correct, tighten the adjustment screws, drill pilot holes through the round holes in the hinge leaves, and drive screws there to fix the door in position.

HANG THE DOORS

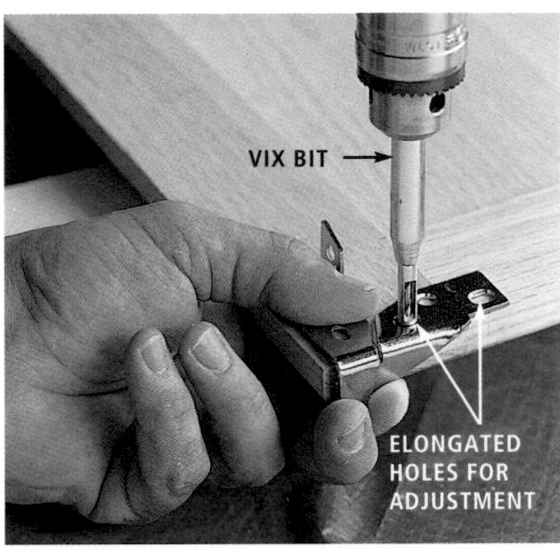

Photo 14. Use a self-centering Vix bit to make pilot holes. Drill only through the elongated adjustment holes in the hinge leaves for the first installation.

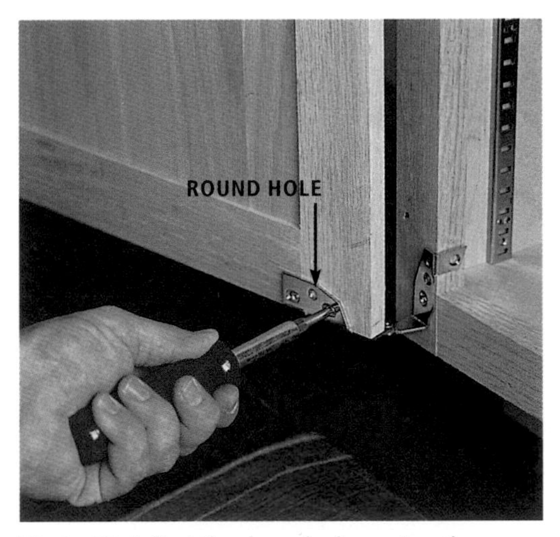

Photo 15. Adjust the doors by loosening the screws in the elongated holes. When finished, drive pilot holes and screws through the round holes in the hinges.

BUILD THE WINDOW SEAT

In this project, a window seat with a lift-up lid is placed between cabinets to provide additional storage space. Construction details are shown in the diagram on the opposite page. Here's what to do:

▶ Build a face frame of 1x4's with openings to be covered by decorative panels. If you bought ready-made cabinet doors at a home center, you can probably get matching drawer fronts to use as panels.

▶ Screw 1x4 braces to the rear wall studs and the adjoining cabinet sides so their top edges will be at the same height as the top of the face frame. The lid rests on these braces and on the face frame.

▶ Attach the face frame flush with the cabinet face frames and with the bottom edges aligned. Clamp it in position, drill pilot holes, and drive 3-inch drywall screws through the cabinet frames into the edges of the window seat frame (Photo 16).

▶ Make the lid of 3/4-inch plywood with finished edging on the front edge. Attach it to the brace on the wall with a piano hinge (Photo 17). Install a toy chest lid support to hold the lid safely in an opened position (see detail in diagram, opposite).

▶ Attach the decorative front panels with screws driven through the face frame from behind (Photo 18).

▶ Cut a plywood bottom for the window seat, put it in position, and fasten it with screws driven into the base stringers below, as you did with the cabinets.

Photo 16. Clamp the window-seat face frame to the adjoining cabinet frames and screw them together edge to edge. Make sure the front faces remain flush.

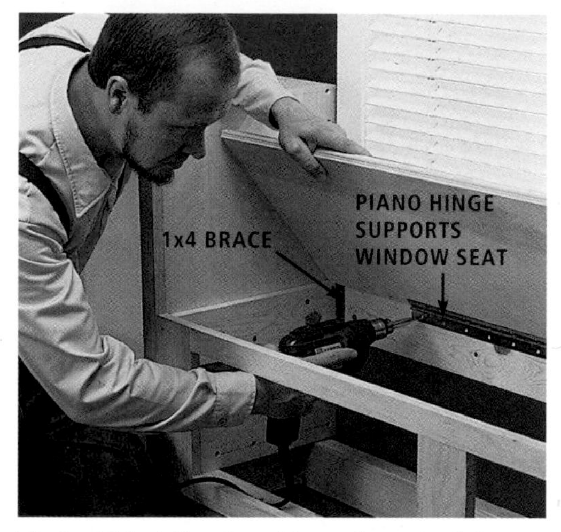

Photo 17. Install a piano hinge along the full length of the window-seat lid. The lid rests on the back and side braces and the top edge of the face frame. Then add a lid support.

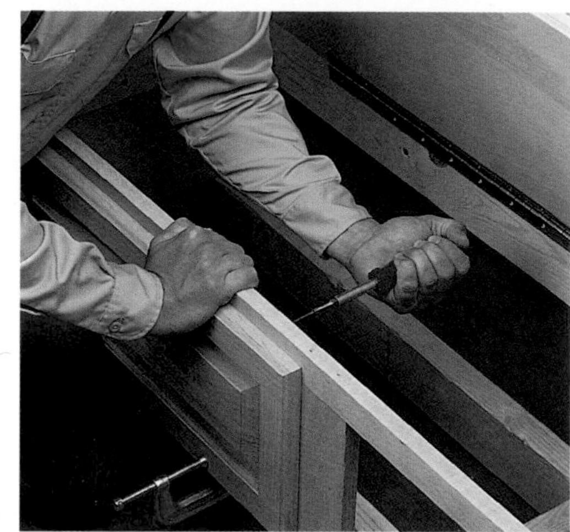

Photo 18. Fasten drawer fronts or other panels to the face frame with screws driven from behind. Screw a plywood bottom to the floor frame to complete the window seat.

Window Seat Construction

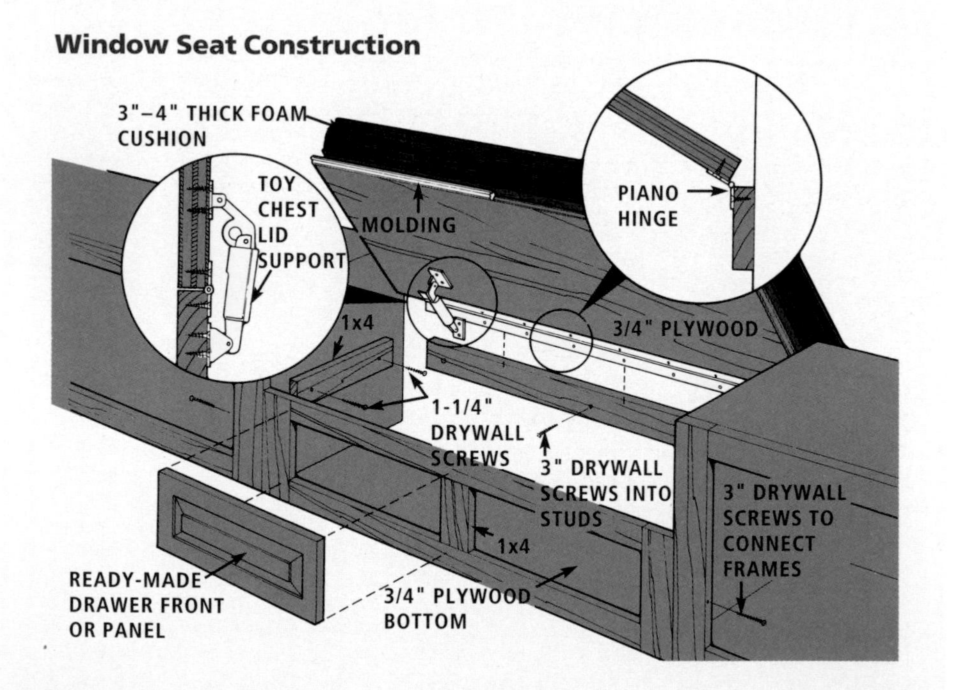

FINISH THE PROJECT

Remove cabinet doors and all hardware such as hinges and knobs before finishing. Sand all surfaces with fine-grit paper; pick up sanding dust with a vacuum cleaner and a tack cloth.

For painted cabinets, brush on a coat of primer, then fill all cracks, nail holes, and dings with spackling compound. Sand again and spot prime where necessary. Apply two coats of latex enamel, sanding between coats.

For a varnish-only or a stain-and-varnish finish, follow the product instructions carefully. Be sure to use compatible products; some stains and finishes cannot be used together successfully.

When the paint or finish is thoroughly dry, rehang the doors and reattach the hardware.

The Living Room and the Dining Room

Floor to Ceiling Bay Window

A bay window will add light and floor space to a room, provide a panoramic view of the outdoors, and improve the look and value of your home.

138

A New Face for the Fireplace

Custom-build a mantel and facing unit to transform your fireplace. This design looks richly complex, but it is really easy to construct.

150

Add a Bay Window

A bay window is a marvelous addition to a house. It makes the exterior more attractive, brings light into a room, and provides a panoramic view of the outdoors.

Adding a bay window doesn't involve a large area of the house, but it's certainly a big project in terms of the advanced DIY skills it requires. If you can handle the work, this miniature addition can transform a room as no other project can.

Open a view, add more space, and let in light with a floor-to-ceiling bay window. It's a job that calls for many skills, but the rewards are well worth it.

LOCATION AND STYLE

The bay window in this project was installed in a dining room, but it could have been added to almost any room—first or second floor, front, back, or side. Favorite spots for a bay window include the dining room, a study or family room, and a room facing the garden.

The model shown at the right is called a "45-degree bay" because the side windows meet the house at a 45-degree angle. Other common styles are bays with 30-, 60-, and 90-degree side windows.

The large center window of this bay is fixed; the side windows are casement sash that open outward. You may prefer to have double-hung sash windows at the sides, or perhaps a double-casement window in the center. There are many window options.

There are two points in particular to note in evaluating this project:

▶ The roof of this bay window is built against the second-story wall of the house. On a single-story house, you can either tuck the window under a wide eave or construct a roof that ties into the existing roof.

▶ The instructions on these pages deal with a specific bay design incorporating a specific style of window. Your project will almost certainly be different in a number of ways, depending on the brand of window used, the space available, and structural limitations. Whatever style of bay and type of window you choose for your house, the building principles, design and structural considerations, and basic steps will be essentially the same as those illustrated and explained here.

PROJECT SCOPE

This project ranks close to the top of the difficulty scale for do-it-yourselfers. It calls for just about every skill required to build a house: framing, roofing, siding, insulating, heating and cooling, electrical wiring, and sometimes plumbing. Drywall skills and finish carpentry also come in handy.

If you doubt your construction abilities, hire a professional carpenter to build the structure to the point where the roof is on and the windows have been installed. Similarly, it may make sense to hire professionals to put in ductwork, wiring, or plumbing rather than struggle with unfamiliar tasks. Even if you do only the finish work you can save money.

The total cost and the time needed to install a bay window varies with every house. The size and type of windows; whether you need to reroute pipes, ductwork, and wires; and what types of siding and interior finishes are needed to match the existing house will all affect the final cost and how long it will take.

If you do it yourself, schedule the various stages of the work so you don't leave a gaping hole in the exterior wall as you head to work one day. It's also a good idea to check the weather report before you cut a hole in the side of your house. Do as much work as possible—including installing the new header and cantilevering the joists—before opening the wall in the room where the bay will be located.

A bay window improves the exterior of a house at least as much as the interior, and it adds value. It's a project that demands and deserves careful work.

Measure First

Don't begin this project until the windows are delivered. Measure them carefully and verify that the size is correct and double-checked against the dimensions on the floor template.

PLANNING

The first consideration is how to support the floor of the bay. There are three basic ways (see diagrams, opposite page):

▶ If your house is built directly on a concrete slab, without a basement or crawl space, pour a new section of concrete slab to go under the bay. Tie it into the existing slab with rebar as shown in the diagram.

▶ If there is a basement or crawl space and the existing floor joists run in the same direction that those under the bay will run—and if there are no ducts, pipes, or cables in the way—support the bay on cantilevered joists from inside the house.

That is the method used in this project: new joists that extend out beyond the foundation are nailed alongside the existing joists. There is no need to add any type of support beyond the existing foundation.

▶ If you cannot extend cantilevered joists because there are obstructions or because the existing joists run in the wrong direction, you can support the bay on concrete posts. Run short joists from the rim joist of the house to new rim joists for the bay structure, as shown in the diagram.

Get advice

How far you can cantilever floor joists depends on their size—2x8 or 2x10—and how far back under the existing floor you can slide them. This very basic consideration requires the advice of a building inspector or a structural engineer. For this project, the engineer determined that the 2x10 floor joists could be safely cantilevered 36 inches past the basement wall. The actual bay required an extension of only 28 inches, so there was no problem. You will almost certainly need a building permit for this project, so a building inspector will have to check the calculations and approve your plans in any case.

Draw a plan

With window catalog and graph paper in hand, sketch out two or three window designs that work for the room.

▶ Be precise. Draw in each angle and window rough opening—the height and width of the opening needed for each window unit. The design used here placed the windows as close to one another as possible, with only one stud and one trimmer on each side of each window.

▶ When your sketch is complete, measure the opening needed in the exterior wall to accommodate the bay. The larger the opening, the larger the support header across it must be. For this calculation, you absolutely must consult a building inspector, and perhaps a structural engineer, to determine what size header is needed to support the opening in the exterior wall. In this project, the engineer calculated that a double 9-1/4 inch header of laminated veneer lumber (LVL) was necessary to support the weight of the second story and the bay roof across the 8-foot opening. An LVL header is made from pieces of plywood laminated together into a beam. This kind of construction can carry more weight across a span than conventional lumber headers.

▶ Order the windows through a home center or specialty window store; they can often take four weeks or more for delivery. Take your sketch along when ordering. Experienced salespeople may offer some helpful hints.

Make a template

When your plans have been approved by the building inspector, draw a full-size template of the bay window on a 4- x 8-foot panel of 3/4-inch plywood (Photo 1).

▶ Lay out the positions of the nailing plates for the walls, and mark the stud and trimmer thicknesses on each plate. Note that the plates for the side framing extend to the house edge of the template. Their ends will be cut at the same angle as the sides of the bay—45 degrees in this project.

▶ Don't forget to leave enough room for interior moldings. Work carefully; this template will become the actual floor of the new window bay.

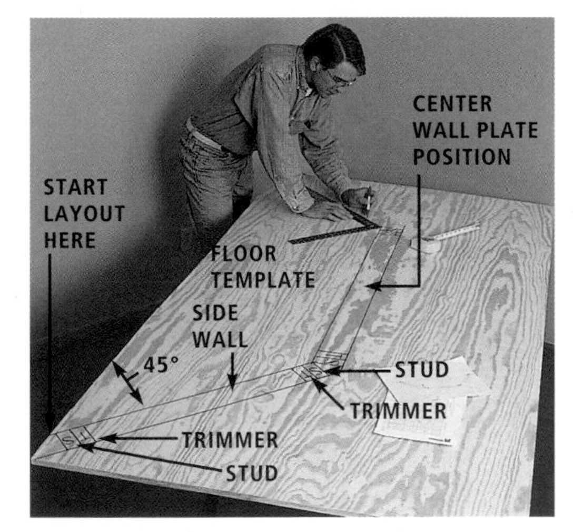

Photo 1. Make a full-size plywood floor template. Draw the correct angle and length of each wall, allowing for the window rough openings, trimmers, and studs.

Supporting a Bay Window

House floor construction largely determines how to support a bay.

Pour a concrete extension for slab-on-grade construction.

Where the floor is above grade, extend the cantilevered joists if the house construction permits.

Support the floor frame of the bay on posts if it is not possible to use cantilevered joists. This method may require considerable excavation. The footings under the posts must lie below the frost line.

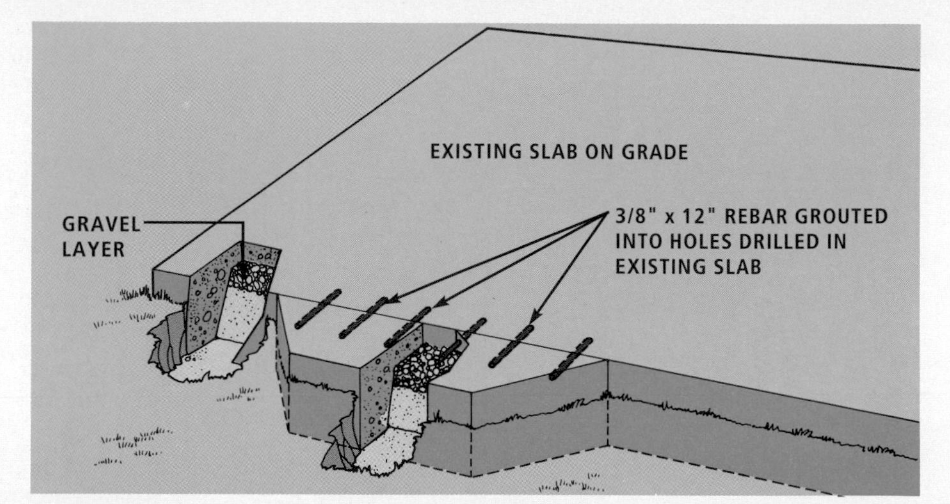

Slab on grade.

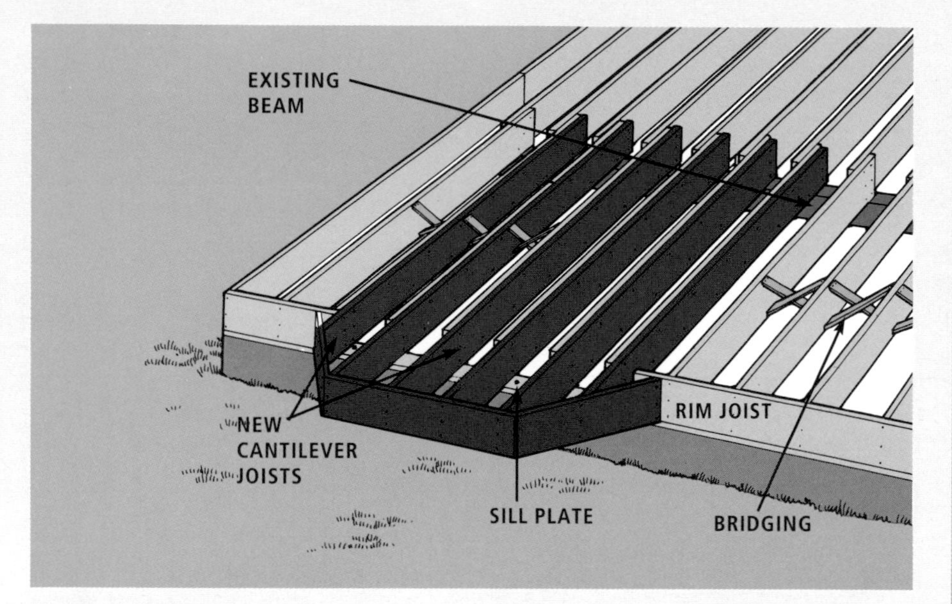

Cantilevered floor.

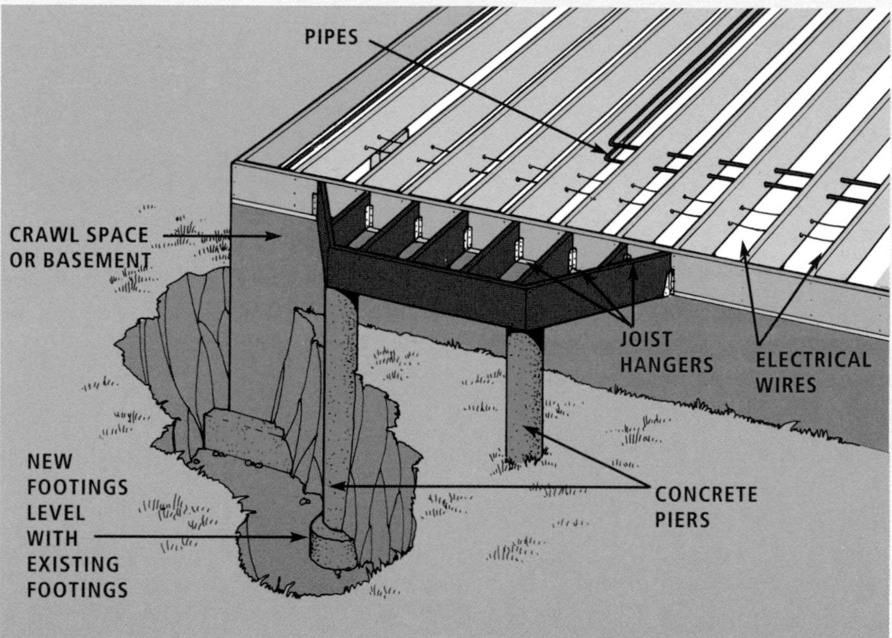

Post-supported floor.

TOOLS

- Circular saw with rip guide
- Reciprocating saw
- Framing square
- Power miter saw
- Hammer
- Sledgehammer
- Chalk line
- Wrecking bar
- Pry bar
- Adjustable T-bevel
- Tape measure

OPEN THE RIM JOIST

In order to extend cantilevered joists to support the bay window you must open up the rim joist of the house, just above the foundation. To do that you first must determine the exact position of the bay window on the interior and exterior walls.

▶ From inside the room, mark the center of the bay on the wall, then open the existing window or door and transfer this center mark to the outside of the house. If the center does not fall within an existing window or door, cut a small hole in the interior wall to find a spot without any obstructions such as pipes or electrical cable. At that point, remove a small amount of insulation and drill a hole through the plywood sheathing and exterior siding. If that is exactly on the center line, fine; if not, measure the distance on the inside and transfer it to the outside.

▶ Using the center line as a reference point, measure and mark the outside of the house where each side of the bay window will meet the exterior wall.

▶ Remove the siding and plywood sheathing from the house's rim joist between those points. Cut through and remove that section of the rim joist to create an opening through which new joists can be cantilevered. Start the cut with a circular saw, then finish with a reciprocating saw (Photo 2). Don't cut through the 2x4 or 2x6 sill plate under the joists.

Photo 2. Cut and remove the section of the rim joist where new joists will be cantilevered. Start the cut with a circular saw and finish it with a reciprocating saw.

BUILD THE BAY FLOOR

Cut the new joists longer than required by the plan; you will cut them to exact length after nailing them in place.

▶ From the basement pull the new joists through the opening in the rim joist into position below the floor (Photo 3).

▶ Rest one end of a joist on the house's support beam and the other end on the sill plate, then tilt it upright alongside the existing joist. Use a small sledgehammer to force it into position if needed, and drive shims under the new joist to get it flush with the top of the existing joist (Photo 4). Nail the joists together with three 16d nails every 2 feet.

▶ Now go outside and position the full-size plywood floor template on top of the new joists (Photo 5). Mark the edge of the template on the top of each one.

▶ Remove the template and make a second set of marks 1-1/2 inches inside the first ones to allow for the thickness of the rim joist around the perimeter of the bay. Use a combination square to extend the second marks straight down the face of each joist.

▶ Cut the joists on these inside lines. Set your circular saw to cut the outer ends of the joists that support sides of the bay at the proper angle—45 degrees in this project (Photo 6). Cut the other joist ends at 90 degrees.

▶ Reposition the plywood floor template so it overhangs each of the cut joists by 1-1/2 inches. Nail it to the cantilevered joists, then cut and nail the rim joists to the ends of the cantilevered joists (see Photo 10, page 145). The outside face of the rim joist should line up exactly with the outside edges of the template.

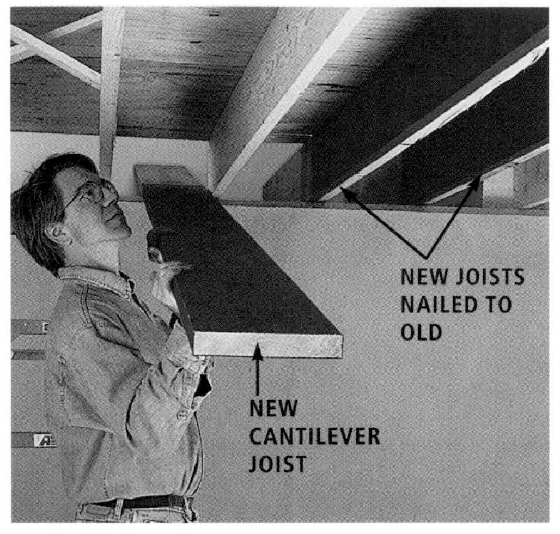

Photo 3. Pull the new joists through the opening in the rim joist. Tilt them up beside the existing joists, resting on the center beam and the sill on the foundation wall.

Photo 4. Nail the new cantilevered joists to the existing joists with 16d nails every 24 in. Use shims as necessary to get the tops of the joists flush with one another.

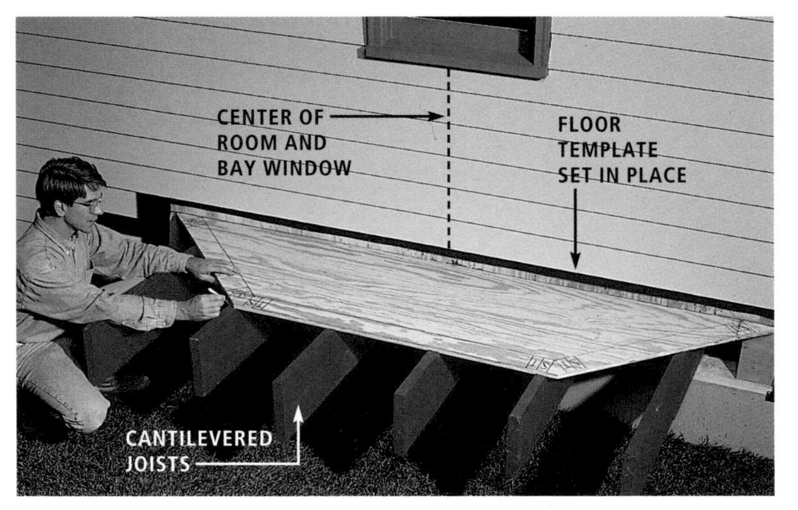

Photo 5. Mark the cantilevered joists to length using the floor template. Remove the template and mark cutting lines 1-1/2 in. back from the first marks.

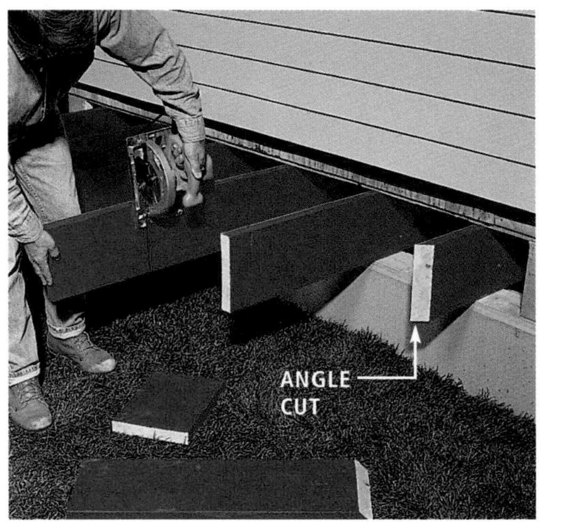

Photo 6. Cut the cantilevered joists to length with a circular saw. Set the saw to cut angled ends on the joists that support the side walls of the bay window.

MATERIALS

- 3/4" plywood
- 3/8" plywood
- 1/2" plywood
- 2x8 or 2x10 boards for joists
- Engineered header (if necessary)
- 2x4's
- 1x6's
- 1x4's
- 1x2's
- Shims
- 16d nails
- 8d nails
- Roofing felt
- Shingles
- Flashing material
- Fiberglass insulation
- 1" polystyrene insulation
- Siding material
- Ductwork (if necessary)
- Drywall
- Electrical cable and outlets (if necessary)

Turn Off Power

At the main electrical service panel, turn off electricity to all outlets, switches, and wires in the room before demolishing the interior wall.

BUILD THE WALLS

Before you erect the walls of the bay window, first erect the new header across the intended bay opening. Then you can build frames for the walls, cut the opening, and put up the frames.

Install the new header

▶ Inside the house, build a temporary support wall of 2x4's located 2 feet back from the exterior wall (Photo 7). Position it so each vertical stud in this wall sits below a ceiling joist.

▶ With a wrecking bar, remove the drywall or plaster (Photo 8), insulation, and vapor barrier to expose the inside of the exterior sheathing. Wear a dust mask and eye protection as you work. Remove the drywall all across the interior wall; it's easier to install all new drywall than to blend new and old together.

▶ Knock out the studs inside the wall where the bay window will be built. A sledgehammer makes quick work of this even though the sheathing and siding are nailed to them. If necessary, cut the studs in half with a reciprocating saw. Use the same techniques to remove the header over the existing window or door, if any. Pound over and flatten protruding nails.

▶ Add the new LVL support header specified by the building inspector or engineer. The header shown here is long enough to span the distance between two existing studs. It is supported on each end with two trimmer studs (Photo 9). Nail the trimmers together.

Build the bay wall frames

Each bay wall is constructed as a separate frame; the frames are then joined together to form the skeleton of the bay. Each frame has top and bottom nailing plates, and a header across the window space just under the top plate. A top plate is added over the top nailing plates when the walls are erected (see diagram below and Photo 12).

▶ Cut pairs of 2x4 nailing plates the same length and angle as the walls drawn on the plywood floor template. Cut the house ends of the side wall plates to meet the house at the proper angle—45 degrees here. Cut the other ends and the ends of the face wall plates at half that angle—22-1/2 degrees here. Mark the

Bay Wall Details

The LVL header across the house wall is supported on double trimmers. The bay window headers are built from 2x lumber and plywood. A top plate covers the nailing plates above the window headers.

Plywood sheathing and roofing felt cover the frame except for the window openings. The plywood and framing over the top of the bay are part of the roof structure; see pages 146–147.

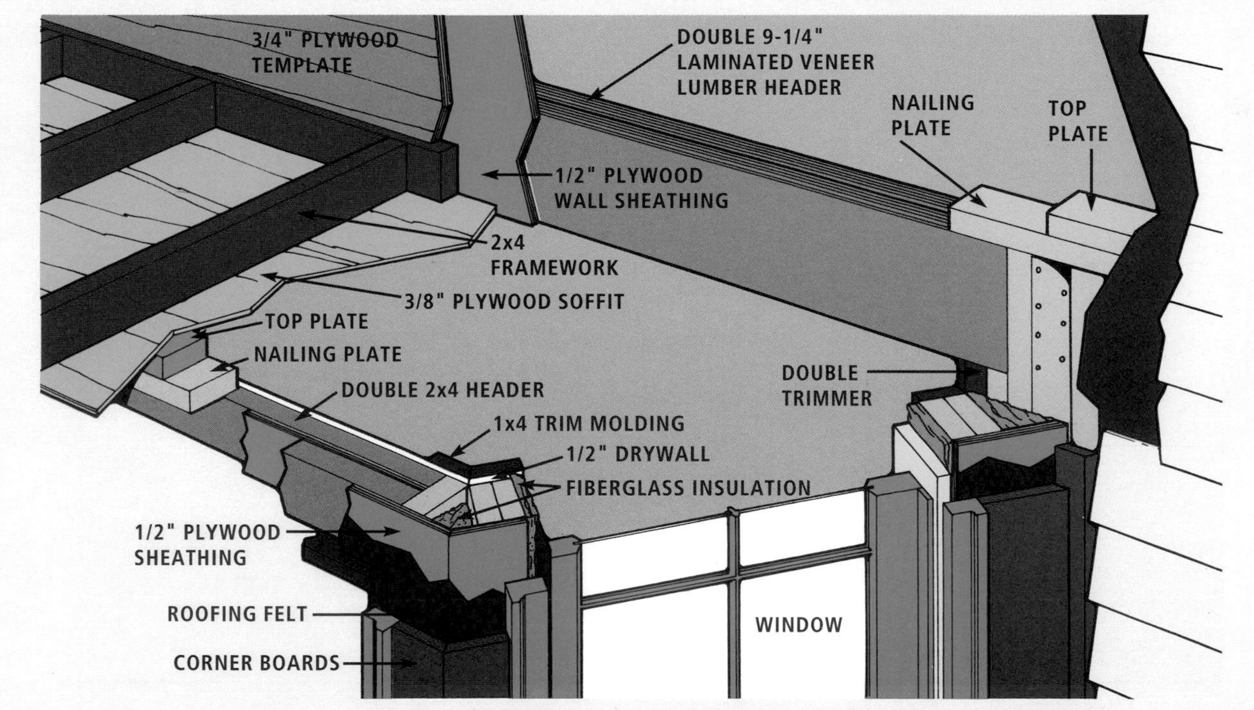

location of studs, trimmers, and the window openings on the nailing plates.

▶ Cut studs and trimmers. The studs will rest on the bottom nailing plate and must hold the final top plate at the same level as the bottom of the LVL header in the house. The trimmers sit inside these studs and support the individual window headers.

▶ Build the window headers of two 2x4's with 1/2-inch plywood sandwiched between. Large window openings may need a header of doubled 2x6's or larger lumber. Follow the building inspector's specifications.

▶ Nail these frame members together, then add a sill supported on cripple studs under each rough window opening (Photo 10).

Cut the opening and put up the wall frames

▶ Cut through the house sheathing and siding. Working from the inside with a reciprocating saw, cut along the bottom of the LVL header and along both sides of the bay window opening (Photo 11).

▶ Cut back the exterior siding—but not the sheathing—an additional 6 inches to accommodate the bay walls and trim.

▶ Stand the walls in place and nail them to the floor of the bay and to the house. Nail on the top plates, overlapping the corners of the walls to lock them together (Photo 12).

▶ Stuff fiberglass insulation into the open corners, nail 1/2-inch plywood sheathing to the frames under the window openings, and staple on roofing felt over the sheathing (see diagram, page 146).

BUILD THE WALLS

Photo 7. Add a temporary wall to support the second story and roof while installing the new header. Use cardboard to protect the ceiling.

Photo 8. Open the entire wall out to the exterior sheathing. Use a sledgehammer to remove studs where the bay window will be installed.

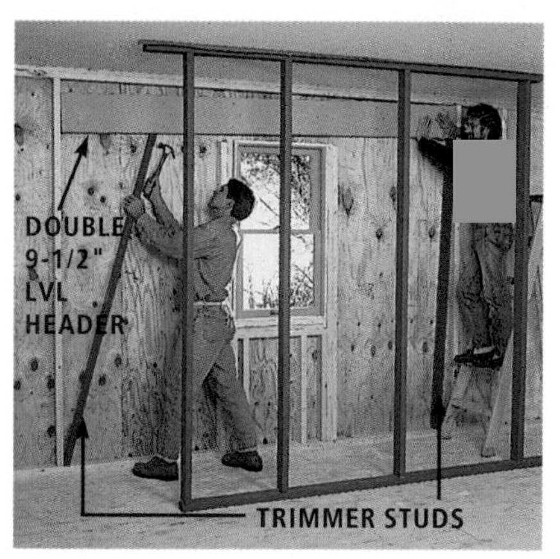

Photo 9. Install the new header on double trimmers at each end. Make the opening larger than necessary and frame the width later.

Photo 10. Build the walls flat on the ground. Cut pairs of nailing plates as drawn on the floor template, then add the 2x4 framework between.

Photo 11. Cut out the window rough opening. Cut back the siding, but not the sheathing, 6 in. more to accommodate the walls and trim.

Photo 12. Nail the wall frames to the floor and to one another. Add top plates that are level with the bottom of the header across the opening.

Roof and Bay Framing

The roof structure is composed of a flat roof framework made of plywood and 2x4's, rafters, and a wall plate. Using 3/4-inch roof sheathing reduces the number of rafters required. The eave edge is trimmed with a fascia and a drip edge. Window and wall framing details are explained in earlier sections of the text. Polystyrene insulation and a plywood soffit are added to the bottom of the structure as a finishing step.

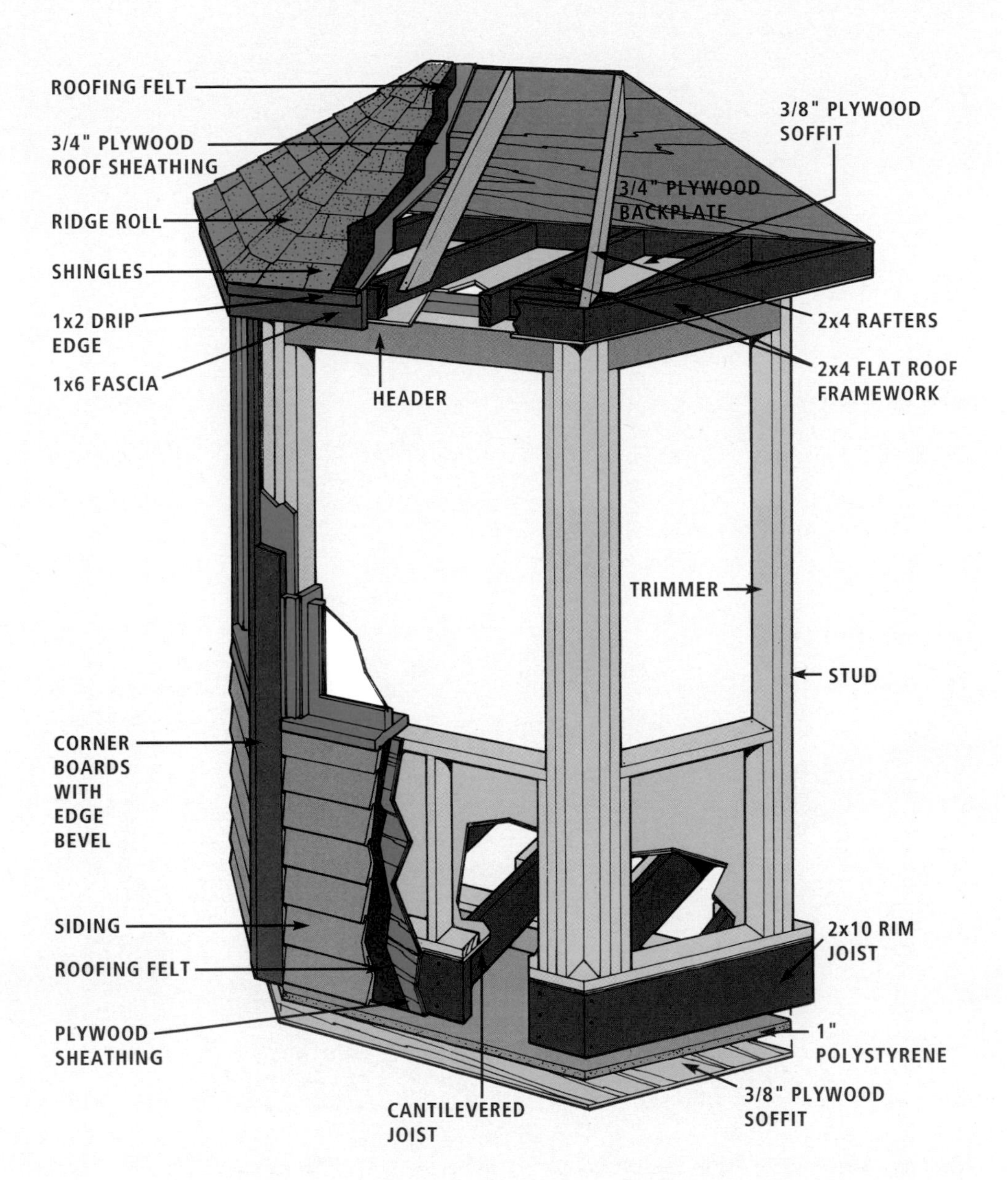

BUILD THE ROOF

Roof construction for the bay window is complex, but plywood templates similar to that used for the floor simplify the task. A flat roof framework supports rafters that in turn support the roof covering.

Construct the flat roof framework

▶ Lay a sheet of 3/8-inch AC plywood on top of the walls. Snap chalk lines parallel to all three walls to indicate the width of the roof overhang—5-1/2 inches in this project (Photo 13). The overhang portion of this plywood becomes the exterior soffit; the interior portion offers a flat surface for attaching the drywall that forms the bay window ceiling.

▶ Remove the plywood and cut out the marked shape. Cut and nail 2x4's to the top of this template. Set them on edge all around and flush with the outside edges. Then add 2x4 "joists" between the front and rear framing pieces, spaced 16 inches on center (see diagrams at left and on page 144, and Photo 14).

▶ Lift this flat roof assembly into position on top of the bay and nail it to the house framing and the bay walls with 16d nails.

Add rafters

Make a 3/4-inch plywood template for a wall plate that indicates the height and slope of the roof where it butts against the house. Experiment with various shapes and sizes until you find a height and angle that appeals to you. The template helps you visualize the roof, serves as a guide for measuring the length and angle cuts of the rafters, and forms a structural backplate against the house.

Photo 13. Mark and cut a roof template that extends to the edges of the eave overhang. Build a 2x4 flat roof framework on top of the template.

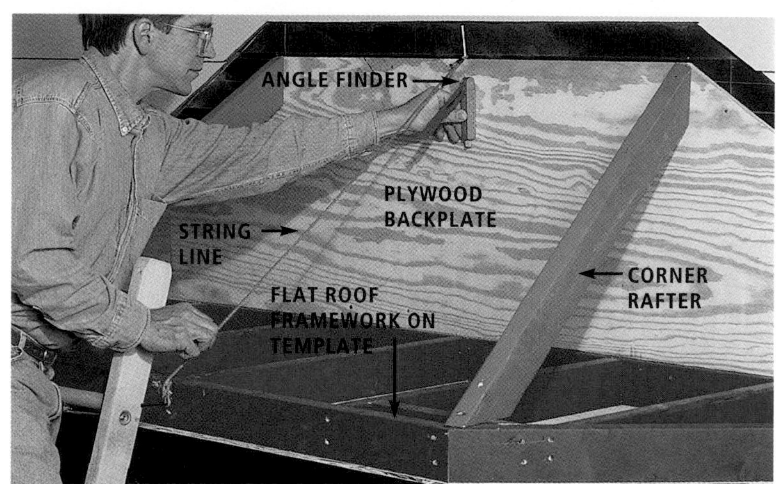

Photo 14. Cut and mount a wall plate for the roof. Then stretch strings to help you determine the length and end angles of the rafters.

▶ Hold the wall plate in position against the house above the bay and mark its outline on the siding. Cut away the house siding to about 3 inches outside the line, but do not cut through the sheathing.

▶ Nail the wall plate in position. Then stretch strings from its top edge to the outside top edges of the flat roof frame (Photo 14). Position the strings where the rafters will go—one from each upper corner of the wall plate to the outside corners of the bay, and at least one in the center. Use a tape measure and adjustable T-bevel to find the length of the rafter pieces and the angle at which they must be cut. The corner rafters have compound angle cuts where they meet the house.

▶ Cut the rafters. You will have to cut some compound angles, using either a power miter saw capable of them, or a circular saw. With either tool, measure carefully and set up your cut so that the blade is tiltled at an angle to its base, while it cuts across the 2x4 at another angle. Then nail the rafters to the flat roof framework and the wall plate on the house.

Finish the roof

▶ Fill the flat roof framework with insulation. Then sheathe the roof with 3/4-inch plywood nailed to the rafters, the flat roof framework, and the wall plate.

▶ Cut and nail in place 1x6 fascia and a 1x2 drip edge (see diagram, below). Staple roofing felt to the roof sheathing, then nail on the shingles. Apply two rows of overlapping cap shingles on the ridges where the roof sections meet one another.

▶ Where the sloped roof sections meet the house wall, slide step flashing up behind the siding and underneath each row of shingles (Photo 15). Install a strip of continuous flashing under the siding and shingles across the top of the center roof section.

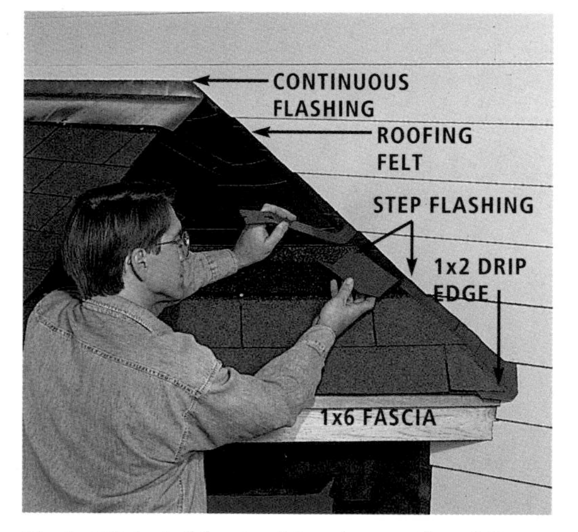

Photo 15. Install fascia, drip edge, roofing felt, and shingles. Slide flashing under the siding and shingles where the roof meets the house along the sides and across the top.

INSTALL THE WINDOWS

Installing the window units in a bay window is a two-person job that calls for careful work and attention to detail (Photo 16). Follow the manufacturer's installation instructions.

▶ Install the large center window first, then the side windows. All the windows must align with one other and be symmetrically positioned in the bay framing.

▶ The worker inside the bay first makes sure each unit is centered in its opening. Then he or she should use a level to check that the sill is level and the sides are plumb. If necessary, shims should be used to get the unit into proper alignment.

▶ The outside worker nails each unit in place. Nails go through the mounting flange into the studs of the bay framework.

Photo 16. Nail windows in place after sheathing the walls in 1/2-in. plywood and roofing felt. The person inside centers and levels the window in the opening before it is nailed.

FINISH THE PROJECT

The final steps in adding a bay window include providing heat, insulating the bay, covering the outside, and finishing the interior.

▶ If you have a forced-air heating and ventilating system, extend a duct into the bay window area to increase air circulation and minimize frost. Otherwise, extend wiring or piping for baseboard heaters. The small length of the extension duct and the relatively small interior volume of the bay window should not tax the capacity of your furnace or air conditioner.

▶ Extend electrical circuits into the bay, if necessary, before adding insulation and drywall. Some municipalities require building permits and inspections for any extension of the electrical system, so be sure to ask about this when consulting the building inspector.

▶ Insulate the floor with fiberglass batts cut to fit between the cantilevered joists (Photo 17). Then nail 1-inch thick rigid polystyrene insulation to the bottoms of the joists (see diagram, page 146). Cover this with a floor soffit of 3/8-inch thick AC exterior plywood.

▶ Install exterior trim at the outside corners of the bay and where the walls meet the house (Photo 18). Use a table saw or circular saw with an edge guide to rip the boards with beveled edges for this trim. For a 45-degree bay, the bevels should be 22-1/2 degrees.

▶ Cut siding to fit between the trim and nail it over the sheathing and building felt on the outside walls of the bay. Use siding that matches the house.

▶ Caulk all exterior joints around the windows and where the bay joins the house.

▶ Inside the house, lightly pack fiberglass batt insulation or spray expandable foam insulation into the spaces under the windows and between the window frames and the house and bay framework. Do not cram it in or otherwise compress it; this reduces its insulating properties. Once the insulation is in place, staple sheet plastic as a vapor barrier over all the insulated sections of the framing.

▶ Nail or screw gypsum wallboard panels to the walls, then apply tape and joint compound (Photo 19).

▶ Apply interior window and baseboard moldings. Then paint the walls and trim and extend the finish flooring into the new bay window area (Photo 20).

Photo 17. Insulate the floor of the bay window. Fill the joist cavities with fiberglass insulation, then install rigid insulation and a plywood soffit.

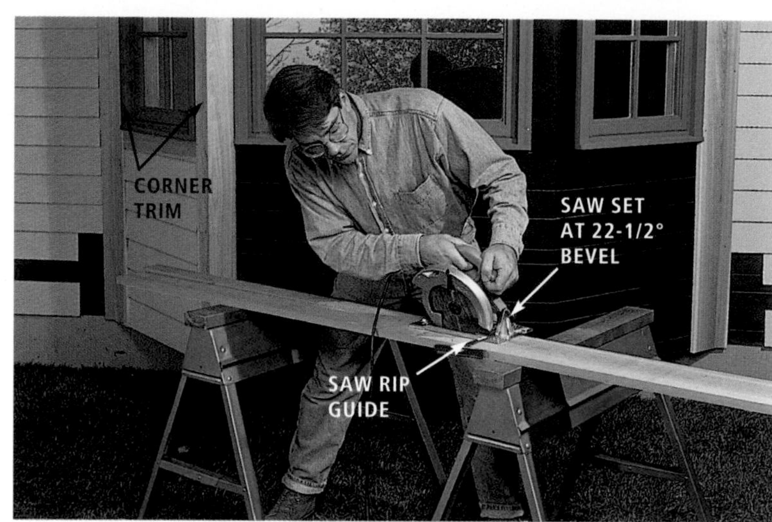

Photo 18. Cut trim with beveled edges to make mitered joints at the corners and the house. Then fill in between with siding that matches the house.

Protect Yourself

Wear a dust mask, gloves, and eye protection during interior demolition work.
Wear gloves, long sleeves, and a dust mask when working with fiberglass insulation.

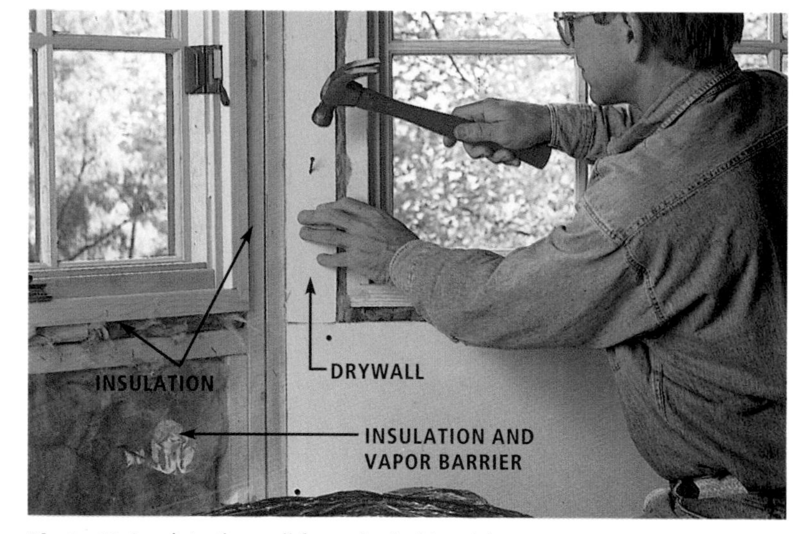

Photo 19. Insulate the wall from the inside with foam and fiberglass materials. Cover with a vapor-retarding barrier, then install drywall.

Photo 20. Cut and fit interior trim after the drywall joints have been taped and sanded. Fill nail holes, then paint the trim and walls to finish the project.

A New Face for the Fireplace

A fireplace looks warm and inviting when there's a fire blazing within. At other times, its appearance depends largely on the facing, which is composed of the mantel and the surround—the columns, panels, and masonry around the firebox.

A new mantel and fireplace surround made of rich, warm-looking wood can add greatly to the style of a living room or family den. It will become the room's centerpiece, a place to display not only family heirlooms but your woodworking talents as well.

This project may look tough, but it's not. A little crown molding, a sheet of plywood, and some slick router work will turn that old, cold fireplace into something warm and inviting.

A bit of molding, some plywood, and intermediate woodworking skills are all that's needed to give an old fireplace a warm and inviting new face. The fire screen was removed for this photo; always use yours.

SCOPE OF THE PROJECT

Building a wood mantel and surround is like crafting a piece of furniture. It requires very careful planning and cutting, and equal care in making close-fitting joints.

One of the appealing features of this project is that you can take your time. There's no need to disrupt the living space by tearing out walls or ripping up floors. Once you have made the necessary measurements, you can cut and assemble most of the mantel and surround in a workshop or garage.

The mantel shown in this project is made with solid oak boards and moldings and oak veneer plywood. It is actually a long, thin box. The columns are also three-sided boxes with decorative faceboards and bases. The facing bridge running between the columns under the mantel can be a piece of plywood or a solid board. Moldings are used to finish the edges and the joints with the wall and the fireplace facing. If you plan to paint the mantel, use birch or good-quality pine plywood and moldings instead of oak. They accept paint better and cost less than oak.

You can install the mantel and surround on the existing facing and hearth, but a new facing will help create a total makeover and is not difficult to install. In the project described here, the original brick was covered with marble tiles. You could use decorative ceramic tile or thin-cut facing stone instead.

Fireplace Checks and Fire Codes

Modern fireplaces are usually quite safe installations; those in old houses may need some work to bring them up to present-day standards.

Whatever the age of a fireplace, it requires periodic inspection and cleaning, to maintain it in a safe condition. The most common fireplace hazards are a dirty chimney flue and cracks in the mortar joints of the firebox lining.

Wood smoke deposits both soot and creosote on the walls of the flue. When allowed to accumulate, these can ignite, causing a very high temperature, and a dangerous chimney fire. If you haven't had your fireplace chimney cleaned in the last year or two, call a certified, licensed chimney sweep. For a quite reasonable charge an experienced professional will clean the flue and firebox and inspect them for cracks and blockages. He will also check the damper for proper operation, too. And of course he can make any necessary repairs.

Between inspections and cleanings, you should clean out the firebox and inspect it yourself. Patch any cracks in the firebrick lining or the mortar joints with an approved fireplace repair compound, sold in tubes like caulking, or with refractory (high-temperature) mortar. Do not use ordinary mortar.

Wherever wood is used around a fireplace opening, there are important safety precautions to be observed. The National Fire Protection Association provides the following guidelines:

▶ Woodwork, trim, and other combustible materials may not be placed within 6 inches of a fireplace opening.

▶ Combustible materials that project more than 1-1/2 inches from the masonry facing—such as a wooden mantel—must be at least 12 inches away from the top of the fireplace opening.

▶ If the fireplace opening is less than 6 square feet, the hearth area in front of the fireplace should extend at least 16 inches in front of the facing material and 8 inches beyond each side of the opening.

▶ If the fireplace opening is more than 6 square feet, the hearth should extend at least 20 inches in front of the opening and 12 inches beyond each side.

The specifications for the required clearances between the fireplace opening and surrounding wood and for hearth dimensions may be different in your local ordinances. Be sure to talk to a building inspector about the regulations in your area, to make sure you create a safe, violation-free installation.

Finally, always keep a fire screen in place when a fire is burning. In the photos on these pages the screen was removed to show off the marble facing and the fire.

ASSEMBLY PLAN

TOOLS

- Circular saw
- Router
- Drill
- Measuring tape
- Hammer
- Nail set
- Socket wrench
- Power miter saw
- Stone-cutter's tub saw (optional)

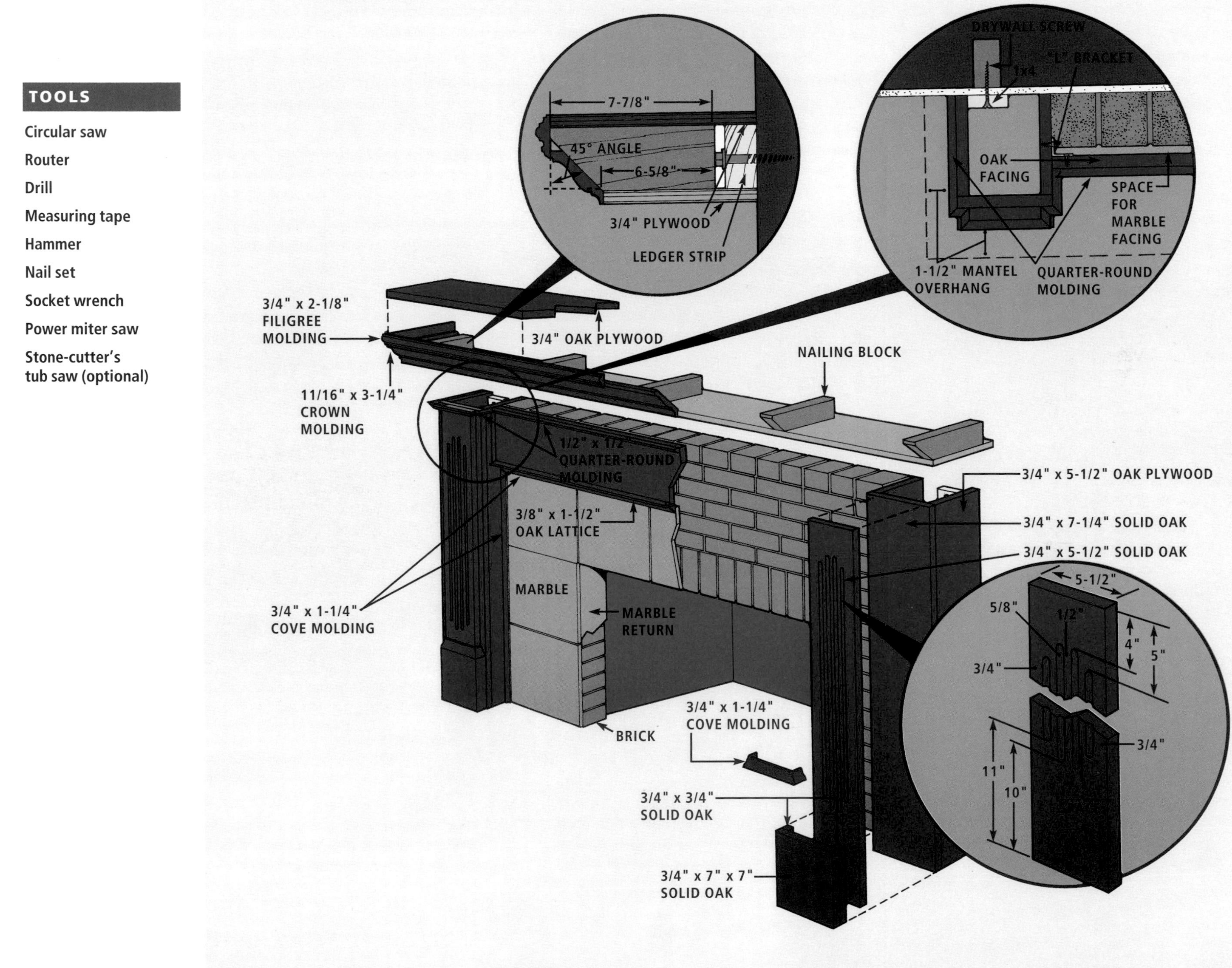

DESIGNING A FIREPLACE FACE

There is a wide range of fireplace sizes and designs. The fireplace shown in this project—with a brick facing 4 feet high and 5 feet wide—is very much like the millions that were built in the 1950's, 1960's, and 1970's. If your fireplace is different from this one, the mantel and surround shown in the plans on the opposite page and in the photographs can be adapted to fit.

To design a complete installation for your fireplace, remove the old mantel (see Getting Ready, page 154) and make careful measurements to establish the following dimensions:

▶ The height of the columns should be the same height as the masonry facing, allowing for the thickness of any new facing on the hearth below (Photo 1).

▶ Columns should extend 3-1/2 inches out from the new facing on the fireplace. The depth of the column boxes will depend on how they are to be placed. If they go flat against the fireplace facing (see box, page 157), the columns can be just 3-1/2 inches deep. If they wrap around or if they fit outside the ends of the masonry facing (see plans, opposite), the columns must be deep enough to reach to the wall around the fireplace.

▶ For columns that wrap around or fit outside the ends of the existing masonry facing, the length of the wood bridge between the columns should be 1/4 inch longer than the horizontal measurement of the fireplace. This will provide a bit of clearance for moving the assembled columns and bridge into position. If the columns are to mount against the face of the masonry, the extra 1/4 inch fitting clearance is not necessary.

▶ The bottom board of the mantel should overhang the column sides and faces by about 1-1/2 inches (Photo 2). The top board will be larger, to join with the built-out molding that covers the thickness of the mantel box.

You may not wish to build an entire surround, but only to replace an existing mantel or install a mantel where there is none at present. In that case, make the necessary measurements described above, then start with the section Build the Mantel Frame on your project page 158.

MATERIALS

- 3/4" hardwood veneer plywood
- 1x8 and 1x6 hardwood boards
- 2x4's
- Wood glue
- Metal L-brackets
- 3/4" x 1-1/4" cove molding
- 11/16" x 3-1/4" crown molding
- 3/4" x 2-1/8" filigree molding
- 1/2" x 1/2" quarter-round molding
- 8d finish nails
- 4d finish nails
- 1" brads
- 1/4" x 3-1/2" lag screws
- 1-5/8" drywall screws
- Cement board
- Mastic
- Tiles (optional)
- Tile mortar and grout (optional)

DESIGNING A FIREPLACE FACE

Photo 1. The mantel is a long, thin box with sides built of crown and filigree moldings. Each column is also a box, with a faceboard decorated with routed flutes.

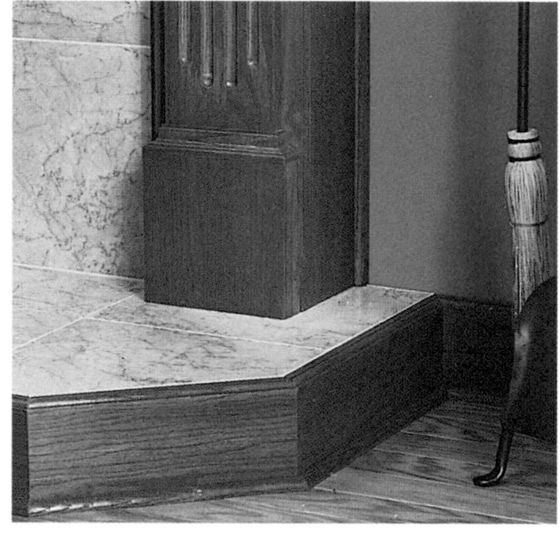

Photo 2. The column base is a simple add-on piece trimmed with molding. New facing material on the fireplace front and hearth complete a total makeover.

GETTING READY

To take measurements and get to work, you need to expose the masonry facing of the existing fireplace.

▶ Remove the old mantel first, if there is one. A single solid timber supported on brickwork is probably secured by nails at the back edge. Drive the nails all the way through with a nail set (Photo 3), then pull and pry to remove the mantel. The mantel could be secured in a number of other ways, especially if it is not a single piece. If so, examine it for traces of nail-heads, plugs over screwheads, brackets, and other clues. If you can't undo a screw, remove the head with a large-diameter drill bit. Pry and hammer as necessary to get the mantle free, but work so that any damage will be covered by the new installation.

▶ Level the top of the masonry. It does not have to be smooth, but should not vary more than 1/2 inch. Chip away any protrusions with a cold chisel and small sledgehammer, or fill in with mortar.

▶ Remove any other trim and facing material that would interfere with the new installation.

▶ Measure the outside dimensions of the fire-place facing and the firebox opening and draw them to scale on graph paper. If you plan to cover the hearth with additional material, place spacers of the same thickness on the hearth when you measure the height (Photo 4). This is important, because you must build and install the wood columns with enough space for the new hearth material below them.

▶ Draw in the layout of the new marble, stone, or tile facing and trim moldings to make sure every part of the old masonry facing will be covered. Depending on the size of the facing units, you may have to plan narrow courses around the outside edges.

▶ Draw up cutting plans for each of the pieces you will need. Refer to the Assembly Plan on page 152 and Designing a Fireplace Face on page 153. Then look through the instructional photos on the following pages to make sure you account for everything.

▶ Purchase the materials for the project, based on your plans. Stain the moldings and plywood before assembly for a consistent look and to reduce mess. For clarity some of the pieces are shown unstained in the photos.

GETTING READY

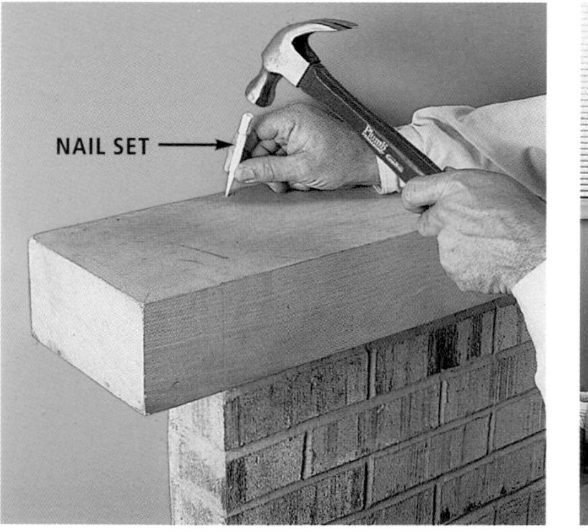

Photo 3. Punch nails through with a nail set to remove the existing mantel. It may be held with other fasteners as well. Use a pry bar with care to avoid wall damage.

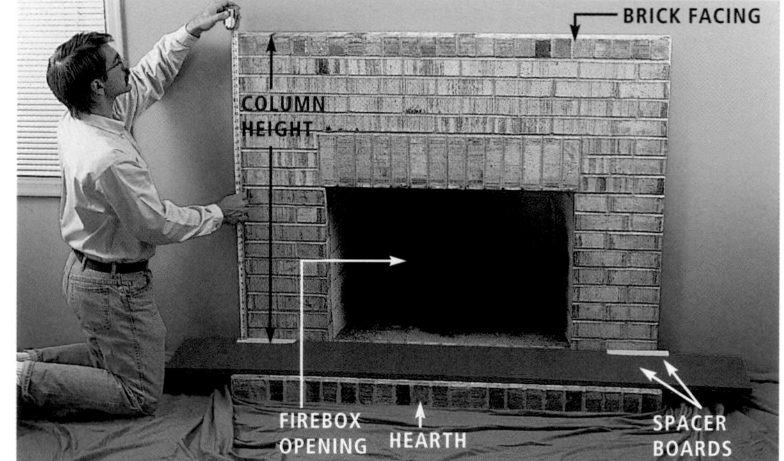

Photo 4. Measure the height and width of the masonry facing and the firebox opening. Use spacers to represent the thickness of new hearth facing material.

BUILD THE COLUMN BOXES

The columns are U-shaped boxes with sides of 3/4-inch veneer plywood and a matching solid board across the front. The front is then covered with a decorative faceboard with routed flutes.

▶ Cut the pieces for the sides of the columns to width, then cut them to length. For information about techniques for finish-cutting plywood, see page 117.

▶ If necessary, rip the solid front boards to width. Turn the best face down if you are cutting with a circular saw. Cut the front boards to the same length as the sides.

▶ Predrill nail holes every 6 inches along the solid front boards and fasten the fronts to the column sides with carpenter's glue and 8d finish nails (Photo 5).

▶ Cut four 2x4 backer blocks to fit inside the columns. Get the ends square, because they hold the columns square. Install them about 10 inches from the top and bottom of each column with a narrow side against the front boards. Position the nails in the front board so they will be covered by the fluted face.

▶ Cut two 3/4- by 5-1/2 inch (nominal 1x6) faceboards the same length as the columns. Also cut a practice board the same size. Mark out the centerlines and end points for four equally spaced 5/8-inch wide flutes on the boards. The two middle flutes extend 1" farther than the outside flutes at both the top and the bottom (see detail in the plans).

▶ Cut flutes in the practice board first, to get the feel of it and establish the required router settings. Use a 5/8-inch core box router bit.

Although you can use a standard router, a plunge router is much better for this kind of work (Photo 6). It is similar to a standard router but the motor and bit ride up and down on spring-loaded legs. You preset the bit to a specified cutting depth—1/2 inch in this case—then lower (plunge) and retract it precisely where you want each cut to begin and end. Use the router edge guide to make straight cuts at a preset distance from the edge of the board. Since the flutes are symmetrically spaced, you can set the guide to cut the two outside flutes first, working from opposite edges of the board, then reset it to cut the inside flutes, working from opposite edges.

Routing Tips

When the edge guide is running along the edge of the board closest to you, move the router from left to right. When the edge guide is against the far edge, move the router from right to left.

If you make a mistake when routing the flutes in the column face-boards, turn the boards over and try again; the back side will be hidden.

BUILD THE COLUMN BOXES

Photo 5. Glue and nail the solid column front to the plywood sides. Predrill holes in the front for 8d finish nails. Then glue and nail backer blocks inside the column.

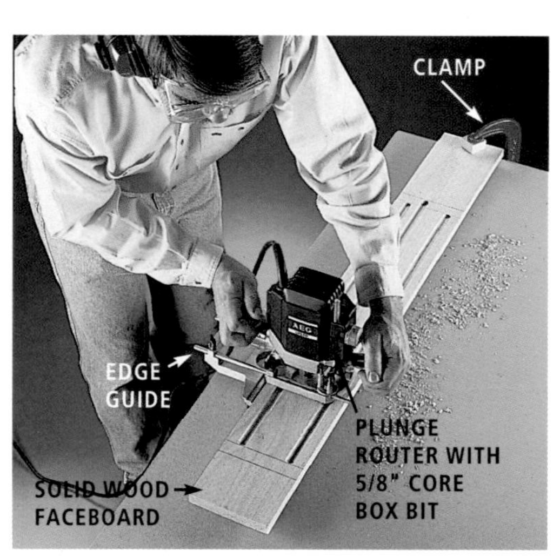

Photo 6. Rout the four flutes onto the 1x6 face-board using a plunge router, 5/8-in. core box bit, and edge guide. Flute spacing is shown in the Assembly Plan on page 152.

ASSEMBLE THE SURROUND

The surround consists of the two columns and a bridge faceboard that connects them at the top. Complete the faces of the columns before attaching the bridge board.

▶ Fasten the fluted faceboards to the column fronts. Use carpenter's glue and 8d finish nails, and position the faceboards so there is an equal space on each side.

▶ Cut pieces of solid board to length for the column base pieces (Photo 7). Use the same stock as the solid (unfluted) fronts of the columns. Add return pieces at the edges the same thickness as the fluted face piece and attach the bases to the columns, again with glue and finish nails.

▶ Cut and install 3/4- x 1-1/4 inch cove molding on the top edges of the bases. Cut the ends at 45 degrees so you can make miter joints at the corners.

▶ Cut the bridge from 3/4-inch veneer plywood that matches the columns. Cut it to the length appropriate to the placement of the columns, as explained in Designing a Fireplace Face (page 153).

▶ Attach the bridge to the sides of the columns, using screws and pairs of metal L-brackets on the back (Photo 8). Set its top edge flush with the tops of the columns. On columns that fit outside the ends of the existing masonry, leave space behind the bridge for the thickness of the masonry plus the new facing you will add. For columns that mount on the face of the masonry or wrap around the ends (see box, opposite page) you need leave only enough space behind the bridge for the thickness of any new facing.

ASSEMBLE THE SURROUND

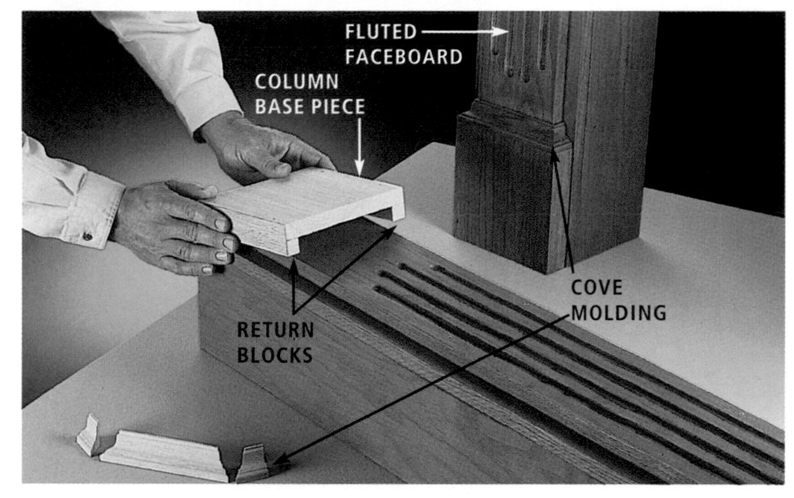

Photo 7. Glue and nail the fluted faceboard in place, then cover its bottom end with a U-shaped base piece. Trim the base piece with cove molding.

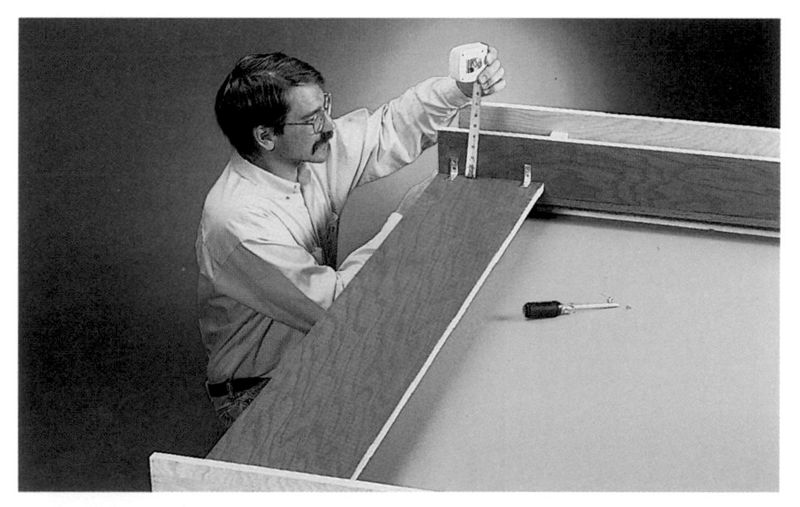

Photo 8. Attach the bridge between the columns with L-brackets. Set it forward of the fireplace facing according to how the columns will be mounted; see text.

INSTALL THE SURROUND

You will need to install nailing strips on the wall or on the masonry in order to fasten the surround in place.

▶ For columns that fit outside the masonry, put the surround temporarily in position and press it flat against the wall. Prop it up on the spacer boards if you intend to add hearth facing under the columns. Trace the outer edge of each column onto the wall.

▶ Remove the surround and draw parallel lines 3/4 inch inside the traced lines; these mark the thickness of the column sides.

▶ Screw 1x4 nailing boards to the wall framing; use toggle bolts where there is no wall framing (Photo 9). Align each nailing board with the inside line of the column side.

▶ For face-mounted or wrap-around column positions, draw lines on the masonry and install nailing boards as shown in the diagrams at right. Use screws and masonry fasteners.

▶ Put the surround into final position, again with spacers if needed (Photo 10). Fasten it to the 1x4 nailing boards with 2-inch finish nails driven every 8 inches through the sides of the columns. For wrap-around columns, fasten the wide side of the column to the masonry.

INSTALL THE SURROUND

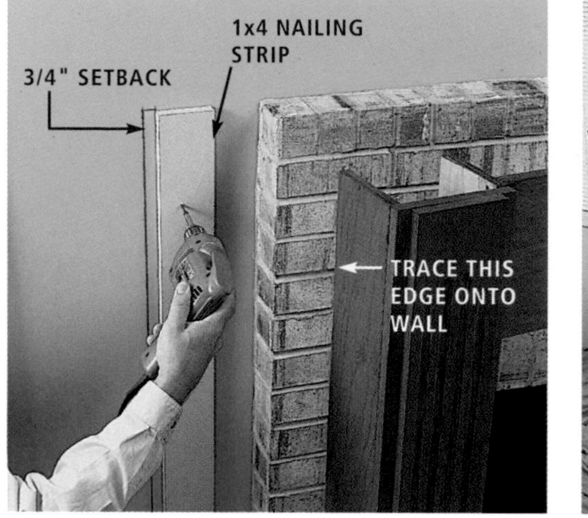

Photo 9. Mark the thickness of the column side on the wall. Then attach a nailing strip along the inside line. Use screws, or toggle bolts if necessary.

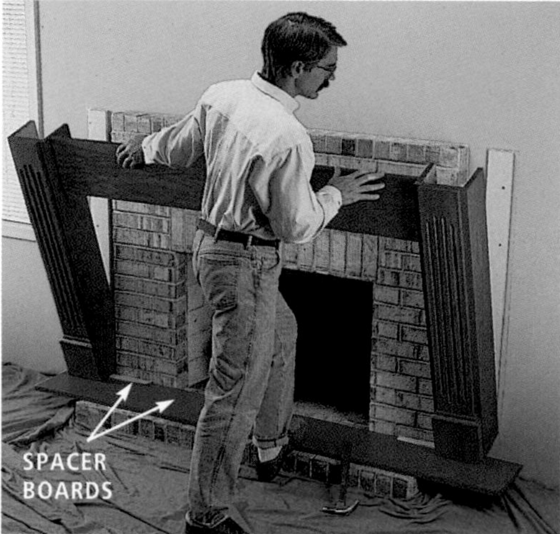

Photo 10. Guide the surround into place and secure with 8d finish nails. Use spacer boards to install the surround high enough to allow adding hearth facing later.

Installing Face-mount and Wrap-around Columns

Secure nailing strips to the masonry with masonry fasteners and screws. Use a full-width strip for face-mounted columns; use a narrower strip for wrap-around columns. Fasten columns as described in the text.

Face-mounted column.

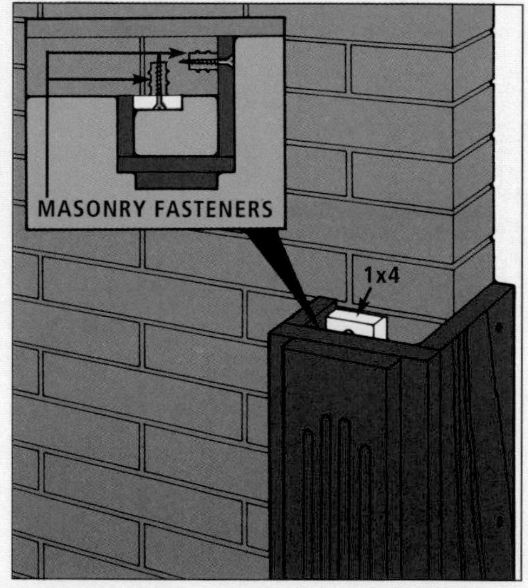

Wrap-around column.

Firm Molding Joints

Firm up corner joints and where the crown and filigree moldings meet—especially along the mantel ends—by gluing small scraps of wood to the backs of the molding.

BUILD THE MANTEL FRAME

The mantel is a long, thin box. The basic frame is a bottom board and nailing blocks to which crown and filigree edge moldings and a top board are attached.

▶ First, determine an exact profile for the mantel. Then cut 2-inch sample pieces of each of the moldings and the 3/4-inch plywood bottom board. The bottom board sample should be the length required to reach from the wall to the desired overhang beyond the faces of the columns.

▶ On a flat surface, lay out the bottom board sample with its back edge against a reference line (Photo 11). Position the crown molding against the front edge, then overlap it with the piece of filigree molding. Use a square to make sure that the back of the filigree molding is at right angles to the surface of the bottom board.

▶ Now measure from the back of the filigree molding to the reference line. This is the required width of the top board. Cut a sample piece to length and fit it in place.

▶ Finally, cut a piece of 2x4 as a sample nailing block. Angle-cut the lower front corner to fit against the back of the crown molding. Cut the block short to leave a 2-inch space at the rear, for a ledger piece that will be mounted on the wall.

▶ Now cut the parts for the basic frame. Cut enough nailing blocks to place one at least every 16 inches. Then cut a piece of plywood to width and length for the bottom of the mantel.

▶ Mark out the spacing of the nailing blocks on the bottom board. Fasten the board to the blocks with 8d finish nails and glue (Photo 12).

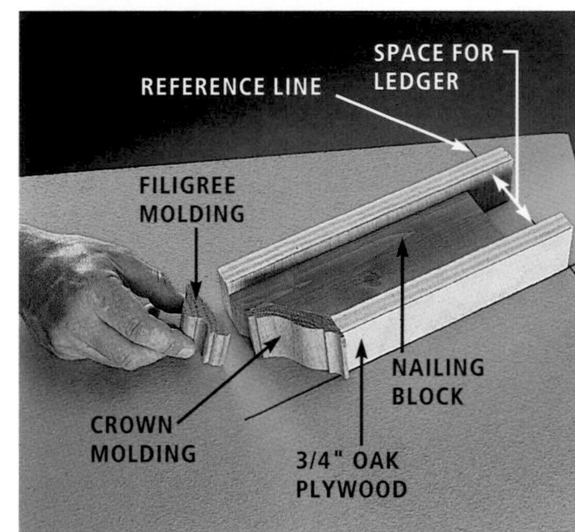

Photo 11. Use sample pieces to lay out a cross section of the mantel. Flats on the back of the crown molding set its angle; keep other pieces straight and square.

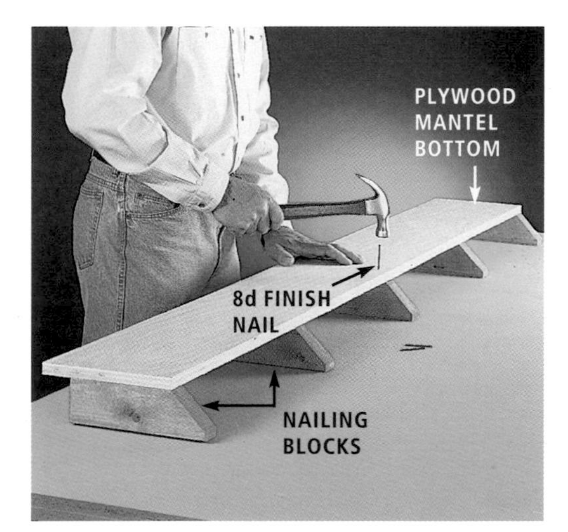

Photo 12. Nail the mantel bottom to nailing blocks positioned about 16 in. apart. Align the front edges precisely so the crown and filigree moldings will mount properly.

ASSEMBLE AND INSTALL THE MANTEL

To assemble the mantel, first cut crown molding with mitered ends for corner joints. Use an angle block to hold the molding in the miter box at the same position it will be installed (Photo 13).

▶ Fasten the crown molding to the edges of the bottom board and the backer blocks using glue and 4d finish nails (Photo 14).

▶ Turn the mantel over and install the filigree molding (Photo 15). Overlap it onto the crown molding 1/8 inch and line up the corner joints exactly. It must extend 3/4 inch above the nailing blocks to be flush with the surface of the top board.

▶ Cut the top board to fit exactly inside the filigree moldings when its rear edge is aligned with the rear edge of the bottom board (Photo 16). Fasten the top to the nailing blocks with glue and 8d finish nails.

▶ Cut a ledger from 2x stock just wide enough and long enough to fit between the top and bottom boards of the mantel.

▶ Mount the ledger on the wall with lag bolts (Photo 17). Leave a 3/4-inch space above the columns and bridge; the bottom board of the mantel fits into this space.

▶ Place the mantel in position with the top and bottom boards fitting above and below the ledger strip (Photo 18). Check the fit against the wall. If necessary, scribe the back edge, remove the mantel, and use a belt sander to shape the edges of the top and bottom boards to the marked contour. (For scribing instructions, see page 20.) When the mantel fits in place with no gaps, secure it to the ledger with 8d finish nails every 8 inches.

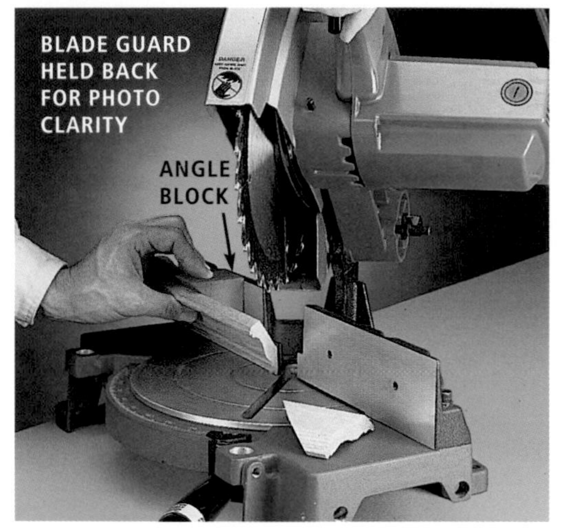

Photo 13. Cut crown molding in a power miter box. An angle block holds the molding at its mounting angle for the cut.

Photo 14. Glue and nail the crown molding with 4d finish nails. Predrill, and then fasten the corners with 1-in. brads.

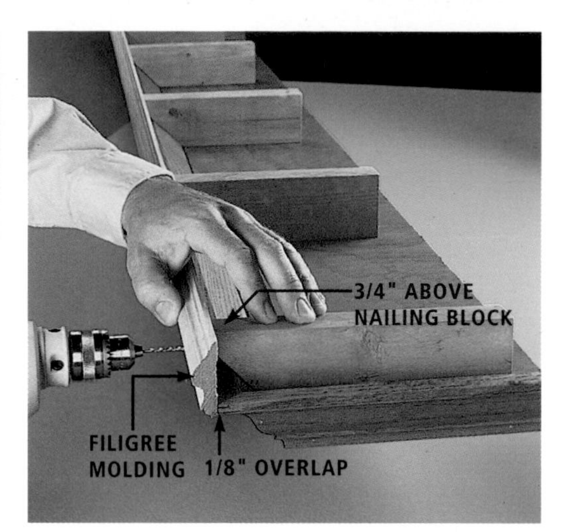

Photo 15. Add filigree molding. Overlap the crown molding 1/8 in.; extend it 3/4 in. to conceal the edge of the top board.

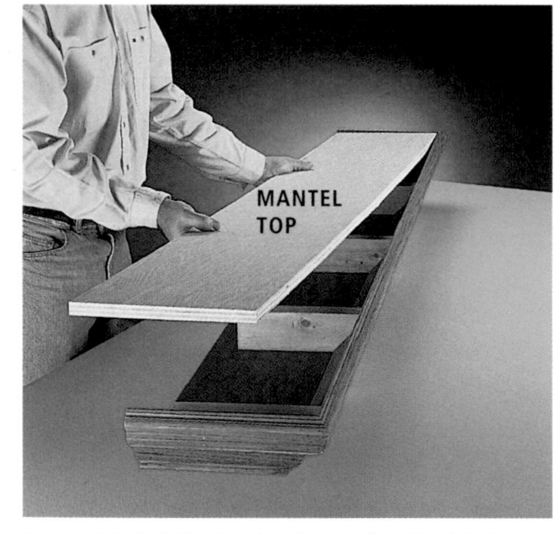

Photo 16. Put the top in place, align it with the back edge of the bottom board, and secure it with glue and 8d finish nails.

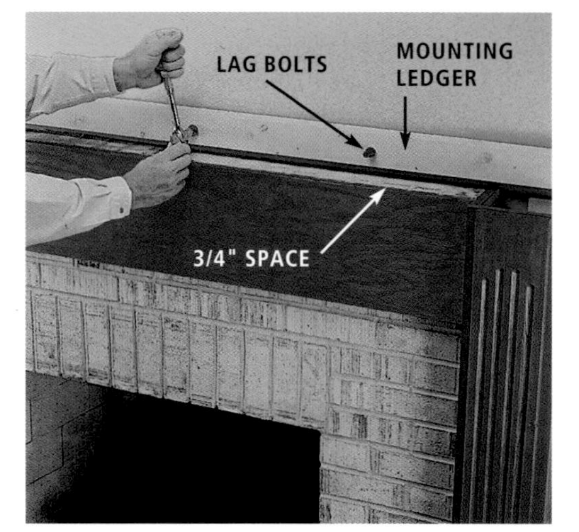

Photo 17. Attach the mounting ledger to the wall using lag screws and a socket wrench. Leave a 3/4-in. gap for the plywood mantel bottom.

Photo 18. Slip the mantel in place and check the fit. Scribe and shape the edges, then fasten the mantel in place with 8d finish nails.

REFACE THE HEARTH AND FIREPLACE

If you plan to leave the old brick hearth and facing exposed, all that remains to be done is to trim the edges of the surround, as explained on the next page. But adding marble, ceramic tile, slate, or thin-cut stone veneer is a great finishing touch. Of course you must have planned ahead for this step, as explained at the beginning of the project.

To extend the hearth, build a framework of wood and cover it and the existing hearth with cement board and your new finish material (see diagram, below).

▶ Build the frame to extend a few inches past the sides of the columns and far enough forward to meet the fire precautions discussed on page 151 or the specifications of your local fire code. Use 2x4's or other 2x stock, furring strips, and shims to make the frame surface level at the same height as the existing hearth. Add blocking every 6 inches or closer to solidly support the cement board.

▶ Cut sheets of cement board to size, then secure them to the old brick hearth with mastic and to the wood framing with 1-5/8 inch drywall screws (Photo 19). Make straight cuts in cement board by scoring a line several times with a sharp utility blade, then snapping it over the edge of a board as if cutting drywall. Cut the board to fit underneath the bases of the wood columns and slip it into place.

▶ Experiment to determine the best layout for the marble, tile, or other finish material (Photo 20). The joints on the vertical face of the fireplace should line up with those on the hearth, so you may need to cut some pieces for the pattern to work out. Marble must be cut with a special tub saw, which you can rent. Other materials can be cut with a slate or tile cutter, or with an abrasive wheel in a circular saw.

▶ Set marble with a white mortar mix; gray can bleed through and discolor the marble. Fill the joints between the tiles with unsanded grout. Follow your supplier's recommendations regarding whether to use mortar or mastic to set other materials and what kind of grout to use.

Hearth Details

A wood frame extends the existing hearth. Cement board is held by screws and mastic. The new hearth facing can be laid in mastic or mortar, as recommended by the supplier. A wood facing conceals the frame and protects the edges of the hearth facing.

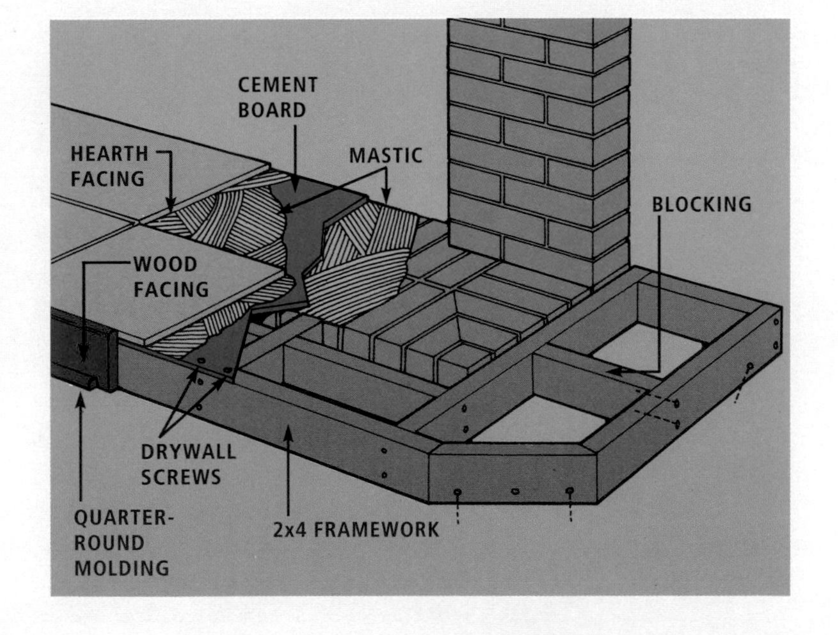

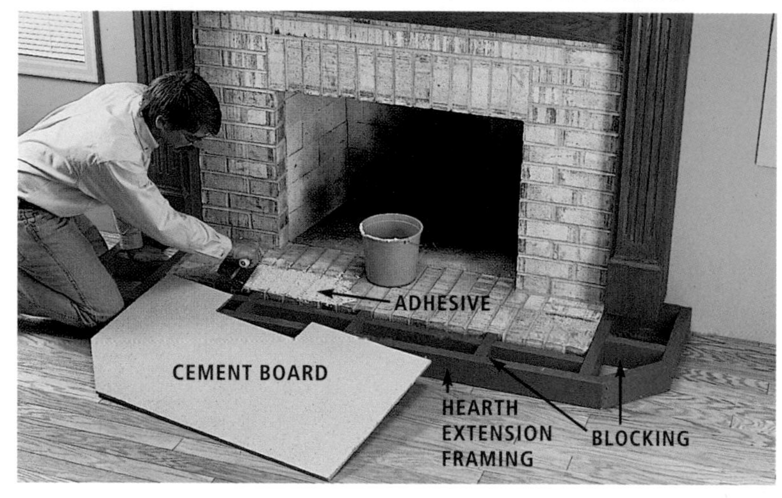

Photo 19. Check your local fire codes to determine how far out to extend the hearth. Cover the old hearth and new frame with cement board, then add facing.

Photo 20. Plan the hearth layout so the joints will align with those on the vertical face of the fireplace. Precut all facing pieces before setting any in mastic or mortar.

TRIM THE EDGES

Finish your fireplace project by gluing and nailing trim to joints and edges.

▶ Cover the edges of the hearth frame with oak boards set flush with the surface of the hearth. Round over the upper edge of these boards with a beading bit in a router.

▶ Add 1/2-inch quarter-round molding where the columns meet the wall (Photo 21).

▶ Add a 3/8- x 1-1/2 inch oak strip to the bottom edge of the plywood bridge between the columns, then add quarter-round molding all around the bridge.

▶ Use quarter-round molding along the bottom of the mantel, and 3/4- x 1-1/4 inch cove molding where the wood surround fits against the fireplace finish facing.

▶ Apply a coat of clear wood finish, fill all nail holes with wood putty, then apply one more coat of clear finish.

Cutting Molding

For the smoothest results, cut molding with a power miter saw and a carbide-tip blade with 40 or more teeth. Work safely: Never try to recut a 2- or 3-in. piece to a shorter length or different angle. Cut the angle on a larger piece, then trim to length.

Photo 21. Install quarter-round molding where the surround meets the wall. Install other trim moldings as suggested in the text and shown in the Assembly Plan on page 152.

The Basement and the Attic

Bring a Basement to Life
Create new living space for much less than an aboveground addition would cost. It's a sizable project—here's how to do it step by step.
164

Brighten a Room with Sunlight
Skylights are a dramatic way to increase the natural light and ventilation to a room. Stock units make installation a feasible project for the experienced do-it-yourselfer.
180

Bring a Basement to Life

Don't let your basement be a dark cavern; convert it into extra living space—a family room, an office or den, a bedroom, or even a second living room. You can do it if you follow the information given here.

This is a big job, but it's less expensive than building a new addition aboveground, because the walls, floor, and ceiling are already in place. They just need to be dressed up. That's a perfect job for the do-it-yourselfer with intermediate skills.

A basement can be remodeled to become almost any kind of room you need or would like to have. It's easier and less expensive than building an aboveground addition. These pages show you how to do it yourself.

EVALUATE YOUR BASEMENT

A remodeled basement, if done right, is warm and comfortable because it's well insulated, evenly heated, dry, and brightly lit. To decide whether your basement can be like that, consider three basic issues:

- ▶ Does the basement meet building code requirements?
- ▶ Is there a persistent water problem in the basement?
- ▶ Is radon gas seeping into and collecting in the basement?

Be realistic. Any of these factors may raise hurdles that will make basement remodeling too expensive. However, before deciding compare the expense with the estimated cost of building a ground-level addition—which will require new foundations and a roof as well as walls, a floor, and a ceiling.

Building code requirements

Building codes set strict standards for such things as ceiling height and window area to make sure all rooms provide comfortable, healthy, and safe living space. A remodeled basement must be up to par on all of them.

Meeting the standard for ceiling height is often a problem in a basement. Measure from the floor up to the undersides of the joists, then add the thickness of the finished floor and ceiling materials to get the *finished* ceiling height. If it does not satisfy the minimum, don't abandon the project yet. Building codes vary, and a local inspector may suggest special ways to meet the requirements. Note, however, that some remedies—such as digging down and pouring a floor at a lower level, or jacking up the house and extending the foundation—can be very expensive.

The building inspector can also help you figure out how to meet the window-area requirements for both light and ventilation. In addition, at least one of the basement windows must be large enough for easy exit in an emergency. You might have to put in two or more windows. But most basements are as dark as medieval dungeons, so enlarging the windows to bring in a flood of daylight makes good sense.

Water problems

A properly designed and constructed basement will be bone dry. Unfortunately, many foundation walls leak to some degree. Seepage, leaks, and dampness will cause mold, mildew, rot, odor, stains, warping, and other deterioration in a finished basement. All water problems must be stopped before you begin any remodeling.

It's best to control wetness from the outside. Establishing good drainage away from the house will solve most moisture problems, but if you live in a poorly drained area or over a high ground-water table and are unable to solve persistent wetness, finishing the basement will just add to your woes. If the foundation walls need repair, doing the work from the outside is expensive.

While interior solutions aren't as good, they can adequately deal with moderate moisture problems. Repair is usually a two-step process. First, plug cracks to block leaks and then seal the walls and floor to prevent dampness. There are many good commercial products available from concrete suppliers and home centers for these projects.

Radon

Basements tend to be concentration points for radon, a radioactive gas that occurs naturally in many soils. It can cause lung cancer, so test the basement following Environmental Protection Agency guidelines, available from the local public health department or from the regional EPA office. There are various do-it-yourself tests (Photo 1). Correcting a radon problem before finishing the basement is usually easy; afterward, it will be a good deal more difficult and expensive.

Photo 1. A prepared charcoal canister is the most common short-term radon monitor. Leave it open for exactly the time specified in the instructions.

MATERIALS

- Concrete sealer
- Concrete paint (optional)
- 2x4's
- Pressure-treated 2x4's
- 2x2's
- 1x4's
- 3/4" rigid insulation
- Caulk
- Fiberglass insulation
- Electrical cable
- 1/2" gypsum wallboard
- 16d nails
- 4d nails
- 1-1/4" and 3" drywall screws
- No. 6 sheet metal screws
- 5/16" bolts
- Metal ductwork and registers
- Sheet-metal panning

Interior Wall Construction

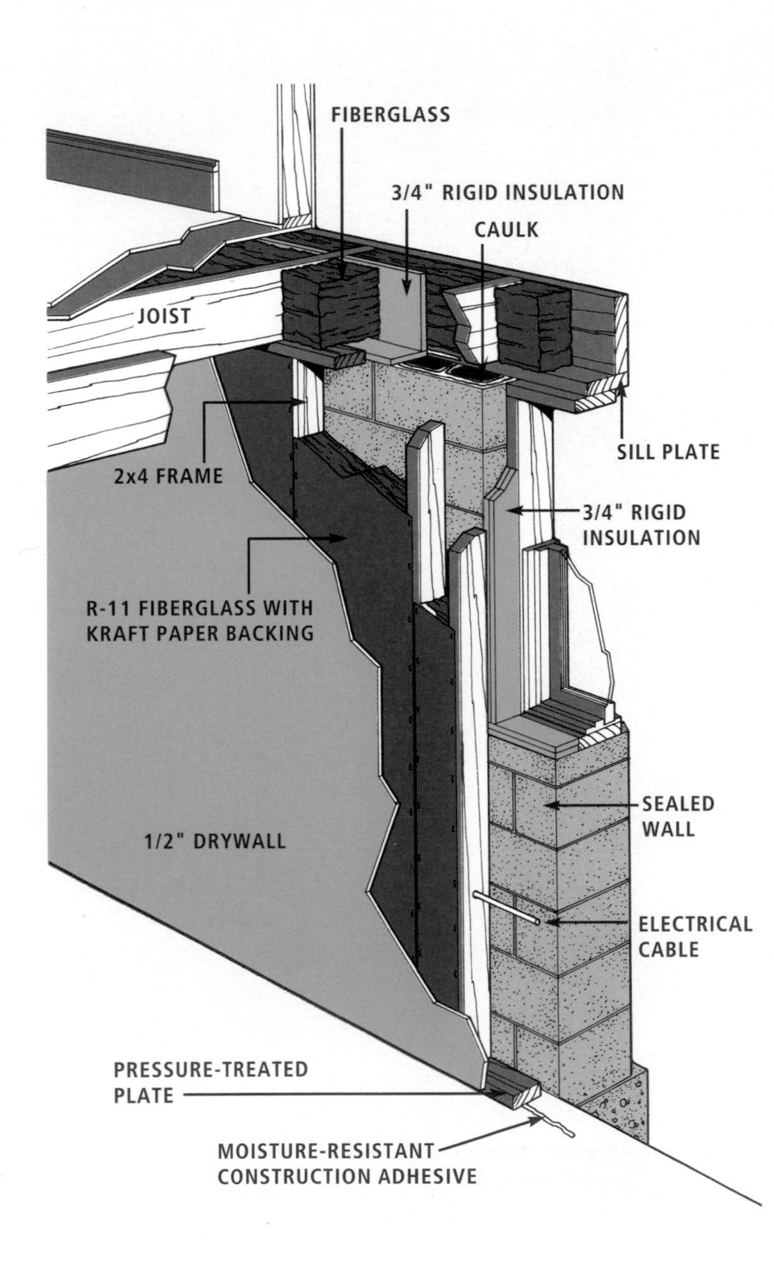

BUILD THE WALLS

Framing basement walls is a quick, easy task, but taking care of the preliminary details is the most time-consuming—and important—part of the job. The most painstaking chores are sealing and insulating the foundation walls.

Seal the foundation

▶ Fill all cracks with waterproof mortar and prepare the surfaces properly. Remove all peeling paint and get the surface truly clean—free of dust, oil, or other matter that would prevent a new coating from taking hold.

▶ Seal the walls to keep dampness from working its way through the concrete foundation (Photo 2). Many types of brush-on sealers are available from home centers. In general, use a cement-base product on bare poured concrete or concrete blocks, and a paint product over a previously painted surface.

Insulate joist cavities

Most houses waste valuable energy by heating or cooling air that quickly leaks away. In a basement, the point where the floor joists meet the foundation is usually the leakiest spot of all (see diagram at left).

▶ To cut most of this loss, use caulk to attach rigid insulation over the open cores of concrete blocks (Photo 3). Seal another piece of insulation against the outside rim joist (Photo 4), and a third piece against the subfloor above the foundation. Use a long-lasting, flexible caulk like silicone, butyl, or urethane.

▶ Where the ceiling joists are parallel to the rim joist, it may not be possible to seal the joist cavity in this way. In that case, fill it with fiberglass insulation. You'll insulate the interior wall framing later in the project (see page 178).

Frame the walls

Use 2x4's spaced every 16 inches on center for wall studs. A 2x4 wall is thick enough to run electrical wires through it with room for 3-1/2 inches of fiberglass insulation. If you want to add thicker insulation, use 2x6's spaced every 24 inches. They don't cost much more, but you will sacrifice a little more interior space.

▶ Nail the wall frames together on the floor in large sections. Use pressure-treated lumber for the wall soleplates to avoid rot if moisture should develop in the basement floor.

▶ Snap layout chalk lines on the joists and floor. Where a wall will run parallel with the joists, attach 2x4 nailing blocks to the joists. Then raise the walls into position (Photo 5).

▶ Where the walls run across the joists, shim any gaps for a tight fit. Drive nails through the top plates into the joists and nailing blocks to secure the walls (Photo 6).

▶ Use a power nailer, available at tool rental stores, to fasten the soleplate to the concrete floor quickly and easily. Or run a bead of construction adhesive on the floor and drive masonry nails through the soleplates with a 3-pound sledge.

▶ After installing the walls, build rough window openings (Photo 7) with 2x4's.

Photo 2. Seal the foundation walls after repairing or caulking cracks to retard moisture migration through the concrete. Cover the wall thoroughly.

Photo 3. Cap the open cores of concrete blocks in the foundation walls with rigid insulation and caulk. Seal all edges to make them airtight.

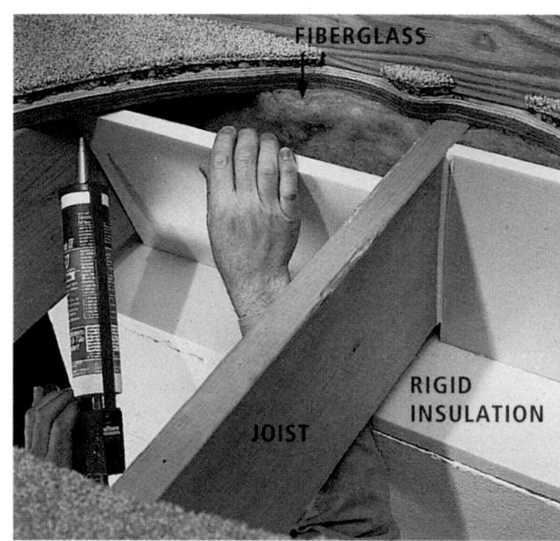

Photo 4. Use caulk to secure rigid insulation to the rim joists, the subfloor above, and the sill plate on top of the foundation wall. Seal all gaps.

Photo 5. Frame walls with 2x4's spaced 16 in. on center. Where a wall parallels a joist, put in nailing blocks before raising the frame into place.

Photo 6. Fasten wall frame top plates to joists or nailing blocks with 16d nails. Shim where needed to make the plate fit tightly before nailing.

Photo 7. Frame windows and other wall openings with 2x4's or 2x6's. Support sills with short cripple studs that reach to the soleplate on the floor.

TOOLS

- Paintbrush
- Tape measure
- Level
- Drill
- Screwdriver
- Socket wrench
- Circular saw
- Hammer
- Caulking gun
- Power nailer (optional)
- 3-lb. sledge
- Straightedge
- Metal snips
- Heavy-duty stapler
- Chalk line
- String line
- Staple gun

CEILING OPTIONS

There are two practical choices for a basement ceiling: a suspended ceiling and a standard wallboard ceiling. They cost about the same.

A suspended ceiling is easy and quick to hang; a wallboard ceiling requires some installation experience but looks more finished. A suspended ceiling lowers the ceiling a minimum of 3 inches, while wallboard lowers it by 1/2 inch plus the thickness of the furring strips needed for the job. The inch or so difference might be significant. There are other considerations with each type of ceiling as well.

Suspended ceiling

A suspended ceiling is first and foremost functional. It hangs below heating ducts, electrical wires, and plumbing, effectively hiding them. The ceiling panels can easily be removed to provide access to these utility lines.

Suspended ceiling systems are inexpensive and widely available as kits through home centers. They're easy to install, too. You first suspend a metal grid below the joists on wires, adjusting their lengths so the grid hangs flat and level. Then you drop lightweight 2- x 2-foot or 2- x 4-foot panels into the grid spaces.

A suspended ceiling has some disadvantages, however. Basically, it has the look of commercial or office space and it can appear temporary. The panels sit loosely in the grid. Airflow around their edges can cause dust streaking on the surface—a problem more likely in a basement than in other rooms of the house. While fine for a home office, workroom, or recreation room, a suspended ceiling would not be a first choice for a more formal room such as a living room.

Uses of Furring

Furring provides a level framework low enough for a wallboard ceiling to clear obstructions (Figure A).

Used with shims, furring can adjust for irregularities in individual joists (Figure B) and for differences in the depths of joists (Figure C).

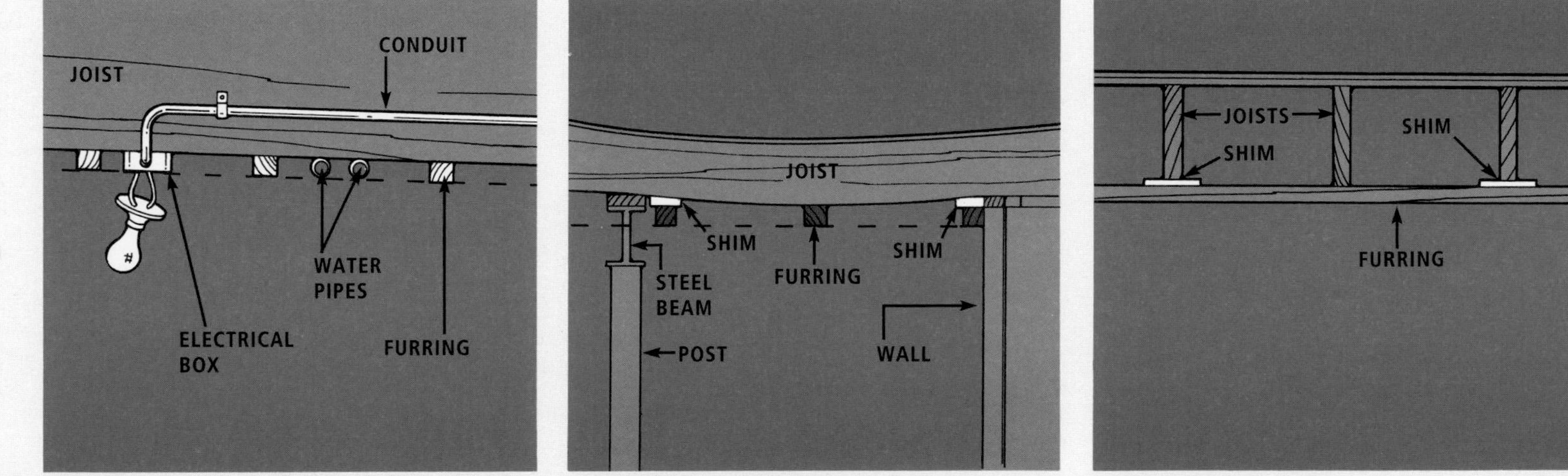

Figure A. Obstructions.

Figure B. Sagging joists.

Figure C. Uneven joists.

Wallboard ceiling

A finished wallboard ceiling provides a sealed, smooth surface that lends itself to detailing and trim. It's not expensive, but you need some experience in installing drywall to ensure a smooth, finished look.

Wallboard has some drawbacks. You can't screw it directly to ceiling joists because pipes and ducts are often in the way. Before hanging it, you must either reroute plumbing and wiring or use furring strips to create a level framework below the obstructions, as shown in the plan on page 170. Rerouting utilities can get expensive, so it's usually easier to fur the ceiling down, usually with 2x2's. Furring is also often necessary to adjust for variations or faults in the ceiling joists, as shown in the diagrams on the opposite page. Instructions for installing furring are given on pages 170–171.

Boxing large obstructions

No matter which ceiling option you choose, you'll probably have to deal with large obstructions such as heating and ventilating ducts, big drain pipes, and structural beams. In a basement you can rarely lower the entire ceiling to hide them. Instead, you can *box* them—build a frame around them as shown at the right. It's easiest to cover the frame with wallboard, even if you're using a suspended ceiling in the rest of the room.

Boxing beams and ducts makes part of the ceiling a good deal lower than the rest, which can be both awkward and unsightly. But with luck, low spots will occur where they can help serve as natural room dividers. If you have an obstruction too low to be boxed, you may be able to reroute it. If that is too difficult or expensive, you'll have to leave it exposed and paint it to match the ceiling or wall.

Boxing Large Obstructions

To box a ceiling obstruction, build two frames from 2x2's about 1 inch deeper than the obstruction. Nail them to the joists on either side, getting the bottoms level. Nail 1x4's across the bottom to complete the box (Photo A). Space the crosspieces in the frames and across the bottom 16 inches apart on center.

To box a hollow post, drill 3/8-inch holes through the post near the top, middle, and bottom. Drill matching holes in 2x4's or 2x6's with countersinks for bolt heads and nuts. Clamp the pieces to the post with countersunk 5/16-inch bolts (Photo B). For a concrete-filled post or other solid obstruction, build vertical boxes with solid sides of 2x lumber and 1x4 crosspieces on the open sides.

Photo A.

Photo B.

FURRING PLAN

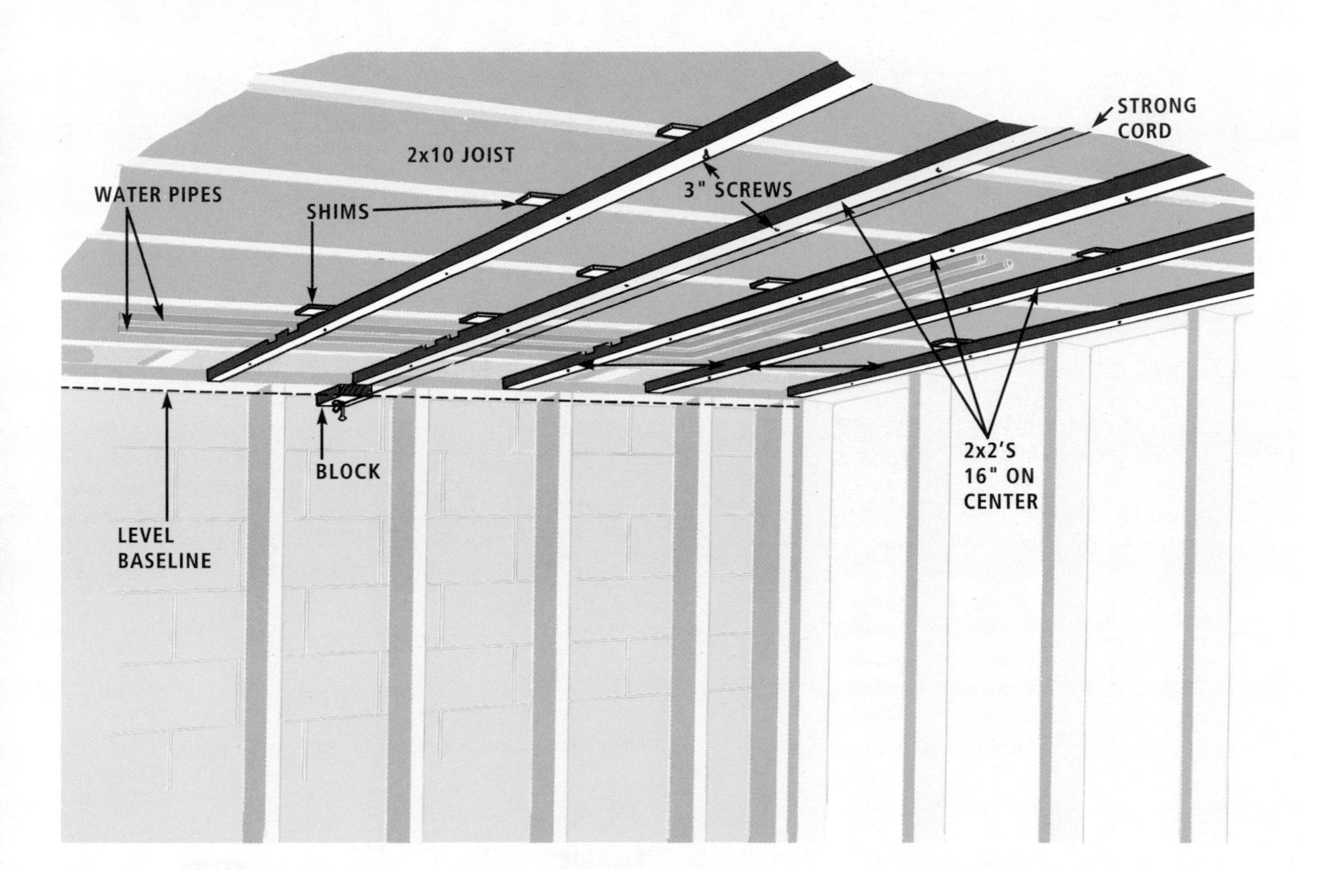

Plan the layout to be sure furring strips will be placed where the joints between panels will fall. Start at one wall and mark off 48-inch intervals to the opposite wall. Then mark off 16-inch spaces between these positions. Install 2x2 furring as described in the text.

If the final interval is less than 16 inches, do not begin with a full-length panel when you put up the ceiling. Instead, start with a panel cut 72 inches long. Follow that with full-length panels until the last one. Measure and cut that to the required length. Start the second row with a panel cut 48 inches long and the third row with a 72-inch panel, so the joints between rows will be staggered.

Some carpenters prefer to put 2x3 furring strips at the locations where the joints will fall. The extra furring width makes it easier to fasten the panel edges without difficulty.

INSTALL CEILING FURRING

Install 2x2 furring strips running at right angles to the direction of the ceiling joists (see plan at left). Space them every 16 inches on center, carefully placing the strips where the edges of adjacent panels will meet.

▶ Find the lowest spot in the joists or ceiling obstructions. Stretch a cord from there to each end wall that runs parallel to the joists. Get the string level and mark the wall framing at that height. Then use a chalk line to snap level baselines at the marked height across the studs of both end walls (Photo 8).

▶ Starting at one side wall, mark off 16-inch intervals on the top plates of both end walls, above the baselines. These indicate the centers of each furring strip.

▶ At every third mark—48-inch intervals—tack a block to the top plates; the bottom of the block should be about 1 inch below the marked baseline. Stretch strong cords across the room between opposite pairs of blocks.

▶ Fasten the ends of the 2x2 furring strips to the wall framing centered above each cord. Get the bottom faces of the strips flush with the baselines. Measure the distance from the cord up to the furring strip. Then measure at each joist and insert shims to keep the furring strip an equal distance above the cord (Photo 9).

▶ Drive a 3-inch drywall screw through the furring strip and shims at each joist (Photo 10).

▶ Now install additional furring strips at the marked 16-inch intervals. Hold a 4-foot straightedge across the installed strips and shim each new strip down to it before screwing it in place (Photo 11).

INSTALL CEILING FURRING

Photo 8. Find the low ceiling point and snap level baselines at that height on the studs of the walls that run parallel to the ceiling joists.

Photo 9. Stretch a strong cord at a measured distance below the baseline. Shim furring to keep it that distance above the cord at all points.

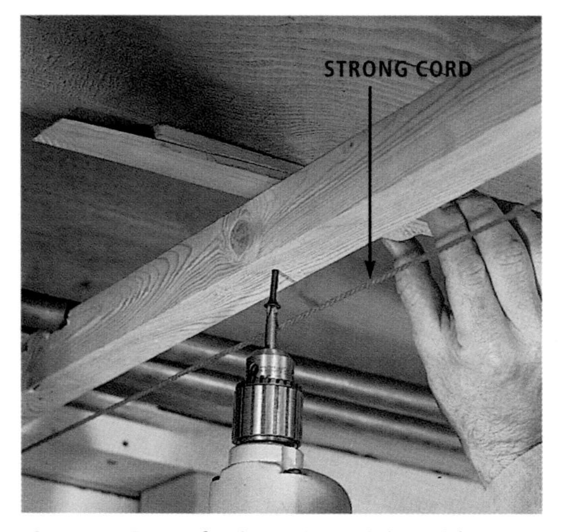

Photo 10. Fasten furring strips to joists with 3-in. drywall screws. You can notch furring a maximum of 1/2 in. to clear some obstructions.

Photo 11. Install furring at 4-ft. intervals first. Then add furring every 16 in. between. Use a long straightedge to check that the faces are even.

CLOSING UP

Before installing wallboard on the ceiling and walls you should provide heating for the room, install electrical wiring, and insulate the walls. These topics are covered on the following pages. When that work is complete, cover the ceiling and walls.

▶ Do the ceiling first, running the length of the panels at right angles to the furring. You may need to start with a partial length panel (see instructions with the plan, opposite page). Make sure the end joints between panels fall on the furring, and stagger joints between adjacent rows.

▶ Snap chalk lines on the panel as guides for driving screws into the furring. Get a helper or use a T-bar made of 2x4's to support one end of a panel as you raise the other end.

▶ Press the panel tightly against the furring as you fasten it with 1-1/4 inch drywall screws. Drive pairs of screws about 2 inches apart along the middle furring strips, with 12 inches between pairs. Drive single screws 8 inches apart along the edges.

▶ Install wall panels horizontally, with end joints falling on studs. Space screws as in the ceiling. Cover any boxed obstructions last.

▶ Finish the joints using metal corner beading on outside corners and self-adhesive fiberglass mesh tape in inside corners and on flat joints. Cover the tape with three coats of taping compound. Let each coat dry and sand it smooth before adding the next.

▶ Finish the walls with paint or a wallcovering, as you prefer.

Marking Level Lines

To extend a level line across a room, fasten one end of a cord at the marked height, stretch the cord taut, and hang a lightweight line level in the center. Adjust the free end of the cord up or down until the bubble is centered in the level, then mark that height on the wall. Even if the cord sags slightly, as long as the level is in the middle of the cord the end positions will be accurate.

MAKE HEATING DECISIONS

A basement will never be comfortable if it's cold and drafty. Many basements have uninsulated, cold floors. Good flooring methods (see page 179) can solve that problem, but the air must be heated to make the living space comfortable. There are two basic methods of heating a finished basement—baseboard radiators or forced-air registers.

Baseboard heating

Baseboard heating uses hot-water or electric radiators or convectors (see diagrams below).

Houses with hot-water heating systems pose a difficult choice. Tapping into and extending the system and installing new radiators is a job for a professional.

Electric baseboard or wall heaters are cheaper to install, but they are usually the most expensive to operate. On average, radiant electric heat costs three or four times as much as gas, oil, or the amount of electricity consumed by a heat pump, although there are large regional variations.

In the long run, electricity is a poor choice for energy conservation and for the pocketbook, but in the short run the initial expense is low, and using it makes sense if it is turned on only to raise the temperature to a comfortable level when the room is in use.

If you do the installation work yourself, check the requirements in your local electric code as well as in the installation instructions for the heating units. Be sure to run the correct size cable for the heater. It will require a circuit of its own. Have a licensed electrician check your work and make the connection at the main electrical service panel.

Forced-air heating

Forced-air heating in a basement should be provided by a well-designed system like that illustrated on the opposite page. Heat is introduced through registers close to the floor near windows so it can rise and mix with cooler air from the windows, setting up good air circulation in the basement. There is a good deal of work involved in extending a forced-air system into a new area, but it is definitely something a do-it-yourselfer can handle. Pages 174–175 show you how.

An alternative, and somewhat less effective design, uses smaller ceiling registers to blow heat downward into the room. The registers are most efficient when placed about 12 inches from windows. This approach is less expensive, because there is no need to extend heating ducts down the walls.

In both designs a cold-air return duct helps balance the system and makes heating more consistent throughout the room.

To make sure a forced-air system will work well, you might have to call a professional heating contractor to determine if the present furnace is large enough to heat the new living space. When a basement is well insulated, there is very little additional heating load. However, he might have to reset dampers in the ductwork to allow the system to work more efficiently because of the extra space.

If you have a gas- or oil-burning furnace or water heater, have a professional check for proper drafting in your chimney after the basement has been remodeled. Improper flow, called backdrafting, could allow exhaust fumes—perhaps containing deadly carbon monoxide—to collect in the living space.

Baseboard Heating

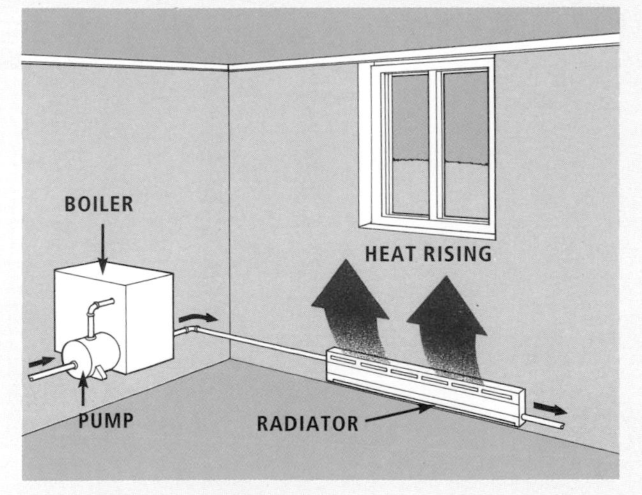

Hot water.

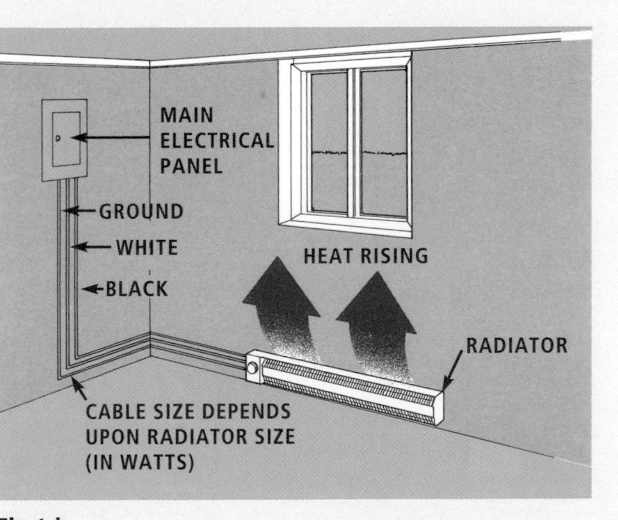

Electric.

Forced-Air Heating

A forced-air system (see diagram at right) has sheet-metal ducts that carry warm air from the furnace to wall or ceiling outlets called registers. Separate cold-air return ducts carry cool air from the living space back to the furnace, where it is reheated.

Most components of a forced-air system (see diagram below) are usually sized to fit between existing ceiling joists and wall studs so they can be concealed.

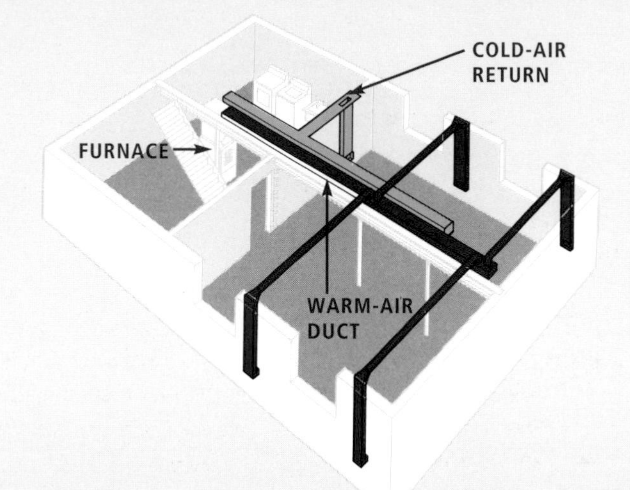

System layout.

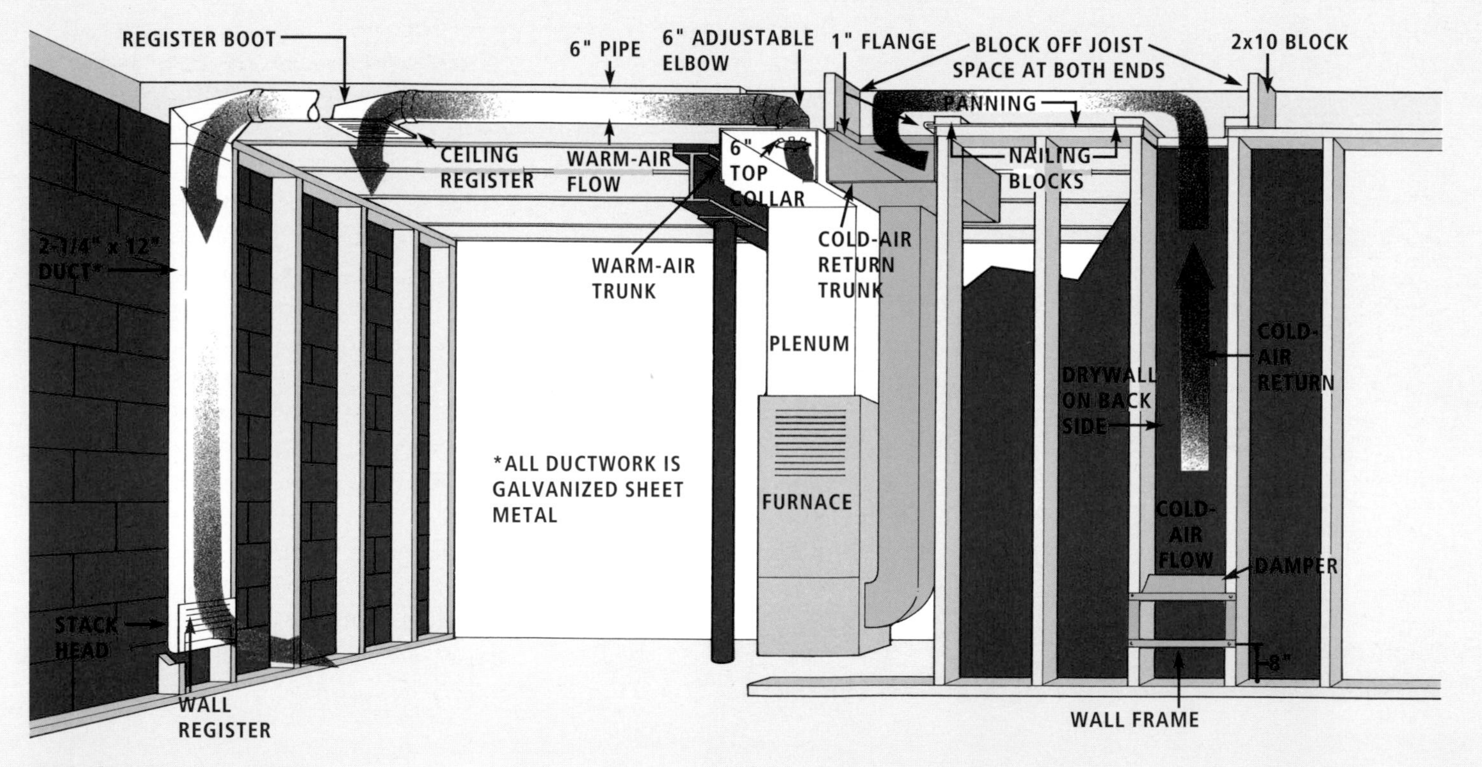

Typical system components.

INSTALL A FORCED-AIR SYSTEM

Make a rough sketch of the basement, including all measurements, before shopping for ductwork and other materials for a forced-air system. Study the components diagram on page 173 to identify the parts you will need—boots, stacks, panning, transitions, collars, and so on—so you can ask for them by name as you buy materials.

Don't forget to plan a cold-air return system and buy materials for it. The cubic footage of the cold-air duct should equal the total cubic footage of the warm-air ducts to balance the air outflow with the inflow at the furnace.

Each register stack, boot, or frame should have a damper to adjust airflow and help balance the system. If the basement feels too hot while other rooms feel cold, adjust the dampers yourself or have a professional balance the system.

You'll need metal-cutting shears for this part of the project. They come in three types: straight-cutting, left-cutting, and right-cutting. As their names imply, the blades are shaped to cut in one direction. Use straight-cutting shears to trim lengths of duct to size. The left- and right-cutting shears make cutting out circles much easier. Always wear thick work gloves when handling and cutting sheet metal.

Cutting Sheet Metal

Use compound-leverage snips to cut sheet metal and ducts. The three types of snips have color-coded handles:

- **Yellow: straight cuts**
- **Green: right curves**
- **Red: left curves.**

You'll use all three to install the ductwork for a forced-air heating system.

Run ducts

Rectangular duct sized 2-1/4 by 12 inches fits into a 2x4 stud space, and 6-inch round duct fits between the ceiling joists.

▶ Begin installation from the wall register (Photo 12) 8 inches above the floor or, from the ceiling register (Photo 13) and work back toward the warm-air trunk connected to the furnace. Fit the joint of each new piece inside the previous piece so hot air blown from the furnace is funneled from section to section without leaking out.

▶ After fitting two sections of duct together, drive a No. 6 sheet metal screw through the joint to secure it (Photo 14), then seal the joint with high-quality duct tape.

Tap into the warm-air trunk

Cutting into the top of the warm-air trunk can be difficult because of cramped space between the trunk and the floor above.

▶ Put a collar in position on top of the trunk and mark its outline. Use a hammer to drive the edge of a screwdriver tip through the trunk to tear open a starting slot. Then insert metal-cutting shears and clip out the circle (Photo 15). Use left-cutting shears for cutting one direction of the circular mark and right-cutting shears for the remainder.

▶ Put the collar in the opening and bend the tabs to secure it. Then install a 6-inch elbow over it. Limited joist space may make it difficult to drop the elbow directly over the collar. Instead, rotate it into place (Photo 16).

Add a cold-air return

The cold-air return trunk usually runs alongside the warm-air trunk on the furnace. Air leakage usually isn't critical here, so return ducts are often made by closing off joist and stud spaces with sheet metal panning, wood or metal headers, and wallboard.

▶ Begin by nailing 2x10 headers between joists to close off each end of the return space. One 2x10 header must run alongside the cold-air return trunk (see diagram, page 172).

▶ Cut a rectangular hole in the top of the cold-air return trunk one inch from each joist and two inches in from each adjacent side. Bend three edges up and nail them to the joists and header with 4d nails. Bend the fourth edge over to receive the sheet metal panning.

▶ Beginning at the return trunk, staple panning between joists (Photo 17). At the far end, staple the panning to the 2x10 header that closes off the joist cavity.

▶ Erect a stud wall centered under the panning at the far end and parallel to the joists. Cut out a section of the wall's top plate between two studs and cut out the panning in that same space (Photo 18).

▶ Install a return register collar and damper at the bottom of the open stud space, 8 inches above the floor (Photo 19). When you install gypsum wallboard later it will form the broad sides of this stud cavity.

Photo 12. Nail a register boot between studs and fit a rectangular duct to it. Install rigid insulation in the cavity first.

Photo 13. For an overhead register, nail a ceiling register boot in position in the ceiling framing.

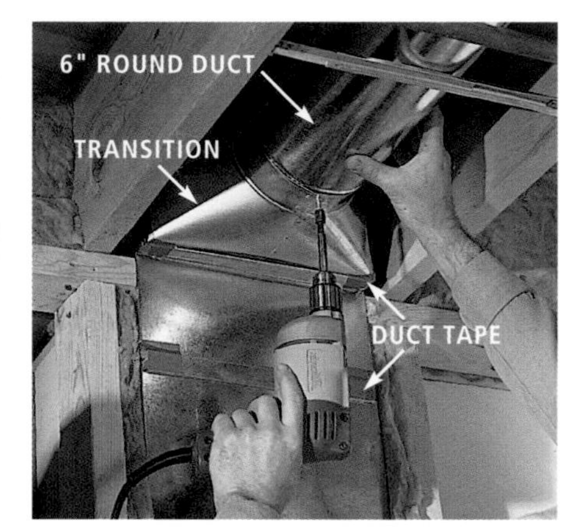

Photo 14. Fit and screw a section of 6-in. round duct to a rectangular transition piece. Cover joints with duct tape.

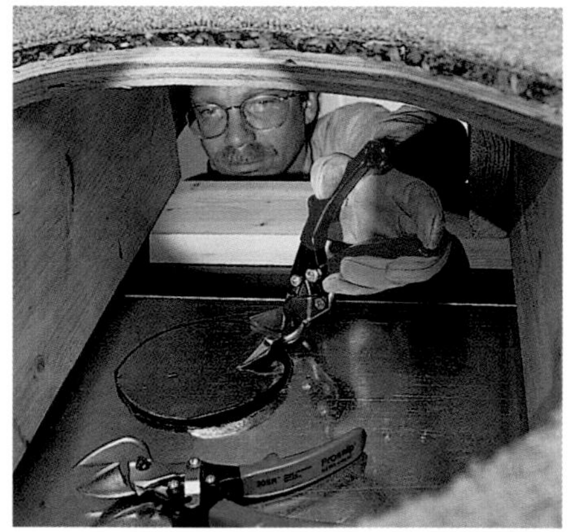

Photo 15. Mark and cut a hole for a circular collar in the top of the warm-air trunk. Use compound-leverage snips.

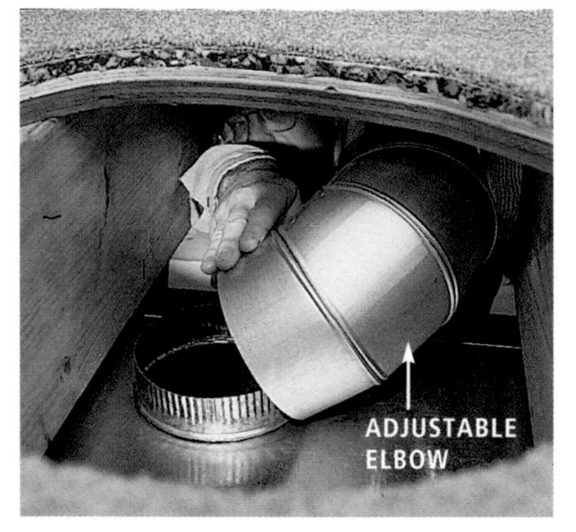

Photo 16. Rotate a 6-in. elbow, connected to the entire duct, onto the collar. Secure with a screw and duct tape.

Photo 17. Cut an opening in the return trunk, then staple sheet metal panning to close off a joist space as a cold-air duct.

Photo 18. Erect a stud wall, remove a section of top plate, and cut open the panning above the stud cavity.

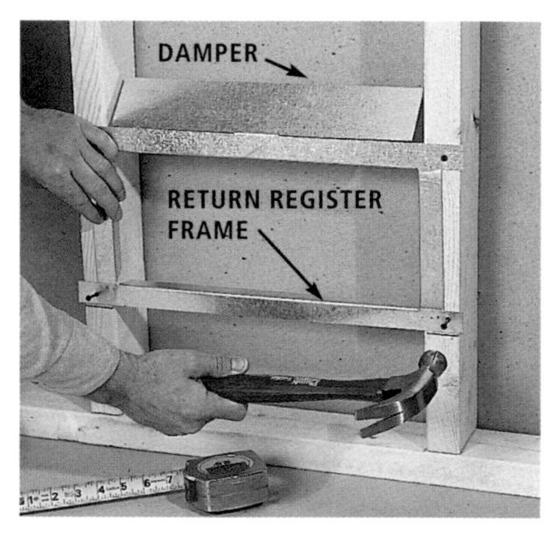

Photo 19. Nail a return register collar to the studs. Wallboard will close the back and front of the stud cavity.

BASEMENT LIGHTING AND WIRING

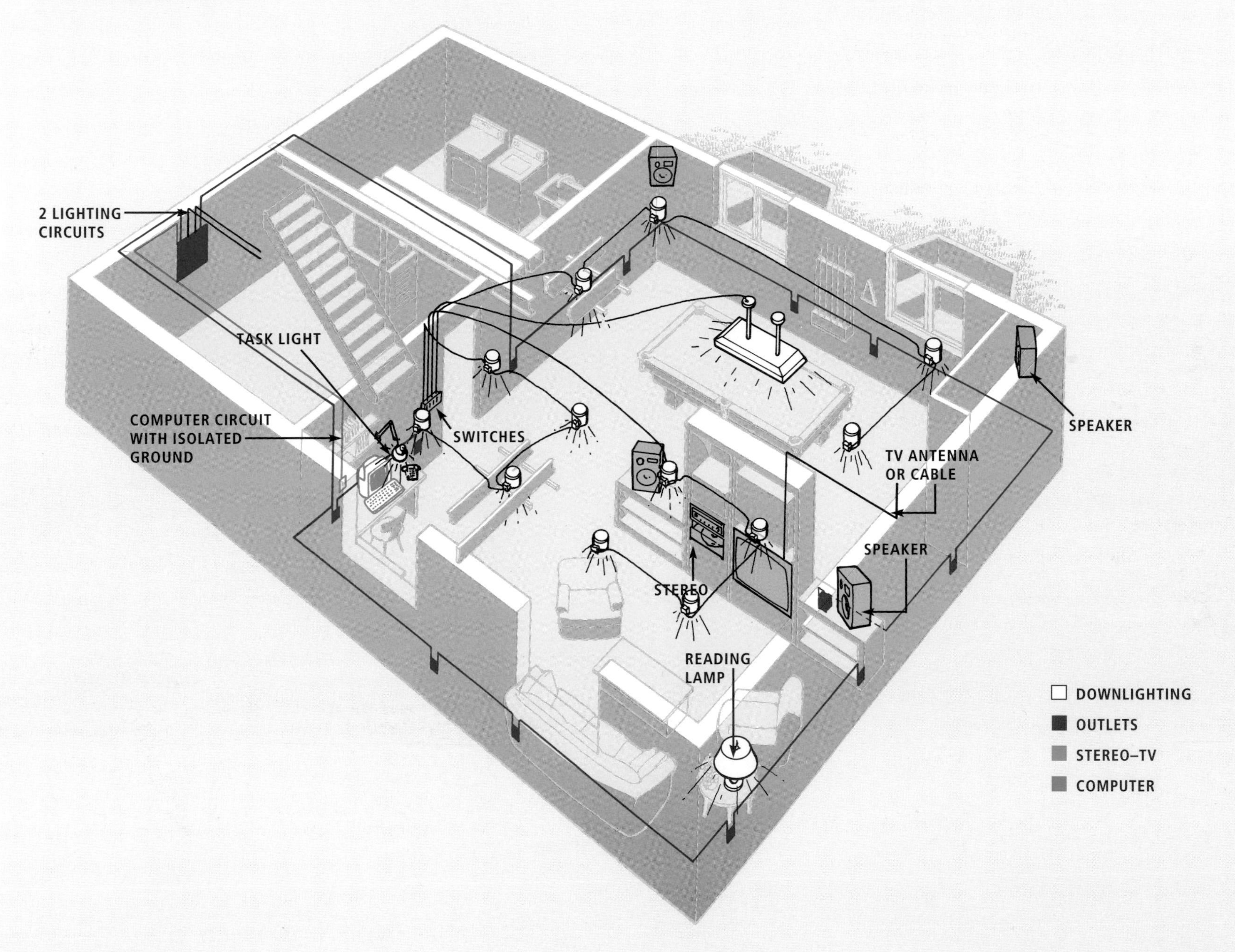

PLAN THE LIGHTING

A good lighting plan is perhaps second only to windows in making a finished basement a first-class living space. The diagram on the opposite page illustrates a well-planned system. Not only is there plenty of light, but more important, the arrangement of switches provides maximum flexibility. It is possible to light selected areas or the entire basement by flipping switches just inside the door. In addition, you can find plenty of receptacles in convenient locations.

Circuits

This basement lighting plan features five separate circuits running from the main service panel. Two marked in red serve receptacles, two marked in black feed lights, and a single circuit marked in green is dedicated to a computer. Power surges, often caused by fluctuating demand from other fixtures on a circuit, can damage a computer; providing a separate circuit minimizes that problem.

When planning the circuits for your basement, figure a maximum of eight receptacles and/or lights on a 15-amp circuit and ten on a 20-amp circuit. Install a receptacle within 6 feet of each side of a door; remaining receptacles are about 12 feet apart.

Appliances that draw a lot of power, such as refrigerators, electric heaters, and air conditioners, usually require their own circuits, so if you include any of these items plan an additional circuit for each one.

Lighting

This basement uses four types of lighting—area, task, reading, and decorative. Depending on the furnishings and contents, some accent lighting might also be desirable. For a discussion of these kinds of light and a number of suggestions that are applicable in a basement, see Lighting Your Kitchen, pages 62–65.

Floor and table light fixtures are useful as reading lights, but the limited ceiling height in a basement may make a hanging fixture impractical. Surface-mounted lights for general lighting are relatively inexpensive and easy to install, but they cast a lot of light against the ceiling, making it seem lower.

In general, overhead recessed fixtures, called downlights, are the best choice for most of the lighting in a basement. The three major downlighting options—spot, general area, and wall—are shown in the diagram below. All three use the same kind of housing, which will fit easily in the joist spaces above the ceiling. Choosing different bulbs and baffles determines the kind of illumination they provide. For uniform general lighting, space area downlights about every 5 feet. It is also possible to use recessed fluorescent fixtures for general area lighting. They have the advantage of lower operating cost and they produce less heat than incandescent fixtures.

Recessed Downlighting Options

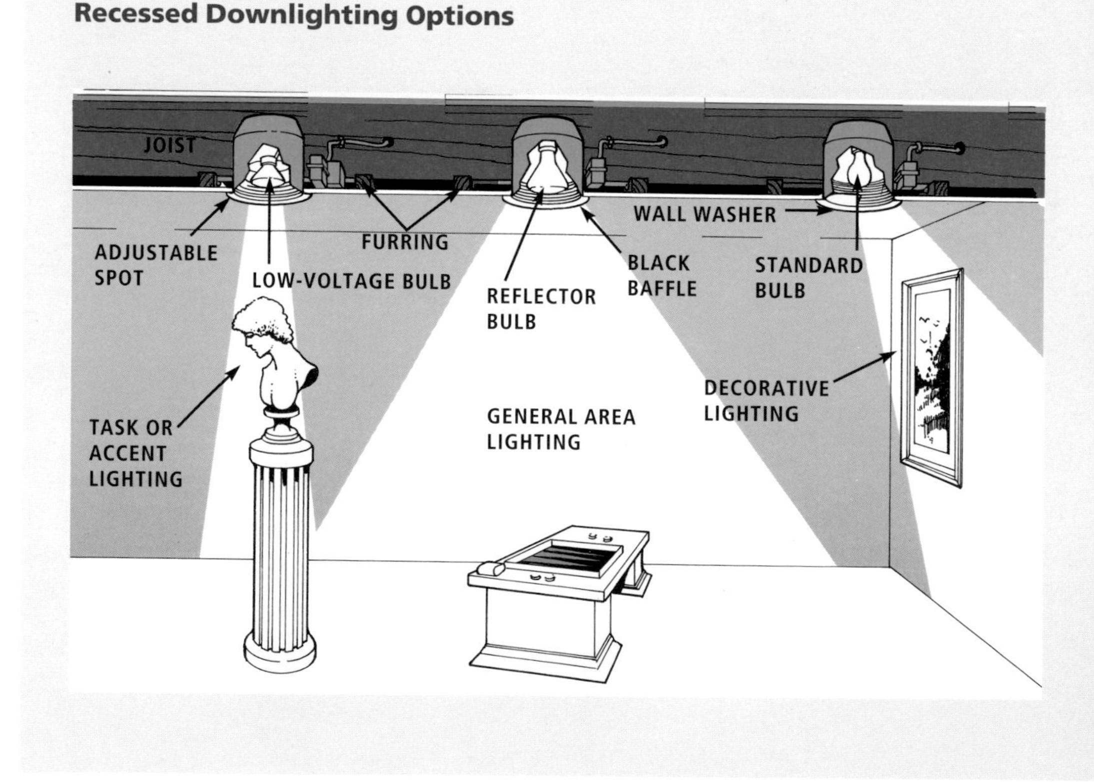

Adjusting Wall Framing

To create flat, uniform wall surfaces, position all of your studs crowned or bowed-side up before nailing them together on the floor.

Installing wiring

There's nothing unique about wiring a basement. The joists in the ceiling and 2x4 framing along the walls provide plenty of room in which to run wires and install electrical boxes and light fixtures.

Most municipalities require approved plans and a permit for doing electrical work. Even if your community doesn't, it's a good idea to ask a local electrical inspector to check your plan. If you run the cable and install the fixtures and receptacles yourself, hire a master electrician to check your work and connect the system to the main service panel.

While the wall stud spaces are still exposed, consider running a telephone line, a TV antenna or cable, and speaker wires to several remote locations in the room before insulating and putting up the wallboard.

COMPLETE THE WALLS AND CEILING

After running cables through the ceiling and wall spaces and mounting electrical boxes, you can finish up with insulation and wallboard, and provide access panels.

▶ Add insulation between all wall studs; split the insulation around cables where necessary (Photo 20). Then staple a vapor barrier over the wall framing. You do not need insulation or a vapor barrier in the ceiling, because there is heated living space above.

▶ Close up the walls and ceiling with gypsum wallboard. See Closing Up, page 171.

▶ Provide access to all electrical boxes where wires are spliced together and to plumbing valves. Frame an opening with 2x2's at each such location. To minimize the danger of cracking the wallboard, cut the opening after a panel is in place. After painting, screw on an unobtrusive cover. A return air grille works well as a cover (Photo 21).

▶ It's even better if you can eliminate unused electrical boxes by rerouting wires. Many water valves are shutoffs for outside faucets to prevent them from freezing in cold weather. You can eliminate shutoffs by installing freezeproof faucets.

COMPLETE THE WALLS AND CEILING

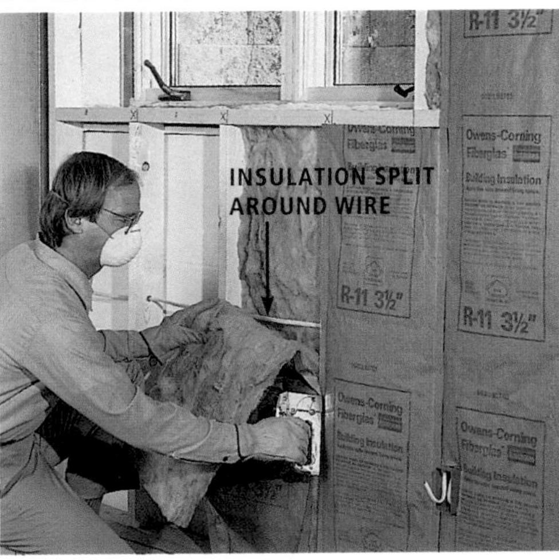

Photo 20. Staple insulation into the stud spaces, splitting it around wires. The kraft paper backing is a sufficient vapor barrier on below-ground walls.

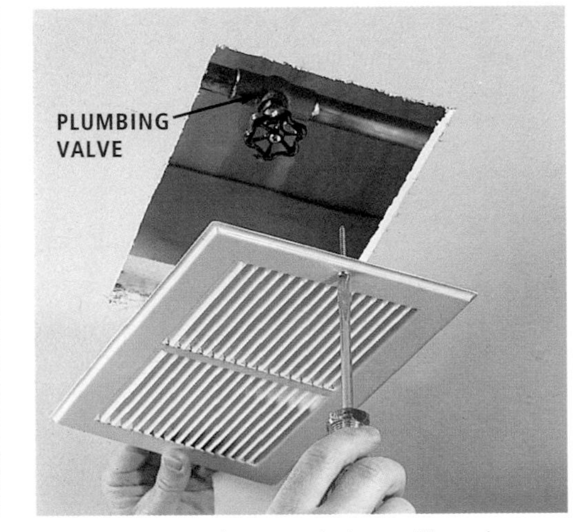

Photo 21. A metal return air duct grille makes a convenient and easy-to-remove access panel. Electrical splice boxes must have individual solid metal covers as well.

FINISH THE FLOOR

A finished basement floor has to deal with cold and dampness. The two approaches to finishing the floor are shown at the right. A pad and carpet laid directly on the floor is cheapest and easiest; a floor on sleepers is more work, but easier underfoot and warmer. For either method, first apply a concrete floor sealer to block most of the moisture.

Pad and carpet

▶ Fasten a tack strip with construction adhesive and cut masonry nails around the perimeter of the room.

▶ Lay a carpet pad over the floor, up to the tack strip. Choose a pad that is at least 1/2 inch thick and that will allow moisture to dry out through the carpet. A pad that traps moisture will allow mold and mildew to grow.

▶ Install carpet over the pad, hooking the edges on the tack strips. Don't install glue-down or cushion-backed carpets; they will trap moisture.

Floor on sleepers

▶ Lay down sleepers—pressure-treated 2x4's—in construction adhesive around the perimeter of the room and across the room, spaced 16 inches on center. Shim the sleepers to maintain a level surface.

▶ Lay rigid insulation between the sleepers, then cover everything with a 6-mil plastic sheet as a vapor barrier.

▶ Screw 5/8-inch plywood to the sleepers as a subfloor. All joints should fall over sleepers.

▶ Cover the plywood with finish flooring—wood, carpet, or vinyl tile or sheet flooring.

Floor Treatments

A pad and carpet (right) are adequate where cold and dampness are not significant problems.

An insulated floor on sleepers (below) provides better protection and makes it possible to use a variety of finish flooring materials.

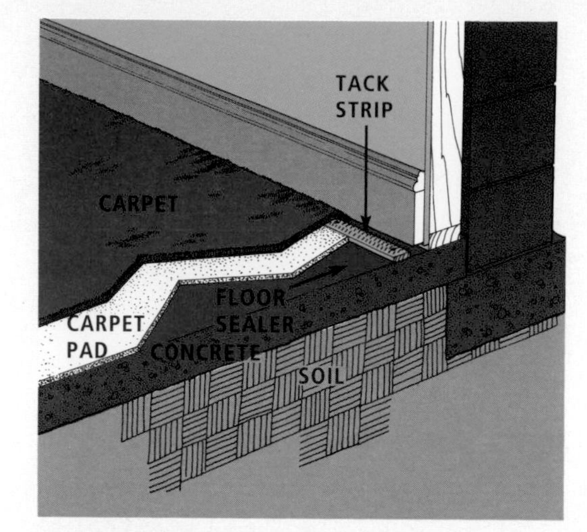

Pad and carpet.

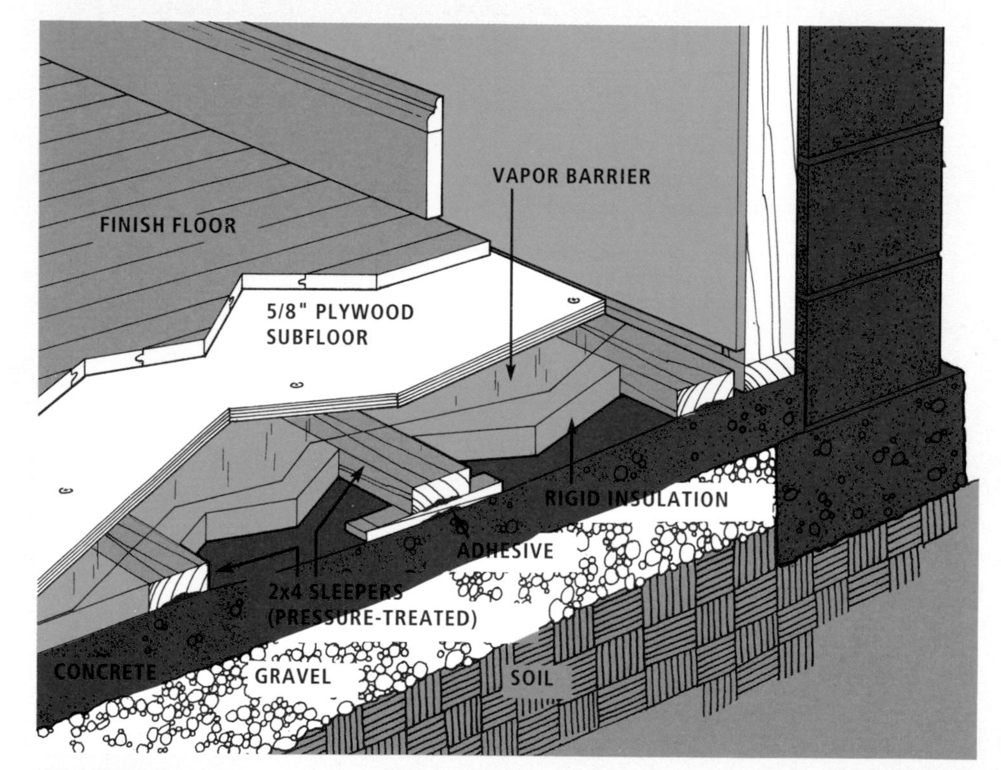

Floor on sleepers.

Brighten a Room with Skylights

Adding natural light has a dramatic effect on a room. A skylight can bring in an abundance of light you could never obtain with a traditional window. In addition, a skylight gives the illusion of more space.

Installing a skylight is less complicated than it looks. The fear of cutting a hole in the roof may be the biggest obstacle to overcome—the intermediate skills required are well within the capabilities of many homeowners.

Brighten up a room and bring in a piece of the sky. Single or multiple skylights do both. Installation of ready-made units requires only a moderate amount of skill.

PLANNING FOR SKYLIGHTS

A skylight must of course go into a room that is directly under the roof, such as an upstairs bedroom or a finished attic room. When choosing a location for the skylight, take into account any plumbing stacks, chimneys, or roof valleys that may be in the way.

When you consider how big a skylight to install, a good rule of thumb is to obtain a total glass area of at least 10 to 15 percent of the room's floor area. You might be able to do this with a single unit, but in a room of much size you will find it easier to use a combination of smaller units, especially if you would like to spread light over a wider area. In the project shown on these pages an attic room was remodeled using two long skylights side by side. Each filled two rafter bays, spaced with a single bay between (see plan, page 182).

Choosing skylights

Before going shopping, use a stud finder to locate the rafters in the roof. Manufacturers make skylights to fit common rafter spacings, and the spacing in your roof will help you determine both the size of the units to buy and where to install them. By buying units that fit neatly within two or three rafter bays you can minimize the number of rafters that need to be cut and avoid extra construction of framing around the skylights. If your rafters or trusses are 24 inches apart, you may want to choose a skylight that will fit between them, allowing you to skip much of the structural remodeling.

In addition to size, you must consider what type of skylights you want, fixed or ventilated.

▶ Fixed skylights. Skylights of this kind do not open. They are used where light is the primary concern and air movement is impractical or not needed. If the room is served by a central heating and air conditioning system, fixed units are probably your best choice.

▶ Ventilated skylights. Skylights that open to provide ventilation are very useful, especially where heat buildup and lack of circulation are problems, which is often the case in an attic room. Some ventilated units are hinged at the top and the entire sash opens like an awning window. Other units have a section near the top that opens to allow airflow. Some units can be tilted inward for easy cleaning.

Ventilated skylights are opened and closed in a variety of ways. Crank-operated windows may be installed so they can be opened by hand, like those in the photo on the opposite page. Crank-type units that are installed out of easy reach may be opened or shut with a pole that lets you reach them from the floor. Skylights with small motor drives are operated by a switch on the wall. You'll need to install wiring before closing up the walls if you choose this type.

With ventilated skylights, you have to watch the weather, to close them in case of wind or rain. Peace of mind is available at a price by installing motor-operated skylights with sophisticated moisture sensors that automatically close the windows at the first sign of rain.

Installation factors

Some ventilated skylights can be installed without climbing onto the roof because the skylight's sash can be removed from the frame. That means you can mount and seal the frame by working through the opening from the inside, as shown in the installation photos in this project. If you must do any work that requires standing on the roof, work safely, as explained in the section on outside work, page 185.

Check your local building code for permits or any restrictions on skylight installation, especially with motor-operated skylights. Some municipalities require an inspection of new electrical work, and others may require an inspection of the installation before you close up the walls and ceiling.

Procedures

Whether you choose fixed or ventilated skylights, installation is basically the same:

- ▶ Prepare the location.
- ▶ Install the framework.
- ▶ Reinforce the kneewall.
- ▶ Cut the opening.
- ▶ Install the skylight.
- ▶ Finish the interior.

The procedures for these project stages are explained on the following pages.

TOOLS

- Stud finder
- Straightedge
- Framing square
- Combination square
- Reciprocating saw
- Circular saw
- Adjustable T-bevel
- Screwdriver
- Drill with 1/2" bit
- Utility knife
- Pry bar
- Hammer
- Stepladder
- Staple gun

CONSTRUCTION PLAN

MATERIALS

- 2x4 lumber
- 2x lumber for rafter doublers
- Insulation
- Caulk
- 16d nails
- Metal step flashing
- Drywall
- Corner beading
- Drywall tape
- Taping compound

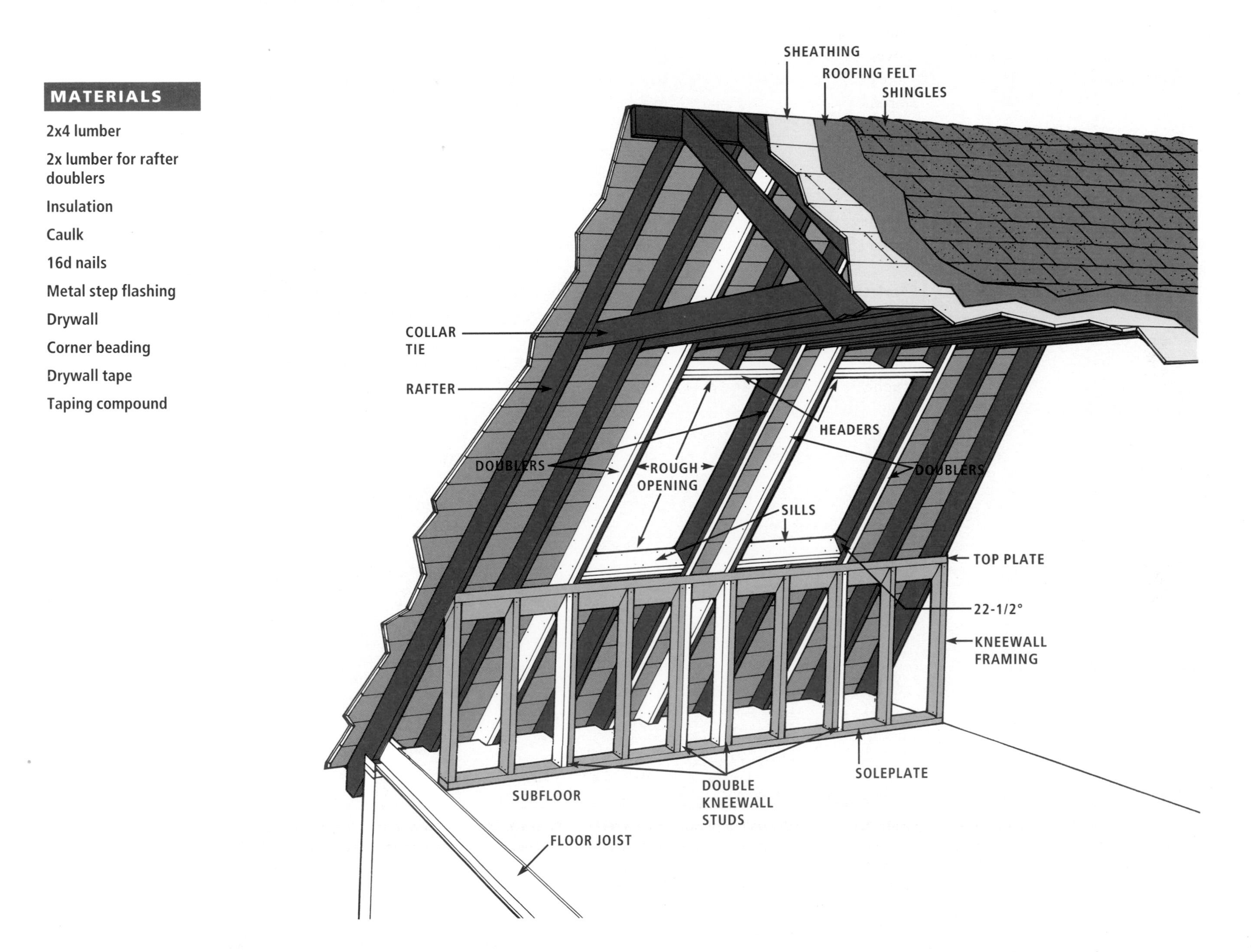

PREPARE THE LOCATION

You must open up the interior wall where the skylights will be installed and then mark the positions of all new framing members before you can begin any construction.

Open the wall and ceiling

▶ First mark the position of all the rafters in the work area (Photo 1). Also use your stud finder to locate and mark the studs in the kneewall below, if there is one. They may not all lie directly under rafters.

▶ Turn off the electrical supply to all switches and receptacles in the area where you will be working. Test them with a circuit tester.

▶ Wear a dust mask, goggles, hearing protection, and long sleeves as you work. A reciprocating saw makes quick work of the job. Set the blade of the saw just deep enough to cut through the drywall (Photo 2). You'll be able to feel the kneewall studs as the saw moves across them; try not to cut into them more than 1/4 inch. If you meet resistance, stop and open the wall to investigate. Don't cut through anything blindly.

▶ Remove the wall covering one full bay beyond the outside edges of the skylights, so you can double the rafters alongside the skylight openings. Then remove the vapor barrier and the insulation.

Mark the framing

Determine the locations for the bottom and top of the rough opening of each skylight—the distance between the sill and header or, roughly, the skylight frame size.

▶ For a clear view of the sky, the top of the skylight should be at least 78 inches above the floor. The bottom must of course clear the kneewall.

▶ Mark the sill and header locations on the rafters (Photo 3). Both the sills and the headers must be doubled, so mark the edges of the rough opening, then mark lines for two pieces of 2x material (3-inch total thickness) outside the opening. Measure and mark carefully; you'll be cutting a hole in the roof based on these measurements.

The sills and headers can be perpendicular to the edges of the joists, or angled to expand the opening on the room side a bit. For example, in the project shown, the sills were tipped down at a 22-1/2 degree angle to provide plenty of room for operating the skylight crank handles.

Handling Insulation

Wear eye protection, a dust mask, gloves, and long sleeves to remove insulation. Put the insulation directly into large plastic bags, to prevent fibers from being carried throughout the house. Do not attempt to reuse it; install new insulation instead.

PREPARE THE LOCATION

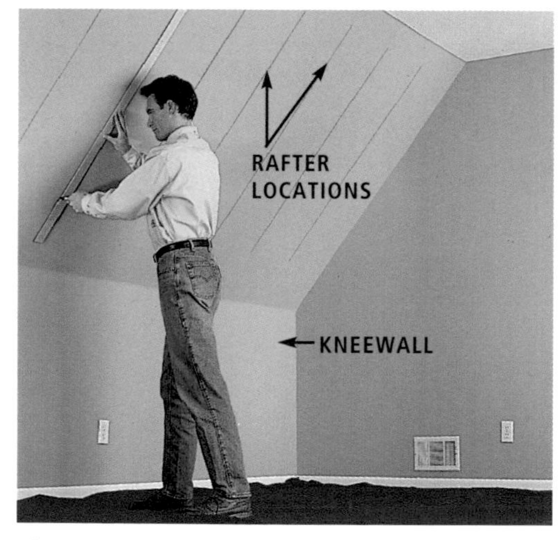

Photo 1. Locate and mark the locations of rafters to determine the placement of the skylight. Also mark the locations of studs in the kneewall, if there is a kneewall.

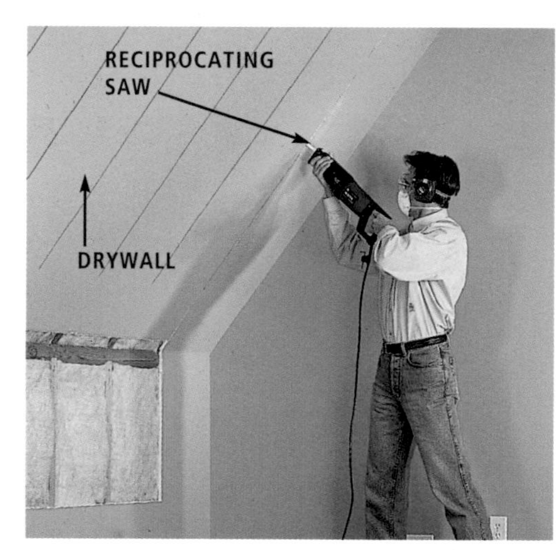

Photo 2. Cut away drywall or plaster using a reciprocating saw. Be sure to turn off the electricity in the wall, and protect your sight, hearing, and breathing with goggles, earplugs, and a mask.

Photo 3. Mark the locations of the doubled sills and headers on the rafters, and determine which rafters need to be cut to form the rough opening. Measure and mark carefully.

INSTALL THE FRAMEWORK

To frame the skylight openings, first install the headers and sills, then double the rafters alongside each opening.

Do Not Cut Trusses

If your house was built in the 1960's or later, it may have roof trusses instead of rafters. These are engineered as a unit and must not be cut. With trusses, select a skylight that fits between them.

Headers and sills

▶ Cut the rafter sections that you intend to remove. Start by cutting exactly along the header or sill line closest to the opening with a reciprocating saw (Photo 4). Finish the cut with a handsaw. Be careful not to cut through the roof sheathing.

▶ If you are installing more than one skylight, install the sill and header for the first window before cutting the rafter for the next. This prevents excess stress on the roof framing.

▶ Use lumber the same size as the rafters—2x6, 2x8, or 2x10—for the sills and headers. Cut two pieces for each sill and two for each header. Drive 16d nails through the rafters into the ends of the first, inside, sill, and header pieces. Nail through these pieces into the ends of the cutoff rafters. Then add the second sill and header pieces. Be sure the header and sill are exactly on your marked lines and that the rough opening measurements are correct. It's easier to correct an error now than later.

Doubled rafters

▶ Remove the insulation from the entire opened section of the kneewall. Then cut out the top plate of the kneewall in the bays that flank each skylight opening, to make it easier to install the doubler rafters. Cut directly along the rafter sides and save the cutout sections; you'll replace them later.

▶ Use lumber the same size as the rafters for the doublers. The doublers strengthen the skylight rafters to help make up for those that were cut. Cut the doublers so that they fit along the full length of the rafters on each side of the opening (Photo 5). Use an adjustable T-bevel to transfer the roof and sill angles to the ends of the doublers so they can be cut to fit.

▶ Nail the doublers to the sides of the rafters with two 16d common nails every 16 inches. If a collar tie is in the way of the doubler (see plan, page 182), cut it off along the edge of the rafter. Then nail a 2x thickness piece to it about 12 inches long and nail a 1x6 splice plate to this piece and onto the face of the doubler rafter.

INSTALL THE FRAMEWORK

Photo 4. Cut through the center rafters at the top and bottom to make room for the header and sill. With multiple skylights, frame one opening before starting the next.

Photo 5. Install double rafters along each rafter flanking the opening; nail them every 16 in. Cut away the top plate of the kneewall to make room for the doublers.

REINFORCE THE KNEEWALL

To finish the framing, reinstall the top plate sections of the kneewall.

▶ Nail through the top plate sections up into the edges of the doubler rafters.

▶ Next, cut doubler studs for the kneewall. Use an adjustable T-bevel to find the top angle, then cut the doubler studs to fit between the top plate and the floor.

▶ Nail the doubler studs to the originals, directly under the doubler rafters (Photo 6).

▶ If there is no kneewall but you want one as part of the finished room, now is the time to put in the framing. See the Construction Plan on page 182. Put in doubled studs under the doubled rafters, as shown in the plan.

REINFORCE THE KNEEWALL

Photo 6. After replacing the top plate sections of the kneewall, use 16d nails to nail a new stud under each rafter doubler. To build an entire kneewall, see the plan, page 182.

CUT THE OPENING

You are now ready to cut through the sheathing to create each skylight opening. In modern houses the sheathing will probably be plywood; in others it will be boards as shown in the photographs. By far the safest way is to cut from inside the house.

Inside work

▶ Drill a 1/2-inch hole in each corner of the framed opening to allow room for starting the blade of a reciprocating saw.

▶ Wear eye and hearing protection when you make the cut. Use a long blade—10 inches or longer—in the saw so you can cut directly alongside the framing (Photo 7). Be prepared to change blades about halfway through the cut, because the roof shingles will rapidly dull a saw blade.

▶ If the roof has board sheathing, be careful, because boards and shingles will fall through as you cut. Stop frequently, pull the debris in, and let it drop to the floor. The work will be easier as you go along because the opening will become larger.

▶ With plywood sheathing, cut across the top and bottom of the opening first and tack 2x4 blocks on the sill and header located about 4 inches from each corner and against the sheathing. Then make the cuts down the sides. The blocks will support the cutout piece so it will not fall in and bind the saw or cause injury as you complete the cut. Remove the bottom blocks and use a pry bar if necessary to bring the bottom end of the plywood piece inside. Work it free, then remove the top blocks.

Outside work

▶ If you must work from the outside, take no chances. Get a pair of roof jacks and a safety plank along with a sturdy extension ladder. Roof jacks are available from tool-rental stores.

▶ Drill 1/2-inch corner holes from the inside, as described above, or drive nails up through the corners. Then go on the roof and snap chalk lines to mark the opening.

▶ Use a circular saw with a carbide-tip construction or general cutoff blade that can cut through the roofing material and sheathing and any nails that might be in the way. Cut along the chalk lines. With plywood sheathing, use support blocks as described for inside work.

Roof Safety

If you must cut the skylight openings from outside, stay on the safety plank and be very careful not to kneel or lean on the area being cut open.

CUT THE OPENING

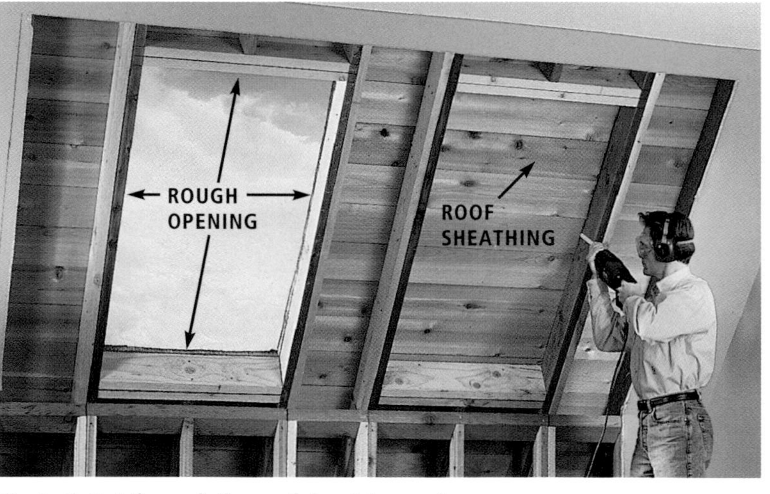

Photo 7. Cut through the roof sheathing and shingles with a reciprocating saw. Use a 10-in. or longer blade and cut flush with the edges of the framing. Wear eye, lung, and hearing protection.

Cordless Convenience

Consider buying or renting a cordless drill for installing the skylight. Roof work is awkward enough without having to keep moving an electrical cord out of the way.

INSTALL THE SKYLIGHTS

Follow the installation instructions supplied with your skylights. You can install a ventilated skylight by standing on a stepladder through the roof opening. With a fixed skylight you must work from outside, on a safety plank set on roof jacks.

▶ First, remove the shingles for at least 6 inches all around the opening (Photo 8). Use a pry bar. You'll need to pull the nails from the shingle just above as well as the one being removed. Stack the shingles in order so they can be trimmed and put back in place when the frame has been installed.

▶ Screw angle clips to the skylight frame, position the frame, and screw the clips to the roof sheathing (Photo 9). Check the corners with a framing square as you work to make sure the frame remains square.

▶ Cut 12-inch wide strips of No. 15 roofing felt for a moisture barrier. Place one across the bottom, stapling it to the roof and the skylight frame. Then work up the sides of the frame, overlapping strips as you go. Finish with a single strip across the top.

▶ Flashing is supplied with each skylight. Install the bottom flashing, overlapping the shingles. Nail it to the skylight frame but do not nail through any flashing into the roof.

▶ Replace shingles up the sides of the skylight, trimming them 3/8 inch back from the frame. Insert step flashing under the shingles, nailing it only to the skylight frame (Photo 10).

▶ Install head flashing across the top of the frame, slipping it under the shingles there (Photo 11). Nail it to the frame, then trim and nail the last course of shingles.

▶ Install the skylight sash in the frame, following the manufacturer's directions.

INSTALL THE SKYLIGHTS

Photo 8. Remove shingles with a pry bar and set them aside. Stack the shingles in the order in which you removed them so you can reinstall them later in the same locations.

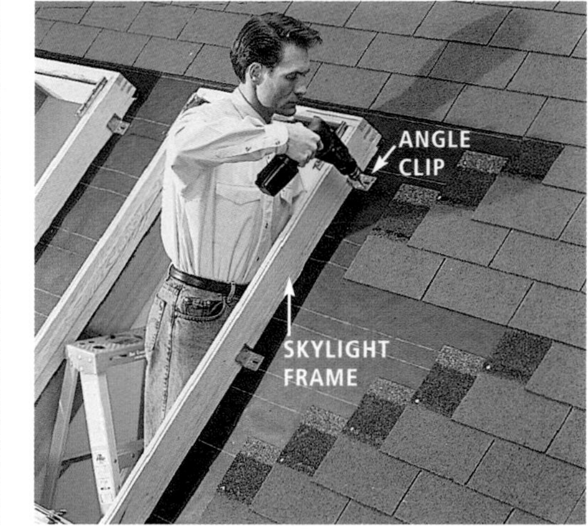

Photo 9. Screw the skylight frame to the roof sheathing. Center the frame over the opening and check the corners with a framing square as you fasten each one.

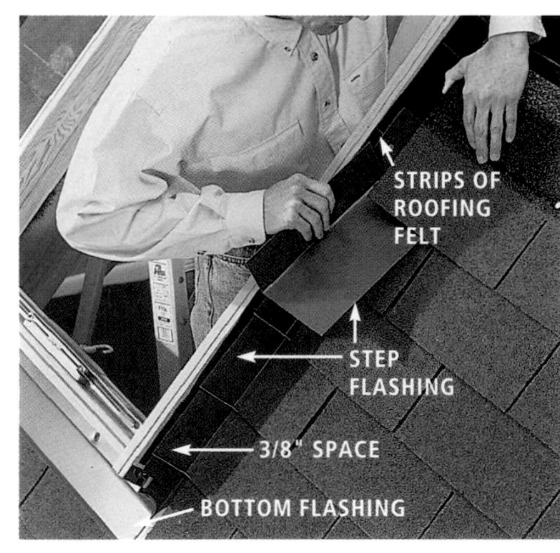

Photo 10. Replace shingles and install flashing around the frame, working from bottom to top. Cut shingles 3/8 in. short of the frame; nail flashing only to the frame.

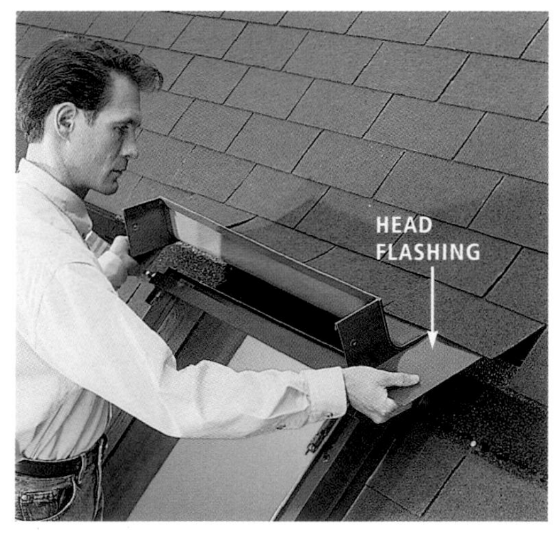

Photo 11. Lift the shingles near the top in order to slip the head flashing under the shingles. Nail down the last row of shingles after the head flashing is installed.

FINISH THE INTERIOR

Insulate the roof and kneewall again before putting up drywall.

▶ Install insulation in the wall and rafter cavities carefully (Photo 12). As always when handling insulation, wear a mask, eye protection, long sleeves, and gloves. Do not crush or cram the insulation into place; that will diminish its effectiveness. Consider using a thin foil insulation, available at home centers. It has a high R-value to minimize heat loss. You can also use fiberglass, although it's less efficient. If there was originally an air space between the insulation and the roof, be sure to maintain it with the new insulation.

▶ Install a plastic vapor barrier and cover the framing opening.

▶ Close the wall with drywall and add strips to cover the rafters, sills, and headers in the skylight openings (Photo 13). You may need to use small furring strips behind these pieces to bring them flush with the wall surface at the outside corners. Finish all seams and joints with drywall tape, corner beading, and taping compound, then paint or put up a wallcovering. Finishing the walls in a light color will accentuate the open, airy feeling in the room.

▶ Another attractive finishing method is to use wood to create jambs similar to a window or door and then trim the edges with wood casing. If you install fixed skylights, consider finishing the wood in a light color to maintain a light, airy feel.

FINISH THE INTERIOR

Photo 12. Reinsulate the wall and ceiling and install a plastic vapor barrier securely along the edges of the framing. Be sure to insulate all the way to the skylight frame.

Photo 13. Trim drywall to fit tightly against the window frame. Add thin furring strips if necessary to position the drywall uniformly around the skylight framing.

Index

Acknowledgments:

Charles Avoles, Darwin Baack, Ron Chamberlain, John Emmons, Bill Faber, Bruce Folke, Jon Frost, Al Hildenbrand, Duane Johnson, Bruce Kieffer, Mike Krivit, Phil Leisenheimer, Don Mannes, Susan Moore, Doug Oudekerk, Mary Jane Pappas, Don Prestly, Dave Radtke, Art Rooze, Phil Rzeszutek, Rich Sill, Mike Smith, Dan Stoffel, Eugene Thompson, Mark Thompson, Bob Ungar, Alice Wagner, Gregg Weigand, Gary Wentz, Michaela Wentz, Gordy Wilkinson, John Williamson, Marcia Williston, Donna Wyttenbach, Bill Zuehlke.

This book was produced by Roundtable Press, Inc.,
for the Reader's Digest Association
in cooperation with The Family Handyman magazine.

If you have any questions or comments, please feel free to write us at:

The Family Handyman
7900 International Drive
Suite 950
Minneapolis, MN 55425

Measuring the Metric Way

Use these guides and table to convert between English and metric measuring systems.

Fahrenheit and Celsius

The two systems for measuring temperature are Fahrenheit and Celsius (formerly known as Centigrade). To change from degrees Fahrenheit to degrees Celsius, subtract 32, then multiply by $\frac{5}{9}$. For example: 68°F - 32 = 36; 36 x $\frac{5}{9}$ = 20°C. To convert degrees Celsius to degrees Fahrenheit, multiply the degrees by $\frac{9}{5}$, then add 32 to that figure. For example: 20°C x $\frac{9}{5}$ = 36; 36 + 32 = 68°F.
(See also Some Rules of Thumb.)

Some Rules of Thumb

Temperature:
If the Fahrenheit temperature is between 0° and 100° and you want to know the approximate degrees Celsius, subtract 30 from the number of degrees Fahrenheit, then divide by 2. For example: 70°F - 30 ÷ 2 = 20°C.

In fact, 70°F is slightly more than 21°C.

The "10 Percent and Up" Rule:
1 meter is 10% longer than 1 yard
1 liter is 10% less than 1 quart
1 kilogram is 10% more than 2 pounds
1 tonne is 10% more than 1 short ton (2,000 pounds)
1 square meter (m^2) is 20% greater than 1 square yard
1 cubic meter (m^3) is 30% greater than 1 cubic yard

The "30" Rule:
1 foot is slightly more than 30 centimeters
1 ounce is just under 30 grams
1 fluid ounce is almost 30 milliliters

The "About" Rule:
1 inch is about 25 millimeters or 2.5 centimeters
4 inches are about 10 centimeters
A 2-inch by 4-inch piece of lumber (a 2x4) is about 5 centimeters by 10 centimeters
3 feet are about 1 meter
10 yards are about 9 meters
100 yards are about 90 meters
1 mile is about 1.5 kilometers
5 miles are about 8 kilometers
1 pound is about 0.5 kilogram
1 imperial gallon is about 4.5 liters (1 U.S. gallon is about 4 liters)
1 quart is about 1 liter (the imperial quart is 1.136 liters; the U.S. quart is 0.946 liter)
1 pint is about 0.5 liter (the imperial pint is 0.568 liter; the U.S. pint is 0.473 liter)